DEFINING BUDDHISM(S)

Critical Categories in the Study of Religion

Series Editor: Russell T. McCutcheon, Associate Professor, Department of Religious Studies, University of Alabama

Critical Categories in the Study of Religion aims to present the pivotal articles that best represent the most important trends in how scholars have gone about the task of describing, interpreting, and explaining the position of religion in human life. The series focuses on the development of categories and the terminology of scholarship that make possible knowledge about human beliefs, behaviours, and institutions. Each volume in the series is intended as both an introductory survey of the issues that surround the use of various key terms as well as an opportunity for a thorough retooling of the concept under study, making clear to readers that the cognitive categories of scholarship are themselves historical artefacts that change over time.

Published:

Syncretism in Religion
A Reader
Edited by Anita M. Leopold
and Jeppe Sinding Jensen

Ritual and Religious Belief
A Reader
Edited by Graham Harvey

Defining Hinduism
A Reader
Edited by J.E. Llewellyn

Religion and Cognition
A Reader
Edited by D. Jason Slone

Mircea Eliade
A Critical Reader
Edited by Bryan Rennie

Myths and Mythologies
A Reader
Edited by Jeppe Sinding Jensen

Defining Islam
A Reader
Edited by Andrew Rippin

Defining Religion
A Reader
Edited by Tim Murphy

Forthcoming:

Readings in the Theory of Religion
Map, Text, Body
Edited by Scott S. Elliott
and Matthew Waggoner

Religious Experience
A Reader
Edited by Russell T. McCutcheon

Defining Judaism
A Reader
Edited by Martin S. Jaffee

What is Religious Studies?
A Reader in Disciplinary Formation
Edited by Steven J. Sutcliffe

DEFINING BUDDHISM(S)

A Reader

Edited by

Karen Derris and Natalie Gummer

Published by

Equinox Publishing Ltd.
UK: Equinox Publishing Ltd., Unit 6, The Village, 101 Amies St., London SW11 2JW
USA: DBBC, 28 Main Street, Oakville, CT 06779

First published 2007

British Library Cataloguing-in-Publication Data
A catalogue record for this book is available from the British Library.

ISBN	1 84553 231 7	(hardback)
	1 84553 055 1	(paperback)
ISBN-13	978 1 84553 231 4	(hardback)
	978 1 84553 055 6	(paperback)

Library of Congress Cataloging-in-Publication Data
Defining Buddhism(s) : a reader / edited by Karen Derris and Natalie Gummer.
p. cm. -- (Critical categories in the study of religion)
Includes bibliographical references and index.
ISBN 1-84553-231-7 -- ISBN 1-84553-055-1 (pbk.) 1. Buddhism. 2.
Buddhism--Historiography. 3. Buddhism--Doctrines--History. 4.
Identity
(Psychology)--Religious aspects--Buddhism. I. Derris, Karen. II.
Gummer, Natalie. III. Title: Defining Buddhisms.
BQ4034.D45 2007
294.3--dc22

2006025271

Typeset by CA Typesetting Limited, Sheffield
www.sheffieldtypesetting.com

Printed and bound in Great Britain by Lightning Source UK Ltd., Milton Keynes and Lightning Source Inc., La Vergne, TN

Contents

Acknowledgements

We are grateful for permission to reprint the essays included in this volume, which have been edited for stylistic consistency. The original publication information follows.

Schopen, Gregory. [1991] 1997. "Archaeology and Protestant Presuppositions in the Study of Indian Buddhism." In *Bones, Stones, and Buddhist Monks: Collected Papers on the Archaeology, Epigraphy, and Texts of Monastic Buddhism in India* (Honolulu: University of Hawai'i Press, 1997), 1-22. Originally published in *History of Religions* 31: 1-23. © 1997 University of Hawai'i Press. All rights reserved. Reprinted with permission of the University of Hawai'i Press.

Walters, Jonathan S. 1999. "Suttas as History: Four Approaches to the *Sermon on the Noble Quest* (Ariyapariyesanasutta)." *History of Religions* 38/3: 247-284. © 1999 by The University of Chicago. All rights reserved. Reprinted with permission of the University of Chicago Press.

Wright, Dale S. 1992. "Historical Understanding: The Ch'an Buddhist Transmission Narratives and Modern Historiography." *History and Theory* 31/1: 37-46. Copyright © 1992 by Wesleyan University. Reprinted with permission of Blackwell Publishing.

Hallisey, Charles. 1995. "Roads Taken and Not Taken in the Study of Theravāda Buddhism." In *Curators of the Buddha: The Study of Buddhism under Colonialism*, ed. Donald S. Lopez, Jr., 31-61. Chicago: University of Chicago Press. © 1995 by The University of Chicago. All rights reserved. Reprinted with permission of the University of Chicago Press.

Lewis, Mark Edward. 1990. "The Suppression of the Three Stages Sect: Apocrypha as a Political Issue." In *Chinese Buddhist Apocrypha*, ed. Robert E. Buswell, Jr., 207-238. Honolulu: University of Hawai'i Press. © 1990 University of Hawai'i Press. All rights reserved. Reprinted with permission of the University of Hawai'i Press.

Snodgrass, Judith. 1998. "*Buddha no fukuin:* The Deployment of Paul Carus's *Gospel of Buddha* in Meiji Japan." *Japanese Journal of Religious Studies* 25/3-4: 319-344. Reprinted with permission. The original article is also available for viewing at www.nanzan-u.ac.jp/SHUBUNKEN/publications/jjrs/jjrsMain.htm.

Germano, David. 1998. "Re-membering the Dismembered Body of Tibet: Contemporary Tibetan Visionary Movements in the People's Republic of China." In *Buddhism in Contemporary Tibet: Religious Revival and Cultural Identity*, ed. Melvyn C. Goldstein and Matthew T. Kapstein, 53-94. Berkeley: University of California Press. Abridged with permission of the author. © 1998 The Regents of the University of California. Reprinted with permission of the University of California Press.

Hansen, Anne. 2003. "The Image of an Orphan: Cambodian Narrative Sites for Buddhist Ethical Reflection." *Journal of Asian Studies* 62/3: 811-834. Copyright © 2003 by the Association for Asian Studies, Inc. Reprinted with the permission of the Association for Asian Studies, Inc.

Jaffe, Richard M. 2004. "Seeking Śākyamuni: Travel and the Reconstruction of Japanese Buddhism." *Journal of Japanese Studies* 30/1: 65-96. © 2004 Society for Japanese Studies. Reprinted with the permission of *The Journal of Japanese Studies.*

Gyatso, Janet. 2003. "One Plus One Makes Three: Buddhist Gender, Monasticism, and the Law of the Non-Excluded Middle." *History of Religions* 43/2: 89-115. © 2003 by The University of Chicago. All rights reserved. Reprinted with permission of the University of Chicago Press.

We thank the authors of these essays for their exemplary work, which has made this volume possible. We are especially grateful to David Germano for allowing us to abridge his article, and to Richard Jaffe for providing us with the images necessary for reprinting his piece in this book. We thank the Center for Business Ethics at the University of Redlands for a faculty seed grant, Beloit College for the Mouat Chair stipend, and the Dean's office at the University of Redlands for book completion funds. Thanks are due as well to Russell McCutcheon and Janet Joyce for the opportunity to undertake this project, and for their advice and guidance through the publication process. Ann Davies, E. Scott Lenihan, Edward Mathieu, Edward Murphy, Nathan Baruch Rein, and especially John Watrous offered insightful comments and assistance in proofreading. Our profound gratitude goes to Sara Kile for her extraordinary and meticulous bibliographic and editorial assistance, and to John Watrous for preparing the index to this volume with such thoroughness and discrimination. We deeply appreciate the care and support of John, Ed, Benjamin and Rebekah. Finally, we are grateful to one another. This book is a monument to the difficult but immensely rewarding process of collaboration, and to the friendship and respect that makes it possible.

Introduction: Defining Buddhism(s)

Karen Derris and Natalie Gummer

The title of this volume suggests a great deal more than might appear at first glance. It invites us to interpret it more deeply. Doing so will take us into the issues that are central to this volume.

"Defining" implies a practice, an activity—a process, rather than a static formulation. Moreover, it implies an ongoing process. It shifts our attention from entities and essences to motion and change. The title prompts us to ask by whom "Buddhism(s)" is being defined. The most obvious answer, in a collection of academic essays, would appear to be scholars, and it is surely the case that scholars of Buddhism, whenever they articulate their understandings of Buddhism(s), contribute to the process of defining it. Of course, Buddhists have engaged with creativity, insight, and no small amount of dissent in the process of defining their tradition for at least 2,500 years, even though they have not always used the term "Buddhism" to name it. When we recognize the range of interpreters involved in the ongoing process of defining Buddhism(s), we come to see it as a dialogical process, a conversation in which both Buddhists and scholars (who do not, obviously, constitute mutually exclusive groups) participate.

To envision defining as an ongoing dialogical process is not only to acknowledge these multiple voices, but also to value the distinct perspective that each voice contributes to the conversation—and to wrestle with the contradictions and complexities that emerge thereby. In recent decades, scholars have begun to reflect upon the ways in which the questions they pose, the sources upon which they rely, and the theoretical assumptions they bring to their studies shape their interpretations and descriptions of Buddhist traditions. As a result, they have sought to engage with Buddhist understandings of Buddhism(s), and have increasingly attempted to represent various Buddhist understandings of Buddhism rather than depicting "Buddhism" writ large.

Studies such as those included in this volume recognize that Buddhists, like scholars, are complex agents who interpret and refashion "Buddhism" in response to the particular circumstances they confront in specific social, historical, intellectual, cultural, political, religious, and other contexts—even as they are themselves shaped by those contexts. Reading these essays together helps us to recognize and attend to the multiple and contradictory perspectives that people have brought (and continue to bring) to the question of how "Buddhism" might be defined. These essays have, in combination and individually, enabled us to recognize the productive possibilities inherent in generating an ongoing dialogue about defining Buddhism(s).

Through this dialogical process of defining, conceptions of "Buddhism" continue to unfold in multiple and distinctive ways that are shaped by both Buddhists and scholars (and others, too, of course). In that sense, Buddhism never "is" or "was" any one thing; the term must encompass so much diversity and contradiction that it breaks at the seams, so that we might talk about "Buddhisms" rather than "Buddhism." Both Buddhists and scholars of Buddhism have, however, at various times and for various reasons, envisioned and promoted the idea of "Buddhism" in the singular. We want to take those visions of an all-encompassing Buddhism into account, and to grapple with the tension between the historical multiplicity that confronts us and the timeless unity that, in numerous times and places, people have ascribed to Buddhism. This tension is embodied in the term "Buddhism(s)."

Defining Trajectories: From Product to Process

The conversation about defining Buddhisms that this volume seeks to illuminate has developed out of recent scholarship that interrogates the study of Buddhism in the Western academy during the eighteenth, nineteenth, and early twentieth centuries.[1] Numerous studies have demonstrated that Orientalist definitions of "Buddhism" reflected to a large degree the assumptions, preferences, and agendas of Western scholars, and have explored the ongoing legacy of these earlier definitions in recent scholarship on Buddhist traditions. Many Orientalists characterized Buddhism as a rational, even scientific, system of thought that provided philosophical and psychological methods for coming to know reality, and that promised an end to suffering. The Orientalist construction of the biography of the historical Buddha portrayed an Enlightenment hero, solitary and self-reliant—a human paragon to be emulated rather than a quasi-divine focus of devotion (Obeyesekere 1997; Almond 1986). Canonical texts in classical languages were the sources privileged by most Orientalist scholars, who saw no evidence of the pure, original Buddhism they had reconstructed in the living Buddhist traditions of Asia or the cultural and religious practices of their Buddhist contemporaries. As Donald Lopez writes, "This hypostatized object, called 'Buddhism,' because it had been created by Europe, could also be controlled by it, and it was against this Buddhism that all of the Buddhisms of the modern Orient were to be judged, and to be found lacking" (Lopez 1995b, 7). Buddhist voices, past or present, were rarely valued or acknowledged as important resources for the study of Buddhism(s). The Buddhism defined by Orientalists was found in the texts that they determined best preserved the teachings of the Buddha. The normative vision of the tradition that scholars derived from these texts became the measure of "true" Buddhism.[2]

While acknowledging that Orientalist scholars were by no means completely unified in their methods and goals, there is nonetheless some validity in characterizing Orientalist scholarship as assuming the existence of a true core of Buddhism, an essence that could be known, captured, and defined. By culling this original essence from the later accretions that obscured it and corrupted its purity, Orientalists sought to define what Buddhism really was, originally and for all time. The definitions created were thus fundamentally shaped by the assumption that this goal—a finished and final product, "Buddhism"—was attainable and desirable. This final product could only be produced through the rational scientific methods of Western scholars.

While several of the essays in this volume engage with the history and implications of Orientalist definitions of Buddhism, most are not primarily concerned with interrogating the ways in which "Buddhism" has been defined as a scholarly category, with uncovering its historical roots and debating its validity or heuristic value. But all grapple explicitly or implicitly with the issues raised by the project of historicizing Orientalist definitions of Buddhism. That project challenges scholars to query the assumptions and objectives that guide them (including those inherited from their Orientalist academic predecessors), the sources and methods they privilege, and the impact of their representations of Buddhism within and beyond the academy. With this self-reflection has come a shift in how definitional projects are conceived and evaluated, a shift away from viewing the process of defining as aiming toward the finished product of a definition that captures and contains "Buddhism," creating "an image that is free-floating and thus apparently true" (Hallisey 2005, 318). The essays collected in this volume, several of which focus on quite specific historical moments, suggest to us a complex dialogical process of definition, the value of which is not located in a final product, but in the ongoing unfolding and interaction of multiple definitions of Buddhisms. This process is shaped by the awareness that both Buddhists and scholars of Buddhism construct and define Buddhism(s) in response to the particular circumstances in which they find themselves. The scholars whose work is included here evince a strong interest in investigating the ways in which Buddhists themselves have defined their own tradition(s) in different times and places—but in doing so, scholars also participate in the ongoing construction and redefinition of Buddhism(s), in ways that are determined by the perspectives and assumptions of their own time and place.

The essays collected in this volume help us to think through a series of questions that open up the possibility of imagining a post-Orientalist methodology for the study of Buddhism. First, how do representations of Buddhism(s) account for the agency of Buddhists, past and present, in representing their own traditions in response to the needs and issues of their own times and places? What implications does this attention to the agency of Buddhists have for the scholar of Buddhisms in reflecting upon her own assumptions, methods and goals in her studies of Buddhisms? How do scholars account for the multiplicity of representations of Buddhisms, even in a "single" time and place, while also accounting for more unified representations of the tradition? And how do we represent the rich historical and cultural contexts that are so complexly intertwined with Buddhism(s) so as to generate "thick descriptions" (Geertz 1973) of Buddhist traditions? The essays in this volume provide us with a wealth of materials and perspectives through which to explore these and other questions.

To explore these kinds of questions provokes us to reflect upon and recognize how we position ourselves in relation to those whom we study. Recognizing that relation—recognizing the ethics of scholarship—might entail reconfiguring our practices. Scholarly studies of Buddhism(s) inescapably contribute to the ongoing process of defining Buddhism(s) and Buddhists; acknowledging this effect necessitates that scholars strive to be aware of their own assumptions and accountable for the role they play in generating representations of Buddhist traditions—but we are unable to interrogate our assumptions or understand the terms of our accountability on our own. Such difficult tasks require vantage points outside the self. If we seek to represent Buddhism(s), then engaging with the perspectives of Buddhists is surely crucial to this reflective process. By conceiving of defining as a dialogical process rather than simply as a product of our knowledge, we recognize ourselves as addressed in some way by the traditions we study and seek to understand: Buddhists can teach us about ourselves even as we represent "them." How we position ourselves in relation to the Buddhists and Buddhist materials that we study determines not only what we learn about Buddhism(s), but also what we learn from Buddhism(s). This mode of engagement may involve rethinking and transforming our methodological approaches, our theoretical assumptions, and, for some of us, the ways in which we understand aspects of our own experience and the world. Taking seriously the critiques of scholarly practices that would surely emerge from such a dialogue entails a degree of vulnerability on the part of the scholar. For all of these reasons, engaging in the dialogical process of defining Buddhisms situates us in the realm of ethics.

To characterize defining Buddhism(s) as an ethical process is thus quite distinct from a simplistic or self-righteous moral condemnation of Orientalist scholars from previous generations; instead, it necessitates that scholars recognize both their responsibility for their representations of Buddhist traditions and the dynamics of power operative in the production of knowledge about Buddhism(s). In this volume, when we deem certain approaches to the study of Buddhism(s) "ethical," we are not suggesting that they are morally "good" (although some may certainly judge them to be so), but rather that they intentionally seek to acknowledge and learn from their relations with the Buddhists they seek to understand.

Defining Context: Questions of Time and Place

To reject the essentializing Orientalist project of accurately defining what Buddhism "is" entails acknowledging the impossibility (and undesirability) of creating a single definition that describes, contains, and sets the limits of "Buddhism." Moreover, attention to the specificity of historical contexts has shown that the internal diversity of Buddhism is so vast, its regional differences so great, and its cultural history so complex that any ostensibly all-encompassing definition would obscure rather than illuminate. Even within a particular historical context, visions of Buddhism have never been static or singular; representations of Buddhist thought and practice have always been debated, rejected, and reformulated by Buddhists, even as tradition has been valued and preserved. Likewise, as scholars have begun the process of constructing and representing the diverse ways in which Buddhists have defined themselves in specific historical contexts, they, too, have generated multiple representations of Buddhism (hence "Buddhisms") that compete with and complement one another.

Many of the essays included in this volume do just that by investigating what Charles Hallisey calls "the local production of meaning"[3]—that is, the ways in which Buddhists have imagined and redefined what Buddhism was, what Buddhism is, and what it means to be Buddhist in response to particular circumstances in particular times and places. The process of reimagining Buddhism very often involves the reinterpretation of authoritative texts, practices, and institutions inherited from past Buddhists. While tradition can function as a conservative, normative force, many Buddhists have found within it the basis for its own creative transformation and skillful application in light of the pressing concerns of the present, as several of the essays in this volume clearly demonstrate. As Anne Hansen's essay in this volume clearly demonstrates, such reinterpretations frequently also provide a means of envisioning the continuity between local forms and practices and the translocal, transhistorical *imaginaire*—the "imagined universe" constituted by the resources in which "tradition" is located.[4] In this process, particular Buddhisms may be produced locally, in response to specific historical circumstances, but their meaning stretches beyond that place and time, laying claim to translocal and transhistorical validity and significance. Indeed, Buddhists have at times identified their Buddhisms with truths and values that they have understood to be ahistorical and universal.

Investigating the "local production of meaning" thus generates some productive challenges. Hallisey notes that attentiveness to the ways in which Buddhism is re-envisioned in particular times and places can obscure the transhistorical value that those constructions of Buddhism might have for their Buddhist architects (111-112) in this volume). Scholars might fruitfully historicize and particularize various definitions of Buddhism, might preserve a certain skepticism regarding historical claims to preserve an ahistorical and universal truth, and might seek to reveal the social and political conditions that motivate those claims—but they will need as well to grapple with the tension between academic angles of vision that currently privilege the study of local and historically situated Buddhisms and Buddhist visions of their tradition as crossing or transcending time and space. The essay in this volume by Mark Lewis provides a vivid example of the ways in which Buddhists themselves have grappled with the tension between their particular historical circumstances and the teachings that they (sometimes) take to be universal; Dale Wright's essay suggests that perhaps we stand to learn something from Buddhists who have negotiated that tension.

It is for these reasons that we have chosen essays that focus on the ways in which Buddhism(s) have been defined in particular times and places by scholars and by Buddhists. These essays might be read most productively as "case studies" that illuminate processes of definition and construction all the more clearly for their specificity. We have attempted in our selection to include essays that examine the definition of Buddhism in a range of different Buddhist traditions, and in a diverse set of places and times. Taken together, the essays display the complexity, multiplicity, and incredible diversity of Buddhist traditions. It is impossible, of course, to be fully inclusive of that diversity; while studies of Buddhisms in Tibet, China, Japan, and South and Southeast Asia are present in the volume, many Buddhisms are only touched upon lightly or are absent altogether. While such omissions are regrettable, it is our hope that the themes and approaches employed in the articles and discussed in our Introductions will enable readers to continue these conversations in their studies of other Buddhisms.

Our decision to include case studies of both premodern and modern Buddhisms warrants brief comment here. Studies of the formation and impact of definitions of Buddhism have generally privileged modern contexts. Attempts to interrogate the Orientalist legacy of Buddhist studies have, for obvious reasons, focused our attention upon the modern period as the locus for the production of the definitions that have shaped categories, assumptions, and approaches in the field of Buddhist studies. Further, the study of modern Buddhisms takes seriously the impact of Western scholars' definitions on how Buddhists themselves have transformed (either receptively or defensively) the ways in which they describe, conceptualize, and evaluate their traditions.[5] The essays by Judith Snodgrass and Richard Jaffe together provide particular insight into the skill and deliberateness with which modern Buddhists constructed their own traditions. Snodgrass illuminates the ways in which Japanese Buddhists rivaled their Western conversation partners in the deft appropriation of ideas, while Jaffe's study of some of the same Buddhists at a slightly earlier time demonstrates that Westerners did not have to be present in order for Buddhists to have such conversations; Buddhists redefined their tradition through interactions with other Buddhists, as well.

Attention to premodern Buddhisms in discussions of how Buddhism has been defined has likewise concentrated on the ways in which Orientalist scholarship constructed early Buddhism through the conceptual frameworks and assumptions of Western scholars. Questions of how Buddhists in premodern contexts reflected upon and represented their own traditions have, however, drawn comparatively less attention in contemporary scholarship. Jonathan Walters's essay is especially helpful for considering the ways in which premodern Buddhist interpretations of received traditions continued to evolve as successive generations engaged with the past. His work also shows how a history of Buddhist interpretations can serve as an important point of comparison with, and potentially as a corrective to, modern scholarly interpretations of the same source material. Several of the essays included in this volumes encourage us not only to consider the ways in which premodern Buddhists constructed representations of their own traditions long prior to the imposition of Western definitions and categories, but also to identify significant continuities between patterns of self-representation in modern Buddhisms and in the premodern past. As David Germano's essay demonstrates with particular force, many contemporary Buddhists view past traditions as possessing ongoing power and validity in the present. One of the great challenges for Buddhists in the present is to determine how best to draw upon that power to address their needs and circumstances.

Defining Questions: A Dialogical Process

Critiques of Orientalist scholarship have enabled us to recognize that the representation of "others" (in this case, of Buddhists and Buddhisms) is necessarily both an ethical and a political enterprise, in that it always also involves the construction of the self, of the scholar, in relationship to that "other," a process fraught with power dynamics. The Orientalist project of defining "Buddhism" is a paradigmatic case in point: in some regions of Asia, scholarly constructions of Buddhism—both the notion of an idealized "original" Buddhism and the representation of modern Buddhists as benighted, irrational, and incapable of self-governance, for instance—served the (multiple) agendas of the colonizers. The perspectives afforded us by our own time and place call into question some of the assumptions and biases of previous scholars. If we insist upon the fundamental difference between "us" as contemporary scholars and "those Orientalists," however, we are in danger of overlooking one of the most important lessons we can learn from them: the recognition of our own finitude in perspective and self-knowledge.

Moreover, the ongoing legacy of Orientalist scholarship is not only to be found in the academic scaffolding of the field of Buddhist studies—in its fundamental assumptions, methodological predilections, and basic terms of analysis—but also continues to inflect the relationship of scholars to the Buddhists, past and present, that they study. As Donald Lopez has observed with regard to his own experience studying in Tibetan exile communities, the scholar finds himself in the patronizing and paradoxical position of retrieving and preserving Buddhist culture because Buddhists themselves are (implicitly or explicitly) viewed as "unequal to the task"—but how could they be otherwise, when "the culture they were charged to preserve was not of their making, but of ours" (Lopez 1995b, 269)? To the extent that "Buddhism" is a scholarly construction, such structural inequalities would seem to be inherent in the relationship between scholars and Buddhists. Orientalist constructions of Buddhism still constitute "the locus of the articulation of our identity" as scholars of Buddhism; from this location, it remains premature to imagine "a post-Orientalist Buddhology and sketch what it might look like" (Lopez 1995b, 21). If we are to continue studying Buddhist traditions, it is necessary to acknowledge this inheritance and location. By doing so, perhaps we can begin to imagine the possibility not of a post-Orientalist Buddhology, but of a post-Orientalist methodology. We suggest that, taken together, the essays in this volume offer up just such a possibility.

While it remains important to continue the work of excavating our Orientalist heritage, the essays gathered here take a different approach, one which we have characterized as a reconceptualization of the scholarly project of "defining Buddhism(s)"—a project in which scholars of Buddhist traditions are necessarily involved—as a dialogical process in which Buddhists, past and present, are centrally involved. We take our cue in part from Michel Foucault's ruminations on the process and purpose of dialogue. Foucault characterizes dialogue as "the work of reciprocal elucidation" (1994, 111), a process of problematization in which each interlocutor, by questioning the other, facilitates "the development of a given into a question" (118). Posing and responding to questions challenges both partners in dialogue to recognize and hold up for examination assumptions that they would otherwise take for granted. For Foucault, a partner in dialogue need not be a person; a text, an institution, or a practice can respond to our questions and pose questions of us, as well.

This difficult dialogical model is founded, then, on the premise that we humans, by virtue of our location in particular cultural, historical, linguistic, and social contexts, are severely limited in our ability to recognize our own fundamental assumptions, the "givens" of our time and place. Through dialogue with an other who can question such givens, we might, slowly, begin to turn our own givens into objects of analysis; we, in turn, have the potential to pose revealing questions of the other. In order for this "work of reciprocal elucidation" to succeed, however, each interlocutor must acknowledge the right of the other to interrogate his or her assumptions, and accept the moral responsibility to ask questions to which we have not determined the answer in advance (Foucault 1994, 111-13). Partners in dialogue must strive to be as open as possible to one another; they must be receptive to the challenging questions they are asked, and must pose in return genuine questions that are not calculated to confirm their assumptions.

The Buddhists we study, past and present, have the capacity to challenge many of the "givens" that the field has inherited from Orientalist scholarship, when we learn to listen to their voices. The myriad ways in which Buddhists have constructed and defined their own traditions call into question scholarly definitions, narratives, and assumptions, both in their broad contours and in their finer details, as the essays in this volume demonstrate. But the potential of this form of dialogue is greater still, as Dale Wright's essay makes especially clear; listening to the Buddhists that we study can challenge not only our conceptions of Buddhism, but also much more fundamental categories that constitute our scholarly cosmology—notions of history and geography, text and object, person and community. Premodern Buddhist voices, uninflected by the assumptions of modernity, have an exceptionally important role to play in this process, although listening to them from our own historical position can be particularly challenging. Like Ronald Inden (2000, 14),

> we wish to establish a dialogical or interdiscursive relationship with the texts we study... we want to see them as living arguments both in their historic usages and by virtue of our reenactment of their arguments, in our own present. We want to see what we can learn from these texts that pertains to our own time and its problems.

Janet Gyatso's essay is a clear example of this kind of constructive scholarship, locating as it does resources for addressing contemporary social challenges in premodern constructions of gender categories. And, as Gregory Schopen's essay in this volume makes clear, establishing a similar kind of dialogical relationship with the material culture of the past helps us both to recognize our predilection to privilege literary culture and to listen to other Buddhist voices, voices that do not always speak through texts. Finally, we can, with Hallisey, reframe our investigation of Orientalist scholarship, as well, by recognizing that it, too, developed through conversation with Buddhists, although not through the difficult "work of reciprocal elucidation" envisioned by Foucault; Orientalists do not seem to have acknowledged or appreciated the impact of their exchanges with Buddhists on the definitions of Buddhism that they created.

Through this ongoing dialogue, scholars are able to formulate different and more productive questions to ask of Buddhist persons, texts, and material culture. As we have noted, those of us engaged in the study of Buddhism(s) are inevitably engaged in defining Buddhism(s), even if we refuse a positivist definitional project; such is the power inherent in representation. Reconceiving of definition as an endless dialogical process does not eradicate that power, but rather places it in service of the (necessarily imperfect and ongoing) ethical project of reciprocal elucidation. Scholarly representations of Buddhism(s) remain the responsibility of scholars; engaging in the dialogical process does not "free" us from the ethical complexity involved in representing others, but rather urges us to acknowledge that complexity more fully. One of the insights afforded us by the problematization of the colonial project and the assumptions of modernity is surely that we humans inhabit the innumerable givens of our place and time. Nonetheless, there remains the potential of thought, when provoked by an interlocutor, to call what is given into question. In this volume, those givens are definitions of Buddhism.

As an anthology, this volume also participates in the process of constructing a dialogue, one that seeks to relate and interpret productively recent scholarship on Buddhism(s). By creating a new context for these essays, we seek to generate a conversation that begins to articulate the contours of dialogical approaches to defining Buddhism(s). By bringing together studies that focus both on distinctive forms of Buddhism, situated in a range of times and places, and on different aspects of thought and practice, this conversation also illuminates the astonishing diversity among Buddhisms. Each of these investigations is carefully attentive to Buddhist agency and ingenuity in the definitional process, and by prioritizing the ways in which Buddhists themselves have defined different dimensions of their traditions, these scholars enable us to imagine how we might begin to construct a dialogue between Buddhist patterns of self-representation and our own definitional practices.

These essays suggest a range of approaches to the process of defining Buddhisms. Some of these are articulated explicitly, while others are made visible primarily through their successful demonstration. While the best description of each approach is to be found in the articles themselves, we do see several important commonalities that allow for these disparate studies to be brought into productive conversation with one another. These essays evince an awareness of the ever-present need to reflect upon the assumptions brought by the scholar (and by the reader, as well) to the interpretation of Buddhism(s), thereby allowing for Buddhist models or instances of self-representation to augment, challenge, and potentially transform previously articulated definitions.

What we learn from these approaches has important implications for our continuing study of Buddhisms. By considering Buddhist models of self-representation, we can contextualize our own methods, thereby giving us a better vantage point from which to consider the strengths and weakness of different approaches. By considering how Buddhists in different times and places have formulated and reformulated ways of interpreting and understanding the world, students of Buddhism (and scholars are, of course, included in this category) may come to reimagine dialogically not only their scholarly practices, but also their responses to the world. The essays in this volume describe Buddhist responses to a range of issues that we presume are of importance to all people, regardless of the differences in our immediate contexts. What might we learn from the ways in which Buddhists have responded to invasion and genocide, from their creative reformulations of tradition in response to modernity and colonialism, or from their engagement with the past as a resource for making sense of and transforming the present and the future? How might the construction and reinterpretation of premodern-Buddhist gender categories offer us resources for reconfiguring gender hierarchies within contemporary institutions? What do we stand to gain from considering Buddhist alternatives to or reconfigurations of empiricism or individualism, or materialism? When we ask ourselves such questions, we open up the possibility of understanding and responding differently to situations that are of tremendous significance in the world in which we live.

Defining Categories: Contexts for Conversation

The categories that structure this volume serve both to designate particular terrains in which definitions of Buddhism are negotiated by Buddhists and scholars, and to provide interpretive frameworks within which the essays included can be read productively in relation to one another. In keeping with the dialogical model we have proposed, we have employed the postcolonial categories that currently frame a great deal of scholarship in the field of Buddhist studies, while at the same time exploring in the introduction to each section related Buddhist categories of understanding that might challenge or nuance the assumptions that scholars bring to these different areas of inquiry.

The three section Introductions discuss each essay in detail; here we provide a brief overview of each section and outline the connections among them.

The essays included in Part I: Defining Buddhist Histories engage critically with the history of Western scholarship on Buddhism and delineate alternative approaches. They begin by recognizing the ways in which Orientalist historiography and the definitions of Buddhism it engendered were shaped by the assumptions and agendas of historians. This recognition prompts some of these authors to investigate Buddhist modes of engagement with the past, to make those engagements themselves the focus of historical inquiry, and to ask how Buddhist historiographies might inform the development of alternative methodologies. These studies provide an important corrective to the frequent Orientalist assumption that Buddhists lacked historical consciousness; they help contemporary scholars to recognize that Buddhist modes of engagement with the past and tradition constitute historiographical models and forms of expression that may differ significantly from those of the modern West. This challenging task necessitates focusing upon the complexities of particular historical contexts, expanding the range of sources consulted for the construction of histories, and considering a variety of strategies for interpreting historical evidence.

Part II: Defining Buddhist Ideologies takes up the postcolonial dictum that the production of knowledge is the exercise of power. The Orientalist representation of "pure" Buddhism as a timeless teaching untainted by worldly concerns—a representation that is itself an illustration of that dictum—lingers on in the popular imagination, but such a definition of Buddhism denies human complexity to Buddhists, who like the rest of us live (and have always lived) in political and social circumstances that demand creative engagement with the ideational and practical resources at hand. The authors in this section recognize and explore the agency and ingenuity of Buddhists in negotiating contests of power. These three case studies together display the radical plurality of Buddhisms as they uncover historical contexts in which Buddhists reinterpreted and reformulated tradition in light of present challenges and anxieties about the future. While the essays explore very different historical contexts and ideological conflicts, a common theme emerges about the ideological power that Buddhist representations of a singular and eternal Dharma have exercised in conflicts. That power has been used both in collusion with and in opposition to state ideologies; it has ensured the survival of some Buddhisms and has brought about the extinction of others. It would be all too easy to misinterpret discourse about the eternal Dharma as indicating the disengagement of Buddhists from the world rather than their active negotiation with it; these authors illuminate how much was at stake in these Buddhist ideological debates.

Part III: Defining Buddhist Identities draws upon the insights of scholarship in postcolonial and gender studies regarding the ways in which defining identity always involves constructing complex and constantly shifting relationships of similarity and difference with others, thereby situating the process of defining identity squarely in the realm of ethics. The ethics of identity formation is such that, in determining who one is and how one should live, one is simultaneously creating relationships with others, relationships of solidarity or opposition. But identities are by no means entirely self-determined; the process of defining identity also involves negotiating the normative identities imposed by society and by others. Likewise, the different dimensions of identity studied in these articles lead us to ask whether any aspect of identity is "natural" or universally experienced. The authors of these articles carefully illuminate the sophisticated and complex ways in which different aspects of identity are constructed in Buddhist discourse in relation to interpretations of tradition and ideological agendas.

These essays demonstrate quite dramatically the close relationship among the categories of histories, ideologies, and identities. To employ these categories as a structuring device, then, is not to seek to differentiate them clearly from one another, but to use them to illuminate particular facets of the process of defining and constructing Buddhism(s) studied in each article. Indeed, precisely because of the close relationship between histories, ideologies, and identities, focusing on one of these categories throws the others into relief. The Introductions to the Parts can be read as three sections of a single essay that enables connections to be made among these categories. Studies in different sections can be fruitfully related in several ways: some share methodological approaches, others reach similar conclusions about the value and implications of attending closely to the self-representations of Buddhists. Read together as different voices in a single conversation, these articles illuminate the central themes of this volume: the great diversity among Buddhisms, the agency of Buddhists in reformulating and representing their own traditions, and the methodological and theoretical implications for the student who positions herself within the dialogical process of defining Buddhisms.

Notes

1. Relevant recent work includes Lopez 1995b, 1998; Almond 1988; Amstutz 1997; Gombrich and Obeyesekere 1988, 202-240. The essays in this volume by Gregory Schopen, Jonathan Walters, Charles Hallisey, and Anne Hansen also examine aspects of scholarship in this period.
2. See the essay by Jonathan Walters in this volume, 44-45.
3. See pages 109-112 in this volume.
4. See Hansen 226 in this volume, citing Collins 1998, 61 and Faure 1996, 11-12.
5. In addition to the articles by Schopen and Snodgrass in this volume, see Hallisey 2005; G. Obeyesekere 1991, 1997; Gombrich and Obeyesekere 1988; Jory 2002.

Part I

Defining Buddhist Histories

Defining Buddhist Histories: Introduction

The engagement with the past is always a project in which present concerns and future aspirations loom large; history is constructed through the interpretive lens of the historian, Buddhist or non-Buddhist. The historian's own theoretical and definitional understandings of history, the sources she privileges, and the values she ascribes to historical narratives for shaping the present and future all significantly determine the construction of historical narratives. Contemporary historians either reject or nuance positivist approaches to history, which proceed from the notion that a historical account can accurately define what "actually" happened in the past; instead, historians now generally acknowledge that histories, even of a "single" context or event, are always multiple and often contradictory and contested. Indeed, as some of the essays in this section suggest, different Buddhist conceptions of the past and its relationship to the present and future have the potential to alter and enrich scholarly notions of history significantly.

These general reflections provide a useful starting point for examining the ways in which Buddhists and scholars of Buddhism have defined Buddhist histories and historiographies. Orientalist and colonial accounts of Buddhism most often pronounced (and denounced) Buddhists as lacking a fully developed historical consciousness of their own tradition. Defining a Buddhist history therefore became the self-delegated mandate of these early scholars of Buddhism, who set a narrow agenda of uncovering Buddhism's origins and the original teachings of the Buddha. The Buddhist history worth knowing—a history apparently unknown to Buddhists themselves—lay in the far distant past. As the articles by Charles Hallisey and Gregory Schopen in this section examine, this narrow prescription for defining Buddhist history has bequeathed a legacy that continues to influence contemporary historians, both within and outside Buddhist traditions.

Scholars have responded in a variety of ways to these early definitions of Buddhist histories. Some historians, led by Schopen's foundational work, seek to deepen and enrich our understanding of early Buddhist social history by challenging Orientalist scholars' almost exclusive reliance on textual sources, which, they assumed, best preserved the "true" Buddhism taught by the

Buddha. Others, like Jonathan Walters, continue to investigate the canonical texts privileged by previous scholars, but rethink in fundamental ways how we might go about interpreting them. Another significant recent trajectory in historical studies of Buddhist traditions involves identifying and describing Buddhist models of historiography. Contesting the Orientalist dismissal of Buddhist historical visions, scholars such as Hallisey and Dale Wright articulate Buddhist models for understanding and constructing the past, and bring those models into conversation with the assumptions and approaches of modern historians. Underlying these varied approaches and focal points is a shared interest in recognizing the agency of Buddhists as authors of their own histories, and in understanding those histories in their local contexts of meaning. This growing awareness of Buddhists as historical interpreters of their own traditions has led scholars of Buddhist traditions to question their own theoretical assumptions about the meaning and value of history, and to investigate the sources of those assumptions. Scholars increasingly recognize and evaluate multiple models for defining history.

The articles in this section highlight the questions that have guided historical inquiry in recent decades, questions that ask how constructions of historical Buddhisms are shaped by explicit or implicit theories of history, as well as by the sources examined and the interpretive methods employed. Concomitant with such avenues of inquiry comes a greater attentiveness to the ways in which accounts of the past (whether Buddhist or scholarly) serve different goals and agendas in the present, and therefore to the historical locatedness of the very concept of history. As these essays demonstrate, scholars of Buddhism increasingly recognize the dialogical nature of the historiographical process, not only in terms of the dialogue between past and present, but also in terms of the dialogue between scholarly and Buddhist conceptions of the past. Each of these essays interrogates the assumptions that have long dictated the ways in which Buddhist traditions have been defined in scholarship, and explores alternative modes of historiographical engagement that emerge from a dialogue with Buddhist conceptions of the past.

Gregory Schopen's essay, by calling into question the sources privileged and the interpretive methods employed in many scholarly constructions of Buddhist histories, illuminates some of the assumptions on which such approaches are founded. Schopen's trenchant critique of scholars' near-exclusive focus upon textual sources in defining Buddhist histories is supported by his argument that canonical texts are "faulty witnesses" to Buddhist history; in his view, texts tend to represent the normative ideals of the tradition, which are often quite different from the ways in which Buddhists actually lived. Schopen shares the perspective of social historians more broadly in critiquing scholarly reliance upon textual sources as having produced impoverished and inaccurate accounts of Buddhist social history. According to Schopen, these textually based accounts reveal more about the assumptions of Western scholars than they do about the history of Buddhism; an unacknowledged Protestant bias rooted in the Reformation informs the notion that the history of religions is to be found in texts rather than in the evidence of material culture, such as inscriptions, architecture, or art. These alternative sources for history have either been ignored by historians or interpreted so as to support the vision of a Buddhist past derived from textual sources. As a result, historians have produced a distorted vision of Buddhist history, ascribing the ideals of the small monastic elite who authored and preserved the canonical texts to all Buddhists rather than investigating the ways in which the vast majority of Buddhists lived. An ethical charge is implicit in Schopen's argument: scholarly definitions of Buddhist history have largely erased the presence of Buddhists from constructions of the past.

By positing a significant disjuncture between lived Buddhism and the normative Buddhism articulated in textual sources, Schopen neither intends to dismiss the canon as irrelevant, nor to represent actual Buddhists as degenerate and at odds with their own tradition. Rather, he seeks to broaden both our conceptions of Buddhism and the sources that we draw upon in order to engage with early Buddhist traditions in all their complexity. Schopen's work represents just such a complicated history, in which Buddhists lived according to varied and frequently contradictory agendas that were often in tension with the normative ideals prescribed in the textual corpus.

Jonathan Walters shares Schopen's concern to shift the focus of historical inquiry to the thought and practice of actual Buddhist communities, and concurs with Schopen's critique of reading canonical texts as transparent accounts of early Buddhist history. Walters, however, argues that canonical sources remain an important resource for defining Buddhist histories—if they are approached through more nuanced and productive interpretive questions. These framing questions effect a movement from a notion of suttas (Sanskrit: sūtras) as straightforward historical accounts to a much more complex vision of suttas as texts that possess their own histories, and that should therefore be viewed as "actions within the sociohistorical circumstances of their production rather than as passive transmitters of neutral information" (133). Rejecting a conception of suttas as static entities that are products of a single historical context, Walters explores the potential for constructing a multilayered history of any text constituted by a complex readership, process of composition, and material transmission.

Walters seeks to deepen our understanding of suttas as dynamic evidence of the ways in which Buddhist self-representations evolve through time by proposing four different "modes" of interpretation. Each of these interpretive strategies (described in detail by Walters) poses a different set of questions and illuminates different aspects of a text's history, as Walters clearly illustrates through close readings of a single sutta. Walters sees value in each of these approaches, and especially in the multifaceted history that emerges through their combination. He finds particular potential in "later reading mode," which asks how subsequent Buddhists interpreted and augmented the texts they inherited. The result of this mode of inquiry is a history of reading, one that significantly challenges historians' predilection to project the motivations and assumptions of modern historiography onto the composers and historical interpreters of the suttas. "Later reading mode" necessitates that historians consider instead how Buddhists engaged with their own canonical tradition according to agendas that emerged from their own sociohistorical circumstances. Such an approach privileges the agency both of Buddhists and of the suttas themselves in the process of defining Buddhist pasts. This approach toward the study of history thus emphasizes the dialogical relationship between the histories produced by scholars and Buddhist engagements with the past: the historian begins from the assumption that the textual history that matters is the history of how Buddhists themselves have interpreted, valued, and lived in relation to the past embodied in their literary inheritance.

These varied modes of interpretation take us very far from the reductionistic vision of a sutta as merely a historical record of its moment of origin; Walters enables us to understand suttas as embedded in and evolving with the cultural worlds that produce, read, interpret, and preserve them. This complex history of suttas proves significantly richer and more illuminating than the pale shreds of history putatively preserved within suttas.

Like Schopen, Walters aims to construct a history of Buddhism that accounts for the complex ways Buddhists have engaged with and continually redefined their own traditions. But if Schopen argues that Buddhists accomplished this in spite of the normative prescriptions dictated in suttas and other canonical texts, Walters argues that suttas were fertile sites for the production of meaning by Buddhists who actively participated in constructing the vision of Buddhism portrayed in their textual traditions. Taken together, these essays challenge core assumptions that have guided previous studies of Buddhist history, and offer fruitful avenues for future inquiry, avenues that privilege the agency of Buddhists in defining their own tradition. The remaining two essays in this section reflect more explicitly on how Buddhist modes of engagement with the past could shape—and have already shaped—the scholarly construction of Buddhist histories.

Dale Wright's study seeks to illuminate the theory of history implicit in an early eleventh-century Chan Buddhist transmission text, and to generate a dialogue between that theory of history and contemporary historiographical practices and assumptions. Through his examination of the structure, terms, and metaphors employed in the text, Wright constructs a model of Chan historical awareness in which putatively ahistorical enlightenment experiences are narrated in chronological sequence and situated within particular times and places. Hagiographical accounts of an unbroken lineage of enlightened masters, beginning with the ancient Buddhas and continuing through Indian and Chinese masters, employ familial terminology and genealogical metaphors to establish ongoing relationships and obligations between the past, present, and future generations of the Chan tradition as they trace the ongoing transmission of enlightenment from one generation to the next. By contextualizing awakening experiences within particular historical moments, the transmission text renders those experiences tangible and meaningful for the self-understanding of the heirs of the tradition. Wright argues that this historicization of the transmission of awakening must be placed alongside, and used to evaluate, the Chan and Zen rhetoric of timelessness that has captured the attention of scholars and contributed to the representation of Chan as a tradition lacking a developed sense of history. To the contrary, Wright suggests, the narratives of awakened masters were constitutive of a Chan understanding of the tradition through time. These narratives also enabled Chan practitioners to strive for enlightenment, an experience described as transcending time, by patterning their lives on the temporally embedded accounts of their lineage ancestors. Wright argues for recognizing this narrative form as a kind of history, albeit a history founded on very different priorities and theoretical assumptions than the histories produced by scholars in the modern West.

Wright proposes that Chan and Western historiographical traditions have much to learn from one another, and seeks to initiate a dialogue between the two. The Chan model of history differs radically in both form and function from modern Western notions of history; Wright highlights in particular the relationship of the historian to the past he recounts. Chan historians envisioned the past as dynamically engaged with the present; the active exchange between past and present allowed for the revision of historical narratives to suit the understanding and needs of the historian's present context. At the same time, the ongoing revision of an idealized past in light of the present precludes a critical engagement with the past. By contrast, Wright suggests, much of modern Western historiography proceeds from the assumption of a rupture between past and present that enables an "objective" and disinterested representation of the past. While this distancing of the historian from her object of study permits a critical engagement with the past, it does not facilitate the use of the past to critique and inform the present. Indeed, Wright contends that comparison with the Chan historiographical tradition reveals the degree to which modern historians "assume the universality and noncontextual truth of their own modern ideas and practices of historiography" (89).

Wright challenges scholars not only to take seriously the Chan affirmation of the past as a valuable resource for the present, but also to recognize the historicity of their own notions of history, re-examining and perhaps altering their practices as a result.

Wright urges us to engage with Buddhist historiographical practices; Charles Hallisey demonstrates that Buddhist visions of the past have already influenced Western scholarship. Hallisey's influential study of eighteenth- and nineteenth-century Orientalist scholarship on Theravāda Buddhism challenges the assumed division between "Western" and "Buddhist" accounts of the past. His work not only significantly enhances our understanding of the complex processes by which Orientalist representations of Buddhist traditions were constructed, but also proposes alternative approaches to the history of Buddhism that emerge from the Orientalist encounter with Buddhism. Inspired by Edward Said's mandate that the scholar must be ever vigilant in the face of received ideas, Hallisey constructs a nuanced history of the methods, sources, and priorities of early Western scholars, whose definitions of "Buddhism" still constitute a complicated inheritance for scholars today.

Hallisey concurs with those who critique Orientalist scholars' essentialist representations of a "pure" Buddhism of the past in relation to which the lived Buddhist traditions that these scholars encountered were deemed degenerate, but his approach takes us in an important new direction by investigating the ways in which Orientalist scholars (some of whom were colonial officers in Sri Lanka and Southeast Asia) were influenced by the modern Buddhists and Buddhist traditions that some scholars denigrated. Hallisey questions the assumption of an unbridgeable divide between "West" and "Orient," a paradigm he identifies as still operative in post-Orientalist critiques of the West, and seeks instead to "develop more nuanced accounts of the interactions between Europeans and non-Europeans, ones which are able to avoid a Manichaean division between East and West and remind us that cultures are not only different but connected" (94). Hallisey demonstrates such connections by illuminating the mutual interaction and transformation of scholarly and Buddhist practices in the colonial period. His critique is thus directed not only at Orientalist scholarship on Buddhism but also at recent scholarship on Orientalism: studies of Orientalist representations of Buddhism have yet to take into account the Buddhist influences on colonial-period scholarship.

Hallisey suggests that we can begin to challenge the assumed division between West and non-West, between scholars of Buddhism and Buddhists, by identifying the patterns of "intercultural mimesis" and "elective affinity" at play in the colonial context. A closer comparison of the methods and assumptions of early scholars of Buddhism with those of colonized Buddhist communities reveals the ways in which Buddhist practices and representations shaped scholarly assumptions and emphases. Such instances of "intercultural mimesis" illuminate the presence and agency of modern Buddhists in the very works that locate "pure" Buddhism in the far distant past. Moreover, Hallisey identifies instances in which the predilections of scholars and Buddhists coincided to a significant degree (for instance, in the privileging of Buddhist origins found both in the positivist historiography of European scholars and in Theravāda commentaries and anthologies). Recognizing these "elective affinities" significantly complicates the study of Orientalism by calling into question the ascription of agency solely to the colonizers and the assumed passivity of colonized Buddhists in the refiguration of their traditions.

Hallisey also proposes that contemporary scholars of Buddhism can derive alternative approaches to historical study from early works on regional Theravādin traditions written by Western colonizers. These "amateur" scholars, lacking academic training, focused their studies upon the local, vernacular texts of Theravādin traditions not because they disputed the Orientalist obsession with the origins of Buddhism, but because they were acquainted with vernacular rather than classical languages. Hallisey urges us to cast aside their assumptions about Buddhism, but to follow their attention to later periods of Theravādin history and literary traditions that have been all but ignored until very recently in Buddhist studies.

Hallisey asks us to locate the production of historical meaning not only in the complex exchange of multiple voices with varying agendas, but also in multiple places and time periods. Focusing upon the ways in which local Buddhist communities have refigured the tradition in light of their particular circumstances, like Walters's "later reading mode," provides an important corrective to the Orientalist tendency to locate the legitimate history of Buddhism almost exclusively in its origins—yet Hallisey's attention to intercultural mimesis cautions us against moving toward a reactionary extreme in correcting historiographic practices. The vision of a transhistorical Buddhism not precisely bound by time or space is not only the production of Orientalist imaginations, but profoundly present in Buddhist self-representations as well. Post-Orientalist and postcolonial histories must, then, consider how local circumstances and concerns engage and shape the vision of a translocal Buddhism that transcends boundaries of specific contexts. If we fail to recognize the ways in which particular Buddhisms are sometimes envisioned as having universal validity and significance, we ignore dimensions of Buddhism that are highly valued in the self-understanding of many Buddhists.

As these essays indicate, current approaches to Buddhist histories continue to reflect upon and respond to the legacy of Orientalist scholarship; realizations about the collusion of power and knowledge that emerge from the critique of colonialism determine the questions that current historians ask and the approaches that they take. Each of these authors challenges us to attend to the history of Buddhists and to Buddhist histories as we construct the history of "Buddhism," rather than locating that history in the murky origins of the tradition. Read together, these articles articulate a process aimed at greater self-awareness, whereby the historiographies both of the Western academy and of Buddhist traditions are interrogated and integrated in order to recognize the implicit assumptions shaping the theories, methodologies, and goals that guide the study of Buddhist pasts. As we have seen, this charge is ethical as well as historiographical: scholars participate in defining Buddhist histories as they investigate those histories, and with that power comes the responsibility of attending to and engaging with Buddhist conceptions of and relationships to the past. In asking how histories of Buddhism have been (and are being) defined, then, we need not only to interrogate the scholarly historical tradition, but also to listen to the Buddhist voices, past and present, that have much to teach us both about the past and about the different ways in which we might engage with and represent the past in the present. As these essays suggest, when we listen to those voices, we begin to move toward conceiving of the writing of history itself as a form of dialogue.

1

Archaeology and Protestant Presuppositions in the Study of Indian Buddhism

Gregory Schopen

The way in which the history of Indian Buddhism has been studied by modern scholars is decidedly peculiar. What is perhaps even more peculiar, though, is that it has rarely been seen to be so. This peculiarity is most readily apparent in what appears at first sight to be a curious and unargued preference for a certain kind of source material. This curious preference, although it may not be by any means uniquely characteristic of the study of Indian Buddhism, is particularly evident there; so too is the fact that it has no obvious scholarly justification. We might first look at a small sample of statements expressing this preference and at its consequences. Then we must at least ask what can possibly lie behind it.

When Europeans first began to study Indian Buddhism systematically there were already two bodies of data available to them, and the same is true today. There was, and is, a large body of archaeological and epigraphical material, material that can be reasonably well located in time and space,[1] and material that is largely unedited and much of which was never intended to be "read."[2] This material records or reflects at least a part of what Buddhists—both lay people and monks—actually practiced and believed.[3] There was, and is, an equally large body of literary material that in most cases cannot actually be dated[4] and that survives only in very recent manuscript traditions.[5] It has been heavily edited,[6] it is considered canonical or sacred, and it was intended—at the very least—to inculcate an ideal.[7] This material records what a small, atypical part of the Buddhist community wanted that community to believe or practice. Both bodies of material, it is important to note, became available to Western scholars more or less simultaneously.[8] The choice of sources for the scholar interested in knowing what Indian Buddhism had been would seem obvious. But the choice made was, apparently, not based on an assessment of the two kinds of sources as historical witnesses, but on some other kind of an assumption. This assumption, it appears, more than anything else has determined the status and use of archaeological and epigraphical sources in the study of Indian Buddhism, and this assumption, apparently, accounts for the fact that an overriding textual orientation was in place very early in Buddhist studies.

In discussing Burnouf, who died in 1852 and whom he calls "the brilliant founder of the study of Buddhism," de Jong, himself the most recent historian of Buddhist studies, says:

> Burnouf stressed the fact that Indian Buddhism had to be studied on the basis of the Sanskrit *texts* from Nepal and the Pāli *texts* from Ceylon .... Burnouf was well aware of the fundamental importance of the study of *texts* for the history of Buddhism. His idea with regard to India at the time of the Buddha, the doctrine of the Buddha and its later development, the relation of Buddhism to caste, etc., which he develops in the *Introduction*, are all based on a careful study of the *texts*. (de Jong 1975, 21; 1987, 20, emphasis added)

De Jong himself has made a number of statements that clearly indicate that the position he ascribes to Burnouf in the first half of the nineteenth century is very much his own position in the second half of the twentieth:

> Each of these vehicles [the three main "divisions" of Buddhism] has produced a rich literature. Undoubtedly, this literature is the most important source of knowledge of Buddhism. Buddhist art, inscriptions, and coins have supplied us with useful data, but generally they cannot be fully understood without the support given by the texts. Consequently, the study of Buddhism needs first of all to be concentrated on the texts . . . (de Jong 1975, 14)

De Jong's statement is of interest both because it is recent and representative and because it makes explicit some of the assertions and assumptions that lie behind it. Notice first that de Jong gives a variant version of the all-too-common, simplistic view of archaeology as "the handmaiden of history."[9] But he goes even further: not only must archaeology be the handmaiden of literary sources, it and the evidence it brings forth can only be "fully understood" with "the support given by the texts"; not only must archaeology support and amplify the literary sources, it must also be supported and amplified by them; otherwise, it has no real use. It cannot be an independent witness. It cannot, therefore, tell a different story.

But notice too that this position, which gives overriding primacy to textual sources, does not even consider the possibility that the texts we are to study to arrive at a knowledge of "Buddhism" may not even have been known to the vast majority of practicing Buddhists—both monks and laity. It is axiomatically assumed that the texts not only were known but were also important, not only were read but were also fully implemented in actual practice. But no evidence in support of these assumptions, or even arguments for them, is ever presented.[10]

Notice too that no mention is made of the fact that the vast majority of the textual sources involved are "scriptural," that is to say, formal literary expressions of normative doctrine.[11] Notice, finally, that no thought is given to the fact that even the most artless formal narrative text has a purpose, and that in "scriptural" texts, especially in India, that purpose is almost never "historical" in our sense of the term.[12] In fact, what this position wants to take as adequate reflections of historical reality appear to be nothing more or less than carefully contrived ideal paradigms. This is particularly clear, for example, in regard to what these canonical texts say about the monk. But in spite of this, scholars of Indian Buddhism have taken canonical monastic rules and formal literary descriptions of the monastic ideal preserved in very late manuscripts and treated them as if they were accurate reflections of the religious life and career of actual practicing Buddhist monks in early India. Such a procedure has, of course, placed archaeology and epigraphy in a very awkward position. If, then, archaeology and epigraphy are to be in the service of a "history" based on written sources of this kind, then they are going to have to "support and amplify" something that very probably did not exist: they are going to have to sit quietly in the corner spinning cloth for the emperor's new clothes.

That this is largely what has happened and continues to happen is again not difficult to document. We might, as a simple example, cite a series of passages from a variety of scholars that address in one way or another the question of whether individual monks owned personal property—a question of considerable importance, since it bears on the character of Buddhist monasticism and because Buddhism has been presented as "the world-renouncing religion *par excellence*" (Zaehner 1974).

Bühler, in discussing the second or first century BCE donative inscriptions from Sāñcī, said:

> Proceeding to the inscriptions which mention donations made by monks and nuns, the first point, which must strike every reader, is their great number . . . *As the Buddhist ascetics could not possess any property*, they must have obtained by begging the money required for making the rails and pillars. This was no doubt permissible, as the purpose was a pious

> one. (Bühler 1894, 93, emphasis added; cf. Marshall and Foucher 1940, 34 and n. 2).

Discussing the Bhārhut donative inscriptions, which may slightly predate those from Sāñcī, Lüders said much the same thing: "It is perhaps striking to find monks and nuns making donations, *as they were forbidden to own any personal property* besides some ordinary requisites. Probably we have to suppose that they collected the money required for some pious purpose by begging it from their relatives and acquaintances" (1963, 2, emphasis added).[13]

Arguing that a "small jar" from Haḍḍa that had a Kharoṣṭhī inscription on it containing the name of a monk was not a gift made to that monk but rather "a funerary jar" intended to hold his ashes, Fussman said, in part: "Above all, it seems surprising that the gift would be given to a monk in particular. *It goes against the prescriptions of the vinaya* . . . One can then assume that the jar was intended for the monks' burial"—to which he adds in a note: "*In this case it would not be a violation of the rules of the vinaya*" (Fussman 1969, 8-9, emphasis added).[14] Marshall, commenting on one of the numerous hoards of coins found at the monastic site surrounding the Dharmarājikā at Taxila, said:

> Probably the hollow block of kañjūr was merely a secret hiding place where one of the monks hid his store of coins . . . the possession of money by a monk *was contrary, of course, to the rule of the Church,* but the many small hoards that have been found in monasteries of the early medieval period leave little room for doubt that by that time the rules had become more or less a dead letter. (Marshall 1951, 240)[15]

Finally, Spink, in an overview of Ajaṇṭā, said:

> A number of inscriptions at Ajaṇṭā also prove that some of the caves, and numerous separate images, were donated by the monks themselves. This is an interesting commentary on the changing of Buddhism in India, for it suggests that monks, far from having renounced all worldly goods, were sometimes men of considerable wealth. It is doubtful that Buddhabhadra, the chief donor of the elaborate cave 26—a man who proclaims himself the friend of kings—spent very much time humbly wandering from village to village with his begging bowl *as his predecessors in the early days of Buddhism certainly did.* (Spink 1972, 51, emphasis added)[16]

The point here is not whether individual monks or nuns did or did not possess private property; the evidence we have, from all periods, indicates that they did. The point is that every time epigraphers, archaeologists, or art historians encountered evidence that even suggested the possibility that monks or nuns owned personal property, they first signaled their surprise ("It is perhaps striking, . . ." "Above all it appears surprising . . .") and then immediately invoked either explicitly or implicitly the rules in the canonical monastic codes against it to assert, in one way or another, that they were not really seeing what they saw. Either that, or they neutralized what they were seeing by attributing it to a "late change" or implied "decline" within the tradition. They all axiomatically assumed that the textual ideal either was or had been actually in operation, that if it said so in a text it must have been so in reality.

There appears to be, however, no actual evidence that the textual ideal was ever fully or even partially implemented in actual practice; at least none is ever cited. And even though the mere existence of rules against it might suggest that monks did own personal property,[17] and even though it is clear that in the textual ideal itself the infraction of those rules was a "minor offence,"[18] and even though it is almost certain that in a strictly legal sense "the monk might retain the ownership of the property that he had abandoned" (Lingat 1937, esp. 431ff.; cf. Oldenberg 1882, 355 and n.), still all material evidence that monks did have personal property must be explained away: Bühler's "they must have obtained by begging," Lüders's "Probably we have to suppose." This is an archaeology truly in the service of written sources, no matter how idealized the latter may be, an archaeology that will find itself forced to retire in the face of frequently indelicate situations. One example must suffice.

We know that Longhurst's Monastery 1 at Nāgārjunikoṇḍa was the gift of a lay sister (*upāsikā*) named Bodhiśrī, and that it was the property of "the Theravādin teachers of Ceylon." These same "teachers" are further described in the epigraphy of Nāgārjunikoṇḍa as "skilled in the exegesis of both the letter and meaning of the ninefold instruction of the teacher and the preservers of the tradition of the holy lineage" (Vogel 1929–30, 22-23). It is of some significance that it was in this monastery, belonging to this group, that Longhurst discovered in one of the cells "a large number of small lead coins of the usual South Indian type of about the second century A.D." But he also found, together with these coins, "a lump of lead ore and an earthenware die for the manufacture of coins of this size and pattern." Longhurst says simply that this indicates "that the monks made their own coins" (Longhurst 1938, 10).[19] No mention is made of the fact that the authority for minting coins in early India was vested in the state, or in guilds of traders or "moneyers" by the power of the state (Bajpai 1963, 17-21; Sircar 1968, 277-78; etc.). This would suggest either that the monk or monks who lived in Monastery 1 at Nāgārjunikoṇḍa were involved in trading and commercial enterprises and were empowered by the state to do so, or that they were involved in counterfeiting. It is difficult to say which possibility is the more likely, but either alternative is interesting for what it might say about the character of actual, historical Buddhist monasticism. Evidence for such activities is, moreover, by no means limited to Nāgārjunikoṇḍa.[20]

The question of ownership by Buddhist monks of private wealth is, of course, not the only question that has been handled in this curious way. Another important example we might look at concerns the so-called doctrine of *karma*.

There are hundreds of short, simple donative inscriptions on the railings surrounding the *stūpas* at Sāñcī and Bhārhut that have been assigned to the second or first century BCE. Almost every one of them says something like *vajigutasa dānaṃ*, "the gift of Vajiguta," or *ghosāye dānaṃ*, "the gift of Ghosā," or one or another of hundreds of names, frequently with a title added indicating the donor's religious or secular status. That is all. The intention of the donor, the reason behind the gift, is—with only one exception—simply never stated. Confronted with this situation, Lamotte, in a book entitled *Histoire du bouddhisme indien*, a book that is *the* standard authority in the field, was able to say:

> At this time the mentality remains strictly orthodox, that is to say it conforms to the spirit of the Buddha. By their charity, the generous donors [at Bhārhut and Sāñcī] never hope to reach the level of *Nirvāṇa*, but simply intend to benefit from the five advantages of the gift signaled by the *Aṅguttara* (III, p. 38-41). (Lamotte 1967, 456)[21]

Putting aside the fact that it is difficult to know how Lamotte knew exactly what "the spirit of the Buddha" was, still it is interesting to notice what happens here. The inscriptions themselves—again with one exception—say nothing about intention, nothing about what the donors "hope" or what they "intended." There is, moreover, no evidence that the *Aṅguttara* was ever known at either Bhārhut or Sāñcī. Nevertheless, Lamotte not only imputes to actual individuals very specific intentions where none are actually expressed, he also assigns these intentions to a very specific text that he cannot, in fact, actually place at either site. This is at best a curious kind of history, a kind of history that—to put it most simply—seems to assume if it says so in a canonical text, it must have been so in reality. It does not seem to matter, again, that there is no actual evidence that this formal doctrine was ever a part of actual Buddhist practice.[22]

If this assumption is able to override the absence of evidence, it is also important to notice that it is also able to override the presence of contrary evidence. After ascribing to the donors at Bhārhut and Sāñcī the very specific intention of "benefiting from the five advantages" described in the canonical *Aṅguttara*, Lamotte goes on to say: "There can be no question [at Bhārhut and Sāñcī] of transferring the merit [of their gift] to someone else, nor moreover of formulating intentions which the mechanism of the retribution of acts would render inoperative" (Lamotte 1967, 456). Notice again that there can be no question either of transferring the merit or even of formulating a particular intention because, by implication, the mechanism of the retribution of acts would render both inoperative: that is to say, real donors—actual people—could only intend or want what was in conformity with a textual doctrine. There are, of course, a number of problems here, not the least of which is that it has never been established that a strict doctrine of retribution of acts was ever actually recognized outside of texts; it has never been established that it had any impact on actual behavior. In fact, what we know from contemporary anthropological studies of both Buddhist and Hindu communities where this doctrine is officially recognized suggests otherwise. It suggests that, where the doctrine is known at all, it is generally invoked in very limited and specific contexts, and people's behavior and their motivations are largely governed by other ideas or forms of a doctrine of *karma* that differ, sometimes very markedly, from the classical, textual doctrine.[23] Moreover, epigraphical data suggest that this has always been the case. Oddly enough, this is clear even at Bhārhut and Sāñcī, the sites Lamotte is specifically referring to.

As we have seen, the vast majority of donors at both sites do not record their intentions. There is only one exception. But in this single case in which the donor actually states his own intention, that intention is exactly what Lamotte says is impossible: it is exactly what the textual doctrine of the retribution of acts would render inoperative. However, Sagharakhita, the donor in question, does not seem to know that. He makes his gift *mātāpituna aṭhāyā*, "for the benefit of his mother and father" (Lüders 1963, 55, A 108). This, in fact, is one of the earliest expressions of and the *only* actually attestable form of the actual—as opposed to the ideal—Buddhist doctrine of *karma* and giving current at Bhārhut and Sāñcī. But because it does not conform to and confirm the existence of the textual doctrine, it is said, "It cannot possibly be." Textuality overrides actuality. And actuality—as expressed by epigraphical and archaeological material—is denied independent validity as a witness. It may not be altogether surprising to note that the more we come to know about what real donors actually did, the clearer it becomes how defective our textual sources can be as historical witnesses.

Since Lamotte wrote the remarks quoted above, a number of important early inscriptions have come to light. In 1968 a number of donative inscriptions on what was a railing surrounding a *stūpa* were discovered at Pauni in Maharashtra. In both style and paleography they are very similar to the inscriptions found at Bhārhut and Sāñcī, and like them, have been assigned to the second or first century BCE. At Pauni, again as at Bhārhut and Sāñcī, the majority of donors do not express their intentions, but there is at least one exception. This exception indicates that the donor, one Visamitā, gave her gift "for the happiness of all beings" (*{yā}ya visamitāya dana sukhāya hotu savasātāna*) (Kolte 1969, 174 (D); Deo and Joshi 1972, 38, no. 2). The other early inscriptions of interest to us come from Sri Lanka and are almost certainly even earlier than those from Bhārhut, Sāñcī, and Pauni. One of these inscriptions, according to Paranavitana, is among "the earliest in Ceylon that can be definitely attributed to a particular ruler" and dates to the period between 210 and 200 BCE. It reads: *gamaṇi-uti-maharajhaha{jhita abi-ti}śaya leṇe daśa-diśaśa sagaye dine mata-pitaśa aṭaya:* "The cave of the princess (Abi) Tissā, daughter of the great king Gāmaṇī-Uttiya, is given to the Saṅgha of the ten directions, for the benefit of (her) mother and father" (Paranavitana 1970, no. 34; lii-liii). Additionally, we now have four virtually identical inscriptions that record gifts of caves and that may even predate Abi Tissā's inscription. All four end by saying that the gift was given *aparimita-lokadatuya śatana śita-śukaye*, "for the welfare and happiness of beings in the boundless universe" (Paranavitana 1970, nos. 338-341; lii-liii).

Known epigraphical evidence, therefore, proves that the earliest actually attestable Buddhist doctrine of *karma* and giving—and this is now attested from the third century BCE and at very widely separated geographic sites—always involves exactly what Lamotte, on the basis of textual sources, said "could not possibly be the case." The intentions of actual donors at Bhārhut, Pauni, and very early Sri Lanka, whenever they are actually expressed, indicate that they all wished in one sense or another "to transfer the merit to another": to their parents, or to all beings, or to "all beings in the boundless universe." These same inscriptions give no indication that any other doctrine, textual or otherwise, was ever known at these sites.

A final example we might cite concerns the disposal of the dead. Here, the assigning of primary status to literary sources has not so much determined how the archaeological record should be read. It has, rather, determined that it should not be read at all.

We know from the scholarly secondary literature on literary sources the precise views of several obscure monk-scholars on exactly how many angels can dance on the head of an abhidharmic pin, and yet that same literature tells us nothing about how the Indian Buddhist community disposed of its dead. Even de la Vallée Poussin, in writing the entry entitled "Death and Disposal of the Dead (Buddhist)" for Hastings's *Encyclopaedia of Religion and Ethics*, was able to say almost nothing about disposal of the dead and filled the entry instead with scholastic definitions and descriptions of the process of death itself (1911, 446-49). Again, the reasons for this are not difficult to determine. T. W. Rhys Davids says:

> Nothing is known of any religious ceremony having been performed by the early Buddhists in India, whether the person deceased was a layman, or even a member of the Order. *The Vinaya Pitaka, which enters at so great length into all the details of the daily life of recluses, has no rules regarding the mode of treating the body of a deceased bhikkhu.* (1900, xliv-xlv, emphasis added)

Rhys Davids, writing in 1900, makes it clear at least why nothing is known about the ritual disposal of the monastic dead: because the canonical literature known to him says nothing about it, the inference being, of course, that it therefore did not occur. But evidence that it did occur, that early Buddhist monastic communities were, in fact, preoccupied not only with disposing of their dead but with ritually and elaborately housing them as well, had been published nearly 50 years before Rhys Davids and 60 before de la Vallée Poussin. But this was only material, physical evidence of what actually occurred—archaeological evidence—not canonical evidence.

As early as 1854, Cunningham published the results of his cursory excavations of the Central Indian monastic sites around Sāñcī. Here already was clear evidence that indicated the existence of an extensive "cemetery" associated with the Buddhist monastic site at Bhojpur before the common era; here too at Sāñcī itself and at Sonārī and Andher was clear evidence for the elaborate housing and worshiping of the remains of the monastic dead.[24] The epigraphical material we have makes it clear that the construction and embellishing of the monumental reliquaries that contained these remains resulted from activity undertaken and paid for by a disproportionately large number of monks and nuns.[25] Only eight years later, in 1862, West published the first description of what he correctly identified as an extensive monastic cemetery that formed a part of the Buddhist monastic complex at Kānheri on the western coast of India (West 1862, 116-20; Gokhale 1985, 55-59). In 1883 Burgess published a description of what is clearly another monastic cemetery in the midst of the monastic cave complex at Bhājā (Burgess 1883, 7; see also Mitra 1971, 153). All of this evidence was available to both Rhys Davids and de la Vallée Poussin, but for them, it seems, Indian Buddhism and Indian Buddhist practice were contained in canonical texts. What Indian Buddhists actually did was of no consequence. And since this was true, Buddhist archaeology and epigraphy also were of no consequence.

It would appear, then, that the ascription of primacy to textual sources in Buddhist studies not only effectively neutralizes the independence of archaeological and epigraphical sources as witnesses, it also effectively excludes what practicing Buddhists did and believed from the history of their own religion. We can see something more of this in, for example, another statement of de Jong's:

> Missionaries came into contact with Theravāda Buddhism in Ceylon, Burma, Siam, and Indochina and with different forms of Mahāyāna Buddhism in China and Japan. Their knowledge was based upon what they observed, and on discussions with Buddhist priests, but very rarely on the study of Buddhist literature itself. For these reasons it must have been very difficult to gain a clear notion of the main Buddhist ideas. A

> religion like Buddhism which is based upon principles which are very different from the guiding principles of Christianity cannot be understood without a thorough study of its scriptures. (1987, 11)

Without wanting in any sense to defend "missionaries," still there are a number of statements here that one would like to unpack, although we can deal with only a few of the most important. Notice only that it is again clear that, for this position, Buddhism is based on texts, that it can be really—do we dare to say "correctly"?—understood only by a study of its scriptures. The implicit judgement, of course, is that real Buddhism is textual Buddhism. Notice that "Buddhist ideas"—at least "correct" "Buddhist ideas"—apparently do not reside in what Buddhists actually did or in what their "priests" said in conversation. Notice that knowledge based on observation of actual behavior is not adequate. But if actual religious behavior cannot tell us about religious "ideas" then this, again of necessity, has radical implications for the uses of archaeology and epigraphy: since archaeology and epigraphy tell us what people actually did, they cannot tell us about "real" or "correct" religion. "Real" or "correct" religion, we are given to understand, and it is assumed, resides in scriptural texts, in formal doctrine.

It is precisely this curious assumption concerning the location of real religion that lies behind the equally curious history of the study of Indian Buddhism. But the fact that it is so firmly fixed in Buddhist studies, and was operational from the very beginning, and the fact that this is a discipline largely formed—if not fully founded—within the Western intellectual tradition, might well suggest that this assumption too is rooted there, and that it might occur elsewhere as well. And indeed it does. It is not only found in fact in a variety of similar disciplines, it is much more nakedly expressed in other fields. I cite here only three examples.

Charles Thomas, one of the foremost figures in the archaeology of Early Britain, starts his book entitled *The Early Christian Archaeology of North Britain* with some important observations. He says:

> It would now be possible to build, slowly, a reliable framework for the Christian events of those centuries [the fifth to the sixth], using no more than archaeological, artistic and architectural data . . . So much that we can today detect through the exercise of archaeological methods—the primacy of the Christian cemetery, the direct Mediterranean contacts, the introduction of full monasticism, and the interplay of art styles in different media—is nowhere explicitly described in what literature has survived. Conversely, much that *is* contained in literary guise alone is not, as yet, reflected in visible or tangible evidence from this period. (1971, 1)

These observations—all of which point toward the importance of archaeological remains as independent sources for the history of a religion—are, however, followed by an otherwise curious *apologia*:

> The Christian reader may find many features of insular Christianity explained below in terms of pagan or prehistoric monuments . . . This requires, perhaps, a short clarification. The central message of the New Testament, that redemption and the means of grace were provided for us, the priesthood of all believers, through God's assumption of manhood and his crucifixion in the person of Jesus Christ, remains untouched. It is a message conveyed by the Gospels, by patristic writing, and additionally through the means of symbols; these apart, it does not and cannot require any material reflection. On the other hand, the outward and visible form assumed by humanly constructed burials or burial-grounds, by the commemoration of dead humans by living humans, by the retention of skeletal fragments and like trivia as relics, and by the building of structures specially designed for the ceremonies of worship, are man's accretions in response to this message. As such, they are independent of the Word, and for the most part devoid of direct biblical authority. They are no more than the handiworks of what Professor Mircea Eliade has called "religious man." They are, moreover, the Christian versions of certain ideas . . . which prove, upon examination, to occur widely and commonly in the outward manifestations of most known religions both past and present. (Thomas 1971, 3-4)

Thomas's statements, taken from a work of historical archaeology published in 1971 by Oxford University Press, provide us with a startling example of how the assumption as to where religion is located neutralizes the significance of material remains and, *ipso facto*, the role of human behavior in the history of a religion. Thomas makes it very clear that because "they are independent of the Word, and for the most part devoid of direct biblical authority," the material remains that characterize the early *Christian* archaeology of North Britain—"the primacy of the *Christian* cemetery" (emphasis added), etc.—cannot be, paradoxically, in any way essentially and historically *Christian*. In fact, he hastens to assign them to some bloodless, ahistorical abstraction called "religious man" who seems to have behaved much the same everywhere and at all times.

Virtually the same position—though made even more explicit—is maintained by Snyder in an even more recent work on "the archaeological evidence of church life before Constantine." Snyder makes a number of moves that are similar to those of Thomas, although they are more neutral in their expression. He too seems anxious to make sure that "the central message of the New Testament . . . remains untouched," but he goes about it in a somewhat different way: "In this study," he says, "there is a resolve to use only archaeological data as derived from the early Christians themselves. For a study of the New Testament, there is no such possibility. It is a basic assumption of this study that there never will be such data available for the study of the New Testament period" (1985, 10). This, of course, rather effectively neutralizes the significance of any material remains that might turn up from early first-century Capernaum, for example, simply because they could not be Christian.[26]

If this suggests to the disinterested reader that what early Christian people did or how they lived has nothing to do with the history of early Christianity, Snyder is quick to confirm this when he finally encounters material remains that are clearly "derived from the early Christians themselves" and therefore indicative of what they actually did: they are, in the end, also not allowed any significance for the history of Christianity.

Snyder first asserts that "the interpretive edge today rests with the Bonn School, which proposes to study early Christian remains contextually as a *Volkreligion*." He then goes on to say:

> If archaeological data belong to the realm of popular religious practice, the interpreter, or historian, must state clearly how the evidence of archaeology does relate to the literary material, or, to state it another way, how the popular religion relates to ecclesiastical tradition. The issue raised belongs not to the disciplines of patristics, history, or theology, but to the sociology of religion. (1985, 7, 9)

The position here is as straightforwardly contradictory as was that of Thomas. The historian must clearly relate the archaeological evidence to the literary material, but that relationship—"The issue raised"—does not belong to the discipline of history. Early Christian remains and archaeological data belong, according to Snyder, "to the realm of popular religious practice." They must represent then, at the very least, what early Christian people actually did. But again according to Snyder, the relationship of what early Christian people actually did, or actually believed, to "the literary material" falls outside the purview of the historian of Christianity. Christianity, like Buddhism, apparently only exists in texts.

It is here also worth noting incidentally that, as Thomas's reference to Eliade suggests, the same assumption concerning religion and where it is located occurs in widely different kinds of work. The fact that a scholar like Eliade, whose concerns differ widely from those of Thomas and Snyder, also implicitly accepts this is only confirmation of how pervasive and perverse it has been.

Eliade, in speaking about "the customs and beliefs of European peasants," says:

> It is true that most of these rural European populations have been Christianized for over a thousand years. But they succeeded in incorporating into their Christianity a considerable part of their pre-Christian religious heritage, which was of immemorial antiquity. It would be wrong to suppose that for this reason European peasants are not Christians. But we must recognize that their religion is not confined to the historical forms of Christianity . . . We may speak of a primordial, ahistorical Christianity; becoming Christian, the European cultivators incorporated into their new faith the cosmic religion that they had preserved from prehistoric times. (1959, 164)

Although there is much here that would require clarification, for our purposes it is sufficient to notice that like Thomas and Snyder—but toward a very different end—Eliade separates what Christians actually did or do, their "customs and beliefs," from "the historical forms of Christianity." What European Christian peasants do or believe is excluded from the history of their own religion and is assigned to something called "ahistorical Christianity." Once again the implications are clear: the historical forms of Christianity—whatever they are, and these are assumed to be self-evident—have little to do with actual Christians.

It is a curious fact that Thomas, Snyder, and Eliade—although each deals with a different period, a different location, and different kinds of evidence—all end by doing the same thing: they all want to exclude in one way or another actual Christian behavior and belief from the history of Christianity. Thomas wants to assign it to generalized "religious man"; Snyder assigns it to "popular religious practice," the domain of the sociologist of religion; and Eliade attributes it to "immemorial antiquity" or "ahistorical Christianity." None of them will admit it into the history of Christianity, and this can only be because they all share a common conception of where "essential," "real," or true Christianity is located. For them it appears to reside in texts. It would appear, then, that Buddhist scholars, archaeologists of early Britain, and historians of religion are all working from the same assumption as to where religion is located. But at least in its origin, this may not be an assumption at all.

Although most Buddhist scholars, archaeologists, or historians would probably resist the suggestion, this assumption in regard to the sources for the understanding of religions looks, on closer inspection, very much like it might itself be a religious or theological position. Embedded, for example, in apparently neutral archaeological and historical method might very well be a decidedly non-neutral and narrowly limited Protestant assumption as to where religion is actually located.[27]

The methodological position frequently taken by modern Buddhist scholars, archaeologists, and historians of religion looks, in fact, uncannily like the position taken by a variety of early Protestant reformers who were attempting to define and establish the locus of "true religion." The unknown author of the tract "On the Old and the New God" proposes, according to Eire, "that Christians should not seek religion in outward things, but rather in scripture" (1986, 76). Karlstadt, again according to Eire, "began to strike out against the prevailing religious externalism of his day, hoping he would be able to reassert the primacy of the Word." His position "is clearly revealed in this dictum: Only the Spirit vivifies, and the Spirit works through the Word, not through material objects. 'The Word of God is spiritual, and it alone is useful to believers'" (1986, 55, 59). In his *Commentary on True and False Religion*, Zwingli declared that "we ought to be taught by the word of God externally, and by the spirit internally, those things that have to do with piety, and not by sculpture wrought by the artist's hands" (1981, 331-32). Calvin too saw material things—"images and like things"—not as integral and vital parts of "religion," but as "innumerable mockeries . . . which pervert religion" and must be excluded from it. They are not "spiritually ordained by the Word" (1954, 36).

There are other and probably better passages that could be cited, but the point at least, I think, is clear: there is a remarkable similarity between the value assigned literary sources in modern historical and archaeological studies and the argument of Protestant reformers concerning the location of true religion. This suggests, at least, the distinct possibility that historical and archaeological method—if not the history of religions as a whole—represents the direct historical continuation of Reformation theological values; it further suggests that if Karlstadt's hope was to "reassert the primacy of the Word," he may have succeeded in doing just that in some very unlikely and unforeseen ways.

There are other considerations that point in the same direction. It is not just the assigning of primacy to literary materials in the study of religion in both modern archaeological and historical studies that shows several signs of possibly being rooted in sixteenth-century Protestant tracts. The concomitant disinclination of archaeologists and historians to consider material remains as independent, critical sources for the history of a religion also looks very much like a more recent manifestation of the sixteenth-century Protestant distrust and devaluation of actual religious and historical human behavior. Sixteenth-century material objects—reliquaries, shrines, and images—were for Protestant reformers apparently irrefutable evidence of what Christian people were actually doing. They refer to them constantly in their polemics: Calvin, in fact, drew up "an inventory of relics" to show, from his point of view, just how bad things were (1844, 289-341). This inventory, ironically, is an extremely valuable historical document because it allows us to see what was actually occurring during his lifetime in specific geographical locations.

But what is a boon for us was a bane for Calvin. In fact, the problem for the reformers was, in part at least, precisely what was actually occurring and what had been historically practiced. Given the nature of the case they were trying to advance, they did not—more pointedly, could not—allow actual religious practice to have any meaningful place in defining the nature of true religion. To have done so would have been to concede to their perceived opponents the validity of a substantial portion of the argument from "tradition." Proponents of this new and historically peculiar conception of religion, therefore, were of necessity forced to systematically devalue and denigrate what religious people actually did and to deny that it had any place in true religion.[28] This devaluation, not surprisingly but in fact almost obsessively, focused on material objects. The religious power and importance of these objects are, however, only underlined by the fact that they frequently had to be forcefully removed and destroyed and always had to be fulsomely denounced with an otherwise curious ardor. We, it seems, may have inherited both tendencies: the unwillingness to allow actual practice a meaningful place in the definition of religion and the devaluation of any sources that express it.

Merely stating the striking similarity between the arguments of sixteenth-century Protestant reformers and the assumptions of modern Buddhist scholars, archaeologists, and historians of religion, does not, of course, prove anything. It does, however, suggest some possibilities. It is possible that the curious history of the study of Indian Buddhism is neither curious nor unique. It begins to appear as only one instance in which a particular assumption concerning the location of religion has dictated and determined the value assigned to various sources.[29] It is possible that what originated as a sixteenth-century Protestant polemical conception of where "true" religion is located has been so thoroughly absorbed into the Western intellectual tradition that its polemical and theological origins have been forgotten and now it is taken too often entirely as a given.[30] It is possible, then, that it is this conception that has determined the history of the study of Indian Buddhism and that—as a consequence—our picture of Indian Buddhism may reflect more of our own religious history and values than the history and values of Indian Buddhism. It is possible, finally, that the old and ongoing debate between archaeology and textual studies is not—as is frequently assumed—a debate about sources. It may rather be a debate about where religion as an object of investigation is to be located. It is possible, perhaps, that the Reformation is not over after all.

Notes

1. There is, of course, no single, systematic survey of Buddhist archaeological remains in India. The best attempt so far is Mitra 1971. It, however, was not only not intended to be exhaustive but is now also some 20 years out of date. For inscriptional remains we

have, for the period up to 1910, Lüders 1912. It is, though, by now badly outdated and, as its title indicates, does not list material beyond "about AD 400." Both more comprehensive and much more recent is Shizutani 1979, but it too is already dated and contains serious omissions—cf. Shizutani's listings of the Kharoṣṭhī inscriptions, e.g., with those in Fussman 1989, 444-51. Shizutani is especially unreliable now for important sites like Mathurā (only one of the finds from Govindnagar is included) and like Amarāvatī (none of the early inscriptions brought to light in the "clearance-operation" in 1958–59, e.g., are included; see Ghosh 1979, 97-103).

2. On the curious fact, e.g., that a considerable number of Buddhist inscriptions were never intended to be seen, let alone read, see Lüders 1909, 660; Konow 1929, 31; Naik 1948, 3-4; etc.
3. This point in regard to archaeological evidence in general has been made a number of times. See, for example, Grenet (1984, 7), who, in referring to Zoroastrianism, contrasts "canonical or clerical texts—always untiringly scrutinized although the narrowness of the milieux which produced them is ever more clearly evident," with archaeological materials "which allow us the most direct access to the religion as it was lived and practised by all social classes." Much the same has also been said of epigraphical sources. For example, L. H. Kant, in speaking of Jewish inscriptions from the Greco-Roman world, says "inscriptions, in contrast to most other written records, reflect a broad spectrum of society—from nearly illiterate poor, who wrote many of the Roman catacomb inscriptions, to the apparently wealthy patrons of funerary poetry and from tradesmen such as shoemakers and perfume sellers to educated persons such as rabbis and disciples of sages. It is also striking that, unlike many written texts, the inscriptions express for us religious views that have not been filtered by a subsequent normative literary tradition" (Kant 1987, 674). Likewise, in regard to "les inscriptions latines chrétiennes," Sanders has said: "De la sorte, les inscriptions nous renseignent aussi de manière privilégiée sur la masse, sur la majorité oubliée par la littérature à hauts talons, le majorité silencieuse, l'homme de la rue, sa vie privée, son imbrication dans son monde à lui, telle qu'elle fut définie par les coordonnées du temps, de l'espace, des conditions sociales, du climat religieux et émotionnel . . ." (Sanders 1976, 285). For the points of view represented in Indian Buddhist inscriptions and the role of the "lettré," whether "moine ou sculpteur," see the important remarks in G. Fussman's review of *Epigraphical Hybrid Sanskrit*, by Th. Damsteegt (Fussman 1980, 423-24). It should be noted, finally, that inscriptions are, of course, written sources, but they are most easily and clearly distinguishable from literary sources by the simple fact that they were not meant to be circulated.
4. For some representative recent views, see Norman 1984, 1-9. He points out that it is now known that "the Pali canon is a translation from some earlier tradition" (4), that, in fact, "all traditions which we possess have been translated at least once" (5). See also Gomez 1987, 352ff.: "Textual sources are late, dating at the very least five hundred years after the death of the Buddha"; Schopen 1997, 23-25.
5. This, ironically, is especially true for the so-called early canonical literature. For Pāli, see Hinüber 1983c, 75-88: "most of the surviving [Pāli] manuscript material is hardly older than the late 18th century" (78); see also Hinüber 1978; 1983b; 1985; 1987a; 1987b; Fernando 1985. For Central Asian Sanskrit material, see Sander 1968, 51: "Unter den in die Tausende gehenden, von den vier preussischen Expeditionen [1902-1914] im Norden Ostturkistans gefundenen fragmentarischen Sanskrithandschriften gibt es, soweit mir bekannt ist, nur sieben mit den charakteristischen Merkmalen der Kuṣāṇa-Brāhmī," and so on.
6. Horner 1930, xx: "Still another inherent difficulty in dealing with the Pāli texts arises from the various editions, glosses, and revisions which they have undergone at the hands of the monks"; etc.

7. A. K. Warder, e.g., starts his discussion of the Pāli canon as a "historical record" by saying "the Buddhists . . . were ready to turn everything to account in developing and popularizing their ideas and in presenting a comprehensive 'world view,'" and ends it by saying: "The bias of the repeaters [of the canon] sometimes intrudes itself, often very clumsily" (1961, 46-47).
8. For the history of the study of the archaeological and epigraphical material, see Chakrabarti 1988; there is also some interesting material for the earliest period in Mitter 1977; and some useful data in Imam 1966. For the study of literary sources, the most recent and reliable work is de Jong 1987; see also de Lubac 1952; Schwab 1984; Halbfass 1988.
9. Archaeologists themselves have contributed heavily to the currency of this view; see Daniel 1981, 13; Alexander 1979, 215; cf. Dymond 1974.
10. Epigraphical evidence, at least, does not support the idea that Buddhist literature was widely known in actual Buddhist communities, but in fact points in the opposite direction; see, most recently, Schopen 1989, 149-57, and the sources cited in the notes there.
11. In speaking about "early Christian archaeology," G.F. Snyder refers to "three mistaken assumptions" about "sacred" literature: "It is assumed the literature represents rather accurately the historical situation when actually it may have a tendentious purpose . . . It is assumed the literature speaks *cum solo voce* when actually other voices have been ignored, repressed, or assimilated . . . It is assumed the literature represents a reflective or literary level of popular religion whereas actually literature and practice often stand in tension with each other" (1985, 8). Snyder's formulation is, of course, suggestive of what has been assumed in Buddhist studies as well; but cf. below 34-36.
12. It is worth noting that even those South Asian Buddhist literary sources that have been taken to most closely approximate "historical" documents in our sense of the term were intended, by their authors or transmitters, to fulfill a very different function. The chapter colophons of the *Mahāvaṃsa*, e.g., uniformly say: Here ends such and such a chapter "in the *Mahāvaṃsa*, compiled for the faith and exhilaration of good men" (*sujanappasāda-saṃvegatthāya*). See Geiger 1908, 11, 15, 20, etc.; see also the opening exhortatory verses in Oldenberg 1879, 13.
13. Like Bühler before him, and in similar terms, Lüders points out that a comparison of Buddhist with Jain inscriptions makes it very difficult to avoid the fact that, in Buddhist inscriptions, the monks themselves appear as donors—they are not acting as organizers or agents of others: "The wording of the Bhārh[ut] inscriptions refers to the Buddhist clergyman in such a way, as if he himself had made the donation" (1963, 2).
14. The original reads: "Surtout il paraît surprenant que le don soit fait à un moine en particulier. *C'est contraire aux prescriptions du vinaya*; . . . On peut donc penser que la jarre était destinée à l'inhumation du moines . . . *En ce cas il n'y aurait pas violation des regles du vinaya." Ed.*
15. Such hoards are, in fact, found in Buddhist monasteries that are very much earlier than "the early medieval period"; see Sahni 1937, 21-22; D. B. Diskalkar 1949, 12ff.; etc.
16. For yet other examples, see Kosambi 1955, 52-53; Gunawardana 1979, 81-86; Falk 1989, 223, n. 2; Ray 1986, 104.
17. Compare Wassilieff 1896, 321: "pour le vie en communauté, même dans les autres religions, les règles établies ne peuvent sortir du cadre connu."
18. See, for the sake of convenience, Prebish 1975, 13-14, 70-71; Horner 1940, 268-91; Wijayaratna 1983, 93-104.
19. Cf. Sarma 1973, which deals with an even earlier mold from the site.
20. Evidence for the manufacture of coins at Buddhist monastic sites is both early and widespread. For such evidence at Kasrawad, see Diskalkar 1949, 15; for Nālandā, Kumar 1987, 212; Prakash 1986, 202ff.; and so on.

21. I have elsewhere discussed this same passage from a somewhat different point of view; see Schopen 1997, 41-42.
22. There has been very little discussion of the assumptions and method that lie behind this important book. The only serious attempt to get at some of the problems involved is, as far as I know, Pye 1973, 1-58, esp. 31ff. At least some of the problems, moreover, appear to be directly related to Lamotte's declared intentions, which, on the surface, appear to be mutually contradictory. He first says, "Notre premier souci a été de replacer le bouddhisme dans le cadre historique qui lui manquait, de le retirer du monde des idées où il se confinait volontairement pour le ramener sur terre," but then says: "En laissant au merveilleux la place qu'il a toujours occupée dans les sources, on pense donner un reflet plus fidèle de la mentalité des disciples du Buddha. C'est cette mentalité qui constitue l'objet propre de notre enquête et non une fuyante et insaisissable certitude historique" (1967, vi, x). Note that H. Durt has already pointed out that "certes, l'*Histoire du bouddhisme indien* n'est pas une 'histoire des mentalités' au sense contemporain du terme" (1985, 14).
23. Even the most steadfastly conservative have had to admit this in regard to contemporary Buddhism. See, for example, Gombrich 1971, 243: "The canonical theory of *karma* survives intact—cognitively; affectively its rigour is sometimes avoided. Similarly, though the doctrine of *anatta* can be salvaged by the claim that the personality continuing through a series of births has as much reality as the personality within one life, *prārthanā* for happy rebirths and the transfer of merit to dead relatives show that the *anatta* doctrine has no more affective immediacy with regard to the next life than with regard to this, and that belief in personal survival after death is a fundamental feature of Sinhalese Buddhism in practice." Interestingly, something very like this had been pointed out more than a hundred years ago; see Foucaux 1884, xvi, n. 2, and xvii, nn. 1 and 2. For the Hindu context, see, among many possibilities, Sharma 1973, 347-64.
24. Cunningham 1854, 211-20, Bhojpur—at which *Stūpa* 8c, e.g., contained numerous large bones; 184-89, Sāñcī, *Stūpa* no. 2; 203-205, Sonārī, *Stūpa* no. 2; 223-26, Andher, *Stūpas* nos. 2 and 3.
25. This is beyond doubt, for example, in regard to Sāñcī *Stūpa* no. 2; see Schopen 1997, 92 and n. 32. Bénisti (1986, 165-70) has recently argued that this *stūpa* is older even than Bhārhut.
26. This same assumption also makes it impossible for archaeological investigation to critically comment on the nature of the New Testament as a historical document; cf. the remarks in Meyers and Strange (1981, 58-59) on the absence of a first-century synagogue at Capernaum in spite of the fact that Mark 1:21 places one there. For other problems concerning Capernaum in the New Testament, see Blenkinsopp 1989, 201-202.
27. "Protestant" is used here in the broadest and most general sense, and the assumption involved is probably only meaningfully so-called in regard to its origins. It has, it seems, been so generalized and fully assimilated into Western intellectual and cultural values that, in its present form, it is probably most simply characterized as "Western." Elements of this assumption were, of course, much older. There was, to begin with, the "Second Commandment" and its long and convoluted history; see Gutmann 1961, 161-74; 1977, 5-25. There was Vigilantius, of whom Saint Jerome, at least, was not fond and the later Iconoclastic controversies; see Fremantle 1983, 417-23 and, among an immense bibliography, Sahas 1986, along with the select bibliography given there. There was Guibert of Nogent's *De Pignoribus sanctorum*; see Guth 1970, but see also J. F. Benton's discussion of Guibert's character (1970, 1-33); and even Erasmus in *Ten Colloquies* 1979, 56-91. But none of these in and of themselves had lasting cultural influence, and almost all are more significant in retrospect—that is to say, in the way in which they were perceived and used during and after the Reformation.

28. This can be illustrated by a number of passages from the *Institutes of the Christian Religion by John Calvin* (Calvin 1843). In reference to the intercession of saints, 3.20.21: "Therefore, since the Scripture calls us away from all others to Christ alone . . . it would be a proof of great stupidity, not to say insanity, to be so desirous of procuring an admission by the saints, as to be seduced from him, without whom they have no access themselves. But that this has been practised in some ages, and is now practised wherever Popery prevails, who can deny?"; 4.9.14: "Of purgatory, the intercession of saints, auricular confession, and similar fooleries, the Scriptures contain not a single syllable. But, because all these things have been sanctioned by the authority of councils, or, to speak more correctly, have been admitted into the general belief and practice, therefore every one of them is to be taken for an interpretation of Scripture"—a position Calvin, of course, denies; 4.10.1: "Whatever edicts have been issued by men respecting the worship of God, independently of His word, it has been customary to call *human traditions*. Against such laws we contend."
29. This, of course, is not to deny that other factors were involved. P. C. Almond, for example, has recently discussed the textualization of Buddhism as an instrument of colonialist ideology: a "Victorian Buddhism . . . constructed from textual sources increasingly located in and therefore regulated by the West" (1988, 24ff.). A striking example of the effects of this textualization may be seen in Hardy 1880, 412: "The difficulties attendant upon this peculiar dogma [the textual conception of *anatta*] may be seen in the fact that it is almost universally repudiated. Even the sramana priests, at one time, denied it; but when the passages teaching it were pointed out to them in their own sacred books, they were obliged to acknowledge that it is a tenet of their religion." See also Rocher 1978, 221-35. That the textualization of Hinduism by Indian "reformers"—in imitation of the Protestant missionary model of religion—had the same consequences for the evaluation of Indian religious practice as the Protestant location of religion had had on the evaluation of European practice, at least at the intellectual level, is painfully clear from a number of sources. Rāmmohan Roy said, e.g., "My constant reflections on the inconvenient, or rather injurious rites introduced by the peculiar practice of Hindoo idolatry which more than any other pagan worship, destroys the texture of society, together with compassion for my countrymen, have compelled me to use every possible effort to awaken them from their dream of error; and *by making them acquainted with their Scriptures*, enable them to contemplate with true devotion the unity and omnipresence of nature's God"; quoted in Richards 1985, 5, my emphasis; see also Richards 1985, 6-9, 24, 30-33, 45, 48-50, etc. It is undoubtedly and notoriously difficult to separate the religious and the political in colonialist ideology, but since both were also at work in founding the *Archaeological Survey of India* (Imam 1966, 40-41), the ideological concern could not itself have been a sufficient cause for the dominance of the textual orientation.
30. This, again, is not to say that there were not powerful competing conceptions, but only to say that they did not culturally win. Early on, the "Catholic" conception held its own and produced, as a consequence, some important scholarly works: "Catholic scholars tended to anchor their investigation of Christian religious observance in ancient tradition. It was the study of this tradition that inspired the monumental and often reprinted *Annales Ecclesiastici* and the work on the Roman martyrs by Cesare Baronio, as well as Bosio's *Roma sotterranea*, the first major archaeological account of the Roman catacombs. On the other hand, when Protestants discussed the practice of Christian piety, they most often appealed to reason and to theological and philosophical principles . . . In the words of John Calvin, a Christian should have 'no use [for] place apart from the doctrine of godliness' which could be taught anywhere at all"; see MacCormack 1990, 8-9. But recent scholar-

ship, which has tended to see "the Counter-Reformation and the Protestant Reformation as analogous social and religious processes" (Badone 1990, 12), has also pointed clearly to the strong textualizing responses in the former; "De l'extraordinaire intérêt qu'on marqua pour les choses de la religion, au moins dans le public qui savait lire, témoignent les statistiques concernant l'édition . . . l'histoire religieuse et celle des mentalités ne peuvent négliger ce fait quantitatif: jamais autant les livres de spiritualité—souvent de petits formats et en langue vulgaire—, jamais autant d'éloges de la vierge n'avaient été mis en circulation" (Delumeau 1971, 84); "Surtout, l'époque de l'humanisme vit l'essor de la théologie *positive* . . . qui est l'étude de l'Ecriture, aidée par les interprétations des Pères et des conciles" (85); "En 1654, Godeau, évêque de Vence, donna dans ses mandements des listes de livres à lire à ses prêtres. En 1658 l'archevêque de Sens, Godrin, demanda à ses curés de se procurer 47 ouvrages qu'ils devaient, le cas échéant, présenter lors des visites pastorales et, parmi eux, une Bible, le catéchisme romain" (271); cf. also Baroni 1943. Delumeau's remarks raise, as well, the question of sheer influence of the development of printing on the location of religion in texts, and it undoubtedly played a role. But any argument contending that printing in itself is a sufficient explanation must take into account the fact that printing served a very different function in the Far East—especially in the earlier periods. There, sacred texts were printed not so they could be read, but so they could empower sacred objects. The earliest extant examples of printing in Japan, e.g., contain "versions of Sanskrit charms [*dhāraṇīs*] transliterated into Chinese characters," and, even if they had been seen, they would have had little or no literal meaning for a literate Japanese. But they, in fact, were never intended to be seen. They were meant to be inserted into miniature *stūpas*; see Tsien 1985, 336-37; 321-22.

[For some further observations on the early inscriptions from Sāñcī see now: Schopen 1996b, 58-73. For monks and private property, see Schopen 1995, 101-123. For Buddhist disposal of the dead, see Schopen 1997, chs. 7, 9, and 10.]

2

Suttas as History: Four Approaches to the *Sermon on the Noble Quest* (*Ariyapariyesanasutta*)

Jonathan S. Walters

The study of Theravāda Buddhist history was born of a nineteenth-century enthusiasm about the ancient suttas, or sermons, attributed to the Buddha, which Theravāda Buddhists have preserved in the major "Divisions" (Nikāyas) of the "Sutta Basket" (Suttapiṭaka) of their "Pāli Canon" (Tipiṭaka). As early as the 1830s George Turnour had argued for the "historical accuracy" of traditional Theravādan claims about the great antiquity and unique authenticity of the Pāli version of early Buddhist history.[1] Following from that argument, the suttas (and partly overlapping texts of the Vinaya, or monastic discipline) were once thought to be veritable windows into the original Buddhist community. From them historians of earlier generations spun out a biography of the "historical Buddha," a social history of India in the time of the Buddha, and an impressive array of contradictory opinions about a supposed "original" Buddhist teaching.

But during the present century, and especially during the past several decades, Buddhologists, anthropologists, and historians of religions have raised serious doubts about this naive use of the suttas as sources for reconstructing Theravāda Buddhist history. Thus, it is now widely recognized that the form in which the suttas survive today, like Pāli itself, is the result of grammatical and editorial decisions made in Sri Lanka centuries after the lifetime of the Buddha. An extreme version of this view would argue on that basis that it is impossible to fix the texts of the suttas before the time of Buddhaghosa's commentaries on them, a full millennium after the Buddha. Comparison with parallel material in non-Pāli canons makes certain that parts of the suttas are indeed translations of texts considerably more ancient than that, probably as ancient as we will ever possess, but this move simultaneously guarantees the lateness and nonrepresentativeness of those parts of the suttas without such parallels, especially the contextual stories within which the Buddha's teachings are framed. As these stories have supplied the bulk of detail for social historians and biographers of the Buddha, the problem becomes immediately apparent. Moreover, the historical claims made by Theravāda Buddhists (in the *vaṃsas* or chronicles, and in the commentaries) now appear to tell us more about the time in which they were made (c. fifth century CE) than they do about the ancient periods of history they narrate (see Walters 1997a, 100-19; Walters 1999; and Walters 2000). More important still, historians and anthropologists have pointed to a rift between the Buddhism constructed as "canonical" on the basis of the teachings in the suttas and the actual practices and ideas of contemporary Theravāda Buddhists.[2] As similar divergences from this "canonical Buddhism" are evidenced as early in Buddhist history as our evidence itself, namely the time of Aśoka Maurya (third century BCE), the question emerges whether the reconstructed "early Buddhism" ever existed at all.

As a result, though the suttas remain immensely important to comparative philosophers and philologists, for whom these concerns may seem at best tangential, I think it fair to say that among contemporary historians of the Theravāda there has been a marked shift away from attempting to say much of anything at all about "early Buddhism." Whereas earlier scholars tended to ignore post-Aśokan Buddhist history as corrupt, more recent scholars have tended to regard early Buddhist history as unknowable. In recent decades we have become increasingly concerned with recovering the later premodern and modern Theravāda histories for which more reliable evidence does exist. Though a handful of suttas have remained central in more recent understandings of the historical development of Theravāda tradition, the bulk of the seventeen-thousand-odd suttas in the Tipiṭaka have become increasingly irrelevant to historians working in the field.

As one of those historians, and despite my wholehearted support for attempts at recovering a postcanonical Theravāda Buddhist history, I find this fact unsettling. Of course, in thinking of the suttas as foundational while simultaneously all but ignoring them (except in the classroom), I curiously parallel the practices of the "medieval" Buddhists whom I study. But like those of them who continued to draw on suttas in liturgical contexts or commentarial traditions, I feel that there *should* be something more to the Tipiṭaka than, to borrow Steve Collins's (1990) lovely phrase, "the very idea" of it. Has all the scholarly labor devoted to editing and translating the suttas been for naught? Must historians relinquish these ancient documents to the nonhistorical analyses of comparative philosophers and philologists? Is there nothing more for historians to learn from the suttas? If we are to answer these questions in the negative, we must define historical approaches to the suttas which can still be viable today. And I suspect that historians of religions working in other areas of Buddhist and even non-Buddhist history face similar challenges in rethinking parallel "canonical" texts in the traditions they study.

This article attempts to define such approaches for the Theravāda case. An American Academy of Religion-sponsored collaboration on "Pāli Texts in New Contexts" (a conference held in Chicago, May 1998) forced me to confront the problem of reading suttas as history in light of one specific sutta that has captured my imagination over the years, namely the *Ariyapariyesanasutta*, or *Sermon on the Noble Quest* (henceforth NQ). After a brief introduction to the basic themes of NQ and its position in the Tipiṭaka, I use it as a basis for exploring four different, but certainly not unrelated, "modes" of historical study of the suttas. I refer to these with the inelegant but descriptive titles, "historical source mode," "text of its day mode," "textual whole mode," and "later reading mode." My identification of these modes is not original; I merely attempt to describe generally the range of options that I find in the existing scholarship and in the process to articulate some of the potential opportunities as well as the difficulties entailed by each. The original contribution is in my new readings of NQ according to each mode, focusing in particular on that portion of NQ which is concerned with the Bodhisatta's pre-enlightenment training. After showing that each of these programs for studying suttas historically does in fact allow us new insight into NQ, I return in the conclusion to more general questions surrounding the historicity of the suttas and, by implication, the study of all such "canonical" texts.

Ariyapariyesanasutta (NQ) is contained as the 26th sutta in the "Middle Length Division" (Majjhimanikāya) of the Sutta Basket of the Tipiṭaka. Running 16 pages in the Romanized Pāli edition,[3] the sermon is remembered, like most of the suttas, to have been preached while the Buddha was dwelling in the Jetavana Monastery at Sāvatthi (Śrāvasti, modern Saheth Maheth, Uttar Pradesh, India). A group of monks approaches the Buddha's chief attendant, Ānanda, in order to express their desire to hear a sermon "face to face with the Blessed one." Ānanda instructs them to wait at the hermitage of a Brahmin named Rammaka, to which he leads the Buddha after the latter's afternoon bath. When he arrives, the Buddha praises the assembled monks for their diligence in studying the teachings (Dhamma), then proceeds to distinguish between ignoble (*anariya*) and noble (*ariya*) forms of questing (*pariyesanā*). In the former case, a person who is attached to things of the world nevertheless clings to things of the world, thereby failing to escape his or her destiny to be born, to grow old, to die, to grieve, and to be defiled in the perpetual cycle of *saṃsāra*. In the latter case, a person who is destined to those eventualities realizes the danger (*ādīnavaṃ*) in the things of the world that are likewise so destined and renounces them in search of "the unborn [unaging, undying, ungrieving, undefiled] unexcelled Nirvana, which is bound up with peacefulness" (Trenckner 1888, 163).[4]

The Buddha proceeds to tell the monks an abbreviated autobiography, using his own spiritual journey as an illustration of the progression from the ignoble to the Noble Quest. He details his movements from his initial rejection of the world through his encounters and ultimate dissatisfaction with two teachers (named Āḷāra Kālāma and Uddaka Rāmaputta), his attainment of enlightenment (*bodhi*), his initial aversion to preaching, his honoring of God's request that he preach anyway, his search for an audience, an odd and unproductive meeting with an Ājīvika named Upaka, and finally his preaching of the First Sermon to the "Group of Five" monks (*pañcavaggiyabhikkū*) with whom he had practiced austerities and to whom he had decided to preach after learning (from certain deities as well as a survey by his Buddha-eye) that his first choices (the two former teachers) were already dead. He then delivers to the monks assembled at Rammaka's hermitage what I take to be the sermon proper, namely an extended explanation that the Buddhist saint (*arahant*), being free from the snares of Māra (Death), is comparable to a free-roaming beast of prey, whereas a person ensnared in worldly passions is as much subject to Death as a trapped beast is subject to the hunter. The text concludes with a typical statement that, on hearing this sermon, those monks rejoiced at the Buddha's words.

I. Historical Source Mode

In his 1894–95 American Lectures in the History of Religions, Pali Text Society founder T. W. Rhys Davids, discussing the topic of the Bodhisatta's teachers, refers to the good fortune that "we have an account in the *Ariya Pariyesana Sutta*, given by Gotama himself, of the essence of the teaching of . . . Āḷāra Kālāma, and of the reasons which led Gotama to be dissatisfied with the result" (Rhys Davids 1896, 102). Implicit in such statements is the assumption of scholars in Rhys Davids's generation that the suttas provide us a transparent window into the events and ideas of the early Buddhist community and, by extension, the events and ideas of the Buddha's own life. Like NQ, virtually all the suttas are framed as particular moments in the Buddha biography and, of course, as expressions of the Buddha's own teachings; some of them also narrate parts of the Buddha biography itself. As NQ is one of those suttas promising access to the Buddha biography on both levels, it is little wonder that Rhys Davids highlighted it in his narration of that biography.[5]

One hundred years later, however much we still rely on the testimony of the suttas in reconstructing "the historical Buddha" and "what the Buddha taught," we all feel a certain need to qualify Rhys Davids's statements. As mentioned, according to a strict standard for historical evidence we should be treating the suttas as products of the tenth rather than the first century of the Buddha Era (fifth century CE rather than fifth century BCE). Yet I think there is also general agreement that that standard is *too* strict. Texts of the fifth century CE (e.g., Buddhaghosa's *Samantappasādikā*), and even a little earlier (the earliest is *Dipavaṃsa*, c. CE 302) claim that the suttas were by then already very ancient indeed. And even if we ignore these claims and fix the texts nearer the time of the commentaries, we still must admit that at least by that time they were already being read as windows into the time of the Buddha himself. There is moreover plenty of evidence—namely parallel transmissions of suttas and parts of suttas in non-Pāli traditions, for example, in the famous manuscript finds of North India and Central Asia, the early translations of the sūtras preserved in the Chinese Tripiṭaka, and in Buddhist Sanskrit works like *Lalitavistara* and *Mahāvastvavadāna*—that at least portions of the suttas are considerably earlier than the fifth century CE. According to this line of inquiry, it is possible to place one portion of NQ in the earliest layer of the tradition; at least this portion of NQ can still be treated as a document of, and therefore as evidence for, the early Buddhist period.

This portion of NQ is what I will designate (in Sec. II below) the "inner frame" or "frame III." It is that same autobiographical fragment which commences with Gotama's renunciation as "a bodhisatta who had not yet become the Sambuddha, who . . . being a young man with very black hair, auspicious with youth, at the prime age, while [his] parents who did not approve were weeping and wailing, did cut off [his] hair, put on yellow robes and go forth from home to homelessness," and which continues through his encounters with two teachers, his (unstipulated) period of asceticism, attainment of *bodhi*, journey to Benares, and preaching of the First Sermon (Majjhima-nikāya 1: 163-73). There are several lines along which this autobiographical narrative's comparative antiquity can be argued.

First, the language of the text itself belies its age. On one hand, it includes much weird, obscure, and troubling material that might better have been excluded had editorial discretion in fact enjoyed the upper hand. Among the points that I can explain only as a faithfulness to exact transmission are the inclusion of the Buddha's "un-marvelous verses" (*anacchariyā gāthā*) uttered after enlightenment;[6] the problematic initial hesitance of the Buddha to preach his message[7] and the apparent need of anonymous deities to inform the newly awakened Buddha that his former teachers were already dead;[8] the failure of Upaka, followed at first by the Group of Five, to recognize the extraordinary state of his being; the rather un-Buddhalike, half-boastful, half-defensive tone in which he declares himself Buddha to Upaka and the Group of Five; and seeming inconsistencies with accepted biographical tradition, such as the statement that he was in "the prime of his youth" (no indication of being a 29-year-old married father) and that his parents (in the plural) were weeping and wailing when he renounced the world (whereas later Buddha biographies insist that his mother was long-since dead). On the other hand, there is something very human about all this: doubt, arrogance, lag times in reaching enlightenment or convincing others, a remembered youth when the Buddha was not yet Buddha, the physiological reference to his "very black hair" (*susukālakeso*), and so forth. This seems to reflect a certain genuineness. Little wonder that Rhys Davids could treat it as true autobiography (despite the fact that this same early fragment details such "mythological" realities as chats with God and gods and all-seeing Buddha-eyes).

Perhaps more persuasively, second, this portion of the narrative is repeated almost verbatim at other points in the Tipiṭaka. The whole narrative is repeated in three other suttas of the Majjhimanikāya[9] while other parallels are found elsewhere in the Tipiṭaka (some of the narrative has been joined with an early Mārakathā to create the opening of the *Mahāvagga* of the Pāli Vinaya,[10] while the words uttered to Upaka the Ājīvika reappear often in the form of quotation).[11] These are large narrative segments, suggesting that they belong to a different class from the repeated stock phrases, clichés, lists, and so on, that are well known in the sutta texts. Whereas the latter could all have been editorial innovations, I agree with E. J. Thomas that in the present case the editors likely had an extant narrative that they reworked as these suttas, *Mahāvagga*, or *Kathāvatthu*; this narrative fragment would therefore predate the initial compiling and editing of the Tipiṭaka in the form we have it today.[12]

Third, in addition to being present in sutta form in Chinese and Japanese canons, this narrative fragment has also been used by the compilers of the *Lalitavistara* and *Mahāvastvavadāna*. In Thomas's estimation, this too would mean that the narrative is very old ([1927] 1975, 64). I have compared in detail only the passages that relate to the Bodhisatta's teachers, so I hesitate to generalize about the incorporation of the entire narrative fragment, but at least with regard to the teachers I think it quite clear that the Buddhist Sanskrit authors have worked from a Pāli or more likely related Prakrit version rather than the other way around (which in many cases, such as the parallels between *Lalitavistara* or *Mahāvastu* and supplements in the commentaries, is more likely the direction of the borrowing). Thus, in the *Mahāvastu* we find a number of grammatical errors that are best explained as bad translation from the Prakrit (Senart 1897, 2: 117-20).[13] Although these slips do not appear in the *Lalitavistara* version, others give away its origin, too, in a Pāli-like prototype.[14] *Mahāvastvavādana* contains virtually nothing that is not in the Pāli;

Lalitavistara supplements the terse statements about Uddaka Rāmaputta (here Sanskritized as Rudraka Rāmaputra) by making the Buddha already have a philosophical rebuttal before meeting him and meeting Rudraka only in the interest of showing him up. Both Sanskrit versions omit the "conjoining frame" of NQ (about destiny to rebirth, etc.), which further suggests the greater antiquity of the embedded portion, the Buddha autobiography.

Fourth, the great antiquity of this narrative fragment can be argued from its apparent use, as a basis for supplementation, in later Buddha biographies. Though I will deal with the question of supplementation more fully below, here it is important merely to note that subsequent Buddha biographies all supplement this text to the extent that they take up the pre-enlightenment/Bodhisattva stage of the biography at all, given that this is our *only* early version of those events.[15] But this is not merely a matter of supposition; the use of actual phrases or scenes from NQ and parallel Majjhimanikāya suttas betrays the reliance of later Buddha biographies on the Pāli or Pāli-like original. I have already shown this for *Mahāvastu* and *Lalitavistara*, but in this context I should also point to some obvious parallels in *Buddhavaṃsa* (c. second century BCE),[16] Aśvaghoṣa's *Buddhacarita* (c. first century CE),[17] the Chinese *Abhiniṣkramaṇasūtra* (translated sixth century CE; the Sanskrit original was doubtless earlier),[18] and the travels of the Chinese pilgrim Xuanzang (seventh century CE),[19] as well as numerous later Theravāda biographies in Pāli and the vernacular languages. The consistent incorporation of bits of our text, whether verbatim or paraphrased, in these later supplements supports the view that the fragment is an early one and also that it is a narrative that in later centuries continued to be of "practical" or actual importance to Buddhists.

If one or more of these arguments for the antiquity of this portion, at least, of NQ is persuasive, then we can place *this* sutta in a period anterior to the time of Buddhaghosa (which anyway seems quite clear in the radical distance between Buddhaghosa's readings and those of the original, as I suggest below in Sec. IV). It can at least be antedated to the time of the Buddhist Sanskrit literature, the first or second century CE (which in any event is as early as any known Buddhist manuscripts). And given that this narrative appears to have existed as a unit prior to the editing of the suttas and Vinaya in the form we have them today, it presumably can be located as early into Buddhist history as we ever are likely to get.

Yet fixing the text at an early period does not in itself yield any significant historical information. If in fact in this instance we can circumvent the doubts raised about the antiquity of the suttas en bloc, we are still left with the question of how the autobiographical fragment ought to be interpreted. Within "historical source mode," the next move would be to ask whether the narrative as such can be taken as "accurate," a designation requiring that the reported information be the result of eyewitness observation and "objective" recording. Here the problems inherent in "historical source mode" are not so easily overcome.

On one hand, the evidence does not prove (though it also does not disprove) that even this autobiographical fragment is old enough to be counted as an eyewitness report by the Buddha or of the Buddha's words. As studies of the historical Jesus have made only too clear, what adepts thought about the founder a century or two after his death can be at great remove from the historical biography of the founder himself. The best our evidence allows us to say is that this autobiographical fragment accurately records the thoughts that somewhat later Buddhists had about the Buddha, or their beliefs about the words he spoke.

On the other hand, even if we allow the fragment to survive from the mouth of the Buddha himself, via the memories of the selfsame monks who heard the sermon at Rammaka's hermitage, there are still reasons to doubt the "historical accuracy" of the passage in question. Three different sorts of objections have been articulated.

1. The first is a pseudoscientific skepticism about the authenticity of the "mythic portions" of this ancient fragment, namely the chats with God and the gods and the Buddha-eye that surveys the whole world. These elements are integral to the narrative in all its appearances and in most of its supplements, meaning that there is no basis for trying to portray them as later accretions from which an even more original core can be separated out. Their presence casts doubt on a historicist reading of the fragment, for it suggests that something more than a commonsense nineteenth-century "objectivity" was at work in the original composition.[20]

2. A second (and less easily dismissed) argument is raised by Thomas, namely that the Bodhisatta's encounters with Āḷāra Kālāma and Uddaka Rāmaputta are reported in formulaic fashion, nearly word for word the same in both instances. Moreover, he points out, the two teachers are made to claim specific meditative achievements that Thomas maintains were inventions of later Buddhist tradition. Thus Thomas concludes that the narrative of the Bodhisatta's training bears no historical relevance.[21] In virtually ignoring the teachers of the Bodhisatta altogether, Etienne Lamotte seems to concur.[22]

3. A third argument against the historicity of the text has been raised by A. Foucher, who in good Orientalist fashion imputes bad motives to the compilers of that portion of the fragment which details the meetings with the teachers. These compilers, says Foucher—inexplicably unaware of their own cultural mores—maligned the Bodhisattva:

> Another fault of our biographers was their incapacity to imagine the future Buddha in any way but as invested with shining glory . . . Our

> authors have tried to reduce to a minimum the Bodhisattva's period of study as well as the need of it. If we are to believe them, he guessed all the answers before they were given to him, and was quick to make his teachers feel their incapacity to teach him. He soon decided to leave Arāda Kālāpa [a Sanskrit spelling of Āḷāra Kālāma], even though the latter offered to share with him the direction of the community of scholars. Thus our authors, blinded by fanaticism, failed to see that, according to Indian ethics, they were portraying the most unfaithful and insolent of pupils. The Lalitavistara even attempted to put this unworthy version in the mouth of the Buddha, but sometimes forgot to change the verbs from the third to the first person.[23] Having left Arāda's community in Vaiśālī, the Bodhisattva came to Rajāgṛha [*sic*] where, as we have seen, he at once met King Bimbisāra . . . The story goes on much as the above, attributing the same kindliness to the master [Rudraka Rāmaputra] and the same presumption to the so-called disciple. This time we are even told that the Bodhisattva only became Rudrāka's [*sic*] pupil in order to reveal the faults of his teacher's doctrine both to himself and to others. Because we feel that the foolish biographers, not the Bodhisattva, were responsible for these unfortunate statements, we need not spend more time on these particular readings.[24]

Of course by historicist standards, this argument that the reporting was "biased" is as damning as the second argument, above, that the reporting was not done by eyewitnesses; both of these would explain/bolster the first argument that the thing reported is unhistorical/mythic.

Nevertheless, the agreed-on solution seems to be the uneasy compromise of treating the narrative as true in substance—*everyone* has the Buddha meet teachers prior to enlightenment, and almost everyone stipulates them as these two (and/or others who have been named elsewhere) and as teachers of yogic trances and Hindu philosophy—while basically ignoring, in addition to all that "mythic" material, also the full detail of the stories of the encounters with Āḷāra Kālāma and Uddaka Rāmaputta (or, as with K. D. P. Wickremesinghe, reverting to the old naiveté of simply treating it all at face value as historical reporting) (Wickremesinghe 1972, 53-56). Of course in "historical source mode" there is no way to do anything else, these being the only sources we have.

"Historical source mode" is based on what I believe to be an erroneous assumption that the compilers of the suttas were somehow *trying* to objectively report historical facts in a would-be nineteenth-century European way. So long as this assumption remains operative, there is nothing to do except judge the suttas as though they had been compiled by Edward Gibbon; and given that they were not, the impasse reached by scholarship in this mode seems inevitable. But rather than abandon the baby with the bathwater, we can disagree with Thomas's assertion that this is the only point of importance in the study of this portion of NQ (see Thomas [1927] 1975, 229). Rather, we can turn to alternative interpretive strategies that make the motive of the compilers a question rather than a given. In Sections II and III I examine two such alternative interpretive strategies that take as their starting point the conclusions about the antiquity of NQ, made possible by "historical source mode," but that lead, I think, to much more productive questions and answers about the text under consideration. In Section IV I examine an additional interpretive strategy to which this first mode of study is altogether irrelevant. Thus, even if we finally retire "historical source mode" as outdated, unproductive, and—let us be frank—boring, still there remain exciting ways in which a historian can make use of NQ.

II. Text of Its Day Mode

In "historical source mode" the reader of the text is the scholar himself or herself, interpreting directly on the basis of standards for historicity characteristic, not of the period in which the suttas were composed, nor even of the later Buddhist history in which they were preserved, but rather of the period in which the scholar herself or himself lives and thinks. In the past I have assumed this flaw to be virtually fatal to the attempt at finding history in suttas like the *Sermon on the Noble Quest*. It should come as little surprise that the final results of an enterprise devoted entirely to judging suttas on the basis of standards that do not belong to them turns out to be hand-wringing, uneasy compromise, and ennui. But I now admit that this does not mean that the historian's only option is to give up the attempt altogether. Rather, in the past decade I think it has been sufficiently well shown that different sorts of historical analysis, far more promising, solid, and interesting, become possible once we remove ourselves from the position of reader and ask instead how people in the tradition itself would have read such-and-such a text.

While in greater or lesser degree I think this shift has been made by many different scholars, maybe even most of us, in many different keys, if not by members of the contemporary Theravāda establishment, I shall nevertheless try to focus my comments on three scholars whose work strikes me as emblematic of three (no doubt related) directions in which this shift from interpreting reader to interpreter of readership allows us to move. In the present and subsequent parts I examine two approaches to the study of the readership of the suttas in the time of their own production/composition, one of them focusing on an external readership or a context of recitation to and about outsiders, represented by the sociohistorical reconstructions of Greg Bailey. The other of them (in Sec. III) focuses on an internal readership or a context of composition and/or interpretation by and for fellow Buddhists, represented by the literary analyses of Steve Collins. In the fourth part I discuss another approach to the study of the suttas, which shifts attention to readers within the tradition in times posterior to the time in which the suttas themselves were produced. While Collins's literary analyses presumably carry over to later members of the tradition as well—indeed, if I read him correctly, the point is precisely the degree to which the ideologies of the producers of the suttas shaped later readings and ideological and sociopolitical realities—the fourth mode is more pointedly represented by Anne Blackburn's exciting work with the culture of manuscript production and education in a late premodern setting (eighteenth-century Kandy) admittedly far removed from the early Buddhist community and, for that matter, from any original meaning of the suttas.

Bailey's work begins from a frank admission that we are on thin ice trying to use the suttas for the social history of Brahminism in the time of the Buddha, given that Buddhist representations of Brahmins of the day are virtual "caricatures."[25] Yet in the end I think he shows persuasively that with a great deal of care this can be accomplished, and I agree with him that in the absence of other sources it must be accomplished. Bailey certainly does not engage, however, in the sort of face-value reading that characterizes "historical source mode," from which perspective, in terms of his question, Buddhist caricatures of Brahmins would be treated as true representations of what Brahmins then were actually like (or else, and more likely, they would be denounced for failing to be such representations). Rather, he delicately fleshes out his social history from between the lines of the earliest and most difficult suttas, in *Sutta-nipāta*, engaging in a sort of hermeneutical suspicion of both the presences and absences in them. I find compelling his argument that the stories of conversions of Brahmins in *Sutta-nipāta* "illuminat[e] aspects of the Buddhists' self-consciousness of their own fragility and apprehension in the face of the overwhelming cultural opponent they faced in the form of brahmanical culture, the chief symbol and advocate of which was the brahmin himself" (Bailey 1991, 19). From this perspective, the texts give proof, not of their caricatures, but of the fact that early Buddhists felt a need to caricature in the first place. The fact that such a need was apparently not felt by Brahmin writers of the early Buddhist period, who recorded no mention of the Buddhists at all, reinforces Bailey's sociohistorical conclusion that Brahminical culture really did have an overwhelming advantage over the incipient Buddhist community, which appeared to be just one more, no doubt extreme, Upaniṣadic group.

Quite apart from the interesting perspective this gives us on the relationship of Buddhists to theists during the early Buddhist period—and from the light, I might add, which it sheds on the eventual virulence with which theist writers, beginning with the authors of the *Bhagavad-gītā*, felt compelled to sling insults at Buddhists—I find Bailey's work promising because it suggests the possibility of reading the suttas as artifacts of the times and places that produced them. Rather than view them as passive purveyors of historical truth qua nineteenth-century encyclopedias, it becomes possible to view them as actions within a particular set of sociohistorical circumstances. Of course, there are all sorts of problems in trying to determine just what those circumstances were, especially because there is already a certain unsteadiness in a method based on second-guessing ancient texts, and here the question of the relative antiquity of the suttas becomes absolutely critical. But we do have an enormous amount of textual material on hand both Buddhist and Brahminical—and, it is crucial to add, Jain, for they too were actively attacked by and attackers of the Buddhists from an early date[26]—such that, even in the absence of any hard evidence predating the time of Aśoka Maurya, so long as our historical linguistics is accurate we should be able to capture the dialogical moments or intertextual relationships on which historical reconstruction becomes possible.[27] For an obvious example, the *Tevijja Sutta* names several Upaniṣads known from our extant collections, including *Chandoka* for *Chāṇḍogya*, *Addhariya* for *Aitareyya*, *Tittiriya* for *Taittirīya*, and so on (Rhys Davids 1969, 171), an extremely important link which helps date both bodies of literature by placing them in the same general milieu.

The importance of the external, the non-Buddhist—whether these "others" were assumed to have been among the readers/hearers or merely the object of representation by Buddhist readers/hearers—is evident in NQ. When we consider the sequence of events that is actually narrated in the autobiographical fragment under consideration, it is possible to view the entire Buddha biography, in this possibly earliest, original formulation, as little more than a series of encounters with representatives or symbols of the non-Buddhist communities among whom the early Buddhists coexisted: indeed, precisely the groups that are singled out by the Aśokan inscriptions. The fragment begins with Brahmins: Āḷāra Kālāma and Uddaka Rāmaputta, followed by none less than Brahmā the Lord of Creation (Brahmā Sahaṃpati). This encounter with God is followed by a wonderful series of punning references to Jains, as I will discuss in a moment, which are made in a discussion with an Ājīvika named Upaka, after which the now-Buddha returns to Brahmins (the Group of Five) and transforms them with the superiority of his attainments (despite their initial agreement not even to rise to greet him). Indeed, the whole narrative is one of triumph over these non-Buddhists, who are, however, treated reverentially, with a healthy dose of pity for their less exalted state (except perhaps the Jains, who would have been the early Buddhists' closest competitors, whose texts are most directly intertextual with Buddhist texts, and who appear to be attacked directly as a result).

Thus as soon as the Bodhisatta is questing after the good, he is quickly mastering the teachings of first Āḷāra Kālāma and then, almost as an afterthought, Uddaka Rāmaputta, both of whom acknowledge his supreme ability and offer either to make him partner in leading the community (Āḷāra) or leader of the community outright (Uddaka). Yet as Foucher found so upsetting and unlikely, the Bodhisatta is made to abandon both teachers/communities because their attainments, however exalted and close to the goal, are not quite there yet. Without any teacher whatsoever, a point reiterated several times just after the enlightenment, he becomes Buddha and agrees to preach only after the Brahmins' God himself comes to beg him to do so, for the sake of the whole world (including God!). Some anonymous deities—also symbolic of the theist world in which the early Buddhists existed—then confirm what he sees with his Buddha-eye, namely that poor Āḷāra and Uddaka have just died, so he sets out to meet the Group of Five who are staying in the Deer Park near Benares.

Along the way he meets Upaka the Ājīvika, who instantly recognizes that the Buddha is something special but who pathetically fails to believe the Buddha's rather exuberant first self-declaration, shrugs his shoulders, and walks away. In the process of that exchange Upaka somewhat sarcastically responds that in his self-declaration the Buddha makes himself appear to be the unrivalled (*ananta*) victor (*jina*), something along the lines of, "Well aren't you just Jesus Christ?"—to which the Buddha answers with an unabashed "Yes, I am"! Coupled with the odd references, by God himself, to the "stained doctrine, devised by impure minds" which "formerly, among the Magadhans appeared"—no doubt referring to Jainism—there is obviously a polemical stance toward Jains, as well as Ājīvikas, at work here. As mentioned, the final act in this Buddha autobiography is the submission of the Group of Five Brahmin mendicant ascetics to the Buddha. Before hearing the first and subsequent suttas, they are forced to submit to the Buddha's own unique title (Tathāgatha, paralleling in its distinctiveness the epithet Tīrthaṃkara in the Jain world), thereby admitting a level of unique superiority to him, and to submit to his communal rule (begging, studying, meditating, attaining *arahant*-ship). Here, then, there is much material for imagining the sociohistorical position of the early Buddhist community, surrounded as it was by other and likely bigger disciplinary orders of *samaṇas* and *brāhmaṇas*.

The potential of this sort of thinking for moving beyond the impasse of "historical source mode" becomes especially clear in applying it to the question of the Bodhisatta's teachers. Thomas's complaint that NQ's descriptions are little more than caricatures is answered with Bailey's view that caricatures are also part of the history we are trying to reconstruct. Foucher's complaint about the unlikely portrayal of Gotama as an uppity student just a little too smart to be believed is answered with Bailey's suggestion that the early Buddhists were apprehensive and self-conscious about their position vis-à-vis non-Buddhist disciplinary orders. That is, the points raised by Thomas and Foucher become, rather than "faults of our biographers," rather clever strategies in early Buddhist attempts at self-definition and promotion vis-à-vis their own rivals. What if we were to take the caricatures and overkill as evidence that the Buddha's relationship with Āḷāra Kālāma and Uddaka Rāmaputta actually mattered to the early Buddhists (if not the Buddha himself) who composed this autobiographical fragment? Perhaps they were significant teachers of the day, despite the fact that they are otherwise forgotten to history. Perhaps they really did enjoy especially close correspondence to the early Buddhists, such that questions of the Buddha's right to take over both communities could counter an implication that the Buddha is merely a pupil of well-known Yoga masters.

The suggestion that we need to pursue such lines of thought is not as far-fetched as might appear from the fact that the historicity of these teachers has never seriously been engaged in the scholarship. These two teachers are, after all, singled out in the narrative fragment: they are named; their teachings are described; they engage in conversations with the future Buddha; they are clearly achievers of very high states of consciousness; they warrant at least as much attention as the others over whom, I have suggested, the early Buddhist authors of this fragment claimed the Buddha's superiority (Brahmā, Upaka, the Group of Five); the Bodhisatta seeks them out when he first endeavors to learn the truth and seeks to return to them when he first decides to teach it. In terms of sheer quantity in the text, in fact, Āḷāra Kālāma and Uddaka Rāmaputta turn out to be the most important figures in the Buddha autobiography other than the Buddha himself: they deserve more attention than the Group of Five, than the Ājīvika/Jains, and even than God himself (not to mention those weeping parents and unnamed wife and son). It is ironic, then, that "historical source mode" has somehow made their very names irrelevant to the discussion.

If we take seriously Bailey's claim that these texts addressed an external socioreligious reality, the logical assumption to make on the basis of these considerations is that this narrative fragment was composed when Āḷāra Kālāma and Uddaka Rāmaputta were not yet the faceless "Yogic masters" whom later tradition, and Western scholarship, would leave them; it was composed when these teachers were still known, when it still mattered to demonstrate that the Buddhist program is more complete than theirs, when it still mattered that they acknowledged the Bodhisatta's superiority even before he became Buddha, before they died; when it still mattered that he was his *own* teacher. Indeed, the culmination of each encounter with the teachers he is nevertheless admitted to have followed is the expression of each one's desire to have the Buddha take over leadership of his community (which in later sources would appear to have included hundreds of members each).[28] And the Buddha's first thought on enlightenment is apparently to comply after all; to return to these teachers—and their communities—and teach them the higher Dhamma because "for a long time they had little dust in their eyes." When he discovers that each has died, the Buddha pities them, for each one suffered "a great loss; if he had heard this Dhamma he would quickly have understood." There is an almost eschatological promise here: the Buddha could transform these Brahminical teachers and, by extension, their followings.

These claims would have had real weight only in a situation in which members of those communities, in the absence of their now-dead founders, were active rivals and/or were being persuaded that they made the right choice in joining the Buddhist order (or perhaps were being persuaded to join the Buddhist order in the first place). To others who, like the Buddha, were closely connected with Āḷāra Kālāma and Uddaka Rāmaputta, it would indeed matter to know in such absolutely (even painfully) explicit terms whether or not the Buddha taught everything they taught (with those teachers' stamp of approval/offer of succession, after all) but also went beyond them by teaching much, much more.

In this light it seems to me most remarkable to notice, as has not previously been done in this context, that the Pāli texts contain a number of references to the Buddha's interaction with members or former members of both of these communities. Thus, at least one strand of the tradition maintained that the Group of Five monks were in fact followers of Uddaka Rāmaputta; our text, which mentions them as having been there during the period of striving, almost as an afterthought, might similarly be seen to support such a reading.[29] *Mahāparinibbānasutta* (D 2: 130) mentions a Mallian, Pukkusa, who, paralleling the Group of Five in this reading, had been a follower of Āḷāra Kālāma's but later was convinced by the Buddha's superiority to defect to the Buddhists. The Buddha confronts a belligerent group of Uddaka Rāmaputtists, King Eleyya and his bodyguard, in the Vassakāra Sutta of the Anguttaranikāya (A 2: 180) and actively attacks Uddaka in suttas in the Saṃyuttanikāya (S 4: 83-84, where Udakka's claim to have rooted out the source of *dukkha* is refuted) and in the Pāsādika Sutta of the Dīghanikāya (D 3: 126-27, where Uddaka is accused of base thinking). Just as Bailey's work would lead us to see something purposeful in the triumph the Bodhisatta achieves over Brahmins/Brahmā, Jains, and Ājīvikas, so too it would lead us to conclude that, given the great antiquity of this fragment, in the early days of Buddhist history the communities of Āḷāra Kālāma and Uddaka Rāmaputta were serious rivals and probably great sources of aspirants to the new Path.

III. Textual Whole Mode

As interesting as this line of thinking becomes—implying the (I believe) previously unrecognized possibility that our narrative fragment preserves memories of an actual sociohistorical situation in which Āḷāra and Uddaka and their communities were of great concern to the early Buddhists—like "historical source mode" it depends upon fracturing the integrity of the sutta as received, focusing only on that embedded narrative fragment of apparently greatest antiquity. I consider it one of the major contributions of Collins to have shown us so clearly that such fractured interpretation is always incomplete. There is a layer of historicity in the suttas—a history of composition, of aesthetics, of reading—that can be grasped only by treating any particular sutta (or jātaka story, etc.) as a textual whole. In several different contexts, Collins has demonstrated that an analysis of literary devices including frame stories, internal structures, ornamentation, and so forth, can usefully supplement such fragmented readings (see esp. Collins 1990; Collins 1993; and Collins 1998). This of course belies as much a limitation of fragmented philosophical readings as it does of fragmented historical readings; both history and philosophy are enriched by considering the frames within which the fragments are, we assume purposefully, situated. Here, we access a layer of history that does not require historical linguistics to project narrative fragments into remote antiquity; Collins's points are as relevant (or even more relevant) for the time of editing as for the time of earliest/original composition, if any real distinction between those two can or should be made, and are relevant to later readership as well, anticipating my discussion in the next part.

Although this is not a form of reading at which I can claim any special skill—certainly I lack the nuanced eye that has made Collins's readings so rich—still when I think about *Ariyapariyesanasutta* in this mode I find real truth in the argument that much is missed in an exclusive focus on that one autobiographical fragment. Yet this is what *every* scholar who has discussed NQ, as far as I have been able to discern, has in fact done; for all the use of NQ in debating "the historical Buddha," not one scholar has paid attention to the literary qualities of the text. On one hand, this causes us to lose sight of the profound teaching that the monks at Rammaka's hermitage so crave, and of which the autobiography is merely an illustration (albeit a powerfully evocative one), consisting in an analysis of the human condition—attachment to things ("wives and sons, slaves and slavegirls, goats and sheep, cocks and pigs, elephants and cows and horses and mares, silver and gold") (M 1: 162) destining us in their own destiny to birth, old age, disease, death, grief, and defilement—as well as an analysis of the bases of this condition (sense pleasures) and a lovely metaphorical illustration of escape from it. Buddhaghosa titles his commentary on this text "Explanation of the Sermon on the Heap of Snares (Pāsarāsisuttavaṇṇanā), which is named '*Sermon on the Noble Quest*,'" suggesting that what really matters about this sutta is the final teaching, the snares metaphor, rather than the autobiographical illustration of it. (Indeed, as I suggest below, Buddhaghosa is singularly uninterested in the autobiographical details as such; he is concerned instead to supplement them with other details and to articulate a Buddhology that strikes me as quite foreign to the original.)

This fractured reading also causes us to lose sight of the other way in which this is an important text for recovering the Buddha biography. It, like virtually all of the suttas, narrates a particular moment in the life of the Buddha qua Buddha, during the 45 years he spent traveling and teaching and instituting the Sangha. The description of the setting—the Buddha's bath, the meeting at Rammaka's hermitage, the manner in which he addressed the monks—may be a comparatively later addition to the early fragment, but it is a key moment in the massive Buddha biography that all the suttas, together, constitute: a Buddha biography so important to Buddhists at the stage when the Tipiṭaka was being compiled that they chose it as the frame for the entire collected teachings of the Buddha. It is precisely as evidence for the daily habits of the Buddha that Buddhaghosa finds this text biographically interesting, as I explain below. Just as historians of the Theravāda have increasingly shifted their focus away from "early Buddhism," in the interest of recovering the comparably understudied later premodern and modern periods of Theravāda history, so there has been a marked shift away from reconstructions of "the historical Buddha" in favor of studies of what Frank Reynolds calls "the biographical process" in later Buddhist history (Reynolds 1976, 37-61).[30] But as far as I know there has as yet been no attempt to describe and locate the massive Buddha biography that becomes apparent to us when we take the introductory (*nidāna*) portion of each sutta seriously.

Additionally, and here especially I draw inspiration from Collins's work, these different bits of NQ—the teaching, the metaphors, the "one time" at which the sutta takes place, and even that ancient autobiographical fragment—are carefully woven together into a textual whole that has its own integrity, its own beauty, and its own meanings. It will not do to reckon with all the seemingly separate bits and then declare victory; the sutta itself—number 26 in the Majjhimanikāya—is an unfragmented whole. So, too, for that matter, is the Majjhimanikāya itself a whole, and likewise the Tipiṭaka a whole—but an analysis of those wholes obviously lies beyond the scope of this article.

The structure that informs NQ becomes clear when we take up Buddhaghosa's intimation that we should consider the extended metaphor about Māra's snares/beasts of prey as the center or foundation of the text. Treating the actual sermon as a unit (I label it IV below) that is then framed by the rest of the text presents us with a neat structure indeed. The "heap of snares" metaphor (IV) is framed by/told as the culmination of the ancient autobiographical fragment, which I thus deem the "inner frame" (and label III). This was clearly a matter of choice on the part of compilers at some point in the compilation of the Tipiṭaka, for the fragment culminates in other sorts of stories and/or teachings in other versions of it, both in the Pāli and in the Buddhist Sanskrit collections. This inner frame in turn is told as part of a larger narrative about the nature of the Noble Quest more generally, which I call the "conjoining frame" (and label II). But all of these narratives are framed by the monks who are listening to the Buddha's Dhamma-talk at Rammaka's hermitage in Sāvatthi, which I call the "outer frame" (and label I).[31]

The text opens with the monks desiring a Dhamma-talk face-to-face with the Buddha, and their retreat to Rammaka's hermitage toward that end (frame I). The Buddha arrives and begins to discuss the Noble Quest and its opposite, the ignoble quest (frame II). This is the "conjoining" frame because the Buddha identifies the activity of the monks at Rammaka's hermitage (frame I) with the Noble Quest as opposed to the ignoble quest (frame II),[32] then proceeds to narrate the autobiographical fragment (frame III) as an illustration of that same transition from an ignoble to a Noble Quest (frame II). As the culmination of the autobiographical fragment, in which the Buddha and the Group of Five have all attained the perfectly peaceful (*paramaṃ sivam*) goal of the Noble Quest, Nirvana, we then have the sermon proper (frame IV), which hearkens back to frame III (by repeating the elaborate narrative of the progression through and beyond the *jhānas* achieved first by the Buddha and then by the Group of Five), frame II (by analyzing the basis of the attachment that distinguishes the Noble Quest from the ignoble quest, likened to the distinction between the beast who just stands on the snares and the beast who is bound up in them) and frame I (in which the whole thing is, after all, preached, as we are reminded in the concluding statement, "Thus spoke the Blessed One, etc.").

In attempting to chart this out, I find a structure something like this:

I. outer frame, monks listening at Rammaka's hermitage
  II. conjoining frame, the Noble Quest
    III. inner frame, Buddha autobiography
      IV. teaching, the heap of snares
    III. teaching is part of and parallels the inner frame
  II. teaching illustrates the conjoining frame
I. teaching is preached to the monks at Rammaka's

In this configuration, it will be clear that NQ as a whole projects the reader through a series of stages to the teaching of the Buddha contained in the final portion, the heap of snares metaphor, then shoots him or her back to the point of departure. This could be charted in a more elaborate fashion. Thus the forward movement to the teaching proper: the monks gathered together are the monks on the Noble Quest; they are following the Buddha's own paradigmatic illustration of being a monk on the Noble Quest; the validity as well as the possibility of being a monk on the Noble Quest is grounded in the Buddha's enlightenment; the Buddha's enlightenment that grounds the Noble Quest is known because God begged him to preach; by preaching to the Group of Five the Buddha directed them on the Noble Quest; by listening to what he preached the Group of Five also realized enlightenment: what he preached is the heap of snares metaphor. And then the movement reverses, bringing the teaching back to the outer frame: the heap of snares metaphor is the Truth the Group of Five realized, which is what the Buddha preached to the Group of Five, which is what God begged for, which is an explication of what the Buddha realized, which is the distinction between the Noble Quest and ignoble quest, which is what monks ought to be doing, which is what the monks at Rammaka's hermitage are doing.

The symmetry here, I think, extends beyond the text into the community that compiled and preserved it. The monks joined together in Rammaka's hermitage are an unnamed gaggle, in a sense any monks, the monks who compiled and heard this sutta in the early days of the community or the monks who copied and preserved it down into the present; these monks could be any place (the hermitage is otherwise unknown), whether in the center of things (Sāvatthi, where the Buddha spent the bulk of his 45 years) or perhaps somewhere out east of it (this is left ambiguous in NQ). The Buddha's humble entrance, an ahem and a tap on the crossbar, is an entrance into any monastery, any time. He tells the monks, and us readers, that they are doing what monks on the Noble Quest ought to be doing, thinking about the Dhamma. He tells them about the Quest, about his own Quest, about its triumphs. They feel the fear of God that they will never get to hear the teaching; they feel the Buddha's pity for Āḷāra and Uddaka, cheated by death, and Upaka, distracted by sectarianism; they feel the awkwardness of the Group of Five, their ignorance of the real situation, the pull of the Buddha's charisma, their change of mind and subsequent quick attainment of the goal by learning . . . here it comes . . . "Five, monks, are these bases for passion." Recent scholars have suggested that post-*parinibbāna* Buddhists felt a profound longing, like the monks at Rammaka's hermitage, to be in the presence of the Buddha; to hear from him the sort of face-to-face Dhamma-talk which in sutta after sutta proves nothing less than salvific.[33] The *Sermon on the Noble Quest* is structured to satisfy this longing. The Buddha himself *is* face to face with the monks at Rammaka's, with all the later monks who confronted this sutta, and with us, the readers/hearers. And this salvific teaching comes hurtling back through frame after frame to us, sitting here, in anybody's ashram.

A similarly marvelous symmetry can be discerned in the text of that ancient narrative fragment itself. If we consider the various stages of the Buddha biography outlined in this critically important biographical text, we find an easily defined sequence, which could be charted as (1) unenlightened state,

(2) encounters with Āḷāra and Uddaka, (3) fulfillment of the Noble Quest, (4) the decision to preach/God's plea and subsequent boast, (5) encounter with Upaka, and (6) meeting with the Group of Five. But on seeing, in "text of its day mode," that there is something significant about Āḷāra and Uddaka, I was able to realize that they play a considerably more central role in this narrative fragment than this simple listing might suggest.

In this fragment, the two teachers are identified primarily, indeed exclusively, as the teachers of two of the four formless (*arupa*) *jhāna*s recognized in classical *vipassanā* meditation. Āḷāra Kālāma is said to have taught the sphere of boundless space (fifth *jhāna*), while Uddaka Rāmaputta is said to have taught the sphere of neither perception nor nonperception (eighth *jhāna*). Taking these narrative elements—"teacher" and "*jhāna*s"—as well as explicit references to the pair as textual markers of their role in the autobiography, we find that they keep reappearing like a chorus after each discrete moment in the unfolding of the narrative. Thus the ancient fragment is structured as follows, with discrete events indicated by letters and the "chorus" of references to the teachers of the *jhāna*s indicated by asterisks:

(a) the Bodhisatta is in his unenlightened state ("Even I, O monks . . .")
  * encounters with Āḷāra and Uddaka/mastery of the *jhāna*s
(b) fulfillment of the Noble Quest/enlightenment
  * Enlightenment involves a progression through and outside of the *jhāna*s
(c) decision to preach/God's plea and subsequent boast
  * Buddha wants to teach Āḷāra and Uddaka; discovering them dead, he goes to Benares
(d) encounter with Upaka the Ājīvika
  * Buddha's self-declaration as Teacherless Teacher
(e) meeting with the Group of Five
  * Buddha becomes teacher of *jhāna*s (and beyond) to the Group of Five (who happen to be former followers of Uddaka?)

Thus the text itself highlights a certain centrality to the teachers; the story of the Buddha's paradigmatic Noble Quest is intimately bound up with Āḷāra and Uddaka at literally every stage. Without repeating myself, if "text of its day mode" is on track, here we have a very nice overlap of the two modes, in which an appreciation of the text's internal logic and structure speaks to what appears to have been its external audience.

But if that is the case, what is it saying? On one hand it is saying—*pace* Lamotte, Thomas, Foucher, T. W. Rhys Davids, and others who would downplay their significance—that Āḷāra Kālāma and Uddaka Rāmaputta, whoever they were, played a critical role in helping to define the Buddha's distinctively Buddhist teaching and community. On the other hand, these recurring choruses, allusions to the Bodhisatta's teachers, are always allusions to their ultimate inadequacy: these Upaniṣadic gurus have been usurped, they are now dead, their former pupils have come into the Buddhist fold, the Buddhist Path goes beyond their refined versions of mystical wallowing to a self-declared "undefiled, unsurpassed, perfectly peaceful Nirvana," which blinds Māra by leaving him no tracks at all. This is a message intended for all of us—the Group of Five, God, the monks at Rammaka's hermitage, former followers of Āḷāra and Uddaka, monastic compilers, monks seated together in monasteries discussing Dhamma, whomever reads or hears this sutta—which has become obscure only because memory of the teachers thus usurped, and of the independent identity of their communities, has long since disappeared.

IV. Later Reading Mode

It will be clear that I consider the second and third modes described above to be more interesting, and potentially more productive, than I consider the now-outdated "historical source mode" to be. But in one important sense the modes presented in Sections II and III never escape from a problem inherent in "historical source mode." Though these modes shift attention from reading to readership, the scholar still must interpret the original text directly, and any thinking about readership, context, and so forth, must be spun out of that direct interpretation. As a historian, this troubles me: How do we know people read the text in such and such a fashion? In terms at least of evidence, is this not still the same sort of interpretation found in "historical source mode," just knocked back a few notches? I feel myself on much firmer ground when I have evidence of later readership of whatever sutta I may want to study. This is not to deny that history is *always* interpretative, imaginary, and mutable; rather it is to assume that the presence of evidence makes for better interpretation, imagination, and openness to seeing things anew. Thus I am personally most interested in pursuing a fourth mode of interpretation, which asks about how the text was read, on the basis of whatever evidence might actually exist as the remnant of such readings. In my experience, this evidence takes one of three (sometimes overlapping) forms.

First, there is what we might call the manuscript record. In addition to the sheer quantification that a catalogue of existing manuscripts of some particular sutta can provide, giving us some rough idea of its popularity, regional distribution, and so on, when we work closely with manuscripts there is always much the object itself can, even wants, to tell us. It bespeaks, whether in its physical condition (wear and tear, quality of production, materials, script, etc.) or in its contents (colophons, titles, name inscriptions, etc.), or in both, a great deal about where it came from, how it was treated, and how it was understood. Anne

Blackburn's project of reconstructing eighteenth-century monastic education through an examination of the holdings in period temple libraries is unprecedented in the field and promises to tell us more than we have ever known about actual textual practices in any period of Theravāda Buddhist history (Blackburn 1996; Blackburn 1997, 76-99; Blackburn 1999a; and Blackburn 1999b).

However, in terms of the suttas there is a major problem here. Except for certain suttas prized for particular reasons (*Mahāsatipaṭṭhānasutta* for meditation training, *Dhammacakkappavattanasutta* for foundational doctrine and historical uniqueness, *Ratanasutta* and the other *paritta/pirit* texts for supernormal efficacy, etc.), most of the suttas do not have a manuscript record as such. Thus, even as important a sutta as NQ does not appear as a separate piece in any of the 50-odd Kandyan temple preaching manuscripts (*bana pot*) that I have collected, nor have I been able to locate a single manuscript in any of the available catalogues of palm-leaf manuscripts holdings anywhere in the world. Of course, there are manuscripts of the Majjhimanikāya in which NQ obviously appears—and in which that ancient fragment appears four times—but this is not the same thing as, say, the independent record of the growth of the *pirit* liturgy which manuscripts provide.

The fact is that most suttas, like NQ, do *not* have their own manuscript records. Thus NQ is in some ways more typical of the suttas in general; we would like to study the material culture of their reading and use, but we have no evidence that such a culture even existed. This would seem a terrible impasse indeed, that this most exciting avenue for future work on suttas is closed to the vast majority of them. But in fact I think there are two ways out of this bind. On one hand, the very absence of a separate manuscript culture tells us something important about the use (or, more precisely, non-use) of this sutta, and probably of most suttas, in the late premodern period that produced the great bulk of our extant manuscripts. We can agree with both Collins and Blackburn that there was more an *idea* of canon than a consistent interest in reading the suttas themselves. We could even conceive a social history of not reading and studying most suttas, against which we could interpret in new ways the desire of major temples and royal patrons to see them preserved in sometimes rather ostentatious fashion.

But these sorts of reflections are not the only way out of the problem because, as mentioned, material remains constitute only one of at least three different (but overlapping) forms of evidence on which a historically grounded interpretation of the later readership of particular suttas could be based. The second and third forms, by which I mean "supplements" and "commentaries," respectively, do not require a manuscript record as such. As long as one copy of a text that supplements or comments on a particular sutta exists, we can pursue "later reading mode" with reference to the authors (and/or compilers, transmitters) of the supplements or commentaries in question.

In terms of supplementation, I showed in Section I that many later Buddha biographies—even all later Buddha biographies, including scholarly reconstructions—implicitly and often explicitly draw on NQ as their source. In this sense, "historical source mode"—namely, extracting chosen bits of the biographical fragment and supplementing them with other sorts of evidence, pertinent or not—is merely the most recent contribution to a long-standing literary tradition.[34] Because this text has been supplemented so regularly, it occupies its own sort of special place among the suttas and is therefore not entirely typical of them. Indeed, if we question *why* this sutta does not have its own manuscript tradition, we can go beyond the generic answer that like most suttas it simply was not very relevant to the concerns of the people who produced our extant manuscripts. In this instance it seems likely that the need for a special manuscript tradition was obviated by the ever-greater finesse with which NQ was supplemented. If we ask about the manuscript record of the biography conveyed in the sutta, rather than of the sutta itself, then we find it in ever-proliferating abundance. Yet to the extent that much of the sutta material was at least transmitted in other canonical traditions and some post-Tripiṭaka texts, a wider application of this sort of interpretation remains open.

In terms at least of NQ, supplementation is clearly an important avenue for investigation. As shown in Section I, portions of the text's actual language have been embedded in a variety of later supplements, or frames. Whereas in "historical source mode" this was important only by way of demonstrating that the autobiographical fragment is indeed very ancient, in "later reading mode" each and every supplement is a site for further questions that, when we pursue them, turn out to be some combination of "text of its day mode" and "textual whole mode." That is, each supplement is the relic of a process of reading this autobiographical fragment, whether directly or on the basis of an already-supplemented intermediate form, and thinking about what it means: framing its relevance according to the concerns, agendas, styles, tropes, and hopes of the day.

Thus, for example, in earlier work I have shown that the Buddha biography was supplemented with details about the Bodhisatta's previous lives and the existence of previous Buddhas in a historical context of Buddhist expansion (Buddhist empires of the second and first centuries BCE) for which these details had profoundly important political, economic, and religious implications (Walters 1997b). Recognizing *that* some particular detail is added to the original at some particular moment in time-space allows us to ask in meaningful ways *why* such supplementation occurred.

To raise another example of the value of identifying stages in the process of supplementing the original NQ Buddha biography, it has not sufficiently been recognized that the suttas do not provide us good evidence for the

Buddha's claimed royal status. Though the name of his father, Suddhodana, does appear in a text of the Vinaya (establishing the rule that one must have parental permission to go forth) and in a sutta of *Sutta-nipāta* (about his birth), there is otherwise no canonical indication that he was even worthy of note, let alone a powerful (or even world-conquering!) monarch. While there is canonical evidence that the Buddha was believed to be Śākyan (though even this is lacking in NQ), there is no indication that he was intended to rule that kingdom. In Pāli tradition, details about the Buddha's royal birth and the exalted status of Suddhodana, not to mention the narrative of the princely prison in which the latter tried to constrain the former, are startlingly absent, lacking until, truly, the time of the commentaries and *vaṃsas* (fourth to fifth centuries CE). These details are found in Buddha biographies from other traditions, but they are also texts that are much later than the time of Aśoka and shortly thereafter (which is generally treated as the date of the latest compilations of the Nikāyas and the Vinaya). The earliest text in which I have been able to locate explicit statements of the Buddha's royal birth is Aśvaghoṣa's *Buddhacarita*, in which the Buddha's royal birth, connections, and status are highlighted almost to the point of absurdity. In recognizing this fact, we are enabled to start asking very interesting questions about what it meant to claim royal status for the Buddha at that point in Buddhist history (Aśvaghoṣa is believed to have worked in the court of the Kuṣāna emperor Kaniṣka, no less), about why this claim is made in classical Sanskrit court poetry (rare to have Buddhist classical Sanskrit at all, especially weird because this biography became definitive of a genre of theist court poetry), and so on.

I will not engage in that line of questioning here, except to point out that this is by no means the only addition that Aśvaghoṣa makes to NQ and that might help illuminate the social and/or literary contexts of his day. Thus, for example, Aśvaghoṣa, a converted Brahmin, is as far as I know the first biographer to draw explicit parallels to the Rāmāyana, to justify apparent Buddhist deviance from Vedic precedents with an appeal to different Vedic precedents, and to diffuse the "God begs Buddha to Preach" segment by having Indra come down with Brahmā, more as a sort of friendly call than as a charge to preach (Aśvaghoṣa's Bodhisattva already knows he is going to preach). This, too, would have a sharp social edge in Aśvaghoṣa's context, while adding a level of aesthetic quality and completeness to the Buddha biography that had never been achieved before but that has remained the sine qua non for all subsequent Buddha biographies. Indeed, a number of Aśvaghoṣa's innovations, like the innovation that the Bodhisattva was heir to a powerful kingdom, became absolutely standard in later biographies across the Buddhist world (and in scholarship on "the historical Buddha"). Thus, in addition to illuminating the sociohistorical contexts and literary practices of Aśvaghoṣa's world, reading *Buddhacarita* as a later reading of NQ also raises questions about why some of those innovations, and not others, did become standard across the Buddhist world.

In this vein all the Buddha biographies we have are evidence of particular readings of NQ in particular sociohistorical and literary circumstances; one could write a veritable history of Buddhology, if not of the whole religion, as a process of supplementing the original biography in NQ. But from the perspective of this larger history of Buddha biographies, that ancient autobiographical fragment becomes most significant for its absences. Much more than the missing Śākyan royal connection of the (unnamed) Bodhisatta, NQ is full of startling silences: here we have no Suddhodana, no Mahāmāyā, no Mahāpajāpatī Gotamī, no Yasodharā and Rāhula, no pleasure palace, no women of the harem, no four signs, no Channa, no renunciatory fanfare, no practice of austerities, no Sujātā's milk-rice, no Māra's army at the Bodhi tree, no three watches of the night, no seven weeks after enlightenment, no text of the First Sermon (replaced with the heap of snares, frame IV!). The *Sermon on the Noble Quest* screams out for supplementation, and the tradition is still supplementing it, that same fragment, today. When we make the supplementation itself the object of study, rather than attempt to mix it all together into a complete and "reliable" single account of the biography of "the historical Buddha," literally hundreds of possible histories emerge for investigation.

While we have been blessed with much good work on Buddhist biography in the past decade—including several excellent volumes of essays in which many of these moves toward a sociohistorical and/or literary reading of later Buddha biographies, as texts of their own days, have been made—I do not think that the role of NQ at the base of the whole house of cards has yet been given adequate attention. A failure to see that these later biographies of the Buddha are direct and indirect supplementations of NQ does more than blind us to some of the potentially fruitful sociohistorical and literary analyses that can be made of those texts. Additionally, this failure blinds us to the possibility that many of the supplementations have been spun out of the evidence of the ancient fragment itself.

Thus in the constantly repeated analysis of the ignoble quest and Noble Quest that so bores my students (the language of being destined to birth, death, etc., and the repeated passages about what is destined for these things), we might be able to detect the seeds of a fuller, supplemented Buddha biography: in the phrase "wives and sons are destined for birth" we might find the source for the stories of Yasodharā and Rāhula; "slaves and slavegirls are destined for birth" supplies the Bodhisatta's attendants and harem; "goats and sheep . . . cocks and pigs . . . elephants and cows and horses and mares . . . silver and gold are destined for birth" intimates the opulence of the palace (M 1: 162). Continuing through the ancient autobiographical fragment: "being a young man with very black hair" may have been the source for stories about the Bodhisatta's beauty, skill, agility, and so forth; "while my parents" in the plural (Mahāpajāpatī as second wife/surrogate mother of the Buddha) "were weeping and wailing" (the opposition of the king and the whole cycle that explains it); "recognizing the danger in that which is destined for death . . . old age . . . disease" (the first three signs); "isn't it the case that I ought to quest after the unborn, unsurpassed, perfectly peaceful Nirvana?" (the fourth sign) (M 1: 163). Likewise, "This group of five monks was very helpful to me, who assisted me in my resolution to strive" (the six years' asceticism) (M 1:170); whatever sermon about Māra is attached to the end of this fragment, as here the heap of snares (the battle with Māra); the initial reflection on the subtlety of *paṭiccasamuppāda* (the emergence of Buddhahood over the three watches of the night). It is possible to read all of these details as already there in the original text; the supplements work. And even if there is not so direct a relationship between NQ and the later supplements, at least it is clear that NQ's basic structure (I was unenlightened, I sought the truth, I found it) is the basic structure of every extant or conceivable Buddha biography, which at least should give us pause as evidence of its force.

In this long tradition of supplementation there is a history of thought about Āḷāra Kālāma and Uddaka Rāmaputta, too. As mentioned, today it would seem that this is the one dimension of that original Buddha biography (with the possible addition of the meetings with God and the Ājīvika) that has become overall less relevant than it once was. There certainly were supplements that have all the richness and openness implied in the above discussion: *Lalitavistara* adds a long passage to the effect that the Buddha already had a philosophical rebuttal before he even met Rudraka Rāmaputra and that the only reason he ever sought out a teacher at all was to demonstrate the teacher's incompetence to get to the heart of the matter. (This might have spoken to the sort of context in which the *Gītā* was being promoted along with Yoga as a theistic alternative to Buddhist meditative practices.) Aśvaghoṣa devotes an entire chapter to "the visit to Ārāḍa," in which that teacher is made to be the proponent of a feigned proto-Sāmkhya philosophy; the Buddha soundly argues it down in order to get this theist master's seal of approval. (It goes without saying that this will draw us into the multireligious situation of the Kuṣāna world.) But after this, within the Buddhist world there was not a lot more textual supplementation; there is a contraction, in which it suffices to say "after giving up the teachings of Āḷāra and Uddaka" or "after rejecting heretical teachers" or simply to omit mentioning the teachers at all (a move made as early as *Buddhavaṃsa*). Perhaps precisely the fact that made this so relevant at the time of production—the living memory of Āḷāra Kālāma and Uddaka Rāmaputta and the independent existence of their communities of followers—rendered it meaningless in a situation when those no longer obtained.

As indicated, in addition to the history of supplementation, the commentarial process also left as relics of its occurrence critically important evidence for investigating later readings of any sutta. We have commentaries on all the suttas, which as indicated is the case neither with a manuscript tradition nor with a supplementation tradition. More important, the commentary is intended to transmit just *how* one is supposed to read the original, which is not true of the manuscript record (produced as the transmission, not an explanation of it) or of the supplementations (which bury the original in themselves). Though the commentary is obviously intended to be part of the manuscript transmission—without it, the texts are in places unintelligible—and though it embeds the original within itself, the commentary assumes, even demands a reading of the original in tandem with itself. It is thus the best imaginable evidence for just how later Buddhists read each sutta or, to be more precise, for how one Buddhist whose voice was later taken as authoritative read each sutta. That Buddhist was Buddhaghosa, a fifth-century Indian native who came to Sri Lanka, studied the ancient (and no longer extant) Sinhala commentaries on the Tipiṭaka, and reworked them (and a great deal more material) in Pāli.

On one hand Buddhaghosa is himself a supplementer. Thus in the midst of the usual commentarial explanations, problematizations, etiologies of names, geographical specifications, and so forth, Buddhaghosa adds as putative "background" (*ānupubbikathā*) to the Buddha's question in NQ, "To whom then should I first preach the Dhamma?" a quick tour through the supplemented Buddha biography, including: the renunciation scene (Kanthaka the horse, Channa the buddy, leaving them at the river), the journey to Magadha (meeting Bimbisāra, recognizing the inadequacy and leaving behind [*sāraṃ avindanto tato pakkamitvā*] the teachers Kālama and Uddaka [their whole names are not even given], performance of austerities), preparation for enlightenment (the story of Sujātā, attendance of the deities, the bowl going upstream in the river, resolution to achieve enlightenment, traverse to the Bodhi-maṇḍapa), assault of Māra's army in full detail, the stories of the seven weeks (Mucalinda, *Ratanacankama*, etc.), and the story of Tapussa and Bhallika the merchants (MA 2: 181-86; see n. 6). As a gloss on the encounter with Upaka the Ājīvika he also adds the later details preserved in the Theravāda aṭṭhakathā.[35]

On the other hand, Buddhaghosa always does so much more than confirm my expectation of the details that ought to be included; he makes me hear details that I did not expect ought to be included and puts forth what strike me as rather bizarre readings of his own. These no doubt spoke to the sociohistorical and literary worlds in which Buddhaghosa, like any author, operated. But they also speak to me, starkly. Buddhaghosa is reading the same text I am reading, but he is reading it on the basis of agendas that are so radically different from my own that it takes me great effort even to fathom what he is saying and that in turn cautions me not to be too certain about seeing my own readings "in the text." In a word, NQ always strikes me, despite the chat with God, in the same way that it apparently has struck Buddhists, and scholars, through the ages: as real biography, even autobiography, concerned with a real man, all-too-human, who must strive hard to find the truth he then, somewhat reluctantly, teaches; a man who feels a certain pride in his achievements and who cares what he is called but who speaks in homely metaphors and uses self-revelation as a teaching device; a man who clears his throat and knocks lightly when interrupting a group of his students whom he encounters on the way home from his afternoon bath.

But this is not Buddhaghosa's Buddha, not at all. And as mentioned, Buddhaghosa is not very interested in the details of the ancient fragment, except to explain some of the names and add the more important supplemental material. Rather, Buddhaghosa is concerned with what I have called "the outer frame" (frame I). Buddhaghosa opens his explanation of NQ by asking why the monks asked Ānanda about meeting the Buddha, rather than asking him for a face-to-face Dhamma-talk directly. The answer is startling:

> Out of respect for the Master they cannot say, "Venerable Sir, talk about the Dhamma for us"; Buddhas are to be venerated. Like the solitary lion who is king of the beasts, like an elephant in rut, like a cobra with expanded hood, like a great mass of fire, [Buddhas] are approached with difficulty. (MA 2: 163-64)

The monks are too frightened to ask the Buddha, so they ask Ānanda instead. And how, Buddhaghosa asks, could unenlightened Ānanda have known the intention of the Buddha? The answer: he could not have known it. He told the monks to go to Rammaka's hermitage on the basis of a logical inference about the Buddha's daily habits, which are explained in rather excruciating detail to make the point.

This is merely the beginning of a remarkable series of glosses that establishes nothing less than a docetic Buddha, only pretending to be an ordinary human being. Thus in a gloss on the phrase "to wash" (*parisiñcituṃ*), used in reference to the bath after which the Buddha approaches Rammaka's hermitage, Buddhaghosa argues:

> "To wash" [requires this clarification]: When someone bathes [*nahāyati*] by smearing his limbs with clay and chunnam and scrubbing them with a coconut shell, it is said, "he is bathing". When someone bathes naturally, without doing all of that, it is said, "he is washing." Dirt and grime to be scrubbed away like that do not cling to the body of the Blessed One. The Blessed One only descends into the water for refreshment. Therefore [the sutta] says, "to wash his limbs." (MA 2: 166)

Buddhaghosa actually gets quite worked up thinking about the Buddha's bath. He does some marvelous geographical gymnastics with the layout of Sāvatthi in previous aeons to prove that the bathing ghat where the Buddha bathed was private, specially reserved for the purpose even above the bathing ghats dedicated to the king, the city dwellers, and ordinary monks. And this was no ordinary bath:

> The Blessed One descended into the water. When he descended all the fish and turtles in his water turned gold; [when the fish and turtles moved in a stream] it was like when a stream of solid gold is shot out of the mechanical tube [in the gold-refining process; and when the fish and turtles scattered] it was like when a cloth made of gold is stretched out. (MA 2: 167)

He came out of the water—Buddhaghosa is careful to stipulate the manner in which Ānanda helped him dress in dry robes so that no one, including the attendant, could see him naked—and then he stood there in one robe (that is, bare-chested):

> The body of the Blessed One, standing thus, shined as though [it were] the Coral Tree in Indra's heaven, all covered with flowers and fruit, [or as though it were] the stars twinkling on the surface of the sky, laughing with [greater] splendor at a lake full of blossoming lotuses and lilies. The radiance surrounding his *vyāma*-wide aura and his [body which was an] excellent garland of the thirty-two [marks of a Great Man] shined enormously, like a garland of thirty-two moons held in place and strung, like a garland of thirty-two suns, as though one had placed in succession thirty-two Wheel-turning Monarchs, thirty-two kings of the gods and thirty-two Great Brahmās. This is called "Illumination Land" [*vaṇṇanā bhūmi*]. In such places the color of the bodies of the Buddhas or the quality of their virtues begins to speak, filled with competent Dhamma-talking resorting to meanings and metaphors and analyses on the basis of pithy segments or entire verses. (MA 2: 167)

The commentator is not kidding about this: "The substantiality [*thāmo*, literally, "hardness"] of Dhamma-talking in such places ought to be understood." Nor is this the end of the bath scene: the Buddha "dries out his limbs" so that a wet robe will not immodestly cling to his body, but

> of course, dirt and grime do not stick to the bodies of Buddhas, and water glides off them like a drop of water dropped on a lotus leaf. Even though this is the case, the Blessed One [pretended to dry himself off] out of respect for the disciplinary rule thinking, "that is certainly the duty of a renunciate"; and having taken the outer robe by both corners he stood there, in front of it, with his body covered. (MA 2: 167-68)

At this moment Ānanda seizes his chance to suggest that the Blessed One tarry at Rammaka's hermitage, thinking,

> From the time the Blessed One, having dressed himself in his outer robe, resolves to go to the Palace of Migāra's Mother,[36] it will be difficult to turn him back. Contradicting the resolution of a Buddha is a grave offense, like stretching out the hand to grab a solitary lion, like taking hold of a powerful elephant, intoxicated in rut, and like grabbing a venomous cobra full of power by the neck. So I will mention the character of the hermitage of Rammaka the Brahmin, asking the Blessed One to go there. (MA 2: 168)

Buddhaghosa is still reading NQ biographically, but not as the sort of biography which all of us, in discussing the historical Buddha, inevitably reproduce as though T. W. Rhys Davids's naivety of a century ago stands unchallenged. Buddhaghosa's Buddha is a Buddha of his own day, reflecting an advanced Buddhology that is anything but secular humanism and that offers up such unlikely options as a Theravāda Sukhāvatī, "Illumination Land." His is a treatment that privileges the frame, the textual whole, over the embedded fragments. And his is a later reading by a member, and a pivotal member, of the tradition itself, who lived far closer than we are to whatever originary moment we may seek to understand. This should, if nothing more, serve to check our assumption that we can just pick up a sutta and "get it."

V. Conclusion

This investigation of NQ began with a larger question about the future of historical study of the suttas. Now that the old agendas for studying them—as eyewitness accounts of the Buddha's life and teaching, as manifestos of the world's first scientific humanism or egalitarian democracy, as philological ends in themselves—have increasingly become discredited, I have asked what use a contemporary historian might make of them. The question is a genuine one, to which I will offer no easy answer. But having entertained great skepticism about even the possibility of such a future, and having therefore focused in my own scholarship to date almost exclusively on later periods of history for which precisely datable texts, inscriptions, monuments, and/or external sources exist, I must admit that this exercise, and the contemporary scholarship on which I have modeled my approaches, gives me a hopeful sense that this judgment was too hasty.

Each of the approaches that I have explored yields insight into Buddhist history that is new and, given the limitations inherent in any interpretation, well grounded. The autobiographical fragment is part of the earliest recoverable Buddhist tradition. The early community struggled to define itself in close proximity of religious others in general and of the communities of Āḷāra Kālāma and Uddaka Rāmaputta in particular. The *Sermon on the Noble Quest* is a carefully structured piece of literature designed to bring readers/hearers face-to-face with the Buddha. It is the core of traditions of biographical supplementation that span Buddhist history, and this sutta therefore helps us to identify the stages in the development of the Buddha biography and, by extension, the sociohistorical circumstances in which each was produced. That very epitome of Theravāda orthodoxy, Buddhaghosa, entertained a Buddhological vision far removed from "the historical Buddha" as he has been conceived by many scholars and Buddhist modernists in the nineteenth and twentieth centuries.

Perhaps more important, our collaboration in Chicago suggested to me that my attempt at defining these four approaches to the historicity of the suttas may have wider application. It at least provides a vocabulary within which different approaches can be discussed, refined, and tested on the great wealth of suttas (and commentaries) that we are lucky enough to possess. While I do believe that "historical source mode" is now largely bankrupt as an end in itself, it remains—like many of the staples of the larger historicist project in which it participated (such as chronologies, critical editions, and identifications of archaeological sites)—absolutely foundational in any attempt at treating suttas or parts of suttas historically. But fixing a sutta at some point in the tradition is merely the first step in much more interesting historical projects that scholars like Bailey, Collins, and Blackburn have opened up for us. The suttas make possible a new sort of social history of the earliest stages in Buddhist history, nuanced by treating the texts themselves as actions within the sociohistorical circumstances of their production rather than as passive transmitters of neutral information. The suttas contain a wealth of literary beauty and efficacy and can therefore help us imagine early Buddhist world views with greater clarity than is afforded by the philosophical doctrines and historical facts we have hitherto extracted in bits from them. The suttas have their own biographies, histories of being read and of not being read, which potentially shed great light on later developments in every realm of Buddhist life.

It may of course turn out to be the case that in each of these modes NQ is uniquely significant. It is after all a sutta that has always been privileged, in Buddhist history and in the history of Buddhological scholarship, as a basis for imagining the Buddha's own life. This privilege is no doubt the result of its obviously great antiquity, it being arguably the oldest Buddha biography in existence. At least the autobiographical fragment appears to be intentionally designed as a response to the multireligious society in which the early Buddhists, and all Buddhists, have found themselves; it is of course no surprise to learn that Buddhists discoursed on the biography of the founder in the same breath that they tried to define their identity as a separate religious order. The fact that this is so ancient a Buddha biography may be the reason that in its final form the sutta seems especially well constructed to bring the reader/hearer face-to-face with the Buddha. This antiquity likewise goes far in explaining why this particular sutta has been so elaborated and ornamented in later traditions of supplementation and why Buddhaghosa chose it for some perhaps untypical speculation on the cosmic issues surrounding Buddhahood. In a word, it may be the case that NQ is uniquely significant for historians precisely because it is uniquely historical in its perspective.

This possibility raises an empirical matter: we will only discover what the thousands of suttas (or parallel texts from other religious traditions) may reveal to the historical imagination if we trouble to apply that imagination to them. The Chicago collaboration demonstrated that the four modes, in their various dimensions, will not be equally applicable to all suttas (let alone all religious classics). Only some suttas will have parallels in other suttas or Buddhist Sanskrit works; only some will address external circumstances in explicit or implicit terms; only some will prove to be carefully constructed and powerfully evocative; only some will prove to have been the basis of later supplementation and/or interesting commentary. But even the absence of applicability can address larger questions about the suttas in general, and our discussions did proceed in sometimes useful ways when the questions implicit in one or more of the four modes were raised. Thus it is my hope that, beyond my new historical readings of NQ, this article contributes in some small way to the ongoing history of religions project to understand historically all the "canonical" texts on which religious traditions have been based.

Notes

1. On Turnour's contribution to the historiography of the Pāli texts, see the appendix to my "Buddhist History: The Pāli Vaṃsas of Sri Lanka" (2000, 152-64).
2. Now classic studies include Spiro 1970 and Gombrich 1971. For important counter-readings, which insist that the rift tells us we are wrong in constructing a "canonical Buddhism" rather than that actual Buddhists are somehow corruptions of themselves, see Southwold 1983 and Scott 1994.
3. The *Sermon on the Noble Quest* is found in Trenckner 1888, 160-75.
4. All translations from the Pāli are my own.
5. In fact, as I shall explicate in greater detail below, NQ and related suttas of the Majjhimanikāya are the *only* canonical narratives of many crucial moments in the Buddha biography; NQ is relied on implicitly and explicitly in *all* reconstructions of the Buddha biography from later canonical times to the present, both by Buddhists and by scholars.

6. In his commentary, Buddhaghosa is obviously troubled by this designation; ignoring the obvious meaning, *an* (not) + *acchariyā* (marvelous), he reads the term as *anu* (exceedingly) + *acchariyā* (wonderful), which may be grammatically questionable yet seems rather more appropriate for the first words uttered after the enlightenment. See Woods and Kosambi 1928, 2: 175 (hereafter MA).
7. Many later Buddha biographies wrestle with this incident, which suggests that it did not sit comfortably with the Buddhists who inherited it. Thus *Buddhavaṃsa* omits it in the biography of Gotama proper (and does not make it a stock category in the many Buddha biographies it narrates), choosing instead to make it the occasion for the declaration of *Buddhavaṃsa* itself (again without a hint that the Buddha actually hesitated). Aśvaghoṣa's *Buddhacarita* has God come in an exalted company, more as a social call than an actual plea; the Buddha already knows he is going to preach his message before God arrives. A similar move is also made in later texts such as the *Nidānakathā* of the *Jātakaṭṭhakathā*. In the Lotus Sūtra the Buddha not only knows that he will preach before God arrives but knows it from the veritable beginning of time.
8. In NQ itself this uneasiness is apparent: the gods tell the Buddha that the two teachers are dead, but his knowledge and insight in this regard then seem to arise on their own. Aśvaghoṣa (*Buddhacarita* 14:106) simply omits the deities altogether.
9. "*1. Biographical fragments incorporated into the Sūtras*—In the *Majjhimanikāya*, four suttas which repeat and complement one another all tell us of an important phase in Śākyamuni's life, namely, the period which extends from the flight from Kapilavastu until the Enlightenment: these are the *Ariyapariyesana* (M I, pp. 163-73; T 26, No. 204, ch. 56, pp. 776b-778c), the *Dvedhāvitakka* (M I, p. 117), the *Bhayabherava* (M I, pp. 17-23; T 125, ch. 23, pp. 665b-666c) and the *Mahāsaccakasutta* (M I, pp. 240-49). Against the will of his parents, he left home and donned the yellow robe of the religious; he studied successively under Ālāra Kālāma and Udraka Rāmaputra; the former taught him the way of nihilism, the latter that of neither-perception-nor-nonperception; however Śākyamuni considering their doctrines to be imperfect, abandoned them, passed through Magadha and withdraw [*sic*] into solitude, in the neighbourhood of Uruvilvā (M I, pp. 163-67; T 26, ch. 56, pp. 776b-777a)" (Lamotte 1988, 648-49).
10. I have tried to work some of this out in Walters 1992, 228-30. Parallel passages are: M 1: 167-73 = *Mahāvagga* 1:5-1:6 (with the addition of *Dhammacakkappavattanasutta* at the point where it belongs in the narrative).
11. As at *Kathāvatthu* 289; see Malalasekera 1937, 1: 386.
12. Thomas [1927] 1975, 62, n. 1: "See *Majjh.* i, 23, 117, 167, 247-49; ii 93-94; these are repetitions, and this means that the redactor of redactors of this collection incorporated an older document."
13. We find the Pāli (*akāmakānaṃ mātapitunnaṃ assamukhānaṃ rudantānaṃ* (genitive absolute construction, "while [my] parents who did not approve were weeping and wailing") badly rendered as *akāmakānāṃ mātāpitṛnām aśrukaṇṭhānām rudanmukhānāṃ*, which in addition to being garbled in a way that can only be explained as bad translation ("weep-necked" instead of "weeping" [literally, "faces of tears"]; "wail-faced" instead of "wailing") betrays its Pāli-like origin in the use of the real plural rather than the dual, which an original composition in Sanskrit would surely have employed for "mother and father." The dual, of course, is lacking in Pāli and some related Prakrits. Likewise, mistakes in *sandhi* throughout suggest direct copying from a Pāli-like manuscript or oral tradition, in either of which *sandhi* rules are loose, informal, or nonexistent. There are lines omitted such that the Sanskrit text is almost gibberish without the Pāli (*sa khalvahaṃ bhikṣavaḥ yena Udrako Rāmaputra etadavocat*; cf. the Pāli *Atha khvāhaṃ bhikkhave yena Uddako Rāmaputto*

ten' upasaṃkamim, upasaṃkamitvā Uddakaṃ Rāmaputtaṃ etad avocam). Most telling, the pseudo-Sanskritization of "Uddaka" as "Udraka" is belied in the one-time slip, in all the manuscripts, into the Pāli spelling "Uddaka."

14. Thus, in addition to similar *sandhi* gaffes, *Lalitavistara* employs the common Pāli term *ātāpī*, zealous, which is not ordinarily found in Sanskrit, in rendering the common Pāli description of an *arahant* (*eko vupakaṭṭho appamatto ātāpī pahittatto*) as *eko 'pramatta ātāpi vyapakṛṣto*.
15. "Of his six years' striving we know from the Canon only what the *Majjhima* tells us (above, pp. 62ff.)" (Thomas [1927] 1975, 229-30).
16. The *Buddhavaṃsa* (BV, Morris 1882; citations are to chapter and verse) opens with a scene of Brahmā begging, located in the canon only in NQ and related texts (BV 1:6), and this becomes standard in the account of other Buddhas too (e.g., 2:211); the period of striving also becomes standard of the *type* "Buddha," though note that Āḷāra and Uddaka do not appear in this account; another parallel is the recognition (by Sumedha, however) of liability to birth (*jātidhamma*), etc., and the language of "why then don't I . . ." (BV 2:7-9); cf. Horner and Law 1975, 10, n. 4.
17. The *Buddhacarita* (Johnston [1936] 1992; citations are to chapter and verse) contains the self-recognition of destiny to birth, etc. (4:89; 5:12-13; also the language of seeing the danger in this, e.g., 4:97 and 11:7; also 12:48); black hair/supreme youth of the Bodhisatta (8:52; cf. 10:23: "prime of youth"; 12:8: "flush of youth"), weeping in the palace (8:81; cf. 9:13), visit to Āḷāra (Ārāḍa) Kālāma (9:6; 11:69; ch. 12, esp. 12:83: "Thus he was not satisfied on learning the doctrine of Arāḍa, and, discerning that it was incomplete, he turned away from there"); visit to Udraka Rāmaputra (12:84-88; same language of attainments in each teacher's case); pure bank of Nerañjarā River (12:90); description of Nirvana being sought (11:59: "the stage in which there is neither old age, nor fear, nor disease, nor birth, nor death"); description of the ultimate as *paramaṃ śivaṃ* (12:69 = Pāli *paramaṃ sivam*); description of the eight *jhanas* (12:49ff.); surveying the world with purified eye, people of little or great dust, etc. (14:8ff.); sees Arāḍa and Udraka are dead so decides to preach to the Group of Five (14:106—but now out of the surviving Sanskrit text); the whole thing is predicated on a rejection of the passions, precisely what NQ's sermon proper (see frame IV, below) is actually about; see esp. chap. 11.
18. The *Abhiniṣkramaṇasūtra* (Beal [1875] 1985) is obviously drawing on NQ either directly or indirectly (perhaps via the *Buddhacarita*) in its descriptions of the visit to the teachers (169-77) and of the events after the enlightenment (242-50).
19. Beal [1884] 1981: NQ (probably through *Buddhacarita* transmission?) is clearly presupposed by 2: 54-55 (*stūpa* of reluctance of the Group of Five, also mention of Āḷāra and Uddaka); 2: 139-42 (weird story of Uddaka).
20. Some scholars have actively pooh-poohed this criticism (e.g., C. A. F. Rhys Davids's defensive argument [1938, v] that "who is to say [God's appearance before the Buddha] is any less true than the baptism in the Jordan?") but most scholars (e.g., T. W. Rhys Davids, Étienne Lamotte, E. J. Thomas, A. Foucher) have seemingly confirmed it in their utter silence about these matters (which nevertheless does not prevent them from narrating other aspects of this Buddha autobiography as "historical fact").
21. "*We are told in the legends* that Buddha studied under Āḷāra Kālāma and Uddaka the son of Rāma, but all we learn is that the former made the goal consist in the attainment of the stage of nothingness, and the latter in the attainment of the stage of neither consciousness nor non-consciousness. These are Buddhist terms for two of the attainments, and *there is no reason to suppose that the legend is recording exact details of fact* about two teachers who were dead before Buddha began to preach. The compiler is using the only terms he

knew to express the imperfect efforts of Buddha's predecessors" (Thomas [1927] 1975, 184). Explaining himself, Thomas adds (n. 2): "There is one other reference to Āḷāra in the Canon, which shows that he was looked upon as a practiser of concentration. See p. 150. When we come down to the second century A.D., we find much more detailed accounts of his philosophy in Aśvaghosha's *Buddhacarita,* ch. 12, and they have even been treated as evidence for the sixth century B.C. Their historical value is discussed in ch. xvi." Following that reference, cf. pp. 229-30: "Of his six years' striving we know from the Canon only what the *Majjhima* tells us (above, pp. 62ff.). His two teachers are described as practising concentration, and what they inculcated were two of the so-called Attainments, which are also a part of the Buddhist system, but probably not a primitive part of it. *It seems very unlikely that the compiler of the sutta a century or two later had any real knowledge of the facts* of their teaching. He had to describe their imperfect methods, and he gives them in what are exact descriptions of two Buddhist practices. Nothing about the philosophical systems of these teachers is said either in the Canon or out of it until we come to Aśvaghosha's poem of the first or second century A.D. [BC xii.17 ff.]. There we are told that Ārāḍa or Āḷāra first described his philosophy concisely to Gotama. It has a resemblance to the Sānkhya philosophy, but is without some of its most characteristic doctrines. R. Schmidt calls it an older form of Sānkhya. Windisch supposes that Aśvaghosha introduced only what he needed for this purpose. The point is important only with regard to the question of the origin of Buddhistic principles, and even then only on the supposition that Aśvaghosha is faithfully describing a system in the form in which it existed before Buddha began to preach. This is entirely improbable. *The terminology used is neither that of early Sānkhya nor of early Buddhism.* More important is Aśvaghosha's account of the replies of the two teachers to Gotama's questions about the religious life and the obtaining of final release. Āḷāra's reply consists of a description identical with the methods of the Buddhist monk up to the last Attainment but one. The monk reaches the four trances, and then successively attains *space,* the *infinite,* and *nothingness.* These last three stages are concise statements of the first three of the four Attainments. This account corresponds to the statement in the Pāli that Āḷāra taught the Attainment of the state of Nothingness. The description of Uddaka's doctrine also corresponds with the Pāli in making his teaching the fourth Attainment. Aśvaghosha has thus added nothing essential to the canonical statement beyond giving an independent account of a philosophical system which *has no appearance of being historical*" (my emphasis throughout, except the emphasis on space, the infinite, and nothingness, which is in the text).

22. Lamotte's only mention of the teachers is his brief notice of NQ and related Majjhima suttas in an appendix, cited in full in n. 9 above.
23. Here Foucher inserts a footnote (n. 9) to Warren ([1886] 1992, 334), which contains his translation of the relevant portion of NQ, not *Lalitavistara*! And there is no inconsistency I see in the use of pronouns; the first person is employed consistently throughout.
24. Foucher 1963. The original French edition is Foucher 1949, 96-97.
25. In addition to some detailed correspondence with Greg Bailey in 1995, I base what I say here on Bailey 1991.
26. The Jain case is especially interesting for the obviously intertextual relationship between the biographies of the respective founders, who are interchangeably referred to with the same epithets (Buddha, Jina, Mahāvīra, Arahant) and whose biographies exhibit differences as minor—yet definitive, distinctive, across an unthinkable line—as the iconographic difference of whether or not the genitals show.
27. On dialogical as opposed to monological readings of South Asian texts, generally, see Ron Inden's introduction in Inden 2000. My "Buddhist History" in that same volume applies Inden's insights to Buddhist texts (Walters 2000).

28. According to *Mahāvastu* and *Lalitavistara*, Āḷāra's community contained 300 students, while Uddaka's community contained 700 students.
29. According to *Lalitavistara*, the Buddha met them when he arrived at Uddaka's ashram, from whom he spirited them away; Tibetan versions make them representatives of the 300 (3) and 200 (2) men sent by the Bodhisatta's father and father-in-law, respectively, to attend on him when he went forth; the Pāli *Jātakaṭṭhakathā* makes Koṇḍañña the youngest of the eight Brahmins who prophesied at the Bodhisatta's birth. The previous seven having died, he tried to rile their sons to follow him in serving the Bodhisatta, but only four complied; together with him they are the five. See Thomas [1927] 1975, 80. Buddhaghosa's commentary also treats the five as sons of the Brahmins who first predicted the future greatness of the Bodhisatta.
30. For fruits of this approach, see the wide-ranging collection of articles in Schober 1997; Strong 1983 and Strong 1992 are exemplary in this regard. For a non-Theravādin parallel, see Granoff and Shinohara 1988.
31. Reverting to text of its day mode for a moment, it is worth noting that this hermitage is mentioned only in NQ; this is our only source for thinking about just who Rammaka might have been: a former follower of Uddaka? Is his name a mishmash allusion to Uddaka Rāmaputta himself? Or is his very anonymity meant to represent any Brahmin? The fact that he is Rammaka *the Brahmin* is repeated seven times in the first paragraph of the text. In either event, the setting may have interesting things to say about the content of the autobiographical fragment in this regard, too.
32. This is only implicit in NQ itself. The Buddha, on learning that the monks have been there at Rammaka's discussing the Dhamma, praises them saying, "Excellent, monks! It is proper that you, sons of good family who through faith have gone forth from home to the homeless life, sit down together in a Dhamma-discussion. Monks, when you are sitting together there are two proper courses of action for you: either Dhamma-discussion or else the Noble Silence" (M 1: 161). That this Dhamma-discussion is in fact exemplary of the Noble Quest as such becomes explicit, twice, in Buddhaghosa's commentary: "[The monks] sat down there for a Dhamma-discussion; they were not seated [engaged] in gibberish. Then the Blessed One began this preaching to point out [to the monks,] 'your quest is definitely the Noble Quest' . . . [the statement in NQ that] 'This, monks, is the Noble Quest' should be understood [to imply,] 'this, your own [Dhamma-discussion] for the sake of purity, because it is what ought to be quested after by noble people, is the Noble Quest'" (MA 2: 169-70 [n. 6 above]).
33. I believe that this sense of longing for the Buddha's presence was first noticed by Paul Mus 1935, preface. Manifestations of it have been described, in strikingly different keys, by Schopen 1997; Strong 1983; and Eckel 1994.
34. A recent example of this sort is Carrithers (1983), who explicitly and implicitly embeds most of the NQ narrative (see esp. 20-52) but adds to it an incredible array of material that even my students recognize to be a haphazard collection of tidbits from later Buddha biographies as well as from his own general knowledge (e.g., his digression into the psychoanalysis of altered states as an explanation of the Bodhisatta's encounters with Āḷāra and Uddaka). On the role of "the historical Buddha" more generally, especially in terms of the scholarly construct of pan-Buddhist history, see Walters 1998.
35. Upaka was love-enslaved by a hunter's daughter, married her and lived a normal, if rather low, lay life. But when she turns out to be trouble he renounces the world and sets out looking for "the boundless Victor" (*anantajina*), the epithet that Buddha so unabashedly accepted in their earlier encounter. Knowing that Upaka would come back, he instructed

his attendants to direct anyone seeking "Anantajina" to him, and sure enough Upaka shows up and is quickly initiated into the Dhamma (MA 2: 189-90).

36. This is where the Buddha was then spending his nights. Buddhaghosa is careful to give a layout of the palace lest anyone infer that the Buddha was sleeping anywhere near a woman (MA 2: 165).

3

Historical Understanding: The Chan Buddhist Transmission Narratives and Modern Historiography

Dale S. Wright

In his *Studies in the History of the Early Chan School* (Yanagida 1967, 18), the Zen historian, Yanagida Seizan, claims that the classic Chan "Lamp Histories" presuppose an orientation to history that differs significantly from that of the modern historians who now study them. Focusing on one such text, the classic *Records of the Transmission of the Lamp*,[1] compiled in 1004, this paper seeks to articulate an understanding of the character of historical awareness in Song dynasty Chan Buddhism and to define the difference, suggested by Yanagida, between it and modern historiography.[2] Having done this, the paper will conclude with some reflections on what each historiographic tradition can learn from the other, and how historiographic understanding can be advanced in light of this learning.

The initial difficulty of this task is that, although this voluminous text is thoroughly historical in character, no "theory" of history is explicit in the text, nor, for that matter, anywhere else in Chan literature. Therefore, this paper begins with reflections on the language and formal structure of the text insofar as they enable us to define what understanding of history is presupposed in Chan transmission practices.

I

The historical intention of *Records of the Transmission of the Lamp* can be gleaned from its title: it consists of "records" (*lu*) of "transmission" (*chuan*) as seen from the perspective of a particular historical era—the Jingde imperial era within the Northern Song dynasty. What was being transmitted—a lamp and its light (*deng*)—was the fundamental aim of the tradition, enlightenment or "awakening." The overall narrative structure of the text, therefore, is a story of the origins and dissemination of "enlightened mind" beginning with the ancient Buddhas and continuing through Indian and Chinese patriarchs up to current recipients of transmission.[3] Temporal, chronological structure—earliest to most recent—is maintained throughout the text. Within this overarching historical framework, the actual content of the text employed to tell the story of mind transmission is religious biography.

The historical, narrative structure of the text is therefore twofold: biographical histories, themselves individually temporalized in a narrative order moving from birth through death, are placed within the overarching history of human enlightenment. The text's editors venture no reflections on sacred history as a whole—on its meaning, *telos*, or significance. Aside from genealogical charts that serve as periodic tables of content, all interesting detail enters the narrative on the level of individual history. This detail takes basically two forms. First, we are provided with essential biographical information at the beginning and then again at the end of each account. Typically we get an account of names, origins, early signs of brilliance, circumstances of ordination, and some account of the content of early monastic studies. At the end of biographies we often find a transmission *gāthā* or poem, an account of the Chan master's death, its date, along with subsequent imperial decrees concerning posthumous names, titles, and pagoda inscriptions.

Between these two extremes, however, is content even more pertinent to the transmission of mind—that is, narratives recounting particular events in the Chan master's life in which the power and efficacy of his "awakening" are clearly manifest.[4] These occasions are most often rhetorical occasions, discursive events that in one way or another display the character of enlightened mind. These stories, more than anything else in classical Chan, were understood to demonstrate what it means to be awakened. What this paper highlights, however, is the way in which these enlightened events receive their full meaning and significance only when placed within the overarching context of Chan history. Enlightenment is not figured as an isolated and unrelated event, nor just as an experience of eternity in the present moment. In each case enlightenment is a historical event located in a particular temporal, spatial context. My point here is simple: that the classical Chan interest in history is more central to their concerns than we have taken it to be and that beyond the Chan rhetoric of timelessness, we find historical contextualization to be central to their self-understanding.

In order to specify further the role that history plays in classical Chan, we turn to the key metaphors and symbols that place people and events into temporal relation. How are historical connections construed in this text? Primarily, it seems, through a complex set of metaphors drawn from the domain of family genealogy. Most basic to this symbolic order is that Chan itself came to be understood as a *zong*, a word evolving out of the ancient Chinese sense of ancestry. Interesting work has been done on the concept of *zong* by Yanagida, John McRae, and Griffith Foulk, especially on when and how Chan became a *zong* and what that meant over time (Yanagida 1967; Foulk 1987; McRae 1986). Pertinent to this paper is that in the most general and archaic sense *zong* meant "ancestor" and came by extension to connote anything related to clan or family ancestry. It is clear that throughout the Song and subsequent epochs, the term continued to carry deep pre-Buddhist religious connotations—ancestral spirits oversee and guide the clan. They are to be revered, followed, and honored; it was they who established the clan and made it what it is. In effect, the clan's identity is a gift of the ancestors; only through them can one understand what it is. Similarly, understanding Chan as a clanlike institution meant conceiving it in genealogical terms. Knowing what it meant to belong to the institution entailed knowing from whom it had been inherited, a historical knowledge transmitted and inculcated by means of narratives like the *Transmission of the Lamp*.

In effect, then, we can think of this text as analogous to a document of family history; it communicates a distinct Chan identity by means of significant family stories. Moreover, we see that family lineage and genealogy provide virtually all significant terms of relation within the Chan clan. Bodhidharma, the founding figure of the lineage, is called the "first ancestor" (*chuzu*), the patriarch of patriarchs.[5] Subsequent patriarchs are his "Dharma heirs" (*fasi*), each of whom can be located on distinct branches of the family tree. Relations among later Chan masters are also figured in genealogical terms, basic kinship titles such as uncle, nephew, and cousin, providing the overall framework. Words related to "inheritance" provide the primary symbols for patriarchal succession—the transmission of Chan mind from one generation to the next.[6]

The *Transmission of the Lamp* pictures the Chan master in constant search for an appropriate heir, someone who is seen as capable of being a "vessel" or "receptacle" of the Dharma. The Chinese term here is *qi*, a sacred, ceremonial vessel used in ancient times to make ritual offerings to the ancestors. A *qi* is also a tool or instrument, something that exists for the sake of something else. In this case, the patriarchs exist for the sake of the Dharma and of posterity. Like the ceremonial vessel, they receive, preserve, and transmit the substance of the sacred. Dharma transmission from one generation to the next is also figured as the impression made by a "seal" or "stamp" (*yin*) upon the mind and character of the inheritor. The so-called "mind seal" is imprinted upon the next generation's practice and experience by virtue of long-standing co-practice under the guidance of the master. The Chan practice of issuing certificates of "inheritance" or "authorization" doubles this metaphor of the stamp through the use of an actual seal stamping a document certifying that the holder has in fact received the master's seal upon his mind.

Occasional passages in the text allude to a sense of "debt" that inheritance accrues. Being selected and trained as an heir imposes enormous obligation and responsibility—a debt to be repaid. This responsibility is figured as a form of filial reverence that a descendant owes to the family lineage. "Confession" of this debt is common in the text, where a newly selected successor announces his gratitude and subsequent obligation to others in the lineage. The master warns the recipient not to "neglect posterity," and that "inheriting the Dharma" imposes an obligation to carry out the transmission as the ancestors had done. Being placed in a genealogy establishes relation not just to the past but to the future as well.[7] In order to feel this obligation to past and future generations, the inheritor must have a working understanding of the history of the lineage, not just knowing it but striving to embody it in act and discourse.

All of the genealogical terms that we see applied to patriarchal succession are applicable to the majority of practitioners who have not succeeded to the abbotship. They too stand in a concrete lineage location; they too inherit the Dharma and pass it along to the next generation, primarily through the everyday teaching that socializes a new generation of monks. They are all *Chanzi*, "children of Chan," raised by the family elders and socialized into the lineage. As the offspring of a particular master, raised in this monastic household rather than some other, they all manifest a distinct "family spirit" (*jiafeng*), the particular style of Chan behavior and rhetoric characteristic of the lineage.[8] Given the way in which sense of identity in Chan was structured upon models and terms supplied by family life and lineage, it is not surprising to find that role models, socialization, and mimetic repetition were essential to the way in which Chan practice came to be understood. To practice Chan was to repeat the ancient, ancestral Buddha pattern, and in turn to have its stamp placed upon one's character and comportment.

A subthesis of this paper is that one of the most important forms of this repetition was the repeated retelling, rereading, and rethinking of Chan narratives like those in the *Transmission of the Lamp*. By means of mental repetition, narrative shapes the participant's self-identity. "Narrative selfhood" here means that who the monk becomes, how he fits himself into the world, is to a great extent shaped by the stories into which he has been socialized. As Alasdair MacIntyre puts it: "I can only answer the question 'What am I to do?' if I can answer the prior question 'Of what story or stories do I find myself a part?'" (1981, 216). In the case of classical Chan this would be to say that personal identity or self-understanding was communicated only partly by doctrines concerning the self and much more by narratives, models, and precedents. Moreover, the doctrines themselves are integrally tied to the narratives and can be understood only in terms of particular exemplars described in narrative texts. As in other clans, the *Chanzi*, the "children of Chan," come to understand who they are and what they are doing through the process of hearing and acting out the stories of Chan. Prior to the "practice of presence" are stories weaving the concept of presence into conscious understanding; prior to the practice of *zazen* (meditation) are the narratives of *zazen* telling who did it, how, when, and to what effect. If this is so then narrative, historical identity would have been an essential component of enlightened identity. What I mean by this is that, although the Chan tradition did come to conceptualize and to represent the experience of "awakening" in vocabulary that expresses timelessness and an ahistorical ground, even more prominent in its representation are the genealogical, historical metaphors of relatedness that I have begun to describe here. Furthermore, the ahistorical concept of enlightenment comes to be situated under the overarching structure of genealogy such that belonging to the Chan clan becomes a background, stage-setting factor for the experience of enlightenment—a condition of its possibility. Since "awakening" was figured first and foremost as an "inheritance," the tradition naturally assumed that only well-socialized family members came into its possession. Thus enlightenment and historical understanding were integrally related.[9]

What is intriguing about the *Transmission of the Lamp* as a historical document is the extent to which it has been structured as a montage of earlier traditions, a characteristic which reveals something of the historical consciousness presupposed in it. Editors of the text have essentially gathered together all of the legends, stories, and other texts related to the key figures in the lineage. Then through substantial editing, rewriting, and repositioning, they have organized a new text and through it a revised understanding of the tradition. Furthermore, while drawing heavily on forebearing texts, the editors have made no effort at attribution. Innumerable bits and pieces of other texts are woven together into a new one without citation, quotation, or other devices that might credit the appropriate sources. In addition, editors seem very little concerned over the accuracy or legitimacy of their sources. Epistemological concerns—how do we know that this story about Mazu really did occur—seem to be subordinate interests at best. From our modern perspective, what we notice is that objective authentication of sources is not the reigning criterion of inclusion. What seems to matter is not where the story came from but how good it is and how well it might serve the purposes of transmission. This realization pushes us toward the question: Were these editors really historians, and if so, what kind?[10]

II

When Yanagida wrote that the sense of history among Song "lamp historians" was different from that of modern historiography—of which he himself is a practitioner—what concerned him was the extent to which classical Chan historians seemed to ignore pertinent data in order to construct their own history. How, he wonders, is the Zen tradition to reconcile these constructions with the discoveries of modern historians?[11] Yanagida's dilemma parallels in many ways the situation of modern Christian historians who have had to live in the tension between traditional doctrine and a series of historical realizations about the texts which have served to establish that doctrine. But, as Yanagida suggests, we would miss the productive point of this tension altogether if we were to construe it as an epistemological issue about the accuracy of the traditional narratives. The difference between modern and classical Chan historical consciousness goes much deeper. It concerns fundamental differences, in self-conception, in relation to tradition, and in what history is taken to be. In order to articulate these differences, we will need to ask: From what understanding of history could texts such as the *Transmission of the Lamp* and our own modern histories about those texts, have derived? How does the Chan historian's relation to history differ from that of the modern historian?

Although the differences between these distinct traditions could be shaped in any number of forms and in varying degrees of specificity, I will here characterize the contrast in terms of four basic points.

First, the Chan historian sees himself and his own text as standing in continuity to the tradition. Because he "recapitulates" and "hands down" what has already been handed down to him, his text stands in full continuity with its sources. Modern historians, by contrast, draw a line of separation between the object of study and their own texts about that object. The modern history of Buddhism is not to be considered a re-enactment of that tradition.

Second, feeling this sense of continuity, the Chan historian acts as a participant, fully engaged by the stories he transmits. He assumes that the literature of the tradition addresses him directly. Stories about past actualities are taken to be current possibilities, fully applicable to the historian in his own context. Modern historians shift the context of understanding. The text is to be understood, not in relation to the historian in his or her context, but in relation to its original context in another time and place. Bracketing out the present context of meaning, the modern historian describes what the text once meant to others.

Third, the Chan historian hopes to be freely and thoroughly influenced by the tradition he writes about. Because the text at hand, no matter how ancient in origin, is assumed to be fully applicable to his own context, his posture towards it is responsive, not just open but eager to undergo whatever influence it bears. His ideal is that the language and character of the text have been imprinted upon and joined to his own language and character. Modern historians, by contrast, make a commitment to avoid that influence on the thought that it might invalidate the history that they have written. The principle of objectivity requires that the historian's voice remain distinct from and not overlap with that of the text. The line between what the Buddhist text asserts and what the modern historian asserts about it must in every instance remain clear. While the Buddhist historian strives to learn *from* the text, the modern historian is content to learn *about* it.

Fourth, the Chan historian assumes the overriding truth of the Buddhist tradition and takes himself to be fully accountable for the recapitulation of that truth. His text is not just a report on what other Buddhists once said, but also what he, the historian, now says. Thus accountable, the stories he transmits must in some way accord with the current "sense of the Dharma." Whenever they don't, the stories are either omitted from the new text or appropriately altered.

Modern historians understand truth primarily as representational accuracy. They seek to know what the text really did say in its own context and to describe how people in that epoch really did use it. This task requires that they bracket, at least for the time being, all opinions about whether what was accurately reported is, in fact, true. Modern historians assume that their own views on its truth are irrelevant and that it simply isn't the historian's job to consider that question.

From the perspective of the modern historian, the procedures of the Chan historian are flawed to the point of producing "bad history." Lacking sufficient distance from the tradition, the Chan historian fails to describe the tradition accurately because the position from which his text is written conjoins and confuses how it was with how it is.

The weakness, however, of Chan historical consciousness is not just that it alters the data available to historical narrative. It is rather that its underlying assumptions and desires concerning the continuity and coherence of the tradition structure for the historian a perspective from which the "otherness" and the "disjunctions" of the tradition cannot be seen. If current practitioners model themselves on the ancients *and* the ancients are updated to fit the current image of "awakening," then no fundamental difference remains between the past and the present. The figure of the ancestors evolves along with the understanding of what "enlightenment" could mean to the extent that each new generation projects its highest aspirations on to the ancestors. Thus the ancestors always represent what the current practitioner could conceivably become even though that conception changes over time. Lacking a way to represent the "otherness" of the tradition to itself, the Chan historian has no perspective from which the present understanding can be criticized.[12] Practitioners, therefore, live out of a partially mistaken and typically precritical understanding of their own tradition. As a modern Zen historian, Yanagida Seizan stands within the first generation of practitioners to correct this defect by adopting the methods and procedures of modern, critical historiography.

III

However, critique can run in the opposite direction as well—a critique of modern historical consciousness from the perspective of classical Chan. What can an understanding of the classical Chan sense of history show us about our own practice of historiography and the understanding of history upon which it is based? Two brief suggestions along these lines are salient.

First, compared to the Chan tradition, our historical practices demonstrate very little sense of belonging to a tradition. We imagine ourselves tradition-free observers, representing no particular point of view and responsible to no one. On this point, however, we are mistaken. Like Chan Buddhists, we do, in fact, stand within a tradition and write out of a contextualized point of view. Although lack of self-understanding on this issue does not mean that we stand nowhere, it does mean that the quality and depth of our stance in study is significantly diminished. Knowing where you stand is important, as is understanding the relation between where you stand and what you study. In consequence of our view, we weaken the relation to tradition that we do inevitably have.[13]

Second, studying the various kinds of relationship between reader and text in the classical Chan tradition may bring to our attention a weakness in the extent of reflexivity or self-awareness that we bring to our study. This weakness is a consequence of the modern inclination to take natural science as the model toward which humanistic study should aspire. Valorizing objective disengagement, modern historical studies of Buddhism tend not to relate the Buddhist text at issue and its context to the context of the interpreter. Thus isolated, Buddhist texts tend not to serve as the impetus to seek a deeper understanding of the positions and assumptions out of which our work proceeds nor as encouragement to discover what of significance could be learned "from" these texts. We proceed, in effect, as if we aren't really involved. In this respect the narratives we tell about ourselves are underdeveloped.[14] They fail to locate us in a productive relation to the text, one through which we might be provoked by the text, either to understand more deeply our own position, or to rethink, revise, or expand it. A reflexive relation to the text takes advantage of whatever light the text can shed on its reader. When this reflexive relation is lacking or weak, the very rationale for historical study has become obscured. As the Mazu section of the *Transmission of the Lamp* asserts, the most important answers to our questions about Buddhism can be discovered only in self-conscious relation to "the one who is doing the questioning."

IV

Although the deficiencies highlighted in this paper in both traditions of historiography are at this level of description polar opposites of one another, they can also be understood to share a fundamental similarity: both the Chan Buddhist and the modern Western historical traditions deny implicitly some dimension of the impermanence of history, the radical mutability of temporal movement. Although the Buddhist tradition highlights the deficiency of the present—its unsatisfactory character due to which the ancestral Buddhas need be consulted and imitated—it is unable to consider critically the deficiencies of the past or the possible inapplicability of past truths to present contingencies. And although modern historians understand very clearly the deficiency of the past—the relativity of "outmoded" ideas and practices to their own historical context—they tend to assume the universality and noncontextual truth of their own modern ideas and practices of historiography. One tradition—the Buddhist—experiences the lack or absence of the present in relation to the fullness of the enlightened past, while the other—the modern—maintains that, whereas the full presence of true historical knowledge is now possible, it appears not to have been so in the past.

In both traditions, therefore, one dimension of time stands exempt from the negativity of historical finitude. Locating a kind of historical understanding that overcomes these particular deficiencies is thus a matter of learning to avoid these exemptions. Working toward this kind of self-awareness in our study would, in effect, constitute work toward the development of a new and more encompassing criterion of truth for historical reflection.

Because each tradition of historiography evolves within its own cultural tradition and upon the conceptual and practical bases supplied for it by other dimensions of culture, it should not be surprising that each places its focus differently and orients itself to past, present, and future in a distinct way. The possibility of a significant transformation of historical consciousness in each of these cultures is greatly enhanced in the current setting by the availability of different traditions of historical reflection in relation to which each tradition can understand, evaluate, and critique itself.

Already the social, cultural ramifications of the rethinking of both Chinese history and the practice of historiography in China in light of their encounter with

Marxist and other forms of Western historical reflection have been immense. Signs now exist that some form of alteration has begun to occur in Western historical thinking as a result in part of the twentieth-century encounter with the rest of the world. These signs are promising, indeed, exciting. They push historical imagination to consider possibilities hitherto closed to thinking. However, it would be a mistake (in fact a mistake symptomatic of the modern tendency to exempt its own standpoint from contextualization) to regard this present activity of placing two traditions of historiography in critical relation to one another as itself occupying a position outside of and "beyond" those traditions. In a finite, diverse, and historical world, "nontraditional" and all-encompassing theories of history are not possible. What is possible, however, is that through the encounter with other cultures and epochs, particular traditions of historical reflection will become in some way richer, more comprehensive, more self-critical, and more applicable towards cultural ends which are themselves open to similar transformation.

Glossary

Chan	禪
Chanzi	禪子
chuan	傳
chuzu	初祖
deng	燈
fasi	法司
jiafeng	家風
Jingde chuandeng lu	景德傳燈綠
qi	器
yin	印
zazen	座禅
zong	宗

Notes

1. The *Jingde chuandeng lu* (*Taishō* 1924–32, 2076.51) was compiled by Daoyuan and published in 1004. A partial English translation can be found in Chang 1971.
2. Maraldo (1985) is the first to raise questions of this kind about the Chan tradition. This paper follows the course staked out by Maraldo's essay and is indebted to it in many ways.
3. For an elaboration on this historical structure see McRae 1986, 75.
4. Because all Chan Buddhist masters represented in the *Transmission of the Lamp* were men,

this essay uses masculine gender pronouns when referring to the Buddhist saints of this time period. The essay employs inclusive gender references in all other cases.

5. Yanagida (1967, 214) traces the Chan history of the term "patriarch." See also Yampolsky 1967, 1-23.
6. Yanagida (1978) does a more extensive analysis of the vocabulary of Chan genealogy. Heinrich Dumoulin (1988, ch. 10) draws upon this work.
7. For interesting reflections on themes related to past, present, and future generations, see Ricoeur 1988, 3, esp. 109-116.
8. Ricoeur (1988, 3: 221) elaborates on the relation between language and tradition.
9. Modern interpreters, under the influence of the language of "universality," have ignored this genealogical dimension of "Zen," preferring instead to read it as an excellent example of the transcendence of tradition and history.
10. See McRae (1986, 10-11) on "the distinction between legend and history."
11. For an interesting characterization of modern Japanese Zen historiography see Foulk 1987, ch. 1.
12. This account is overstated in order to highlight one side of a more complex interaction. The texts did in fact serve as an ancient perspective from which the present historical moment could be criticized. This would have been so in several important respects. But at least two factors diminished the extent to which this "difference" between past and present could be recognized. The first, suggested above, is that the texts were altered to bring them into accord with the language and thought of the present era. Thus their "otherness" was erased whenever it seemed to protrude. The second is that, even when the text was not altered, the overriding assumption that past and present are in full correspondence sets up the likelihood that whatever the text says will be given a new and current sense rather than being seen as a "difference" demanding critical judgment between former and current points of view.
13. "Modern historical research itself is not only research, but the transmission of tradition" (Gadamer 1975, 253). Gadamer's work is the primary source for the concepts of "tradition" and "historicity" operative in this paper. See also MacIntyre 1990.
14. For a critique of modern historiography on this point see LaCapra 1983.

4

Roads Taken and Not Taken in the Study of Theravāda Buddhism

Charles Hallisey

> It does not matter whether one generation applauds the previous generation or hisses it—in either event, it carries the previous generation within itself.
>
> José Ortega y Gasset

My title alludes to an essay by Edward Said in which he engaged "in a useful exercise, by which one delineates the critical field in order to propose changes in it or lacks in it" (Said 1983, 140). In a fundamental way, Said's *Orientalism* (1978) was a similar exercise concerned as it was with the necessity for members of an academic community to struggle constantly for critical distance on their own work. As Said warned at the end of *Orientalism*, "Trouble sets in when the guild tradition of Orientalism [or any academic field] takes over the scholar who is not vigilant, whose individual consciousness as a scholar is not on guard against *idées reçues* all too easily handed down in the profession" (326).

Trouble can set in even for those of us who seek to extend the insights of *Orientalism*; it is all too easy to reproduce unwittingly a kind of "latent Orientalism"[1] as can be seen in Philip Almond's *The British Discovery of Buddhism* (1988). As if he were taking as his premise Said's trenchant comment that if "Orientalism makes sense at all [it] depends more on the West than on the Orient," Almond builds on Said's basic argument that Orientalist discourse is a system of representations which is primarily embedded in European culture (Said 1978, 21-22, quote on 22, see also 5, 12). But Almond's own careful analysis of the emergence of this discourse leads him to move beyond the "principles" of Orientalism to the "many concerns of the Victorian age":[2]

> Victorian interpretations of Buddhism, whether of its founder, its doctrines, its ethics, its social practices, or its truth and value, in constructing Buddhism, reveal the world in which such constructing took place. . . . Discourse about Buddhism provides a mirror in which is reflected an image not only of the Orient, but of the Victorian world also. (5-6)

It is worth noting, however, that while Almond refers to an image of the Orient, he makes no attempt to reconstruct Buddhist thought and practice in nineteenth-century Asia. Although this omission would seem to make good sense for a project concerned with "the internal consistency of Orientalism and its ideas about the Orient" (Said 1978, 5), it has the unintended consequence of once again hypostatizing and reifying an absolute divide between "the West" and "the Orient"—a basic premise of Orientalist constructions of knowledge (2, 43)—by proceeding as if a genealogy of the West's account of Buddhism could be made without any reference to the people and places from which it is imagined to emanate.[3] Moreover, this omission has the ironic effect of once more denying any voice to "Orientals" in the Western apprehension of what they are about even as it makes us more aware of the historicity of our concepts of Buddhism.[4]

Said himself was uneasy about positing an absolute divide between the West and the Orient, as is clear at the end of *Orientalism* when he reiterates a question that runs throughout his book: "Is the notion of the distinct culture (or race, or religion, or civilization) a useful one?"

> The notion that there are geographical spaces with indigenous, radically "different" inhabitants who can be defined on the basis of some religion, culture, or racial essence proper to that geographical space is . . . a highly debatable idea. (1978, 322, 325)

Said indicated which side of this debate he was on by showing that it is impossible to define the modern West without reference to the Orient. Referring to the work of Raymond Schwab, he says that "his thesis in *La Renaissance orientale* is a simple one: Romanticism cannot be understood unless some account is taken of the great textual and linguistic discoveries made about the Orient during the late eighteenth and early nineteenth centuries" (Said 1983, 151). Said's suggestions of this sort can help us to see that his basic concern is, as James Clifford has noted, "not so much to undermine the notion of a substantial Orient as it is to make problematic 'the Occident'" (Clifford 1980, 219). This rearrangement of received notions about the constitution of the modern West has been continued by many others in recent years, and "detailing the process by which the West became itself by confronting the Rest is one of the . . . important steps forward in postorientalist intellectual history."[5] But although significant progress has been made in displaying how the self-image of the West in the nineteenth century depended on projecting onto others the negation or inversion of what was taken to be distinctive of "European-ness," this line of inquiry can still paradoxically leave the West–Orient divide in place as a paradigm instead of problematizing it or removing it altogether.[6]

Where can we begin to develop more nuanced accounts of the interaction between Europeans and non-Europeans, ones which are able to avoid a Manichaean division between East and West and remind us that cultures are not only different but also connected? One way of at least making space for accounts of this kind is to show the heterogeneity of interests within those communities called "Europe" and "the Orient" as they encountered each other,[7] and especially among Orientalists themselves (see, e.g., Kopf 1992; Hatcher 1992).

We might also address our task more directly and look for relations between "the West" and "the Orient" that are not characterized by negation or inversion, but instead seem to represent a kind of "intercultural mimesis." That is, we should consider occasions where it seems that aspects of a culture of a subjectified people influenced the investigator to represent that culture in a certain manner (Burghart 1990, 266). Such an exercise would not challenge but rather would nuance Said's argument that the links between knowledge and inequalities of power provided some basic conditions of Orientalist discourse.

In the rest of this essay I will explore some diverse examples of this kind of "intercultural mimesis." It can be found in the work of T. W. Rhys Davids, whose career as a student of Buddhism represents a crucial stage in the study of Buddhism in Europe,[8] but in order to recognize it we will also have to examine the work of some lesser-known contemporaries of Rhys Davids: R. Spence Hardy, Paul Bigandet, and Adhémard Leclère. An awareness of these patterns of mimesis not only will help us to appreciate critically the legacy of Orientalism inherited by contemporary students of Buddhism, but will also suggest a strategy, from within that legacy, for passing beyond it. We will see that a road rarely, if at all, taken in the study of Theravāda Buddhism is indeed a viable option for us.

T. W. Rhys Davids and the Biography of the Buddha

The name of T. W. Rhys Davids (1843–1922) is well known to all students of Buddhism.[9] This "great orientalist," according to Richard Gombrich, "did more than anyone else to introduce [Buddhism] to the English-speaking public, influencing even English-speaking Sinhalese Buddhists," and thus "serious students of Buddhism will never allow [his] name to die" (Gombrich 1986, 121-22). But Rhys Davids is not only a figure of historical interest. He is what Said calls an "inaugural hero," someone who "carved . . . out a field of study and a family of ideas which in turn could form a community of scholars whose lineage, traditions, and ambitions were at once internal to the field and external enough for general prestige."[10] And as an inaugural hero, Rhys Davids has recently been subjected to scorn for promulgating a "Pali Text Society mentality" which "essentialized Buddhism in terms of its 'pristine' teachings."[11] Still, we cannot ignore the fact that he produced tools, such as a Pāli-English Dictionary and editions of Pāli texts, which remain to this day unsurpassed and indispensable for research. His efforts resulted in the creation of institutions, such as the Pali Text Society and the School of Oriental and African Studies, from which all students of Buddhism still benefit, either directly or indirectly. Moreover, many of his ideas continue to be reproduced unacknowledged in the writings of others, an indication of the extent to which his ideas have been naturalized within the tradition of Buddhist Studies.[12]

Among Rhys Davids's lesser writings are two encyclopedia entries, "Buddhism" and "Buddha," which he wrote for the *Encyclopaedia Britannica* at different points in his scholarly career. They are among his more minor and ephemeral writings, and their specific contents are of little interest to us here. They are still useful to us, however, because by the nature of their genre, they give an indication of the scholarly resources available to Rhys Davids at the time they were written, and it is these resources which will draw our attention to an aspect of Rhys Davids's practice as a scholar in which we can see an instance of intercultural mimesis.

In his first entry on "Buddhism," written in 1876, Rhys Davids was limited to four "authorities on the life of Buddha," which he could recommend to his readers.[13] These were R. Spence Hardy's *A Manual* of *Buddhism*, which collected biographical narratives drawn from medieval Sinhala literature; Bishop P. Bigandet's *The Life or Legend of the Gaudama the Buddha of the Burmese*, a translation of an early modern Burmese text; Fausbøll's edition of the Pāli biography found in the Jātaka commentary from the fifth century CE; and Foucaux's French translation of a Tibetan translation of the *Lalitavistara*, a Sanskrit text composed early in the common era. By the time Rhys Davids revised this entry a quarter of a century later, European students of Buddhism had gathered enough material that Rhys Davids was able to add a second entry in the *Encyclopaedia Britannica*, which focused on the life of the Buddha alone. The difference between the two entries, however, is not only the quantity of sources available but the interpretative frameworks in which Rhys Davids ordered his sources. In the first entry, two of the four sources were in vernacular languages, Sinhala and Burmese, and two were in the "classical" languages of Pāli and Sanskrit. By the time of the second entry in 1910, the number of resources in the classical languages had increased dramatically. This was especially true of the canonical Pāli sources which were of unique importance to Rhys Davids. In addition, he was also to make use of the *Mahāvastu* and *Buddhacarita*, two Sanskrit sources, as well as Rockhill's translations from the Tibetan (which themselves were almost exclusively translations from Sanskrit) in *The Life of the Buddha*. In contrast, the resources from vernacular languages had hardly increased at all and Rhys Davids only added Adhémard Leclère's French translation of the Khmer text *Pathama Sambodhian* in *Livres sacrés du Cambodge* to his bibliographies. Unlike the earlier entry, where no distinctions were made among the four works cited, in the later article, Rhys Davids created two distinct categories: one for "modern works," which grouped Leclère and Rockhill together with Hardy and Bigandet (Rhys Davids 1910, 327), and a second for the accounts of the life of the Buddha, which he considered more authoritative. The assumptions behind this distinction are clear in the contents of the entry: Rhys Davids limited his attention to the numerous, albeit fragmentary, accounts of the Buddha's life in the Pāli canon which had been edited and published in the meantime by the Pali Text Society. This approach to the biography of the Buddha is an aspect of Rhys Davids's scholarship for which he is still remembered (de Jong 1987, 27), although it is taken as an approach appreciated more for historical interest, and most students of Buddhism are confident that they have moved beyond it.[14]

In one respect, however, there is a remarkable unanimity between Rhys Davids's approach to the biography of the Buddha and current scholarly consensus. A student interested in the Buddha's biography today is in a better position than Rhys Davids to consider its early development, having the benefit of research by scholars as diverse as E. J. Thomas (1927), Jean Filliozat (1953, 2: 463-92), Alfred Foucher (1949), Erich Frauwallner (1956), Étienne Lamotte (1947, 37-71; 1958), and André Bareau (1963). Furthermore, the field of Buddhist studies has collectively benefited from the discussions which have surrounded the work of such scholars, just as it is currently benefiting from exchanges on the date of the historical Buddha—a direct product of that earlier scholarship (see Bechert 1991). But with respect to later biographies of the Buddha, especially those written in the vernacular languages of Sri Lanka and Southeast Asia, the contemporary student of Theravāda Buddhism has no more access to translations 80 years later than did Rhys Davids.

This neglect of texts written in vernacular languages as sources for the study of Theravāda Buddhism can be explained in a number of ways. The most immediate explanation comes from Rhys Davids himself. Indeed, indifference to vernacular literature seems a natural consequence of Rhys Davids's approach to the study of the biographies of the Buddha:

> [The vernacular texts] are not historical biographies. Milton's *Paradise Regained* is of value not for what it tells us about the life of its hero, but for the literary ability with which it has recast a story derived *entirely* from older documents. The historical value of those documents must be determined by a criticism which will, of course, take no notice of the later poetical version. A corresponding argument ought to hold good with respect to these Pali and Sanskrit poems, and *a fortiori* with respect to the Chinese and Tibetan *reproductions* of the Sanskrit ones. They are literary not historical documents, and such historical value as they have is the very instructive way in which *they show how far* the older beliefs about the life of the Buddha had been, at the time when these books were composed, *developed* (or rather corrupted) by the inevitable hero-worship of the followers of his religion. (Rhys Davids 1877, 88-89, emphasis added)

The approach outlined here, with its split between older and later sources and its positivist concerns for origins, is typical of the historicism which permeated almost all nineteenth-century scholarship in Europe and North America. This historicism aimed to rescue texts from conditions of misunderstanding and reveal their objective meaning for the first time by applying the critical methods of "scientific history" which could disclose the intentions of their author (see Bennett 1989, 69). Thus, knowing the biography of the Buddha was an essential part of any attempt to understand Buddhist texts which were attributed to him. The historian using this historicist approach could safely ignore the later biographies written in Sinhala, Burmese, or Khmer because they could—self-evidently—contribute little to any effort to uncover the origins of Buddhism. It was obvious to everyone that, as Rhys Davids wrote, "the only proper course is to go back, behind these later . . . documents, to the actual text of the Three Pitakas themselves, to collect there whatever is said incidentally about the life, family, and personal surroundings of the Buddha, and to piece them together into a connected whole." Once this was done, the "objective" meaning of the later biographies would also be clear: common and all-too-common expressions of hero worship (Rhys Davids 1877, 89; 1882, 122, 128).

It is worth keeping in mind that there is nothing particularly "Orientalist" about this historicist approach, although it is obvious that it did assume political significance in the colonial contexts in which it was pursued. But we can also see in Rhys Davids's statement the kind of cultural hegemony which was always an absolute presupposition of Orientalism. As Said said, "In a quite constant way, Orientalism depends for its strategy on this flexible positional superiority, which puts the westerner in a whole series of possible relationships with the Orient without ever losing him the relative upper hand" (Said 1978, 7). Buddhist biographies of the Buddha thus were never taken as examples of common interests between Buddhist and European scholars. Instead they were always distinguished from European biographies and turned into evidence of the inability of later Buddhist communities to know the facts of their own origins. George Coedès, for example, traced the existence of the unusually full biography of the Buddha found in a text composed in Thailand to the likelihood that because the "Buddhist peoples of Indochina [are] perhaps less familiar with the Scriptures and their biographical facts, [they] seem to be particularly interested in complete biographies of the Buddha" (1968, 218). It would seem that if we changed the subject of Coedès's sentence from "Buddhist peoples of Indochina" to "European scholars," the sentence would remain equally cogent.

The historicist approach advocated by Rhys Davids is also shaped by another general process which definitively shaped the study of Buddhism in particular and Orientalism in general throughout the nineteenth century. Building on Said's notion of "textual attitude," Almond has described this process as "textualization" in which "the essence of Buddhism came to be seen as expressed not 'out there' in the Orient, but in the West through the control of Buddhism's own textual past."[15] This process of textualization confirmed the claims of Rhys Davids's historicist approach to the biography of the Buddha: an objective biography of the Buddha was something that the Buddhist communities themselves lacked, and were unable to recover for themselves, but European scholars could reconstruct this biography through their textual scholarship. Europeans were thus able to lay claim to the life of "the founder," and hence, in their eyes, to the very origins of the religion. Their apparent success in this task reinforced their impression that the Buddhism they saw around them was the result of a long process of decay.

Asian Assumptions in European Minds

After Said's *Orientalism*, any interpretation of Rhys Davids's approach to the life of the Buddha as exemplifying nineteenth-century historiography may seem to obfuscate more than it illuminates, but there is benefit to limiting any further Orientalist critique of Rhys Davids. Indeed, an Orientalist critique also obfuscates and prevents us from recognizing the impact that Buddhist texts had on his representations of Buddhism. We will be able to delineate one aspect of this impact more clearly if we look more carefully at the sources which Rhys Davids recommended in his second *Encyclopaedia Britannica* entry on "Buddha." Among those, we will only consider the three modern sources from the Theravāda Buddhist tradition which he recommended, setting aside

Rockhill's translations from the Tibetan, which Rhys Davids also included in his category "modern sources." I omit the latter book here for only the most superficial of reasons, on the grounds that it represents material from Tibet and not from the Theravādin world, yet its inclusion among Rhys Davids's modern sources raises an important point. As we will soon see, the other books included in Rhys Davids's modern sources are, like Rockhill's Tibetan tales, translations of translations. Translation was an ever-present cultural practice in South Asian Buddhism, with material constantly flowing between various languages for various reasons. Yet when Rhys Davids groups, without distinction, material using a highly artificial literary Tibetan (which was employed largely for the purposes of translating Sanskrit texts) with material from Khmer (which stays closer to ordinary speech for the purposes of preaching), he obscures the specifics of translation as a cultural practice within the various Buddhist communities. Instead he merely assumes a dichotomy between classical and vernacular texts—perhaps reflecting the distinction between "the classics" and "modern languages" found in university curricula since the nineteenth century—which has no exact counterpart in Buddhist history. Obviously, this distinction should not be taken for granted in the interpretation of Buddhist cultural history, but as we shall see below, it does point to an alternative road for our studies of Buddhism.

Rhys Davids's other modern translators all had extensive exposure to Theravāda Buddhism in situ. R. Spence Hardy (1803–68), who was included in the bibliography in both of Rhys Davids's entries for the *Encyclopaedia Britannica*, served as a "Wesleyan" missionary in Sri Lanka and played an important role in missionary efforts to "disestablish" Buddhism.[16] After his return to England, he published two anthologies of selections from medieval and early modern Sinhala literature (Hardy 1860; 1850). Although he presented his books as mere translations from various Sinhala texts, in effect, he created new works with no real counterparts in the Sinhala Buddhist literary tradition. His anthologies were arranged by topic, with chapters on cosmology and the "various orders of sentient existence" preceding material about the Buddha. As one would expect given the general nineteenth-century interest in the origins of Buddhism, Hardy includes a biography of the Buddha in his *Manual*. But in contrast to Rhys Davids's attempt to reconstruct the life of the historical Buddha, Hardy's *Manual* begins with accounts of previous buddhas, then proceeds to a narration of the Buddha's previous births, followed by a biography of Gotama from his birth to death. Hardy also included biographical narratives about "the dignity, virtues, and powers of Buddha"[17] although they clearly offended his sensibilities. He justified their inclusion on the grounds that even though they did not add any worthwhile information about the Buddha, they illustrated the workings of "the mind of heathendom" (Hardy 1860, 360). Such comments make Hardy's hostility to Buddhism only too obvious, and consequently his work has received if not continuing criticism then what is thought to be a well-deserved neglect.[18]

Despite the apparent liberties that Hardy took in choosing his material, selecting from a variety of texts rather than translating just one, his collection roughly imitates the manner in which *his* sources treated *their* sources: Hardy generally used medieval Sinhala translations of older Pāli commentaries which also freely chose material from diverse texts to create new compositions.[19] Moreover, his emphasis on cosmography in the Buddha-biography mirrors the central place it occupied in traditional Theravāda Buddhism (Reynolds and Reynolds 1982, 11-27; C. Reynolds 1976; Leclère 1899, 35-171; Gombrich and Obeyesekere 1988, 17-22). In this respect, Hardy's biography contrasts sharply with modern introductions to Theravādin thought which are notable in comparison with medieval literature for their absence of any discussion of cosmology (see, e.g., Rahula 1959). While his presentation of the biography of the Buddha mirrors traditional material quite closely too, Hardy's biography is dissimilar in that he cobbled together a sequential biography that was absent in the Sinhala compilations. The Sinhala texts clearly assume a relatively consistent biographical structure, but they also rearrange the biographical material for a variety of purposes. Rather than noting these purposes, however, Hardy felt frustration:

> I have not met with any eastern work that is exclusively confined to the biography of Gotama, or that professes to present it in its completeness. The incidents of his early life are repeated again and again, in nearly the same order, and with little variety of expression; but after he has assumed the high office of Budha [*sic*], the consecutiveness of the narrative ceases; and in the arrangement of the preceding legends, I have had to exercise my own judgment as to the order in which they ought to appear. (1860, 355)

We can see in this passage something of Hardy's divided loyalties. He clearly wanted his work to find acceptance among scholars like Rhys Davids and thus he was willing to try to arrange the Sinhala material in a manner that might match some of the conventions of biography in nineteenth-century Europe, such as narrative sequence. But he apparently was unwilling to go as far as Rhys Davids and abandon the structure of the Sinhala texts altogether, and as a result, we see more of the imprint of Hardy's sources in his work than we do in the work of Rhys Davids.

Another of Rhys Davids's modern sources was the *Life of Gaudama* by Paul Bigandet (1813–94), the Vicar-Apostolic of Ava and Pegu.[20] As Hardy did with his Sinhala materials, Bigandet seems to have followed the creative example of the Burmese sources in his translations more than he adhered to their contents. Bigandet's *Life of Gaudama* is a more structured biography than

Hardy's *Manual*, which never became more than an anthology. This reflects an important difference between Buddhist literary patterns in Sri Lanka and those in Burma. Complete—or extended—biographies of the Buddha were composed in Burma and the rest of Southeast Asia from the late medieval period onwards in both Pāli and different vernaculars (see F. Reynolds 1976, 53). In 1858, Bigandet translated and published one example of these complete biographies, the *Malālaṅkāravatthu* ("The Collection [of Stories that is] like an Ornament of Garlands"), which was popular in nineteenth-century Burma, under the title *Life or Legend of Gaudama the Buddha of the Burmese*.[21] He published a second edition of it in 1866, although this time he actually created a new composite text by incorporating portions of another Burmese biographical work called the *Tathāgata-udāna* ("The Praise of the Lord") or *Tathāgata-udāna-dīpanī* ("The Lamp on the Praise of the Lord").[22] In this, Bigandet effectively mirrored the style of the Burmese texts that he translated, insofar as both he and they created new works in the guise of translation.[23]

Adhémard Leclère (1853–1917),[24] an administrator in the French protectorate of Cambodia who rose to the position of Résident de France at Kratie, seems to have been more alert than Bigandet to the liberties that translators might take with their sources. This awareness stemmed from his recognition that the text which he translated, the *Préas Pathama Samphothian*, was apparently a Khmer version of a text which existed in Thai, the *Pathama-Sambodhikathā*, and which had already been translated by Henry Alabaster.[25] Referring to the monks who produced Burmese and Thai biographies of the Buddha as "*adaptateurs*," he praised the Cambodian "*traducteur*" who "followed the original more closely for the facts, and [unlike the Burmese and Siamese authors] put in his translation the least he could of himself and nothing of his literature." Here too, Leclère seems to have been inspired by the sources he translated, for he claimed to have followed the Khmer original as closely as possible, retaining even what he saw as its defects, saying, "I wanted to be as exact, as impersonal as possible in this translation" (Leclère 1906, 9). But in saying this, Leclère may have been addressing a problem which he shared with Hardy and Bigandet as a researcher seeking a place in the larger field of Orientalism.

It is important to remember that Hardy, Bigandet, and Leclère all worked as students of Buddhism in a context in which research in Oriental studies, like other academic fields, had already been rigorously organized in a manner which left little room for "amateurs" (Said 1978, 190-91). We can see the pressures on them as outsiders to the university-based guild in their ready apologies for the limitations of their work,[26] and in the reviews of their publications by academics.[27] In such a context, it was necessary for researchers like Hardy, Bigandet, and Leclère to find a way of legitimating their work and giving it some authority within this professionalized context. One way that all three did this was to stress the close relation of their own work to the originals which they were translating. As Leclère did when he spoke of his desire to remain impersonal in his translation, Hardy hid his presence as an author when he spoke of his translation work:

> In confining myself, almost exclusively, to translation, I have chosen the humblest form in which to re-appear as an author. I might have written an extended essay upon the system, as it presents a rich mine, comparatively unexplored; or have attempted to make the subject popular, by leaving out its extravagances, and weaving its more interesting portions into a continuous narrative; but neither of these modes would have fulfilled my intention. They would have enabled me only to give expression to an opinion; when I wish to present an authority. (1860, xii)

It is striking, however, that this rhetorical strategy of authorial transparency was one that was found in the texts which these European scholars translated. Each of the vernacular texts translated by Hardy, Bigandet, and Leclère portrays itself as a translation of another text, their authors employing strategies to attract legitimacy by association with a decentered authority that are identical to those which the Europeans later used. For example, the *Saddharmaratnāvaliya* ("Garland of Jewels of the Doctrine"), a fourteenth-century Sinhala narrative collection based on the *Dhammapada* commentary, begins with a similar claim to authorial transparency and decentered authority:

> We have abandoned the Pāli method and taken only the themes in composing this work. It may have faults and stylistic short-comings, but (you the reader should) ignore them. Be like swans who separate milk from water even though the milk and water be mixed together, or like those who acquire learning and skills even from a teacher of low caste, because it is only acquisition of knowledge not the teacher's status with which they are concerned. (Dharmasēna Thera 1991, 3)

The author of the above quotation is clearly implying that the authority of a translation comes not from itself, but from the relation claimed to an absent text. Attention is thus deflected to this absent work but, at the same time, the accuracy of this relationship cannot usually be verified by those who find it necessary to use the translation. This of course could be exploited, as in the case of Buddhist texts composed in Chinese which present themselves as translations from the Sanskrit (see Buswell 1990).

But because the translations claim authority by suggesting or displaying a relation to an absent text, the student of Buddhism following the approach we have already seen with Rhys Davids naturally begins to look for the original which can legitimate these claims. I have already quoted a statement by

Leclère which exemplifies this expectation, but when read in context it shows as well that he assumes a posture of someone who has no automatic right to speak as a scholar within the professional field of Orientalism:

> It is now necessary to say my feeling, I do not say my opinion, on the source from which the Cambodians have derived this text. It seems to me that it is Pāli, Sinhalese, the same one that inspired the Burmese and Siamese *adaptateurs*, but that the Cambodian *traducteur*—always summarizing, more than the Burmese and the Siamese—followed the original more closely for the facts, and put in his translation the least he could of himself and nothing of his literature . . . There are some small details which are found in the Burmese text and not elsewhere which indicate a common source. But what is the text which the Burmese, Cambodian, and Siamese translators have adapted? That I cannot say. That is for a specialist who is capable of indicating the first sources of this vast *propaganda* which extends throughout all of Indianized Southeast Asia [*l'Indo-Chine aryenne*]. (Leclère 1906, 9)

We can interpret such comments as further evidence of the reigning paradigm of positivist historiography which consistently privileged earlier texts in all studies of culture in the nineteenth century. At the same time we should also keep in mind that Theravāda Buddhists themselves subscribed, at least at times, to a similar "metaphysics of origins" (see Collins 1990). This conception of tradition, historicist in its own way, provided the ideological context for the most common genres in Theravādin literature (commentaries, translations, and anthologies), all of which tended to claim authority and purpose from other texts, usually those known by the generic name "Pāli."[28] In this view, commentaries and translations were not the record of the growing understanding of a text, of the accumulation of evolving interpretation over the centuries; instead they were signposts for those in the present to recover accurately the meaning that had already been promulgated in the past. They were instrumentally valuable, but were without interest in their own right.

This suggests that there was something like a productive "elective affinity" between the positivist historiography of European Orientalism and Buddhist styles of self-representation. Most importantly for our understanding of Buddhist studies as a product of Orientalism, this elective affinity shaped the manner in which research in Buddhist studies "became a regular activity [in which] there was a regulated exchange of information, and agreement on what the problems were as well as consensus on the appropriate paradigms for research and its results" (Said 1978, 191). Originally, and of necessity, European pioneers in the field had imitated traditional Buddhist pedagogical patterns in their investigations, and used vernacular commentarial literature as an aid and guide to the meanings of the more authoritative canonical texts. For example, Eugène Burnouf, "the brilliant founder of the study of Buddhism," left at his death a number of massive studies of Burmese commentarial texts (*nissaya*) which he had used as aids in his researches on Pāli material (de Jong 1975, 21; Pruitt 1992, 294). In this he was not unusual. The use of vernacular commentarial material was routine for the first generations of students of Buddhism. This included Rhys Davids, who used the knowledge of Sinhala which he gained as a colonial civil servant in Sri Lanka throughout his career in his translations from Pāli. For instance, in the footnotes to his translations of the *Questions of King Milinda* and the *Dialogues of the Buddha*, we see evidence of his use of Sinhala translations for assistance in deciphering a difficult passage in the Pāli. But, perhaps most importantly, the self-presentation of these commentaries and translations, in which attention is drawn away from the present to the past, encourages their users to approach them as provisional entrées to the "more authoritative" texts of the Pāli canon.

The effects of this elective affinity fell quickly into place, as can be seen in almost every program of Buddhist studies in European and North American universities. The study of the Theravāda became equated with the study of the Pāli canon, and it is still common for a student to finish a graduate program in Buddhist studies without ever having read a Theravādin commentarial text.

It was scholars like Bigandet and Leclère who, recognizing their second-class status among Orientalists as students of vernacular texts, began to articulate a paradigm for research which made commentaries and translations into proper subjects for study. Bigandet, for example, said that:

> the surest way perhaps of coming to at least an exact and accurate knowledge of the history and doctrines of Buddhism would be to give a translation of the Legends of Buddha, such as they are to be met with in all countries where Buddhism has established its sway, and to accompany these translations with an exposition of the various doctrinal points, such as they are held, understood, and believed by these various nations. This has already been done by eminent Orientalists, on Thibetan, Sanscrit, Cingalese, and Chinese originals. A similar work, executed by competent persons among the Shans, Siamese, Cambodians, and Cochin Chinese, would considerably help the savants in Europe, who have assumed the difficult task of expounding the Buddhist system in its complex and multifarious forms, to give a full, general, and comprehensive view of that great religious creed with all its variations. (1911, viii)

Before considering the implications of this paradigm of research, let us look at another instance where it seems that a kind of intercultural mimesis again shaped Rhys Davids's own understanding of Buddhism.

Rhys Davids and Ritual

In addition to being remembered for his approach to the study of the Buddha-biography, Rhys Davids is also well known for his portrayal of early Buddhism as being largely free of ritual. It is thus no surprise that Rhys Davids did not mention in his encyclopedia entries the translations of Buddhist ritual works available to him and his readers at the time. The first Theravādin works to become known in Europe, however, were from various "paracanonical" anthologies of ordination texts (*kammavācā*). These were translated into Italian as early as 1776 and subsequently into Latin, French, German, and English.[29] But after this initial interest in the ordination texts, which intriguingly are an example of a genre of authoritative literature without clear canonical status, very little attention has been paid to the *kammavācā* texts.[30] Only recently have they received the attention they deserve as historical sources in François Bizot's *Les traditions de la* pabbajja *en Asie du Sud-Est.*[31]

As with Rhys Davids's approach to the biography of the Buddha, there are a variety of ways of explaining his vision of early Buddhism as being free of ritual. One explanation relates generally to patterns in nineteenth-century European culture, one is more specifically Orientalist, and one points to aspects of nineteenth-century Buddhism itself which enabled Rhys Davids to represent Buddhism in the manner that he did. As I suggested above, the self-definition of the Modern West in the nineteenth century often involved "a play of projections, doublings, idealizations, and rejections of a complex, shifting otherness" (Clifford 1980, 220). This complex process, which involved defining distinct cultures located spatially and making comparisons between them, did not always result "in self-congratulation or hostility and aggression" (Said 1978, 325). Although inversions and negations between European and non-European cultures depended on the highly suspect assumption that basic patterns and features of human life—rationality, most notoriously—could be completely absent among particular peoples, they did sometimes provide the European observer with an opportunity to cultivate and enlarge an imagined vision of human life alternative to what was then in place in Europe. The idea of early Buddhism was used in just this way: its definition as an agnostic, rationalist, ethical movement inspired those Europeans anxious to find alternatives to religion as a foundation for morality in everyday life. Furthermore, the image of the Buddha produced by European scholarship also served as a heroic exemplar for those concerned about the proper relationship between the rational individual and received tradition. Thus, as Richard Gombrich has said, even though "Rhys Davids was an excellent scholar . . . he naturally stressed the rationalist elements in Buddhism, because they formed the most striking contrast both to Christian, and . . . to other Indian traditions [and perhaps because] he found them the most sympathetic" (Gombrich [1971] 1991, 61).

Gombrich's reference to other Indian traditions invites a more specifically Orientalist explanation of the exclusion of ritual from early Buddhism. The contrast between Buddhism and Hinduism on the basis of the relative prominence of ritual mirrored an Orientalist contempt for Hindu religiousness, in which Hindu social activity was belittled as inherently irrational and politically ineffective (see Inden 1990, 85-130). Moreover, Orientalist claims of having recovered a rational and practical aspect of India's past, but one which was now absent from the present, served to justify the paternalistic imagery through which colonial rule was presented and understood.

The exclusion of ritual from early Buddhism and thus, within the essentialist assumptions of the day, from the very nature of Buddhism, was also key to Orientalist claims regarding their ability to recover the Buddha's true message. The first texts which Europeans were given in their encounter with the Buddhist world, ritual texts for the ordination of monks, however, indicate that whoever gave those texts thought that ritual was key for understanding the Buddha's message. The very capacity for knowledge depended on ritual preparation, and in Theravāda Buddhist communities this generally presupposed ordination. Before modern times, some of the most distinctive ideas of Buddhist thought, such as the denial of an enduring self to an individual, were not usually seen as relevant to the lives of laypeople. The Orientalist understanding of truth rested, of course, on completely different criteria. It was based on the premise that objectivity was both possible and desirable: who it was that knew something did not matter, only what was known. By emphasizing those aspects of Buddhist ideology, especially those which were polemically directed against Hindus, it was possible for Orientalists like Rhys Davids to make it appear that this rationalism was *uncovered* in Buddhism, rather than projected onto it. The appearances of uncovering the rationalist core of Buddhism were strategically supported by comparisons to Protestant and Catholic Christianity, always of course from the perspective of a Protestant representation of Catholicism as a degenerate form of Christianity.

There is a legacy of this contrast between Hinduism and Buddhism in the contemporary study of Buddhism. It remains typical for Buddhism in South Asia to be studied as a thing apart from the rest of the intellectual and cultural history of India, although it is becoming increasingly apparent how artificial this separation is, especially with respect to the study of ritual. Not only does all Buddhist ritual including early Buddhist ritual appear thoroughly Indian, as we see when we compare Buddhist ordination and consecration rituals with Hindu initiation rituals and image preparation ceremonies, but much of India appears very "Buddhist." This becomes apparent when we consider the patterns associated with worship (*pūjā*) in the various Hindu devotional movements, as well as when we consider the more philosophical ideas associated with Hindu schools of thought like Advaita Vedānta.[32]

Even though it remains necessary for future research to integrate the history of Buddhism into the broader currents of South Asian history, an important truth about modern Theravāda Buddhism may be revealed by Rhys Davids's neglect of ritual in his portrayal of the religion. For it appears that Rhys Davids's representation of early Buddhism as rationalist and free of ritual was prompted not only by his own sympathies and Orientalist expectations but by the views and examples of the monks he met while in Sri Lanka, especially the Ven. Waskaduve Subhuti and Ven. Yataramulle Unnanse. These monks served as teachers to Rhys Davids in his first studies of Pāli, but they were also images for him of the ideal Buddhist monk. They were scholarly, aloof from lay life, and thus uninvolved in the rituals of the Buddhist community in which lay people and monks commonly met. These rituals, such as life-cycle ceremonies and merit making, were ones which Rhys Davids as a lay man would have been able to witness; those rituals of the monastic community in which they may have continued to participate were open only to monks. We know very little today about the details of the monastic careers of Subhuti and Yataramulle, but because of the obvious impression they made on Rhys Davids (and also on R. C. Childers, another great Pāli scholar of the nineteenth century) further study of their scholarly and monastic careers is desirable. From what we do know, however, they seem to fit into the general patterns of Buddhist modernism as it emerged throughout the Theravādin world in the mid-nineteenth century.

It has become common in the study of Buddhism in Sri Lanka to assume that its modern developments are due to the impact of Western culture and Christianity. As Gananath Obeyesekere has said, "One of the fascinating problems in the history of modern Theravāda Buddhism is the manner in which the Western scholarly definition of that religion has been appropriated, albeit with a variety of modifications, by the Buddhists of Sri Lanka." The result of this appropriation has been described as "Protestant Buddhism," and it has been the subject of a considerable body of literature.[33] Most of it has focused on the ways in which protests against the British in general and against Protestant Christian missionaries in particular assumed the characteristics of Protestant Christianity and turned into a protest against traditional Theravāda Buddhism as well.

But this explanation, rooted as it is in the circumstances of modern Sri Lankan history, seems incomplete when viewed from the perspective of events in Thailand. Developments quite similar to those which shaped modern Sinhala Buddhism also transformed Thai Buddhism, but without the element of colonial domination or a sharp confrontation between Buddhists and Christian missionaries so visible in Sri Lanka. Beginning in the eighteenth century and continuing throughout the nineteenth century, there was a radical shift in the interpretation of Buddhist thought, a process of reformation which was encouraged by leading members of the Buddhist monastic order, and supported by the authority of the Siamese throne (Keyes 1989, 123). This reformation began after the fall of Ayutthaya as part of the restructuring of Thai society by King Rama I in what Wyatt has called a "subtle revolution":

> All of Rama I's innovations . . . involved a change in focus that brought rational man clearly to the center of the stage of history, mentally in control of his own world through the exercise of his critical faculties. Though it was more a shift in degree than an absolute change, man began increasingly to self-consciously and critically examine the rules by which he lived and constantly gauge them against his improving understanding of the eternal truths of Buddhism. (1982, 40, quoted in Keyes 1989, 124)

This process of reinterpretation included a reform of the Buddhist monastic order, an insistence on strict ritual, canonical fundamentalism, and purity of ordination, and unlike in Sri Lanka, it seemed only coincident with the arrival of Westerners in Thailand (C. Reynolds 1976, 212). The whole process crystallized in the religious reforms instituted by King Mongkut who sought to eliminate many traditional practices in Thai Buddhism as "accretions obscuring the true message of Buddhism." Mongkut's vision of "true Buddhism" "entailed a shift from viewing the world in cosmological terms to viewing it psychologically" and he also effected a "shift from practice centered on communal rituals to practice centered on self-cultivation" (Keyes 1989, 126). The representations of Buddhism articulated by Rama I and Mongkut are in many remarkable ways identical to the representation of early Buddhism constructed by Rhys Davids, especially with respect to their common neglect of cosmology and ritual in favor of individual rationality and morality.

The fact that the Thai developments were clearly not determined by the presence of antagonistic Westerners[34] provides a useful reminder that we should avoid attributing too much force to the "West" (or Christianity, or Protestant assumptions, or Orientalism) in the changes to Theravāda Buddhism which occurred in the nineteenth century.[35] These developments also open up the possibility that, just as there may have been a productive "elective affinity" between the positive historiography of European Orientalism and some Buddhist styles of self-representation which shaped the manner in which research in Buddhist studies became organized, so there may have been an equally productive elective affinity between some European and some Theravādin responses to modernity, in which an attempt was made to both accommodate and contain the instrumental rationality of modernity, which had proven successful in its agility to predict, control, and explain the world, by emphasizing the rationalist and ethical aspects of the Buddhist heritage. This was necessarily done at the expense of cosmology and ritual, but it was a process that occurred throughout the Theravādin world.[36]

From Orientalism to the Local Production of Meaning

The comparison of certain aspects of the scholarly work of Rhys Davids, Hardy, Bigandet, and Leclère with some parallels in the Theravādin world that they encountered which I have presented here is no more than suggestive. The actual depth of these productive elective affinities and the extent of the inter-cultural mimesis suggested by their writings will only be confirmed by more detailed examination of the cultural politics of the Theravāda as they existed in the eighteenth and nineteenth centuries. There are limited resources for going further in this direction in the existing scholarly literature, a reminder that the later history of Theravāda Buddhism is ignored within the paradigm of historiography that still dominates Buddhist studies. One direction for future studies would be to begin to examine the subcommentaries and translations that were in use in various parts of Asia at the time of the first steps in Buddhist studies, and which were consistently utilized by pioneers in the field. Their use by scholars who inaugurated the field of Buddhist studies makes it likely that an investigation of them will enhance our understanding of the interaction between Europeans and non-Europeans in the modern period and thus help us to make a better estimation of the extent to which modern Asian patterns left a mark on European representations of Buddhism.

Thus, this kind of research on the history of the study of Buddhism has an important contribution to make towards extending the history of Orientalism beyond Said. Based on what little we already know, we can see that it will make it more difficult, albeit in a small sphere, to discuss "the West" and "the Orient" as radically distinct entities. But, more importantly, such investigations may make the basic assumption of Said's critique of Orientalist representations problematic itself, by making it difficult to interpret Orientalist representations as being primarily embedded in European culture.

More research on later Theravādin literature will, of course, show the inadequacy of the work by Hardy, Bigandet, and Leclère, and eventually replace it. But returning to their translations now can also make an immediate contribution to the ongoing field of Buddhist studies—as distinct from the study of Orientalism—by encouraging us to articulate a completely different historical paradigm for our research. We noted above that, within the context of professional Orientalism, translators of vernacular texts apparently had to find ways of justifying their scholarly work. One way that they did this was to challenge in their annotations and prefaces the more official representations of Buddhism.

This usually was done indirectly, as when a translation of a vernacular text was justified on the grounds that accounts of Buddhism based on texts in the past were not adequate representations of "real" Buddhism. Leclère, for example, introduces his work on *Le Buddhisme au Cambodge* by saying:

> This book is not a study of Buddhism in general, still less is it a history of Buddhism in Cambodia. It is a simple inquiry into Cambodian Buddhism. I thought that alongside the admirable and learned works of our Indologists, whose purpose has been to make known Sanskrit, Pāli Sinhalese, Tibetan, Chinese, Mongol, and Japanese texts, and to make a synthesis of them, there is a place for some works which are less learned and less general, and that it would not be useless to investigate what Buddhist doctrine has become among the masses of people and what place it occupies in their conscience. (Leclère 1899; see as well Alabaster 1871, lviii)

In a similar vein, Eugène Burnouf explained his interest in the Burmese commentaries of the stories about the previous lives of Buddha by saying that "these little treatises of the Lives of the Buddha, although historically useless, have an interest for me because of the values which they represent."[37] But these apologies of Leclère and Burnouf have a value for us because we see in them the beginnings of an alternative historical paradigm which will encourage us to expect meaning to be produced in local circumstances rather than in the origins of the tradition. These apologies create a space for the study of the full range of Buddhist literature.

The texts which Hardy, Bigandet, and Leclère translated can still give evidence for local productions of meaning, but not directly. The Sinhala works translated by Hardy in his *Manual of Buddhism* have largely fallen into disuse in modern Sri Lanka. Although they were among the first books to be printed in Sri Lanka, most are no longer in print, and the few that are reprinted are for use as literature texts in university classes rather than for use as religious documents.[38] The texts used by Bigandet have apparently suffered a similar fate. The *Tathāgata-udāna*, one of the two texts used in Bigandet's *Life of Gaudama*, has lost whatever authority it had, to the extent that we are not even sure if a manuscript copy of it survives today (Braun 1992, 47). The social and political conditions in Cambodia make it impossible to even determine whether the text translated by Leclère has survived, but at the same time we can be reasonably certain that, if it does still survive, it does not have the significance that it once had. The production of the vernacular texts which were utilized in the nineteenth century by Hardy, Bigandet, and Leclère, together with their neglect or disappearance in the late twentieth century, forces us to ask, "What is it that maintains texts inside reality? What keeps some of them current while others disappear?" (Said 1983, 152)

This question is the inverse of the one more commonly asked by students of Buddhism. We tend to assume that it is a given that texts should be preserved, especially in religious traditions as conservative as the Theravāda. But once we turn the question around and ask what conditions are necessary for the preservation of a text, a range of other historical questions immediately opens out. If the survival of any particular text is not self-explanatory, but in fact it is normally the case that texts fade in their significance as social change occurs, then we need to discover how those texts which do endure are maintained.[39] In part, this will require us to look at the manner in which texts were circulated—the technology, practices, and institutions which made their survival possible—but especially the processes by which certain texts were singled out as worth preserving. Discovering answers to such questions will require investigations about the extent to which the production and survival of a text is both dependent and independent of the audiences which receive it. In the course of doing all of this we will inevitably end up having to rethink our conceptualizations of Buddhism as a translocal tradition with a long and self-consciously distinct history but which is at the same time a tradition dependent on local conditions for the production of meaning. This is one of the most pressing problems for a post-Orientalist study of Buddhism: theoretically, we will need to reconceptualize the Buddhist tradition in comparison with other transcultural phenomena, and practically, we will have to retrieve and reorganize our scholarly heritage in Buddhist studies in the light of that reconceptualization.

We can conclude by drawing one final lesson from Leclère about an important limit to any representations of the Buddhist tradition which we may construct in the future. In an evocative passage, he described the occasions when he heard the text he translated read aloud:

> Two times I have heard it read in the Temple, in the presence of the assembled faithful, themselves silent, by a priest seated in a preaching chair, his legs ritually folded, the *satra* of palm leaves placed on his knees. His voice was raised high, clear, almost singsong, like that of the priests when they say the *gathas* or read the holy books. He pronounced carefully the words of Pāli origin with which the text is sprinkled . . . One felt that he knew that the Khmer letters have another value when they reproduce a word of the holy language.
>
> One thing surprised me, the silence of those assembled, observant, the attention of each faithful person was held, even the children. One felt that for these very believing people, very religious, observant in their religious practices, that it really was the life of the Master, the Teacher . . . the Savior of Beings, that they were hearing. One old woman, at each of the words of the Saint, raised her joined hands to the top of

her head and bowed; another leaned to the ground on her fore-arms, hands joined, staying immobile, her face placed on her wrists; one young girl followed the reading and, from time to time, her glance went from the preacher to an enormous statue of the Saint who amidst the smoke and incense, showed a smile of perfect peace. I felt that she was living a little of this Great Being and that, taken by her faith, she would not have been surprised to hear him speak, or to see him move his lips and eyes. (Leclère 1906, 10)

Leclère's close attention to the scene, to the circumstances of the preaching and reception of a text as well as to the individuals involved, can be taken as a good model for any investigation which would be attentive to the production of meaning in local contexts, but his distance as an observer is instructive as well. As we attempt to restructure our understandings of Buddhism in a manner that will enable us to overcome the distortions of our scholarly inheritance, we should perhaps keep in mind that our new representations also will keep us at a distance from what we hope to understand. We need to keep in mind, like the preacher with the Khmer letters, that the meanings produced in local contexts may also have a transhistorical value to those who produce and receive those meanings. If we are able to do so, we may be able to avoid the mistakes of our predecessors in the study of Buddhism, who we can now see were too quick and too arrogant when they vouchsafed to themselves the right to speak *for* Buddhism.

Notes

I would like to thank Tara Doyle, Donald Lopez, Rachel McDermott, Sheldon Pollock, and Jonathan Spencer for their helpful comments on earlier versions of this essay.

1. Said (1978, 206) makes "the distinction . . . between an almost unconscious (and certainly untouchable) positivity, which [he calls] *latent* Orientalism, and the various stated views about oriental society, languages, literatures, history, sociology, and so forth, which [he calls] *manifest* Orientalism. Whatever change occurs in knowledge of the Orient is found almost exclusively in manifest Orientalism: the unanimity, stability, and durability of latent Orientalism are more or less constant."
2. Almond 1988, 5. In the same vein are Tweed 1992, and Tuck 1990. Tweed, a historian of American religion, concludes that "nineteenth-century Euro-American Buddhist sympathizers had more in common with their mainline Protestant contemporaries" than with their Asian contemporaries (155). Andrew Tuck, a historian of philosophy, argues that Western philosophic ideas influenced the interpretation of Madhyamaka to such an extent that there has been a "sequence of distinct interpretive fashions" dictated more by trends in Western philosophy than anything in Buddhist thought (v).

3. Said, in fact, criticizes this move at the outset of *Orientalism* (5): "It would be wrong to conclude that the Orient was *essentially* an idea, or a creation with no corresponding reality."
4. These points were made to me by Jonathan Spencer, personal communication, 9 May 1993.
5. Pollock 1992, 419. Pollock names Gauri Viswanathan (1989), Sara Suleri (1992), and Ronald Inden (1990) as examples of those who have pursued this line of argument.
6. This, of course, was not limited to encounters with Asia. See Diamond 1974; Kuper 1988.
7. This suggestion was made to me by Jonathan Spencer, personal communication, 9 May 1993.
8. Richard Gombrich ([1971] 1991, 61) has said that the publication of Rhys Davids's book, *Buddhism*, "first published in 1877 and many times reprinted, may be said to mark the close of the pioneer period of Buddhist studies."
9. For a biography of Rhys Davids, see Wickremeratne 1984.
10. Said 1978, 122. It is particularly interesting to note the regret that some students of Southeast Asia express about the *lack* of an independent Orientalist tradition for that region, because it has hampered the creation of a contemporary community of scholars; see Reynolds 1992, 61; Hutterer 1992, 141.
11. Tambiah 1984, 7, and 1992, 3. In the latter work, Tambiah actually speaks of "Pāli text puritans." This rightly removes the sting of the opprobrium from the Pali Text Society, but it also shifts critical attention from a specific emphasis on a certain body of texts to a vaguer morality.
12. For example, a comparison of Rhys Davids's *Buddhist India* (1903) with analogous sections in Romila Thapar's *A History of India* (1966) shows a great deal of close, unacknowledged overlap between the two historical accounts. Of course, Rhys Davids's ideas are still *explicitly* preserved and defended in scholarship; see Gombrich 1988, 92.
13. Cited in Almond 1988, 55. The works cited in Rhys Davids's entry are: Hardy 1860; Bigandet 1866; Fausbøll 1875; and Foucaux 1860.
14. See Conze 1967 and F. Reynolds 1976, 37-61. Reynolds traces his own discussion to Conze's article (58, n. 7), but in content Reynolds's position seems more influenced by general trends in French Indological scholarship, such as are found in Jean Filliozat's discussion in *L'Inde classique* (1953, 464-67).
15. Almond 1988, 3; see also 24, 37: "By the 1850's [*sic*], the textual analysis of Buddhism was perceived to be the major scholarly task. Through the West's progressive possession of the texts of Buddhism, it becomes, so to say, materially owned by the West; and by virtue of this ownership, ideologically controlled by it . . . Thus, during the nineteenth century as a whole, we can discern clearly the process of the textualization of Buddhism.

    Buddhism had become by the middle of the nineteenth century a textual object based in Western institutions. Buddhism as it came to be ideally spoken of through the editing, translating, and studying of its ancient texts could then be compared with its contemporary appearance in the Orient. And Buddhism, as could be seen in the East, compared unfavourably with its ideal textual exemplifications contained in the libraries, universities, colonial offices, and missionary societies of the West. It was possible then, as a result of this, to combine, a positive evaluation of a Buddhism textually located in the West with a negative evaluation of its Eastern instances."
16. For a useful account of the missionary movements to disestablish Buddhism in mid-nineteenth century Sri Lanka and Hardy's role in them, see de Silva 1965, 64-102.
17. This genre of literature, a major one in the history of Sinhala literature, organizes the life of the Buddha not by a natural life course, from birth to death, but by a structure found in the traditional lists of the virtues of the Buddha; examples of the genre are *Amāvatura*,

Butsaraṇa, and *Pūjāvaliya*. This genre is not limited to the Sinhala literary tradition. The *Tathāgataudāna*, one of the texts used by Bigandet in his *The Life of Gaudama*, apparently was similar in scope; see Bigandet 1911.

18. Alabaster, writing only three years after Hardy's death, commented obliquely on Hardy's translations that "to translate agreeably, one must to a certain extent sympathize with the feelings of the author one translates from, and not serve up our glowing Oriental feasts with a cold chill on them" (1871, xxvi). Wickremeratne, the biographer of Rhys Davids, frequently suggests Rhys Davids's "impartiality" by comparisons with Hardy (1984, 146, 147, 182, 184–85).
19. Wickremeratne, however, traces Hardy's arrangement of his material to his hostility towards Buddhism: "Spence Hardy, the Wesleyan missionary in Ceylon, had devoted as many as seven chapters to a detailed exposition of the legendary elements in the life of Buddha which Rhys Davids, in his own treatise on Buddhism, deftly dealt with in a few lucid paragraphs. The result was that in Spence Hardy's work (a typical example) the metaphysical and ethical aspects of Buddhism—the more worthwhile field of inquiry—had received inadequate attention" (1984, 182). Wickremeratne also says that "to Rhys Davids Buddhist cosmological notions were irrelevant because he had a clear grasp of what was centrally important in Buddhism . . . Writers like Spence Hardy, however, saw the matter in a different light. Buddhist ideas concerning cosmogony were to be highlighted as part of a simple and effective strategy designed to show the absurdity of Buddhism, especially as the ideas seemed to be derived from the Buddha's own opinion of the cosmic order" (185).
20. In addition to his translations found in the *Life of Gaudama*, Bigandet translated some monastic ritual texts (*kammavācā*). He also published an article on "Principaux points du système bouddhiste" (1843).
21. The popularity of the *Malālaṅkāravatthu* is suggested by the fact that two European scholars encountered it in their first encounters with Buddhism and subsequently published translations. Bennett, an American Baptist missionary, published a translation of the *Malālaṅkāravatthu* just before Bigandet in the *Journal of the American Oriental Society* (1853). A re-edition of this work can be found in Edwardes 1959. Bigandet's *Life of Gaudama* has gone through many editions and was recently reprinted in Varanasi in 1979.
22. The results of this composite can be somewhat misleading as Heinz Braun (1991, 47-48) has pointed out: "When comparing Bigandet's translation with the Burmese text of *Malālaṅkāravatthu* in the manuscripts and printed editions, the reader will not discover a single date in the Burmese original at passages where Bigandet gives detailed information such as 'on the full moon of Katsun, on a Tuesday' with regard to the Parinirvana, e.g. Bigandet has taken these 'exact' dates from the *Tathāgataudāna(dīpanī)* without clearly distinguishing the two texts in his translation."
23. See Braun 1992, 46-47: "Bigandet was of the opinion that both texts . . . are Burmese translations of Pāli works. Of course, the Burmese authors had translated portions of the relevant canonical and post-canonical Pāli texts but actually they had created Burmese prose works sometimes with Pāli verses interspersed and explained in the usual way by means of a *nissaya*, i.e. a word for word translation into Burmese."
24. Leclère was an author of many works on Buddhism and Cambodian culture, although, like Hardy, his condescension towards his subject is often obvious and the standards of his scholarship leave him open to criticism. Leclère's works include *Recherches sur la Législation Cambodgienne* (1890); *Recherches sur le Droit Public des Cambodgiens* (1894); *Cambodge: Contes et Légendes* (1895); *Cambodge: Fêtes Civiles et Religieuses* (1897); *Le Buddhisme au Cambodge* (1899); *Le Livre de Vesandar, le roi charitable* (1902); *Les crémations et les rites funéraires au Cambodge* (1907); and *Buddhisme et Brahmanisme: Trois petits livres* (1911).

25. Alabaster (d. 1884) was "interpreter of Her Majesty's Consulate General in Siam." Exactly which work Alabaster translated remains unclear, and it is likely that, like Hardy and Bigandet, he took some liberties with the actual structure of the text. The *Pathama-Sambodhi* itself awaits careful study. It enjoyed popularity in a variety of versions in nineteenth-century Thailand, although the version by H. R. H. Paramanuchitchinorot has attained the status of a classic in Thai literature; see F. Reynolds 1976, 53. For a discussion of the composition and contents of a Pāli version of the *Pathama-Sambodhi*, see Coedès 1968. Coedès takes the Pāli as the source of the various Thai versions, but this is far from certain.
26. R. Spence Hardy (1860, ix-x), for example, complains, "Throughout the whole course of my investigations, I have had to exercise a laborious ministry; with the exception of one brief interval, I have been at a distance from any public library; I have received no assistance from any society, literary or religious, though that assistance has not been unasked; my acquaintance with the lore of Europe is limited; and I have had little or no access to recent publications on subjects of Asiatic literature. I have been charged by my friends, with great temerity in risking, unaided, the publication of the present work." For similar statements, see Alabaster 1871, lviii; Bigandet 1911, 2: 151; Leclère 1906, 9.
27. See, e.g., the reviews of Leclère's books by Finot, Huber, and Coedès in *Bulletin de l'École française d'Extreme-Orient* 3 (1903): 91-92; 7 (1907): 384-85; 14 (1914): 47-54.
28. On Pāli referring to authoritative texts rather than to the name of a language, see Hinüber 1977; 1983a. Von Hinüber points out that "Pāli" as the name of a language is a seventeenth-century European "mistake," and traditionally in the Theravāda referred only to a "holy" text.
29. See de Jong 1987, 14-16, for a useful account of the first translations of the *kammavācā* texts. Given that we have just seen how Pāli came to be privileged over vernacular literature in the professionalized Buddhist studies in a way that hid the role that this literature played in the pioneering stages of the field, it is significant that these early translators did not always find it necessary even to indicate whether they were working from a Pāli or vernacular text.
30. They are relegated to anthologies of Buddhist literature (e.g., the translation by E. J. Thomas [1935, 211-16]) and textbooks for instruction in Pāli (e.g., Frankfurter 1883, 141-50).
31. Bizot (1988, 136) summarizes his argument in a manner generally reminiscent of the research paradigm articulated by Bigandet above: "Observation of the usages and study of the manuals (i.e. *kammavācā*) reveal the existence of distinct traditions of the *pabbajja* and show that the introduction of Sinhalese Buddhism to the Peninsula has not been either sudden or simple."
32. The similarities between Buddhism and Advaita are well known, stemming from accusations made against Śaṅkara that he was a "crypto-Buddhist." For discussions of Buddhist backgrounds to Hindu devotional patterns, see Hardy 1983; Hopkins 1994.
33. G. Obeyesekere 1991, 219. See, in addition, his earlier work which introduced the term "Protestant Buddhism" (1972). See as well Malalgoda 1976; Prothero 1990; Gombrich and Obeyesekere 1988; Holt 1991.
34. C. Reynolds 1976, 212: "These two circumstances—the presence of Westerners willing to discuss comparative culture, and a reform monastic order critical of monastic culture—combined to force on more and more Siamese a new awareness of themselves and their past."
35. Kitsiri Malalgoda (1976) has shown with respect to Sri Lanka that much of what occurred in the nineteenth century had already begun to take place in the pre-British period.

36. In this regard, we would have to mention the development of the *vipassanā* meditation movements as participating in the same general trends. See Houtman 1990.
37. Feer 1891, 402. Among Burnouf's papers at his death were a 520-page manuscript translating the Burmese commentary (*nissaya*) on the *Bhūridatta Jātaka*, a 416-page manuscript on the *Nemi Jātaka*, and a 449-page manuscript on the *Suvaṇṇasāmā Jātaka*. These studies were never published but their scope has not yet been matched.
38. Ranjini Obeyesekere has made this point in an autobiographical comment (1991, x): "Looking back on my childhood, I realize that we were never given religious instruction as such, either in school or at home. We participated in Buddhist rituals and ceremonies, mostly with the extended kin group, went to temple on full moon days (that, too, mainly during vacations), and listened to many, many Buddhist stories. That was how we learned to be Buddhists.

    The stories of the *Saddharmaratnāvaliya* and the *Jātaka Tales* have, I think, always performed this function, ever since they were translated into Sinhala. They have been central to the dissemination of Buddhist values and doctrine, copied and recopied by monks, and passed on from generation to generation. In recent years their role has diminished. Buddhism is taught as a subject in schools, in Sunday schools, or *Daham pasäl*, that have sprung up all over the country, and children study doctrinal texts and understandably, are extremely bored with them. Ours was a much more exciting way to come to the Teachings."
39. It is unclear at this point just how long religious literature endures as compared with literature in general. Robert Escarpit has observed that people at any given time generally know about as many contemporary books as books of the past, which suggests a continuous recession of literary works in the cultural memory into oblivion. He has computed that, within one year, 90 percent of the new books on the market have become unsalable, and, in the course of time, another 90 percent of the remainder disappear (Sammons 1978, 98).

Part II

Defining Buddhist Ideologies

Defining Buddhist Ideologies: Introduction

The essays in this section examine the ongoing definition and contestation of Buddhist ideologies. These rich case studies of medieval and modern Buddhist communities in China, Tibet, and Japan illuminate ideological conflicts that reveal Buddhists as social and political actors. They demonstrate how political and religious concerns are inextricably intertwined, and how competitions for power in particular historical circumstances both give rise to new ideological expressions and lead to the suppression of others. As these studies show, Buddhist ideas and ideals are strategically deployed in service of the promulgation of Buddhism during times when fundamental ideologies are understood to be in question or under attack. Conflict, whether it arises among Buddhists themselves or in response to a perceived external threat, frequently generates innovation. In such contestations of power, the very notion of "tradition" is constantly reinvented. Studying the construction of Buddhist ideologies provides us with important insights into the processes by which multiple Buddhisms are generated and transformed in relation to one another and to social and political forces.

As the essays in the previous section show, Buddhist pasts are (and always have been) reconstructed and defined in relation to the complex concerns and perspectives that Buddhists and scholars of Buddhism bring to the task of historical interpretation; the writing of history is intricately connected to the ideological assumptions and commitments of the historian. By focusing on ideological debates within particular contexts, the essays in this section explore how Buddhists make use of tradition in their attempts to assert and subvert particular ideologies, highlighting how the past functions as a resource for negotiating pressing concerns about present sociopolitical circumstances and imagined future trajectories. Through these negotiations, notions of the past and of a transhistorical tradition are themselves recreated.

These complex temporal interactions stand in tension with the pervasive Buddhist conception of the Dharma, ultimate truth, as eternal and unchanging; recourse to the universal Dharma figures prominently as an ideological strategy for asserting power and authority. Examining the construction of Buddhist ideologies draws our attention to the historical specificity of the sociopolitical agendas and anxieties that motivate a re-visioning of tradition, even as the ideologies themselves envision and attempt to articulate a singular and ahistorical Dharma. Far from being extrinsic to Buddhist traditions, this tension between evolving or devolving Buddhist teachings (also referred to as Dharma) and the timeless and incorruptible Dharma figures frequently and explicitly in the articulation of Buddhist ideologies; if the Dharma as ultimate truth is universal and unchanging, historical expressions of the Dharma are not. The eternal and unchanging Dharma is (necessarily) revealed through historical and transitory forms. Such a paradigm provides rich resources for the constant and explicit reinterpretation of an eternal, unchanging, and universal truth in light of present circumstances and perceived future challenges. Anxiety about the decline of the Dharma provides another perspective on how Buddhists engage with tradition. Tradition is not an inexhaustible resource; history will run its course, and the temporal manifestations of the Dharma will undergo an inescapable decline and, eventually, extinction. Taken together, these essays illuminate both the wide variety of potential ideological responses to the imperilment of the Buddhist tradition, and the opportunities for creative reinterpretation to which this threat gives rise.

Each of these essays highlights the crucial significance of textual authority in asserting or undermining ideological claims. The textual embodiments of Buddhist teachings are particularly potent points of connection between the eternal Dharma and its historical manifestations, enabling innovation in response to particular historical circumstances while articulating a link to the timeless truths of the tradition. For any text to be an effective resource for the development of new ideologies, however, it must be granted authority, and ideological conflicts often involve concomitant disputes about the legitimacy of a text or particular textual interpretation. The ultimate authority is granted to texts that are recognized as containing the words of the Buddha, of course, but Buddhists have developed complex (and frequently contested) mechanisms both for conferring the status of Buddha-speech upon texts and for legitimizing the works of other authors, human or divine. Even when a text is granted clear authority, disputes can arise about the correct interpretation of its meaning. While the malleability of texts can enable creative interpretation in some circumstances, in other cases Buddhists have asserted particular ideologies by attempting to constrict legitimate textual interpretation, arguing that a text was authored (whether by the Buddha or by another figure with claims to authority) with a specific intent that should be faithfully followed and defended.

The relationship between Buddhist ideologies and ideologies of the state or nation also plays a prominent role both in shaping ideologies and in negotiating the contests of authority that emerge when ideologies compete. Premodern and modern Buddhist traditions alike have negotiated complex relationships with the state and political power. Buddhist ideologies have offered not only sources of political resistance and critique, but also strong support for state agendas and discourses. When read in relation to one another, these essays demonstrate quite dramatically the sheer diversity of ideological responses to particular historical circumstances. Buddhist ideologies are always multiple and frequently ingenious, and emerge in relation to a still greater variety of political, religious, and cultural ideologies. These essays also make clear that Buddhist ideological strategies can have profound effects beyond scholastic schisms and doctrinal debates, shaping Buddhist identities, practices, and visions of the good life in particular historical moments.

Mark E. Lewis's study of the Three Stages sect demonstrates how much is at stake in ideological battles through his investigation of the conditions leading to the suppression of this Buddhist tradition in eighth-century China. Lewis's investigation of this premodern ideological conflict illuminates the internal diversity of "Buddhism" in a particular place and time, as well as the role of state power in legitimizing—and eradicating—specific formulations of the tradition. The Three Stages sect argued that the decline of the Dharma was already well under way, as evidenced by the moral decline of the Sangha, especially those monastics closely aligned with the imperial court. While most Buddhist groups accepted the notion that the Dharma would eventually decline, where the present moment stood in relationship to that decline was a hotly contested ideological issue. According to the Three Stages sect, the decline of the Dharma was marked by three stages, and the terminal stage, in which people would no longer be capable of distinguishing right from wrong, had arrived. As a result, Buddhists could neither understand nor adhere to the teachings transmitted from the past; the only option remaining was to embrace and revere all beings without discrimination, and to practice a radical form of *dāna* (giving to others). The decline of the Dharma had eroded all other possibilities for Buddhist practice and experience.

The sect's rhetoric of decline thus had a direct impact upon the social roles, visceral experiences, and lived practices of its adherents; ideological stances often have profound concrete effects on daily life. The ideology of the Three Stages sect entailed a thoroughgoing critique of monasticism. Not only were monks incapable of living up to the moral codes of the Vinaya (monastic regulations), but the distinction between monks and lay persons, so basic to the structure and function of most Buddhist communities, was also inherently suspect: to set oneself above others and to live on their gifts were deemed deeply immoral. Those Buddhists who continued to follow received traditions, especially by joining monastic communities or by supporting monastic institutions, were unethical impostors. The effect of this ideology was in many respects to place the sect in opposition to the core institutions and social structures of traditional Buddhism, even though it was derived in large part from doctrines and practices that were widely shared among different Buddhist sects.

Lewis's study provides a dramatic example both of conflicting Buddhist ideologies and of the (sometimes dire) consequences of such conflicts when state power is involved. According to Lewis, those rulers who grounded their own moral and political right to rule in their patronage of the traditional Buddhist Sangha perceived this stinging indictment of monasticism as a direct challenge to their authority and legitimacy, and therefore labeled the teachings of the Three Stages sect heretical and its scriptures apocryphal. State power to adjudicate the authenticity of scriptural texts in medieval China—a power firmly entrenched prior to the establishment of Buddhism—was a decisive tool in eradicating competing and threatening ideological discourses. By labeling the texts of the Three Stages sect apocryphal, the state rejected their authorship by the Buddha, and thereby their claim to authority; the ideological vision of the sect and the social critique it inspired were rendered baseless. As a result, the sect itself fell rather rapidly into decline and eventually faded away.

In light of the other essays in this section, the suppression of the Three Stages sect reveals the significant continuities between premodern and modern Buddhist ideological struggles. As Lewis's article clearly demonstrates, contests regarding the legitimacy of particular forms of Buddhism are not just a product of the encounter with modernity, colonial power, and Orientalist scholarship, but are part of a long tradition of (often highly politicized) debate. The existence of multiple and conflicting Buddhist ideologies illustrates the awareness and agency of premodern Buddhists in shaping their own tradition, as well as the role of state power in determining which ideologies held normative authority. While premodern Buddhists articulated the terms of these debates quite differently from Buddhists in the modern period, similar patterns of encounter, both with other Buddhists and with non-Buddhists, are evident.

Judith Snodgrass's examination of the complex ideological exchange that occurred between Japanese Buddhists and a modern Western scholar in the process of constructing a modern form of Japanese Buddhism focuses on strikingly similar themes despite the profound differences in cultural and historical context. Buddhists in Meiji Japan (1867–1912), too, confronted the suppression and possible extinction of their tradition by a nationalist movement that initially figured Japanese Buddhism as foreign and corrupt. Snodgrass illuminates a particularly rich and complex moment in the prolonged Buddhist response to this threat—a response that successfully realigned some forms of Japanese Buddhism with state ideologies of modernization, nationalism, and imperialism. In the case that Snodgrass examines, the textual locus of

Buddhist legitimation was found not in the word of the Buddha, however, but in a German Christian philosopher's writings on Buddhism.

Snodgrass delineates a dizzyingly complex ideological exchange between Japanese Buddhist leaders and writer Paul Carus, an exchange that might be characterized as mutual appropriation rather than dialogue. Paul Carus, who, encountering the Japanese Zen abbot Shaku Sōen's rational, secular vision of Buddhism at the World's Parliament of Religions in 1893, saw in Buddhism the potential to reconcile religion and science. While his *Gospel of Buddha* purports to present a compilation of canonical Buddhist teachings, it is ingeniously constructed to support Carus's ideological vision of the evolution of Christianity into a monistic form fully compatible with science. Snodgrass argues that this "archetypically Orientalist" appropriation of Buddhism was intended primarily to spur and justify this transformation of Christianity (155-158). But Carus's appropriation of Buddhism was in turn appropriated by Japanese Buddhists, who found in his work a fortuitous combination of claims about Buddhism. Carus not only represented Buddhism as compatible with modernity and science, but also defended Buddhism "against the common charges of nihilism, skepticism, and atheism" (163) and drew upon Mahāyāna Buddhist teachings, thereby legitimating Japanese forms of Buddhism in a time when most Western scholars viewed Pāli Buddhism as the original and pure form of Buddhism. In an increasingly nationalistic Japan intent upon modernization, the skillful interpretation of this Western scholarly voice authorized the representation of Japanese Buddhism as the pre-eminent religion of modernity and the future.

The deft and deliberate selective reading practiced both by Carus and by Japanese interpreters like Shaku Sōen and D. T. Suzuki provides a keen glimpse into the processes by which "Buddhism" is continually constructed anew in light of particular present circumstances and anxieties about the future. For Japanese Buddhists in this period, however, this Buddhism was both quintessentially Japanese and the supreme, eternal, and universal Truth after which all religious traditions were seeking; universalist ideological claims served to bolster the nationalist agenda, and thereby ensured the vitality of Japanese Buddhism. This vision of Japan as the repository of the universal Dharma that is the culmination of all religions stands in tension with the evolutionary model espoused by Carus, according to which the engagement with Buddhism is but a stage in the historical progression toward the perfection of Christianity. Yet Carus's portrayal of Buddhism in the *Gospel of Buddha* permitted such a reading, just as it provided proof of Western interest in Buddhism and attracted modern, pro-Western Japanese readers to Buddhism. Through their shrewd appropriation of Carus's Western voice and idiosyncratic vision of Buddhism, Japanese Buddhists laid claim to the superiority and contemporary relevance of their own tradition. Snodgrass's work challenges any notion that Buddhists were passive recipients of modern Western definitions of Buddhism; these Buddhists guided the transformation of their own tradition with great skill and intentionality.

David Germano illuminates the ways in which Buddhists actively and creatively engage with the past as a critical resource for addressing present crises and the threat of future extinction in his examination of one Tibetan response to the devastation of Tibet's cultural and spiritual landscape during the Chinese invasion of 1959 and the subsequent Cultural Revolution (1966–76). This study displays the enduring power of an indigenous transhistorical movement with deep premodern roots to serve as a vehicle for resisting oppression and generating alternative ideologies in particular times and places. Germano focuses upon the revival of the treasure (Ter) movement by Khenpo Jikphun, a charismatic Buddhist teacher in contemporary Tibet and China. According to the Ter tradition, a great eighth-century Indian master concealed treasures (both physical objects hidden in the earth and textual revelations deposited in the minds of key figures) that would be revealed at a foreseen time by future incarnations of his disciples, known as Terton (treasure finders). By authorizing the continued revelation of the Dharma in time and space, the Ter movement has for many centuries enabled Tibetan traditions, most especially in the Nyingma sect (the sect that claims to preserve the oldest Tibetan Buddhist teachings), to construct and reconstruct ideologies, institutions, and a sacred physical landscape in response to the challenges of particular historical circumstances. Ter are thus invested with authority and power through their origins in a glorious Buddhist past. The ideology of the Ter tradition envisions the world in ways that depend profoundly upon the reconfiguration of space and time, connecting past and present through the particular space where the treasure (mental or material) is discovered. It also endows the eternal Dharma with immediate relevance to the particular place and time in which the Terton is located; timeless teachings are rendered both timely and tangible.

Germano demonstrates how the historical origins of the Ter movement in the crises faced by the Nyingma sect during the eleventh to thirteenth centuries CE find productive parallels (as well as some significant differences) in the circumstances of contemporary Tibetan Buddhists. In both cases, faced with persecution and the threat of extinction, Nyingma Buddhists have found in the authority of the past a source for innovation and legitimation in the present. The discovery of a combination of textual teachings and material objects in particular locales reimagines Tibetan topography and invests it with power and authority. Especially powerful in light of the current crisis is the way in which the Ter tradition locates this past authority in the present physical landscape; because Ter ideology, like that of the modern nation-state, is deeply rooted in the imagination of physical space, it offers particularly apt strategies for subverting the Chinese subjugation of Tibet. The locations of Khenpo's treasure discoveries delineate an alternative spiritual geography that contests the boundaries of the nation-state drawn by Chinese imperialism. The contemporary Ter tradition, Germano argues, asserts the resilience and vitality of Buddhism in Tibet, counteracting Tibetan oppression and depression in the present, nostalgia for the past, and dreams of escape to communities in exile.

Khenpo's ingenuity is evident not only in his use of the Ter tradition, but also in his transformation of the normative values that had been attached to that tradition in the past. Faced with the moral and psychological as well as the material devastation of the Cultural Revolution, Khenpo presents himself as moral leader as well as a charismatic Terton. In contrast to most Tertons, who usually take consorts and engage in tantric sexual practices, Khenpo is a celibate monk who insists upon his followers' strict adherence to monastic moral codes. This stance and repositioning of the Ter tradition within monastic Buddhism is central to his vision for a Buddhist revival in Tibet; in the wake of the moral corruption brought on by the Cultural Revolution, Khenpo claims that Buddhist institutions must be thoroughly purified if they are to be vital sources of moral vision. Khenpo's insistence on celibate monasticism and the importance of maintaining vows functions to assert the purity, and thus the power and relevance, of his refigured Ter ideology in a perceived time of moral degradation.

Germano's study makes vivid the ways in which the past always has been, and continues to be, a resource for the reconstruction of Buddhist ideologies in the present. As Germano suggests in conclusion, however, the gap between the ideologies of the "coercive modernity" in which Tibetans find themselves and the ideological resources of the Buddhist past is vast, and profoundly difficult to bridge; the revitalized and reconfigured Ter tradition "does not yet seem to involve the digestion of new materials, or the performance of the alchemy of cultural transformation" (206). Whether the tradition will be able to assimilate and respond effectively to aspects of modernity remains to be seen, but it will only be able to do so, Germano suggests, if the Ter revelations begin to address more directly the contemporary realities facing Tibetan Buddhists. While the form and process of Ter discoveries show remarkable potential to address the current crisis, the content of the revelations needs to address that crisis directly if this ideological strategy is to fulfill its potential to transform present circumstances as it has in the past; the reinvention of tradition demands that the relevance of the past be actively forged in the crucible of the present. Germano compels us to ask whether the capacity of the past to address concerns of the present might have limitations.

Scholarly conceptions and practices are themselves products of particular times and places, products of the ideological perspectives that are constructed and debated in the contemporary academy. Those perspectives are evident in the way these scholars approach the study of Buddhist ideologies. These essays share an underlying concern to acknowledge and explore the agency of Buddhists as authors of their own traditions who negotiate the political and ideological conflicts of their times with skill and purpose. The essays reveal the ways in which doctrinal categories, which past scholars have frequently invested with ahistorical meaning and value, constitute malleable resources for developing alternative ideologies that address particular historical circumstances. While historicizing the ahistorical and universal claims that Buddhists have sometimes made regarding their ideological visions, these authors also acknowledge and explore the power and value that those visions have had for Buddhists, and recognize that Buddhists, too, have often developed their own historiographical paradigms that allow for and explicate the appearance (and disappearance) of the timeless and universal in specific times and places. In this manner, these scholars elucidate Buddhist processes of defining Buddhism(s) not only by exploring particular contexts and the agency of Buddhists within those contexts, but also by recognizing normative and universal claims that, while shaped by particular contexts, attempt to speak beyond them.

5

The Suppression of the Three Stages Sect: Apocrypha as a Political Issue

Mark Edward Lewis

It has long been recognized that literary texts played a central role in the imperial Chinese polity. The most familiar example of this is the examination system of late imperial China, where the primary road to honor, power, and wealth lay through the mastery of a prescribed body of texts. The link between literary attainments and political power, however, long antedated the formal system of awarding office through performance on written examinations. In fact it dated back to the beginning of the empire and remained, in varying forms and degrees, fundamental to the Chinese social and political order. As Buddhism developed in China, its texts became entangled in this linkage of letters and authority, and the questions of textual authenticity or validity became political issues. Consequently the study of Buddhist apocrypha in China cannot be separated from the broader questions of the relations of "scriptural" texts to political authority.

In this chapter I offer a new explanation of the suppression of the Three Stages sect (Sanjie jiao) based on a textual analysis of its teachings. This sect was one of the most important religious movements in China in the sixth and seventh centuries, but its writings were barred from the canon as "apocrypha" and the sect itself ultimately stamped out. Its very existence was virtually forgotten and all knowledge of its teachings vanished until the discovery of a large number of the banned texts among the manuscripts discovered at Dunhuang. The motives for the suppression and the means by which it was carried out provide a clear example of how the definition of a canon and the adjudication of the "authenticity" of texts became political concerns, and show how the use of the term "apocryphal" in reference to a text was often less a matter of textual origins and transmission than of the exigencies of power. They also suggest how the repeated promulgations of a clearly delimited canon were part of the broader struggle by the imperial court to create an "official" Buddhism that would define the forms and limits of religious expression.

Texts and Imperium

The link between texts and authority in China was embodied in the word *jing*, which has been rendered variously by such terms as "classic," "scripture," or "canon." Etymologically, this character referred to the warp of a fabric and, by extension, to that which provided order or structure. It was employed verbally in the sense of "to order" or "to regulate." In works of the Han and subsequent dynasties it was often glossed with a homophone meaning "path" (*jing*[a]), and was said to refer to the "constant Way that penetrated all things." During the Warring States and early Han periods this term came to be used as a rubric for a body of texts that supposedly preserved the teachings of the sage rulers of the early Zhou and transmitted the fundamental "arts" (*yi*) that constituted human civilization (Honda 1947, 1-13; Hiraoka 1947, 16-30; Matsumoto 1970, 101-103).

The Western Han's "triumph of Confucianism" established the principle that the definition of a canon and the propagation of its truths was a central role of government. Jia Yi (201–169 BCE) argued explicitly that the true purpose of political authority was to preserve and disseminate the social arts delineated in the canons. In his famous memorial proposing the institution of a state orthodoxy, Dong Zhongshu (176–104 BCE) argued that whatever did not lie within the "six arts" and the teachings of Confucius, i.e., within the canons, would disrupt the Way of the true ruler and ought to be proscribed (Qi 1974, 945-58; Ban Gu 1962, ch. 56, 2523). The Han theory of the "uncrowned king" held that the canons transmitted the Way of the former kings, men who had been both sages and rulers. This exemplary rulership had been lost in the world but was preserved through the scholarly labors of Confucius, who assembled the literary remains of the Zhou state and thus became the heir of the kingly Way. As the master of this textual wisdom he was held to be the true king of his day, despite his low political rank. This idea expressed dramatically the link between texts and political authority, for the true understanding of certain texts made a common man a king.

By the end of the Western Han the unique status of canonical texts and their relation to political authority had become conventional notions. When Liu Xin (d. 23 BCE) compiled a bibliography of the imperial library, he listed the canons as a separate category of text and granted them the first and highest position in the empire of letters. This became the standard practice in all subsequent Chinese bibliographic works, and the study of the canons became an independent discipline with its own specialized methods and monographs (Pi 1958). Moreover, in the bibliographic chapter of the *Han shu* ("History of the Former Han"), Ban Gu (32–92 CE) identified every category of text with the work of specific political offices, thus asserting the inseparability of writing and government.

The idea that the key to good government lay in a certain body of texts began to be incorporated into the structure of the imperial government in the time of Gongsun Hong (200–121 BCE). He was both the first scholar to hold the office of chief minister (*chengxiang*) and the primary architect of the government policy that made systematic literary training a prerequisite for holding office. The emperor appointed a group of erudites (*boshi*) who were noted for their mastery of specific canonical texts. Men selected from the various localities of the empire by a system of recommendation became their students, and those who successfully completed their studies were placed in a pool from which official appointments were made. This "imperial university" established two important precedents. First, the government claimed the right to decide which texts constituted the canon to be studied by aspiring officials. Second, mastery of those texts was made a key path to government office and power. The sanctioning of texts and dissemination of their doctrines had become a positive function of government, and mastery of those texts an attribute of the emperor's servants (Ban Gu 1962, ch. 6, 171-72; ch. 88, 3589, 3593; Sima Qian 1959, ch. 121, 3118-20). The fall of the Han dynasty temporarily ended the direct, institutional link between texts and office, but one of the hallmarks of the "great families" that dominated high office in subsequent centuries was the familial transmission of canonical texts and scholarly traditions, and literary education remained an important element of political power and status throughout the Age of Disunion and the Tang (Ebrey 1978, 31, 39-42, 58, 78, 84, 87, 96, 104-105, 116-19; Yan 1968, 3-8, 52-84; McMullen 1988).

As Buddhism developed in China, its sūtras, which were called *jing* in imitation of the indigenous Chinese canon, provided a new vision of the good society and the nature of political authority. Critics of Buddhism argued that these new texts and their principles challenged the truths and values of the existing canon, while Buddhist apologists asserted that they strengthened and extended them (Ch'en 1973, 14-124). This polemic lasted for centuries and is important for any understanding of the history of Buddhism in China, but for the purposes of this article it is sufficient to note that when Buddhism became an important religion in China, its texts were drawn into the political realm through the received idea that the definition and defense of "scripture" was a fundamental role of the state.

In the wake of the collapse of the Han, many dynasts invoked the defense and propagation of Buddhist scriptures and doctrines as a basis for their authority. If one accepts the account in the *Gaoseng zhuan* ("Biographies of Eminent Monks"), Yao Xing (366–416), ruler of the proto-Tibetan Later Qin dynasty, launched an expedition to bring Kumārajīva (344–413, var. 409) to his capital at Chang'an in order to sponsor the latter's activities as a translator of sūtras.[1] The rulers of the Northern Wei (386–534) claimed the status of tathāgata and were vigorous patrons of Buddhism. In the South, members of the imperial family of the Qi dynasty (479–502) engaged in the copying and exposition of sūtras for the explicit purpose of securing blessings for the ruling house and all subjects of the realm. For the same reason competitions between monks were held in the explication of sūtras, and honors were heaped on the victors. The rulers of the Chen dynasty (557–589) claimed to be bodhisattvas and propagated through regular public readings sūtras like the *Renwang jing* ("Book of Benevolent Kings") and *Jinguangming jing* ("Sūtra of Golden Light"), which exalted the ruler as defender of the Dharma (Ōchō 1958, 346, 259-60, 359-60). Thus, by the time of the reunification of China under the Sui (581–618), Buddhism and its scriptures had become an integral part of the intellectual and textual underpinnings of the Chinese state, and the Three Stages sect's proclamation of the end of the Buddha's Dharma constituted a direct challenge to the imperial government as well as to the ecclesiastical hierarchy it now supported.

The End of the Dharma

The argument that the teachings of the Buddha would inevitably disappear from the world of men has been the object of both general surveys and detailed studies of its various aspects (Chappell 1980; Lamotte 1958, 210-22; Przyluski 1923, 161-85; Zürcher 1982b; Tamura 1954; Kumoi 1970; Maruyama 1976; Yamada 1957; Yuki 1936; Sasaki 1957; Hashizume 1969; Kimura 1963). In this section I will only note two points fundamental to my interpretation of the fate of the Three Stages sect. First, this doctrine was a theory of the decay of the Buddha's law and all its manifestations as they existed in the world; it was not a theory of the general decay of all social mores. In a Buddhist context this distinction was not significant, since a society without the truth of the Buddhist faith was by definition benighted and defiled. But China of the sixth through the eighth centuries was not a purely Buddhist realm, and there were alternative bases for the assertion of ethical norms and political authority. Second, as a theory of the decline of the Buddha's Dharma in the world, the doctrine was primarily espoused by those who perceived the Buddhist Order to be in decline and who advocated either a renewal of monastic discipline or a reform of Buddhist praxis.

In Buddhism the Dharma had a dual nature, and it was this duality that led to its inevitable disappearance (Reynolds 1972, 15). "Dharma" referred, first and foremost, to the supreme sacred reality—the law that regulated the totality of existence and the eternal truth that enabled men to break free from the wheel of rebirth. Dharma in this sense was immutable and unchangeable. But "Dharma" also referred to the teachings by which the Buddha introduced his truth into the world, and in this form it was embodied in the sacred texts, the monastic order, and the images of the Buddha. In this worldly aspect it was bound by the laws of inevitable flux and decay that prevail in the realm of contingent existence (see, e.g., Rhys Davids 1922, 21; Feer 1884–1904, 25; Cowell 1886, 27, 100, 486). Thus the most fundamental principles of Buddhism stipulated its own inevitable demise.

The most ancient and widespread account of the end of the Dharma asserted that the true Dharma would have lasted for a thousand years, but because the Buddha allowed women to join the order it was reduced to five hundred. This already shows that the fundamental issue was the purity of the Sangha. Other versions fall under the Pali rubric *okkammaniye dhammo*, the "retractions of the Dharma," in which the Dharma would pass through five phases of declining religious practice. In the first stage men would achieve liberation (*vimokṣa*), in the second concentration (*samādhi*), in the third observation of the prohibitions (*śīladhara*), in the fourth erudition (*bahuśruta*), and in the last only charity (*dāna*), the religious practice of the layman. Here the object of decay was clearly the specifically Buddhist knowledge and practice embodied in the monastic order (Kumoi 1970, 290-92; Lamotte 1958, 217-22; Przyluski 1923, 161-85).

These schematic models of decline were dramatized in narratives of the Dharma's end that appeared in the *Abhidharmamahāvibhāṣā* ("Extensive Commentary"), the *Aśokāvadāna* ("Legend of King Aśoka"), and other texts. These stories prophesied attacks by alien kings hostile to Buddhism, their defeat by the Buddhists' patron king, the increased generosity of lay patrons, and the consequent corruption of monks, who would abandon all discipline and meditation in pursuit of study for worldly glory. On the day of the disappearance of the Law, the laity would denounce the assembled monks for failing in their religious duties despite the laity's faithful performance of their own obligations. That evening the chief of the monastic order, who was thoroughly learned in doctrine (*bahuśruta-pāramitā*), would refuse to recite the complete *Prātimokṣa* because he could no longer observe all its injunctions. Surata, the last *arhat*, would step forward, declare that he could obey the entire *Prātimokṣa*, and then challenge the chief to recite the whole Tripiṭaka. This assertion of the superiority of a clearly defined code of discipline over the study of endless texts would outrage the followers of the chief monk, who would slay Surata. The latter's followers would kill the chief, and the Dharma would thus disappear from the world (Lamotte 1958, 218-20).

These stories clearly demonstrate the point of the theory of the dharma's end and its role in internal Buddhist polemics. First, they deal entirely with the corruption of the monastic order and the disappearance of Buddhism; the lay followers are explicitly exonerated. Second, the stories place the blame for the disappearance on those elements in the Order who intellectually master Buddhist doctrines for worldly glory but can no longer carry out a disciplined, religious praxis. This same preference for discipline and action over intellectual knowledge is also reflected in the standard ordering of the "retractions of the Dharma," in which meditation and the observation of the prohibitions are granted pride of place over wide knowledge. Thus the idea of the decay of the Dharma was invoked by those who perceived the Sangha to be in a state of decline produced by excessive scholasticism in the cause of worldly glory.

This division between an intellectual faith and a faith of praxis is deep-rooted in Buddhism, and it played a major role in the history of the doctrine of the disappearance of the Dharma (Ōchō 1958, 256-89). In his study of the attitudes toward this doctrine evinced by the leading Chinese Buddhists of the sixth and seventh centuries, Takao Giken has shown that, in general, those who were devoted to philosophical speculation and intellectual synthesis tended to ignore or actively deny the disappearance of the Buddha's law, whereas the advocates of the Disciplinary School (Lü zong), the devotional Pure Land sect, and the radical Three Stages sect all spoke of the end of the Dharma as imminent or as an achieved fact (Takao 1937a; 1937b).

The leading philosophical thinkers of the period, such as Jingying Huiyuan (523–592), Jizang (549–623), all the exegetes of the Huayan school, and the Tiantai's founder Zhiyi (538–597) denied the actual or imminent end of the Dharma (Takao 1937a, 6, 8, 9-11; 1937b, 47-50, 67-70; Maruyama 1976).[2] The single prominent exception to this generalization was the Faxiang school, which produced philosophical arguments of great sophistication but whose founder Xuanzang (596–664) and his chief disciple Kuiji (632–682) believed in the imminent end of the Dharma and cited evidence for it in their writings (Hori 1970, 136-39). This apparent anomaly is explained by the fact that both these men were devout followers of the cult of the future Buddha, Maitreya; indeed, some Japanese scholars have argued that the worship of Maitreya was the actual center of Faxiang Buddhism (Yabuki 1927, 547). Since the ultimate coming of Maitreya was necessarily preceded by the disappearance of the teachings of the historical Buddha, Śākyamuni, those who hoped for the former were inclined to look for the signs of the latter. But barring a strong commitment to such millennial expectations, thinkers who were devoted to the interpretation and synthesis of the vast canon attributed to Śākyamuni were not inclined to deal with doctrines or evidence which suggested that those teachings were no longer of value.

In contrast with those of a philosophical bent, men who advocated a restoration of discipline or a new religious praxis generally argued that the Dharma was on the brink of disappearing or had already done so. The founder of the Disciplinary School, Daoxuan (596–667), believed that the world had entered the fourth of five stages in the decline of the Dharma, and that the Buddha's law could be preserved for a further two centuries only through rigorous practice of a revived monastic discipline (Takao 1937a, 12-16). Despite his belief in the continued existence of the Dharma, his works on the Vinaya code contain numerous references to the present corruption of the monastic order, and he argued that meditation was no longer efficacious in his day (15).[3] These arguments clearly reflect his belief that the Dharma was in an advanced state of decay and that its ultimate disappearance was only a matter of time.

Even more radical were those who proclaimed that the Final Age of the Dharma (*mofa*) had already begun. The most important of these were the Pure Land sect and the Three Stages sect (*Sanjie jiao*), both of whose followers believed that the religious order was corrupt, that the teachings of the historical Buddha had lost their efficacy, and that the people of their day required a new religious praxis to attain salvation.[4] However, the Pure Land sect did not carry the consequences of these beliefs to such an extreme as did the Three Stages sect. While agreeing that the saving power of the buddhas had waned, they excluded Amitābha. While concurring that the texts of the Buddha's teachings were no longer efficacious, they claimed a special hundred-year extension for the *Wuliangshou jing* ("Sūtra of the Buddha of Limitless Life"). While acknowledging that true meditation was no longer possible, Huaigan (fl. seventh century), the leading spokesman for the Pure Land sect, argued that men could still obtain a shallow form of *samādhi*, and this made the chanting of Amitābha's name effective. Even in the twilight of the Dharma the Pure Land sect still believed in the continued efficacy of at least one buddha, one sūtra, and one meditation technique.

Such half measures, however, were unacceptable to the adherents of the Three Stages sect, and during the seventh century an increasingly rancorous polemic developed between the two schools (Yabuki 1927, 547-63). Convinced that the Dharma had entered its terminal age, the Three Stages sect declared the bankruptcy of received Buddhism and called for a new form of religion to rescue people from the world of error and sin in which the Buddhist establishment itself was now also caught. It is to the nature of this new practice and their critique of traditional Buddhism that we must now turn our attention.

Buddhism in the Terminal Age

The core of the doctrine of the Three Stages sect was that the Dharma declined through three stages, and the descent of the Dharma into its terminal stage invalidated all distinctions and judgments of value. Cut off from the Dharma's truth, people could no longer distinguish right from wrong, and so, to avoid the crime of slander and false judgments, they had no choice but to affirm and reverence all beings on the basis of their ultimate buddhahood. As Yabuki Keiki, the leading modern student of the sect, has pointed out, the central word in all the teachings of the school was "universal" (*pu*; Skt. *viśva*) (Yabuki 1927, 284). The writings of the sect repeatedly proclaim such ideas as "universal buddhahood," "universal Dharma," "universal reverence," "universal sagehood," "universal truth," and the "universal common man." The foundation of this call for the abandonment of distinctions and universal reverence of all beings was the belief that all existence shared the "buddha-nature" known as the *tathāgatagarbha*. Various passages in the texts of the Three Stages sect proclaimed that all the various buddhas and buddhadharmas spoken of in the sūtras were just different names for the universal buddha, which was the true nature and substance of all sentient beings. The relation of the buddha-nature to sentient creatures was variously compared to that of water to waves, clay or metal to the implements made from them, or an actor to the many roles he plays, for the true nature of all those beings who were not yet buddhas was actually the same as that of the Buddha himself.[5] Since all beings shared the buddha-nature, all were in truth buddhas.

The doctrine of a universal buddha-nature inherent in all beings is common to much of Mahāyāna Buddhism and would, of itself, merit little notice. The radical character of the Three Stages sect's position lay in the belief that because the disappearance of the Dharma invalidated all distinctions or judgments, the "essential" or "potential" buddhahood of all things had to be treated as a reality in the world. This led them to adopt as their model the Bodhisattva Never-Disparaging (Bu qing pusa) described in the *Lotus Sūtra*, who bowed to everything he encountered and proclaimed its future buddhahood. It also led them to denounce all those who uniquely reverenced the buddhas, the Sangha, or the doctrines of the Buddhist canon at the cost of contempt or condemnation for other creatures. In contrast with their own self-proclaimed universalism, all other sects were censured for being "split" or "separate" (*bie*), because they divided all doctrines into true and false, perceptions into correct and incorrect, conduct into good and bad, and men into sages and villains. Each sect proclaimed the correctness of its own teachings and practice, and thereby condemned the ideas and actions of others as wicked. Such divisions and distinctions had once been valid in terms of the true Dharma, but with its disappearance they became destructive illusions. The impossibility of correct perception in the Final Age of the Dharma invalidated earlier Buddhist practices and necessitated the creation of the new, "universalist" Buddhism of the Three Stages sect.

The very first sentence of a central scripture of the sect, the *Sanjie fofa* ("Buddhadharma of the Three Stages"), proclaimed the impossibility of correct perception in the Final Age of the Dharma, and because correct perception was impossible, any judgment would be slander. Men of the first two ages were still capable of correct perceptions, so for them to study the teachings of the various sūtras and pass judgments of right and wrong was correct, but for men of the third stage to do so was a great crime. For men of the terminal age to make distinctions was, as one passage remarked, like a blind man shooting an arrow; they would not hit what they shot at, but only cause harm. Instead they should reverence all things universally, which was like a blind man shooting at the ground; they could not miss. Because of the centrality of this belief in the impossibility of correct judgments, the standard epithets used in the sect's texts to describe men in the terminal age were "born blind" (*sheng mang*), "of perverse views" (*xie jian*), "of broken precepts and views" (*po jie po jian*), or "inverting [the real and illusory]" (*diandao*).

Given the impossibility of correct perceptions, all distinctions—such as those between sage and petty man, good and bad, correct and deviant, large and small, or monk and layman—had to be abandoned.[6] In all cases the man of the terminal age was enjoined to regard all around him positively, out of recognition of their buddha-nature, and to regard himself negatively (*ren e*, lit., "acknowledge evil"), in full cognizance of his own inadequacies. In addition, to meet these new conditions the Three Stages sect propounded new models of action, such as the demand that when securing the necessities of life—food, clothing, and shelter—the believer must always take the inferior role or portion for himself and grant the superior to others; the assertion that giving (*dāna*) was the only true religious practice; and the ideal of zealous self-denial through rigorous performance of the 12 ascetic practices (*dhūta*). However, for the purposes of this article this new praxis is not so important as are the sect's judgments on the traditional Buddhism that it claimed to supplant. I shall divide this discussion into three parts dealing with the sect's assessments of the nature of each of the Three Jewels—the Buddha, the monastic order, and the canon—in the Final Age of the Dharma.

Because the sect's fundamental tenet was universality, which was defined through the negation of separation, its subsidiary doctrines always centered on the denial of distinctions. The case of the buddha-jewel offers an extreme example of this tendency for, as already noted, the premises of universal buddha-nature and universal blindness combined to lead the sect to propose that all creatures should be treated as the Buddha. A clear example of this is found in the biography of an unnamed master of the Three Stages sect collected by Paul Pelliot and now in the Bibliothèque Nationale in Paris (Pelliot no. 2550, Ōtani 1938). According to this text, such was the power of the master's devotions that even ants gathered around his dwelling like disciples, and asses and other beasts of the mountains also joined his worship. He said, "I clearly know that these are all incarnations of the Buddha who have entered into the practice [of the Way]. They ought to be deeply reverenced; one cannot disparage them" (Ōtani 1938, 284.21–.24).

Nor did this new definition of the Buddha simply include the beasts of the fields and forests. An account of the various means of seeking salvation in each of the three stages includes a description of the changing definition of the Buddha. The Buddha of the terminal age included not only the universal buddha-nature, the buddhas (*zhen shen* and *ying shen*; Skt. *dharmakāya* and *nirmāṇakāya*) of previous Buddhist doctrine, and the images of the Buddha, but also the gods and spirits worshiped by heterodox faiths, the demons employed in casting spells and curses, and even Māras and evil spirits.[7] The blind men of the third stage could only find the Buddha by worshiping him everywhere, even in evil demons and in the gods of alien faiths.

Just as the disappearance of the Dharma obliterated the distinction between buddha and non-buddha, so it removed the separation between monk and layman. This change was already foreshadowed in the *Xiangfa jueyi jing* ("Book of Resolving Doubts During the Semblance Dharma Age," i.e., the second stage of the decline), an officially apocryphal text that was accepted as genuine by followers of the Three Stages sect and frequently quoted in their writings. The central teaching of the *Xiangfa jueyi jing* was the idea that giving (*dāna*) was the highest of all the perfections (*pāramitās*) and the only true road to salvation (Makita 1976, 310-313). To understand the significance of this teaching and the way in which it obliterated the distinction between monk and layman, we must note the relation of *dāna* to the other *pāramitās*: *śīla*, "prohibitions, moral conduct"; *vīrya*, "energy, devotion"; *kṣānti*, "patience, resolve"; *dhyāna*, "meditation"; and *prajñā*, "wisdom, knowledge."

In his study on Buddhism in Thai society, Stanley Tambiah described the "asymmetrical and symbiotic pattern" incumbent on monks and laymen. The actual cultivation of a distinctively "Buddhist way of life," i.e., observance of all precepts, meditation, and study, is reserved for the monks, while the laymen earn merit through financing the building and repair of temples and the daily feeding of the Sangha (Tambiah 1970, 141-49). Thus merit-making through *dāna* is the classic lay form of religious action, and the monks consummate *dāna* by accepting the gifts of the laymen and thereby sharing with them the merit earned through the monks' devotions and study. The other five *pāramitās* constitute the distinctive praxis of the monk as a religious specialist, although they might be observed in reduced form by the laity, in such guises as taking lay vows or attending public lectures.

The *Xiangfa jueyi jing*, however, systematically dismantled this classic, asymmetrical structure in which the monk purified himself apart from the world while the layman earned merit by supporting the monastic order. The text accomplished this through three radical propositions. First, it asserted that the object of *dāna* was not to support the monastic order or the Buddha, but rather to save the poor, the orphaned, and the suffering creatures of the world. It is better, the text argued, to feed one mouthful of food to an animal than to nourish all the buddhas, bodhisattvas, and *śrāvakas* in the universe for innumerable lifetimes (*Taishō* 2870.85.1336a24-26, a29-b2). Second, it argued that both monks and laymen were obliged to give *dāna*. All men, it proclaimed, whether high or low, rich or poor, monk or layman, should gather all they could spare and distribute this to whoever was in need (2870.85.1336a27-29, b2-15). Finally, the text claimed that *dāna* was the only road to salvation and that the other five *pāramitās* were, at best, aspects or developments of *dāna*. All the buddhas of the universe had attained their status through lifetimes of giving, and the performance of the other *pāramitās* for "*kalpas* as numberless as the sands of the Ganges" would not lead to nirvāṇa if not based on *dāna*. Masters of monastic discipline, meditation, or study could only succeed in destroying the Dharma and would "go to hell like an arrow shot from a bow" (2870.85.1336b19-24, 1337a27-b1).[8] Thus the *Xiangfa jueyi jing* argued that there was a single, true mode of religious action common to monks and laymen, whereas the explicitly "monastic" *pāramitās* were at best adjuncts to giving and at worst roads to perdition.

The major texts of the Three Stages sect also focus on *dāna* as the primary form of religious action. The *Duigen qixing fa*'s ("The Dharma of Setting Out [on the Way] in Accord with Capacity") discussion of the cultivation of good during the terminal age deals almost entirely with giving, linking the generosity of *dāna* with the self-denial of the *dhūta*. In contrast with earlier stages of the Dharma, the "good" in the final stage was no longer separate from the "bad"; it was entirely "good within bad" or the "good gained in bitterness." The discussion of the "good gained in bitterness" is divided into 12 sections, but the last 11 appear only as rubrics and detailed discussion is devoted entirely to the first topic, "regularly begging for food" (*chang qi shi*). This thus becomes the central discussion of proper conduct in the Final Age of the Dharma.

The discussion is divided into eight sections, and the first one, which deals explicitly with *dāna*, makes four points. First, it argues that by giving away all good food obtained and eating only the bad, a man quells his own desires and benefits other creatures. Second, it stipulates that food received from begging should be divided into four parts: one part was to be eaten by the recipient, the second by his companions, the third to be given to the poor, and the fourth to hungry ghosts and domestic animals. Third, the text states that food received in the two daily meals at a monastery, as part of a vegetarian feast, or at the homes of wealthy patrons of the Buddhist Order should not be eaten but instead given to those in need. Fourth, in begging for all his food and regularly sharing it with the poor, the devotee was to serve as a model and lead other beings to enter the Way of begging and giving. Giving thus culminated in granting all sentient beings an entry into the path to salvation. This passage clearly follows the *Xiangfa jueyi jing* in asserting the centrality of *dāna* to all religious conduct, transferring the charity from the Buddhist Order to the poor, and insisting that monks must join laymen as givers of *dāna*.

The remaining seven sections on "regularly begging for food" list a variety of virtues and attainments, but these are all treated as aspects of the basic duty of denying oneself and giving all to the poor. Thus "patience" (*kṣānti*), originally one of the *pāramitās*, is explained as bearing one's hunger and not eating any food presented. "Compassion" and "pity" are both manifested by feeding or saving the poor, and "renunciation and self-sufficiency" are marked by denying oneself in order to give to others. "Concentration" (*dhyāna*), also one of the six *pāramitās*, is defined simply as a fixed tranquility of mind that is not disturbed by the desire for good food. "Much profit and merit" are explained as the two benefits of regularly begging for food rather than relying on lay patronage. First, when a patron staged a vegetarian feast for monks, only his family benefited from the merit of the deed. However, when many men engaged in begging, begged from many houses, and then distributed what they received to the myriad creatures, the benefits were immense and widespread. Second, by causing all creatures to give *dāna* in an endless circuit, the beggar himself would ultimately obtain more food. Finally, the section on "liberation" describes how the rejection of the old ties of lay patron and monastic client freed the monk from the trammels of the world.[9] In this way all virtues and the cultivation of the good were identified solely with self-denial and charity. In this expanded form *dāna* was to become the unique form of religious praxis, one that was common to laymen and monks.

Not only were monks enjoined to be givers of *dāna*, but any reliance on lay patronage was specifically attacked. This point appears clearly in the biography of the anonymous master of the sect referred to earlier. After expounding to his pupils the doctrine of giving all good food to others and eating only what they left behind, he noted that for a monk to accept charity in exchange for preaching was to sell the Dharma (Ōtani 1938, 289.103). Here the monks' traditional role of sharing merit through receiving lay charity was explicitly attacked in the name of universal participation in giving. This critique of patronage was not only an attack on the distinction between Sangha and laity but also an assault on the corruption of the religious orders that resulted from regular lay patronage, a corruption that was both cause and consequence of the decline of the Dharma in the classic accounts of its disappearance already cited.

In addition to the centrality of *dāna* in the teachings of the sect, its most famous institution, the Inexhaustible Treasury (*wu jin zang*), was based on the model of charity outlined above. As advocated in the *Xiangfa jueyi jing*, the sect established a treasury at the Huadu Temple in Chang'an where all men could give charity that would then be distributed to those in need. As the institution became more popular, branch treasuries were established by members of the sect in monasteries all over the empire, and it became an accepted practice for people throughout the empire to give donations to these treasuries on the fourth day of the first month and again at the time of the Hungry Ghost Festival in the middle of the seventh month. These donations were used to stage religious festivals, to maintain monasteries, and to give relief to the poor (Gernet 1956, 205-212; Hubbard 1986). It was primarily through this practice of empire-wide, organized charity that the Three Stages sect became influential in Tang society, and the practice itself was a direct extension of the new religious praxis for the terminal age outlined in the teachings of the sect.

The merging of lay and monastic modes of religious practice was to be accompanied by the dissolution of physical and institutional divisions between the Sangha and the laity. In its discussion of the places where one could attain salvation, the *Duigen qixing fa* noted that in the first age of the Dharma men could attain the Way anywhere, in the second age they could attain it only in still places removed from human settlements, but in the third age they could attain the Way only in the midst of other men; they could not be separated from lay society (Yabuki 1927, 125.4–.9). This was an explicit attack on the separation of the monastic order from the world at large, and many other passages in the writings of the sect made the same point.[10] In actual practice, the adherents of the Three Stages sect were noted for mixing with lay society in the course of begging and preaching, and their practice of living apart from other monks in special quarters might also have reflected their rejection of the conventional divisions between the monastic order and lay society.

Further evidence that the Three Stages sect preached the end of a distinct monastic order is found in the biography of the anonymous master. When a group of monks upbraided him for not encouraging a group of wealthy visitors to sponsor a vegetarian feast, he replied with a parable comparing the awesome solemnity of a vegetarian feast with the purifying fasts undertaken by a civil official in preparation for a public ritual. For the slightest error the official would be stripped of his rank and sent into exile, and the consequences of an error in sacred ritual for one who had left the world were infinitely greater. Since the men of the terminal age had lost the capacity to perceive the Buddha's truth and no longer knew how to perform rituals correctly, the food offered to monks by lay patrons was like the bait placed in traps to lure animals to their deaths. The other monks were so impressed with the gravity of accepting the *dāna* of lay patrons that they abandoned their vows and reverted to secular status (Ōtani 1938, 290.122–291.131). Indeed, four times in his biography the result of the anonymous master's preaching was to lead monks to abandon monastic life and resume life as laymen (289.92, 291.131, 292.144, 296.212). Since the intent of the biography is clearly hagiographic, we must conclude that the Three Stages sect celebrated the reversion of monks to secular life as one expression of proper religiosity. Another text even tells of five hundred monks in the terminal age who reverted to lay status because they realized that they had broken their precepts; moreover, as a direct consequence of ceasing to be monks, they met the Buddha and were able to attain the Way.[11]

In addition to persuading monks to return to lay life, the anonymous master did not adopt the traditional accoutrements of one who had left the world. One of the conversations that led his interlocutors to revert to lay status dealt with the differences in practice between the anonymous master and Xinxing (540–594), the founder of the Three Stages sect. When the master stated that he was no different from Xinxing, the others objected that Xinxing shaved his head and wore the *kaṣāya*. The master replied that it was not in accord with the Buddhist faith for common men with broken precepts, i.e., the men of the terminal age, to wear the clothing of a sage (Ōtani 1938, 292.141–.144). This clearly shows that many adherents of the sect rejected any distinctions in dress and tonsure between monks and laymen.

Not only did this master of the Three Stages sect denounce lay patronage of the Buddhist Order, refuse to shave his head and wear a *kaṣāya*, and persuade monks to return to lay life, but he also made laymen and -women the primary targets of religious instruction. The biography records that a monk criticized him for preaching only to the laity and not to monks. The master replied that if one wore the *kaṣāya* in the Final Age of the Dharma, all the buddhas would not appear and the consummation of giving would not be accomplished. This was because self-styled monks were all greedy for wealth from the gifts of patrons and enchanted with sensual pleasures, thus embodying that corruption of the religious order which brought about the decay of the dharma. The questioner then asked why the master taught only women, and he replied that the Dharma ought to have been performed by monks, but that their failure had led to its disappearance. Laymen could not perform it, for they were bound to the service of the emperor. Consequently, only laywomen could now attain the Way (Ōtani 1938, 287.70–.74).

In yet another passage, the master observed that anyone who gave away his wealth would become a monk. His interlocutors objected that people who did not shave their heads could not leave the household and become monks, and they asked the master why he called laymen monks. The master cited examples in the Vinaya where monks were allowed to keep their hair, and he then quoted the *Fozang jing* ("Sūtra of the Buddha-Treasure"): "I did not say that those who shave their heads and wear the *kaṣāya* are monks. Those who obey my law are monks; they are my disciples, and I am their master. If they do not obey my law, then I am not their master."[12] The true division was not between official monks and laymen, but between those who obeyed the Buddhadharma and those who did not. And in the terminal age, the Buddhadharma was synonymous with the teachings of the Three Stages sect.

In addition to this evidence from doctrinal and hagiographical texts, other sources also indicate the blurring of the distinctions between laymen and monks in the practices of the sect. Xinxing's biography in the *Xu Gaoseng zhuan* ("Further Biographies of Eminent Monks") records, "At the Fazang Monastery, he renounced the precepts and personally engaged in physical labor."[13] Xinxing's private secretary and close colleague, Pei Xuanzheng (d.u.), remained a layman even while controlling many of the affairs of the sect and its monasteries. Xinxing's "last testament" records that as of his 48th year there were only four men who shared his religious practices, and they had sworn an oath with him to renounce property and life itself to become buddhas. Two of these four sworn comrades were laymen.[14] Inscriptional evidence also indicates that the skeletons of monks of the sect and of lay followers, both male and female, were buried together (Tsukamoto 1975a, 235-36).

The final element to be considered is the fate of the Dharma-jewel, in its narrow sense of doctrine and texts, during the terminal age. To a certain extent, the repudiation of a distinct monastic order with its own religious praxis based on discipline, meditation, and study also denied the significance of texts and scholastic study. In a world where *prajñā* was impossible and *dhyāna* meant simply the ability to keep one's mind off food, texts could not play an important role. Various texts argued explicitly that to speak of anything other than the Dharma of the universal buddha, i.e., the teachings of the Three Stages sect, was to slander the Buddha and his law.[15] Moreover, numerous passages also stated that in the terminal age the Buddhist canon would cease to exist as a defined body of texts, and the study and dissemination of texts would no longer be an aspect of correct religious praxis.

In the section on "taking refuge in the Dharma," the *Duigen qixing fa* notes that during the second age there was one dharma: the Sūtra, Vinaya, and Abhidharma texts of the three vehicles. This "one Dharma," therefore, meant all the texts in the conventional Buddhist canon. In the terminal age, however, the Dharma was divided into eight sections, and only one of these—the sūtras—corresponded to an element of the official canon. The exclusion of the Vinaya codes and the philosophical elaborations of the Abhidharma reiterated the sect's denunciations, cited above, of traditional monastic discipline and academic speculation. In place of the vanished categories of Vinaya and Abhidharma, however, the canon of the terminal age also included the "Dharma of the great vehicle of the perception of universality"—apparently the teachings of the Three Stages sect—as well as "the Dharma of the lay world," the "Buddhadharma which perverts the good," and other dharmas that included the various heterodox faiths and perverted perceptions adhered to by the blinded creatures of the terminal age (Yabuki 1927, 115.6–.9). Just as the universal buddha of this corrupted age expanded to include alien gods and evil demons, and the monastic order incorporated lay society, so the canon encompassed all religious teachings and texts save those of the corrupted, traditional Sangha.

Another discussion of the transformation of the canon appears in the *Sanjie fofa*. This passage cites a sentence in the *Daban niepan jing* (Nirvāṇa Sūtra) which said that 11 of the 12 sections of the canon would disappear, and only the *vaipulya* (*fangdeng*) sūtras would survive.[16] It then explains that this would occur because the *vaipulya* texts were in accord with the Dharma of the terminal age, whereas the rest of the canon was not.[17] Apart from their own texts it is not certain which works the Three Stages sect would have included under the rubric *vaipulya*, which was not a clearly fixed set of texts but a generic term applied to works of a "universalist" bent. Nevertheless, there is no doubt that this passage denied scriptural status to a significant portion of the traditional Buddhist canon.

Not only were significant elements of the Buddhist canon denied legitimacy and much non-Buddhist doctrine accepted—at least for the sake of polemics—by the Three Stages sect, but the study and preaching of conventional Buddhist doctrine was severely criticized by the school. The *Sanjie fofa miji* ("Secret Record of the Buddhadharma of the Three Stages") described the possibility of doctrinal knowledge and preaching in the terminal age, as follows:

> The position in the third age is one of completely perverted views, fixed and unalterable, and cannot be saved through any of the five ways [of salvation, the traditional *pāramitās*]. This is also called the completion of deviant understanding and conduct. The [*Daban*] *niepan jing* says, "The bhikṣu Shanxing recited, chanted, and expounded all twelve sections of the canon, and in meditation attained the Buddha-Way of the four *dhyānas*. But he did not comprehend the meaning of a single sentence or a single word, did not achieve the slightest good root (*kuśalamūla*), and could not avoid slandering the Buddha."[18]

Here again we see how the members of the sect insisted that the blind men of the third stage could not grasp the truth and that their preaching of doctrine would inevitably slander the Buddha and his law. True learning in the third stage was impossible, and the exposition of doctrine constituted a positive danger. As the *Sanjie fofa* stated, "The age of erudition (*bahuśruta*) is past, and we are now in the age of meritorious deeds (*puṇya*) . . . All the creatures of acute faculties . . . will increase every kind of evil, because they are partial to study for erudition and wisdom (*prajñā*)" (Yabuki 1927, 263.14, 265.11–.13). The anonymous master likewise stated that a man who studied texts in the terminal age was like a blind bird with a bean in its beak; it could not understand what it had (Ōtani 1938, 300.269–.272).

Since the study and exposition of texts in the third stage was hazardous, the Three Stages sect cautioned its adherents against teaching and lauded the virtues of silence. The fifth section on "universal reverence" in the *Duigen qixing fa* spoke of the "Buddhadharma of cutting off all speech" thus: "For all creatures we reverence their essence [buddha-nature] and do not speak of their good or evil. We use the same name for all six destinies of sentient beings [i.e., make no distinctions between spirits in hell, hungry ghosts, animals, men, demons, and gods]" (Yabuki 1927, 132.13–.15).

In the practice of universal reverence, no judgments about others could be made, and doctrines that made distinctions and assigned judgments had to be avoided, so the safest course was not to speak at all about religious matters. The importance of this proscription is shown by the fact that in the list of the 26 characteristic evils in the terminal age, the very first one was "impure discourse on the dharma" (*buqing shuo fa*) and the third was "to praise or malign the strengths and weaknesses of the Three Jewels and the Three Vehicles" (Yabuki 1927, 115.15–116.2). All study and disputation in the third stage became slander against the Buddha.

This injunction to silence and the avoidance of doctrinal discussion or dispute appeared in many other forms. The section in the *Duigen qixing fa* on "seeking spiritual masters" during the third stage listed three types of men of good knowledge: the "'mute sheep monk' who understood neither words nor meaning," the "'mute sheep monk' who understood the words but not the meaning," and the man of acute faculties who through recognizing the character of the age imitated the "mute sheep monk" (Yabuki 1927, 124.9–125.3). The model of the perfect spiritual master was a mute monk who could not understand the meaning of texts, and one who through study came to understand the needs of his own age could only hope to imitate this "mute sheep."

No surviving text explains the meaning of "mute sheep," but the biography of the unnamed master contains several passages pertaining to the virtues of muteness. The master placed tremendous stress on not speaking, and indeed taught that the mouth should not be opened:

> When the master presented the Dharma and [rules of] conduct to his disciples, he forbade them all to open their mouths and had them remain silent like dead men. Even if it reached the point that they were beaten or killed, even if they passed through a thousand deaths, ten thousand

> deaths, or a million deaths, they could not speak to defend themselves. If subjected to all sorts of punishments, they could not speak to defend themselves. The only exception was that they could open their mouths to eat. This continued to the ends of their lives, and then they died like wild beasts.[19]

This teaching was so central that it was elaborated in full twice. Moreover, one disciple in the course of a confession remarked that in the three years since she had last seen the master she had opened her mouth not in wasteful speech but only to eat one meal a day (Ōtani 1938, 302.309). A list of those things that disciples had to renounce as part of their beggar's existence included "all fine expositions," "all commentaries on texts and catechisms," and "all flowery knowledge and ornamented words" (301.284–.285). These passages show that the reference to a "Buddhadharma cutting off all speech" was not simply hyperbole.

Several other passages in the text show that this ban on speech was not simply a form of discipline but grew out of the aforementioned fear of all exposition of the Law in the terminal age. One typical story relates how a group of men came from the city and asked the master to talk about the deviant and correct dharmas. The master replied that men had different understandings and practices, and he could not say which were correct. When pressed to reply he offered a parable of a cock who saw that a fox had entered his shed and did not dare to call out lest he attract attention to himself and be eaten. The master compared himself to the cock; as a common man of no perception he could not speak on deviance and correctness without destroying himself (Ōtani 1938, 290.111–.121). People, the master argued, used their mouths to swear the oath to renounce body and life in order to accord with the Dharma. He imposed silence on his disciples as a sign of these vows, and in doing so he also prevented them from harming the Dharma.[20] This ideal of muteness clearly entailed a condemnation of all scholasticism and textual exposition.

The reference to "sheep" is less clear. At least one text often quoted in the works of the sect used sheep as the image of stupidity or ignorance, but a passage in the biography of the unnamed master suggests another line of argument.[21] Someone asked the master to explain the significance of wearing a sheepskin garment and carrying a single gourd, which was apparently the master's standard apparel, and he explained that it was useful to guard against the wind and rain (Ōtani 1938, 296.212–.213). Thus the "sheep" may refer to the humble but sturdy garb worn by the adherents of the sect in their travels and on begging rounds. Another passage tells of a man who wore only a tattered garment, carried a gourd, and would not speak with men. He would only shout loudly: "I deeply reverence all of you and do not dare to disparage you. You are all walking the Way of the bodhisattvas and will become buddhas"

(285.40–.43). This strange figure, who was clearly imitating the Bodhisattva Never-Disparaging and hence was a follower of the Three Stages sect, was perhaps the very image of the "mute sheep monk."

Other evidence indicating that the Three Stages sect denied the efficacy of the conventional canon comes from the writings of hostile schools. In one story, Xiaoci (d.u.), a preacher from the Three Stages sect, told a group of women lay devotees that they would go to hell if they studied the sūtras, especially the *Lotus Sūtra*. Many of the women agreed to give up this sūtra, but one had reservations about abandoning her studies and devotions. She declared that if to chant the sūtra was truly against Buddhism, may anyone who did so contract a terrible illness and be reborn in hell; but if it were not against Buddhism, then may the same happen to the preacher. As soon as she finished speaking, the preacher and his associates were struck dumb.[22]

A vigorous polemic against the Three Stages sect was also conducted by the followers of the Pure Land sect (Yabuki 1927, 547-82). One of the chief issues of this debate was the continued efficacy of scriptures in the terminal age. The adherents of the Pure Land sect held that, through the special grace of the Buddha, the *Wuliangshou jing* still had spiritual potency in the first half of the third stage. This position was denounced by the Three Stages sect, and as a Pure Land spokesman pointed out, this denial of the efficacy of any scriptures led inevitably to the conclusion that "the subtle and wondrous canon of the Great Vehicle no longer circulated in the world" (Yabuki 1927, 559, citing the *Chun yi lun*). Although one cannot place complete reliance on the polemics of rival schools, the accusation that the Three Stages sect denied the efficacy of studying or chanting scriptures closely matches the arguments in the texts of the sect itself.

Thus the Three Jewels, as recognized and invoked by traditional Buddhism, were all declared to be null and void in the terminal age. The ultimate expression of the Three Stages sect's rejection of traditional Buddhism was the doctrine that the beings of the third stage could not be saved by the five ways (*wuzhong bujiu*). These five roads to salvation were the Buddha, the Dharma, the monastic order, the deliverance of other sentient beings, and the cultivation of good/removal of evil.[23] The inability of these five to save the sentient beings of the terminal age is proclaimed on the first page of the *Sanjie fofa* and recurs periodically throughout the text. This doctrine was nothing less than a declaration of the bankruptcy of traditional Buddhism as a path to salvation and as a source of religious power. In this manner the Three Stages sect proclaimed the end of the old order and the rise of a new form of religion, in which the official Sangha, with its codes of discipline, meditative practices, and scholastic pursuits, was to be replaced by a new religious body that joined monks and laymen in the mute practice of universal austerities, begging, and *dāna* (Kaneko 1959).

The Suppression of the Sect

In light of the foregoing, we can now reassess the reasons for the suppression of the school. The accepted explanation was first offered by Yabuki Keiki (1926), who argued that in declaring the corruption of human character and mores in the Final Age of the Dharma, the Three Stages sect challenged the efficacy and legitimacy of all government. Kenneth Ch'en offers a good summation of this position:

> Moreover, its contention that the contemporary age was one of decay, in which people were depraved, lawless, and blinded by folly, was entirely unacceptable to the rulers, who looked upon their dynasty as responsible for the prosperity and well-being of the people. In addition, they further alienated the sympathies of the rulers by stating that in the age of decay no government existed which was worthy of the respect of the people, and that the present dynasty was incapable of restoring the religion or leading the people to salvation. (Ch'en 1964, 300)

This argument, however, has several weaknesses. First, as already pointed out, the doctrine of the disappearance of the Dharma was a theory of decay in religious practice and perceptions; it did not comment on the mores of society at large or the possibilities of secular law. In the classic Indian accounts of the end of the Dharma (also discussed earlier), lay society and the state not only maintained proper order but even continued to perform their assigned religious functions; it was the monks who became lax and corrupt.

Assertions of the possibility and even the virtue of government in the third stage are not restricted to Indian texts. In several places the *Xiangfa jueyi jing* calls upon the ruler to punish the corrupt men who destroy the Buddhadharma and to encourage those who do good. Thus the text urged the authorities in the terminal age to beat and exile all those who sold Buddhist images or scriptures to make money. Another passage says that in the third stage the ruler, his ministers, local officials, and elders had to encourage monks and laity to pity and save all sentient creatures, and that they should use their powers to prevent evil men from doing harm. If they performed these roles, it states, they would gain "inexhaustible merit."[24] Clearly the authors of this text, which was often cited as authoritative by the Three Stages sect, did not believe that the passing of the Dharma rendered impossible the legitimate rule of kings.

Another text, the *Dehu zhangzhe jing* ("Sūtra of Elder Śrīgupta"; Śrīgupta was an elder of Rājagṛha who plotted to murder Śākyamuni with fire and poison but was then converted through the Buddha's miracles), even contained a prophecy that in the terminal age of the Dharma a great king would arise who would lead all the creatures of his land into the Buddha's Way and thereby plant good seeds for their future lives.[25] References in other texts show that this story was widely known, and it was used to praise Emperor Wen of the Sui (r. 589–604) for his efforts to restore Buddhism after the suppression under the Northern Zhou (Ōchō 1958, 1: 377-79). Once again, no necessary connection was perceived between the decay of the Dharma and the possibility or quality of rule. Indeed, the king might actually become even more virtuous and religiously potent as he took on the role once assigned to the now decayed Sangha.

Moreover, the texts of the Three Stages sect themselves positively affirmed the efficacy of lordship in the terminal age. At the end of his testament, Xinxing stated that his unceasing pursuit of buddhahood would both benefit the myriad creatures and also aid the king and state.[26] The *Sanjie fofa* likewise contains an extended discussion of proper kingship that deals primarily with the question of how the ruler's punishments ought to adapt to each stage in the decline of the Dharma (Yabuki 1927, 273.7–283.3). For example, in the second stage the king could force those monks who broke the precepts to return to lay life, but he could not beat or execute them. In the third stage, however, he could impose the five kinds of "light punishments," including expulsion from a monastery, a city, or even the state. He could also still inflict corporal punishment on the laity in the third stage (279.2–.9). One passage even provided an extended justification of the king's taking life in the course of wars to defend the state and the people in the Final Age of the Dharma (283.1–285.1). In fact, the writings of the sect never questioned the need for a ruler to uphold the Law at any stage of the disappearance of the Dharma, and such attacks on government as they made were devoted to criticism of the alliance of the state with an official monastic order.

Yet another weakness of the accepted interpretation of the suppression of the sect is that it does not account for what actually took place. The proscription of the Three Stages sect was not completed by a single act of government, nor was it the consistent policy of all rulers. The sect became prominent during the Sui, and it was first condemned in 600 by the founding ruler of that dynasty, the Emperor Wen (r. 581–604). However, this initial ban did not lead to the disappearance, or even the long-term decline, of the sect. In fact, both Yabuki Keiki and Tsukamoto Zenryū have identified the seventh century as the period in which the sect flourished and reached its apogee (Yabuki 1927, 62-63; Tsukamoto 1975a, 198). Between the decree of 600 and similar decrees in 695 and 699 under Wu Zetian (r. 690–705) declaring its writings to be apocryphal and banning all practices that differed from those of conventional monks, the Chinese government made no recorded moves against the sect. Several monasteries in the capital were dominated by the sect; its texts circulated and were cited in various Buddhist catalogues as well as in the usually hostile writings of other schools; and its Inexhaustible Treasury became the nexus of an empire-wide system of charity. It is difficult to believe that, for almost a century, a sect of such high visibility could have proclaimed a doctrine that was believed to deny the virtue or efficacy of all government without eliciting a response from a dynasty that was then at the peak of its military power and international prestige.

In fact, as Yabuki himself has noted, only three rulers carried out active policies to suppress the school and its teachings: Emperor Wen of the Sui, Empress Wu, and Emperor Xuanzong of the Tang (r. 712–756). To explain this phenomenon, Yabuki has suggested that these three were dynamic, aggressive rulers who resented the Three Stages sect's advocacy of the virtue of "drawing in the head" (*su tou*, i.e., refusing to act as a leader) (Yabuki 1926, 53). This suggestion, however, is highly implausible. First, it is unlikely that monastic calls for humility, any more than those for boundless charity or for ceasing to take life, would have elicited the rulers' notice, much less their active hostility. Second, *su tou* is neither a central teaching of the sect nor distinctive to it, and the standard Buddhist call for "withdrawal from the world" would have been far more threatening to rulers if they thought it applied to themselves. However, the strictures on *su tou* were explicitly applied only to householders and monks, while the necessity of having rulers, as noted above, was fully acknowledged.[27] Finally, this explanation would scarcely account for the indifference to the sect of the emperors Gaozu (r. 618–627) and Taizong (r. 627–650), who were also, by any standards, dynamic and aggressive rulers.

The single factor uniting Emperor Wen, Empress Wu, and Emperor Xuanzong was that all three were patrons of the official Buddhist Order. They all established official, state-sponsored monasteries distributed in accord with the divisions of the empire, wherein official monks performed ceremonies, meditation, and prayers to mobilize the forces of the spirit world in support of the empire and the ruling house. They likewise sponsored the translation of texts and the production of official catalogues of the Buddhist canon that adjudicated their authenticity. The teachings of the Three Stages sect explicitly denied that the official monastic order and the teachings it preserved had any special spiritual potency or significance. Moreover, as Kaneko Hidetoshi has shown, many of the passages added to the *Xiangfa jueyi jing* by monks of the Three Stages sect to compose the *Foshuo shi suofanzhe yujie fajing jing* ("Book Spoken by the Buddha on the Yoga Dharma Mirror that Exposes Transgressors"; see Forte 1990) explicitly denounced monks who became the adherents of civil officials (Kaneko 1959, 49). Finally, with its call for the negation of all distinctions, the Three Stages sect challenged the rulers' right to declare the supreme truth and to justify their rule through the defense of that truth and the honoring of its presumptive masters. Since the sect spoke from a Buddhist perspective and aimed its criticisms specifically at the Buddhist Sangha, this challenge was felt most clearly by monarchs who made the patronage of the traditional Buddhist Order a significant element in their claims to power.

Emperor Wen was just such a ruler. He repeated constantly that he owed his throne to the Buddhadharma, and he strove to drape himself in the trappings of a bodhisattva and *cakravartin* king. With his bodhisattva vows, his sponsoring of state monasteries, his construction of stūpas in imitation of Aśoka, his mass ordination of monks, and his sponsorship of the copying of sūtras, Emperor Wen made Buddhist symbols and the Buddhist Order a fundamental part of his restored empire. Consequently, he could brook no challenges to them.

The early Tang rulers, however, merely tolerated Buddhism and offered it limited patronage—largess to all varieties of subjects being part of the imperial role and the prestige of Buddhism at every level of society being impossible to ignore—but they granted priority in all religious matters to Daoism (Weinstein 1973, 265-67; 1987, 5-37). Some people have sought to claim the second Tang emperor, Taizong, as a supporter of Buddhism on the basis of his generosity toward Xuanzang (ca. 596–664) and claims in the biography of the latter for a near conversion of the aging emperor, but in fact throughout his reign he followed his father's policy of granting ritual priority and more generous patronage to Daoism. Moreover, in a decree that he wrote with his own hand to an ardent Buddhist descendant of the old Chen ruling house, Taizong derided the folly of those who supported a faith which had led every dynasty that adopted it—the Liang, Chen, and Sui—to rapid collapse.[28] From the founding of the Tang to the establishment of the Zhou dynasty by Empress Wu, Buddhism held an adjunct, secondary position in the spiritual hierarchy of the Chinese realm.

Empress Wu, however, granted unquestioned supremacy to Buddhism. Her attempt to rule in her own person rather than through a child emperor, a practice that violated every precept and precedent of the Chinese imperial tradition, found moral justification, intellectual support, and religious sanction only in Buddhism and the Buddhist Order. Consequently, her intellectual and textual claims to rule were founded solely on the Buddhist canon. In his study of the *Dayun jing* ("Great Cloud Sūtra") and related documents, Antonino Forte has with great skill and impressive command of detail reconstructed Wu Zetian's textual campaign to claim for herself the titles of bodhisattva, *cakravartin*, and future buddha (Forte 1976). For such a ruler, any claims that the old had passed, that the monastic order was hopelessly worldly and corrupt, and that the texts of the canon were no longer spiritually potent or authoritative constituted a mortal challenge. A *cakravartin* needed a Dharma and a monastic order in order to fulfill his or her role:

> The Buddhist conception makes the universalistic assertion that dharma (in its manifold aspects as cosmic law that regulates the world totality and as the truth embodied in the Buddha's teaching that shows

> the path to liberation) is the absolutely encompassing norm and that the code of kingship embodying righteousness (dharma) has its source in this dharma and is ideally a concrete manifestation of it in the conduct of worldly affairs . . . The Buddhist position is that dharma informs and suffuses the code of conduct of the righteous ruler and, moreover, that it is his ruling activities (in the domain of political economy) that give form to society . . . The Buddhist slicing is in terms of two levels—the dharma, as cosmic law and as truth (the seeker of which is the renouncing *bhikkhu*), encompassing the dharma of the righteous ruler, which attempts to give order to this world. The former brackets the latter. (Tambiah 1976, 40)

The righteousness of the Buddhist ruler was encompassed by, and found its meaning only within, the higher Dharma of the Buddhist Order. Although for most Chinese rulers the Buddhist ideal of the *cakravartin* king was only an adjunct to or expansion of the indigenous Chinese ideal of the cosmically potent sage-king, for Empress Wu it was absolutely crucial to her claims to rule.

For this reason, Empress Wu and her advisors were acutely aware of the danger posed by the doctrine of the disappearance of the dharma. This is shown by the fact that in one forgery they inserted a passage in which the Buddha predicted that Devaputra, i.e., Empress Wu, would be reborn in China shortly before the end of Śākyamuni's dharma. After restoring it to its full efficacy, she would rule through the true Buddhadharma (Forte 1976, 130).

In these circumstances it was impossible for Wu Zetian not to act against a heresy that undercut her claim to rulership, and the publication of a new comprehensive bibliography of scriptures in 695 provided her with the opportunity to strike. According to the editors of the *Da Zhou kanding zhongjing mulu* ("Catalogue of Scriptures, Authorized by the Great Zhou Dynasty"), they received a decree in 694 that all apocryphal writings and prophetic texts were to be sent to the Department of National Sacrifices and stored away. In fact, this decree was primarily employed to blacklist the writings of the Three Stages sect (Forte 1976, 166-67). In 699 the members of the sect were also forbidden to engage in any practices except for begging for food, fasting, abstaining from grains, keeping the precepts, and sitting in meditation. All practices different from those of ordinary monks were banned.

The very form of this suppression demonstrates that the issue was not direct subversion of the ruler but denial of the monastic order, orthodox doctrine, and conventional Buddhist practice. It was carried out by "official Buddhists" and consisted entirely of banning texts deemed hostile to the official canon and practices deemed inimical to the traditional Way of the Buddhist Order.

The sect was not treated as a rebel movement but as a heresy, for its only defiance of the ruler had taken the form of a spiritual challenge to her right to define the ultimate truth, to support official organs for the propagation of that truth, and to rule as the patron of and defender of the Buddhadharma. The accusation levied against the writings was not that they were seditious but rather that they were apocryphal, not that they challenged the ruler but that they called into question the spiritual authority of the Sangha. However, for a would-be *cakravartin* or patron of official Buddhism, the questions of textual authenticity and orthodoxy of practice inevitably became political questions.

Emperor Xuanzong essentially continued the policies of Empress Wu, although, as Professor Forte (1990) shows, he may have had the added motive that a leader of the Three Stages sect was associated with the participants in a conspiracy to poison him at the beginning of his reign. In 713, the year after the conspiracy, he banned the Inexhaustible Treasury and the associated separate chambers for the monks of the Three Stages sect. This move both extended Empress Wu's ban on all distinctive practices by the sect and provided the new emperor with a huge financial windfall. In 730, a new imperial canon excluded the works of the sect, but this likewise simply carried forward the policies of Empress Wu. Although he was not an avid patron of Buddhism and restored the priority of Daoism, Xuanzong continued the practice of supporting a network of official monasteries in the capital and provinces to earn merit and spiritual potency for the empire. Moreover, he became deeply interested in the use of the magical techniques of Esoteric Buddhism to secure and expand his power and that of his state. For this reason he patronized a coterie of monks at his court and supported the translation of numerous scriptures (Weinstein 1987, 51-57). The hostile activities of the sect at the time of his accession, their attacks on the official Buddhism which he supported, and the precedent of Empress Wu are sufficient to account for his policy of suppression.

After the reign of Xuanzong there are no further records of attempts to suppress the sect. As Yabuki Keiki has noted, the strongest evidence for the prestige and influence of the sect consists of the repeated government attempts to suppress it and the frequent hostile stories and polemics in the writings of other schools (Yabuki 1927, 104). The cessation of these suppressions and attacks in the second half of the eighth century suggests that with the abolition of the Inexhaustible Treasury, the banning of all distinctive practices, and the decades-long suppression of their texts, the sect lost most of its importance and popular appeal. Although there are scattered records until the end of the Tang of activities by adherents of the sect, it appears that they no longer posed a radical challenge to official Buddhism. Indeed, in 800 the writings of the sect were even temporarily included in a catalogue of the

Buddhist canon prepared by a Vinaya master who apparently saw in their denunciations of monastic corruption a useful spur for a program of renewed discipline (Yabuki 1927, 93-94). But such tentative gestures at reconciliation and absorption probably had more to do with the sect's decline than with any acceptance of its doctrine by official Buddhism, and within a century all traces of the sect's activity had vanished, just as its writings disappeared from later editions of the canon.

Conclusion

The fate of the Three Stages sect, and the political aspect of all adjudications of textual authenticity in Chinese Buddhism, can best be understood as one element in the project of a Buddhist empire in China. For several centuries, a series of monarchs attempted to renovate the Chinese political order by building an explicitly Buddhist state, a state that justified itself at least in part through its patronage of Buddhism. Central to these attempts was the creation of an official Buddhist establishment, housed in state temples, performing rituals for the benefit of the ruling house and the empire, and compiling massive, officially approved collections of canonical texts. As the chief patron of such an establishment, the Chinese sage-emperor added to his traditional cosmic role as the earthly double of Heaven a new aspect as *cakravartin* king, the supreme defender of the dharma.

In this context the Buddhist canon became charged with the same political character that infused the traditional Chinese classics; the sūtras joined the other sacred texts whose dictates offered the state its form and whose defense gave the state its purpose. This "politicization" of Buddhist texts was most intense in the reigns of those monarchs who craved or needed the trappings of the *cakravartin*, but it was a general tendency of the entire medieval period. As Erik Zürcher has noted, throughout these centuries all texts that might have been included in the canon were regularly scrutinized, and any doctrines that challenged the interpretations of the official monastic order and their imperial patrons were suppressed as "heretical" (Zürcher 1982a, 163-64). When the Three Stages sect proclaimed the bankruptcy of traditional monastic Buddhism and suggested a new path to salvation, its adherents had not declared an explicitly political program. But for those who aspired to create a Buddhist empire and an imperial Buddhism, this was a political question. Since imperial authority was defined in part by adherence to and defense of a prescribed body of texts, the right to declare textual truth and authenticity was a fundamental aspect of government. In such a realm, the preaching of apocrypha became a form of treason.

Glossary

Bei Xuanzheng	悲玄證
bie	別
boshi	博士
bu qing pusa	不輕菩薩
bu qing shuo fa	不清說法
Chang'an	長安
chang qi shi	常乞食
chengxiang	丞相
Da Zhou kanding zhongjing mulu	大周刊定眾經目錄
Daban niepan jing	大般涅槃經
Dayun jing	大雲經
Daoxuan	道宣
Dehu zhangzhe jing	德護長者經
diandao	顛倒
Dong Zhongshu	董仲舒
Duigen qixing fa	對根起行法
fang deng	方等
Faxiang	法相
Fozang jing	佛藏經
Gaosengzhuan	高僧傳
Gongsun Hong	公孫弘
Han shu	漢書
Huadu si	華度寺
Huaigan	懷感
Huayan	華嚴
Jia Yi	賈宜
Jinguangming jing	金光明經
jing	經
jing[a]	徑
Jingying Huiyuan	淨影慧遠
Jizang	吉藏
Kuiji	窺基
Liu Xin	劉歆
Lü zong	律宗
mofa	末法
po jie po jian	破戒破見
pu	普
ren e	任惡

Renwang jing	仁王經
Sanjie fofa	三階佛法
Sanjie fofa miji	三階佛法密記
sheng mang	生盲
sutou	縮頭
Tiantai	天台
Xiaoci	孝慈
xie jian	邪見
Xinxing	信行
Xu gaosengzhuan	續高僧傳
Xuanzang	玄奘
wu jin zang	無盡藏
Wuliang shou jing	無量壽經
wuzhong bujiu	五種不救
Yao Xing	姚興
yi	藝
ying shen	應身
zhen shen	真身
Zhiyi	智顗

Notes

1. *Gaoseng zhuan* 2, in *Taishō* 2059.50.332a16-25, cited in Tang 1955, 290.
2. This fact was particularly striking in the case of Zhiyi, whose teacher Huisi, a noted advocate of meditation and religious discipline, believed that the world had entered the Final Age of Dharma (*mofa*) and described events in terms of the eclipse of the Buddhist religion. Convinced of the corruption of the Sangha of his day, he vowed to make a copy of the *Mahāprajñāpāramitā-sūtra* in gold letters and store it in a gem-encrusted box to preserve the true teaching. This vow became the prototype for all those who sought to carve the Buddhist canon in stone to preserve it in anticipation of the coming of the future Buddha Maitreya. See Tsukamoto 1938; Michihata 1944, 102-106. His student Zhiyi, by contrast, systematically ignored the idea of *mofa*, and in his commentaries on works that mentioned the end of the Dharma he deliberately distorted the sense of the relevant passages to avoid any mention of the doctrine.
3. See also *Xu Gaoseng zhuan* 20, in *Taishō* 2060.50.596a23-26ff.
4. On the shared historical background and beliefs of these two sects, see Tsukamoto 1975a, 193-94, 144-46; 1975b, 134-75; 1975c, 71-77; Yabuki 1927, 203, 535-78; Tajima 1940; Michihata 1934; Yagi 1942; 1943; Tokiwa 1928.
5. See, for example, *Duigen qixing fa* 131.12-.13, 139.13 and *Pufa si fo* 201-206, both in Yabuki 1927. On the identity of the "eight buddhadharmas" and the idea of universal buddhahood in the writings of the Three Stages sect, see Kimura 1978.
6. *Sanjie fofa* 257.1-.2, 333.14-334.2 and *Duigen qixing fa* 129.11-130.4, 133.10-.12, 149.11-150.2, both in Yabuki 1927.
7. *Duigen qixing fa,* in Yabuki 1927, 111.15-112.1, 113.8, 114.14-115.56.
8. The biography of the anonymous master of the sect also includes a denunciation of

those who would practice monastic discipline and meditation in the age of the terminal dharma. See Ōtani 1938, 295.203-296.205.

9. *Duigen qixing fa*, in Yabuki 1927, 121.13-124.9.
10. For example, a discussion of "taking refuge in the monastic order" during the third age divided the monks into five types, only one of which was "those who shave their heads and wear the *kaṣāya*," i.e., officially ordained monks (*Duigen qixing fa*, in Yabuki 1927, 115.9-.10). One of the five dichotomies in a discussion of "universal conduct" was that between "those who have left the world" and "those who remain in the world." The text stipulates that regardless of whether or not a man has left the world to become a monk, he should think of himself as in the world, i.e., as a layman. In contrast, he should look upon all others, regardless of their status, as if they had left the world (130.14-131.1). One account of the world after the disappearance of the Dharma says, "Creatures of the dullest faculties will exhort all to conversion and the management of the affairs of the monastic order; together with those who have left the household they will be preceptors (*heshang*) and *ācāryas*" (*Sanjie fofa*, in Yabuki 1927, 264.4-.5). Another passage says, "After the one thousand years during which the Dharma is brilliant, the Dharma of the Four Noble Truths will be extinguished, and the *kaṣāyas* will turn white and no longer take the color of the dye" (74.2-.3). Since the saffron dye of the monks' robes distinguished them from the white-clothed laity, white *kaṣāyas* would mark the disappearance of a separate monastic order.
11. *Sanjie fofa*, in Yabuki 1927, 364.1-.5.
12. Ōtani 1938, 295.192-.196. This passage does not appear in the version of the *Fozang jing* in the *Taishō* edition of the Tripiṭaka.
13. *Xu gaoseng zhuan* 16, in *Taishō* 2060.50.560a9-10
14. *Xinxing yiwen*, in Yabuki 1927, 7.8-.10.
15. *Duigen qixing fa*, in Yabuki 1927, 133.10-.12, 149.11-150.2.
16. *Daban niebanjing* 18, in *Taishō* 374.12.472b7-10.
17. *Sanjie fofa*, in Yabuki 1927, 266.14-267.4.
18. Yabuki 1927, 75.4-.8, citing *Daban niepanjing* 33, in *Taishō* 374.12.561c10-13.
19. Ōtani 1938, 297.220-.223. "Died like wild beasts" may refer to dying in silence, or it could refer to the sect's practice of exposing corpses in the wild to allow animals to feed on them—in imitation of the Jātaka tale of the Buddha and the hungry tigers—and then retrieving the bones for burial.
20. Ōtani 1938, 298.237-.239. This passage is framed by two stories on the value of silence. One tells of a man who hid a pearl in his wife's mouth to keep it from a thief, but the thief hid under the bed, tricked the wife into speaking, and thus gained the pearl. The second tells of a disciple who studied the sūtras and Abhidharma for years without attaining enlightenment. He was about to ask the master for help, and in the moment of silence before speaking he suddenly perceived the truth.
21. *Fozang jing* 1, in *Taishō* 653.15.789a12, 24.
22. *Shimen zijing lu* 1, in *Taishō* 2083.15.806b3-23.
23. *Duigen qixing fa*, in Yabuki 1927, 116.13, 134.10-135.3, 257.7ff.
24. *Xiangfa jueyi jing*, in *Taishō* 2870.85.1337c27-1338a2; 1338a10-20.
25. *Dehu zhangzhe jing* 2, in *Taishō* 545.14.849b20-24.
26. *Xinxing yiwen*, in Yabuki 1927, 7.11.
27. The passage on "drawing in the head" states, "In the household you will not be head or take a government office . . . after leaving the household you will not be a master of men or a master of the dharma." See *Duigen qixing fa*, in Yabuki 1927, 124.12-.14. Clearly neither of these strictures applied to rulers who were neither simple "householders" nor monks.
28. Chen 1971, 306-307. For the argument that Taizong was not an active patron of the Buddhist Order, see also Wright 1973, 247, 252-56, 258-63.

6

Budda no fukuin: The Deployment of Paul Carus's *Gospel of Buddha* in Meiji Japan

Judith Snodgrass

Within months of its American release, Paul Carus's *The Gospel of Buddha* had been translated by D. T. Suzuki and published in Japan with a Preface and endorsement by Rinzai Zen abbot Shaku Sōen.[1] This book, *Budda no fukuin*, a conscientiously literal translation of the original text, was imbued with the political concerns of Meiji Japan. Contrary to the assumption of Carus's biographers, the reason for the publication was not that Carus was "one to whom Buddhists throughout the world looked for source material and instruction in their own religion" (Fader 1982, 141), but rather its strategic value in the discourse on Meiji religion. The content of the book, though of use to the reform movement, was of secondary importance to the publication's strategic function in the cause of Buddhist revival.

Carus's work was archetypically Orientalist, appropriating Buddhism to promote his post-Kantian Christian monism, and, as will be shown later, there is no question that Japanese reform Buddhists were fully aware of the shortcomings of the work as a representation of Buddhism. Its value to them lay in attracting the attention of the Western-educated elite of the nation, introducing them to Buddhist ideas presented in a form acceptable by Western standards, and reassuring them of Western intellectual interest in and approval of their indigenous religion. A most important feature of the book was the Western status of its author. As a German philosopher he illustrated reform claims that Western intellectuals were finding Christianity inadequate and were turning to Japanese Buddhism as the religion of the modern world.

The relationship between Paul Carus and Shaku Sōen, and the intellectual consequences of this on the work of D. T. Suzuki, are well documented, but tend to focus on Suzuki's later career. This early event in the history of Suzuki's connection with Carus is relevant in illustrating its political origins. My own research focus is the discursive interaction between Japan and the West in the formation of Western knowledge of Buddhism. The Asian publication of Carus's work—it was also published in a number of other Buddhist countries—was a major factor in the enduring reputation of the book and its author, and the principal reason the book is still circulating as a source of popular knowledge of Buddhism to this day. Every copy, every notice or review from 1895 to the current edition carries the testimony: "The best evidence that this book characterizes the spirit of Buddhism correctly can be found in the welcome it has received throughout the entire Buddhist world" (Carus [1917] 1973, vi). This paper first characterizes Carus's book, then describes its function in the Meiji Buddhist revival to explain its apparent endorsement by Japanese Buddhists.

Paul Carus and *The Gospel of Buddha*

Paul Carus was an American philosopher, editor, and publisher, remembered now as a pioneer in introducing Oriental religion to America and for his incidental role in the transmission of Zen to the West through his connection with D. T. Suzuki.[2] He was born in Germany to a devout Christian family. He obtained his PhD in mathematics and philosophy in Tübingen. In 1887 he migrated to the United States, where he became editor and publisher of *The Open Court*. From the time he arrived in America Carus devoted his life to his mission of resolving the religious crisis of the nineteenth century: the perceived conflict between religion and science. His solution was to restructure Christianity around a new conception of the nature of self, a psychological and scientific conception that he described in his book *The Soul of Man* (1890). He founded *The Open Court*, a weekly journal, with the intention of propagating these ideas. As the masthead of the journal tells us, it was "Devoted to the Work of Conciliating Religion and Science." This project was his life's work. In 1890 he founded a second journal, *The Monist*, which presented similar material at a more philosophical and technical level. Carus himself contributed regularly. His personal output was prodigious. He wrote more than a thousand articles and about fifty book-length monographs covering a wide range of subjects, all without exception related to his mission of reconciling religion and science. While he was working on *The Gospel of Buddha*, Carus published a number of articles, such as "Karma and Nirvāna" and "Buddhism and Christianity," explicitly making these connections. The popularization of these ideas was the task of *The Gospel of Buddha*. The book was therefore an archetypical example of Orientalism, the appropriation of the Orient—Buddhism and the life of the Buddha—to support a decidedly Western and Christian project.

Carus declared in the Preface that the book was not intended to popularize Buddhism. It had been written "to set the reader a-thinking about the religious problems of today and become a factor in the formation of the future." In spite of its title, *The Gospel of Buddha* was written to propagate Carus's post-Kantian Christian religion of science. Carus believed that it was the duty of all true believers to proselytize. There are two reasons for this, both characteristically scientific. The first was his conviction that universal truth would be revealed by comparison. The second was based on evolutionary theory. Since evolution depended on the struggle for existence and the survival of the fittest, Carus believed that progress toward the ultimate universal religion would be hastened by bringing protagonists into greater proximity through active missionary work. He was particularly interested in Buddhism because he genuinely admired it and had no doubt that it was the only possible contender against Christianity for the role of the religion of the future. Comparison and competition with Buddhism in the minds of a Christian audience would force the evolution of Christianity to its inevitable and ultimate perfection.

However, Carus principally appreciated Buddhism because he recognized his own monistic ideas in several Buddhist concepts. From the nineteenth-century orthodox Christian viewpoint both monism and Buddhism were accused of being nihilistic since they challenged the Christian conception of soul and the nature of God, upon which the major religious issues of free will, ethics, and morality depended. Carus used Buddhism to argue the viability of this alternative world view, to unsettle the "popular conceptions of a Creator God and an ego soul" that were considered "the indispensable foundations of all religion" (Carus 1890, 419). One problem was that Carus's monism was unquestionably Christian. He had to argue, therefore, that Buddhism and Christianity were essentially the same. His most radical declaration of this identity was his hypothesis that Jesus Christ was actually Maitreya, the Buddha of the future. To substantiate his argument, Carus used a Chinese reference that predicted the coming of the Buddha Maitreya 5,000 years after Śākyamuni (Carus refers to Eitel 1888, 92). Since Śākyamuni is believed to have lived in the sixth century BCE, by slipping a zero—thereby making the prediction 500 years—Carus concluded that the advent of the Christian Messiah coincided closely enough to fulfill this prophesy. "Christians may be said to worship Maitreya under the name of Christ" (Carus 1897, 195).

Carus's vision of Śākyamuni was equally unorthodox. The Buddha was not only the prototypical Christ, he was also the world's first logical positivist, the first humanist, the first teacher of the religion of science. However, the point is not to indicate errors of scholarship but to demonstrate the author's remarkable control of the text in pursuit of his purpose. The full title, *The Gospel of Buddha, Compiled from old records, as told by Paul Carus*, presented the book as nothing more than a short version of the Buddhist canon; the truth of the life of the Buddha—the gospel truth with all the colloquial connotations of the term—in the same way that the Christian Gospels, upon which the text was modeled, was the truth of the life of Christ. The religious nature of the work was signaled to his Christian audience by the familiar form of chapter and verse, and the King James style of language he purposely adopted.

The Preface, like the title, attempted to efface the presence of the author, stressing the book's reliance on the canon, claiming that many passages, indeed the most important ones, were literally copied. It admitted to modifications, the "trimming of needless repetitions and adornments," but reassured the reader that there was nothing in the book for which prototypes could not be found in the traditions of Buddhism. Carus scandalized his academic contemporaries by dipping indiscriminately into texts ranging over about 2,000 years and belonging to several different cultural traditions.

However, the claim that the book is merely a compilation hardly does justice to what is in fact a most ingenious original composition, a skillfully articulated deployment of a very idiosyncratic interpretation. Carus's claim that the most important passages are copied is not exactly incorrect—just misleading. Carus used the Buddhist texts in a number of ways. Some chapters of the *Gospel* are extensively copied from Buddhist sources, but often with a revised ending that attaches a new lesson to the familiar story. Other chapters begin with a short quote from a canonical text, which is then developed by Carus to form the body of the chapter. Again the lesson is Christian monist rather than Buddhist. Elsewhere, various passages from assorted books are strung together like words in a vocabulary creating totally new statements.

This incredible patchwork is nevertheless beautifully stitched into a continuous narrative, a work in prose that consciously aimed to rival Edwin Arnold's famous poem, *The Light of Asia*.[3] Arnold's epic, based on the life of the Buddha, had been spectacularly popular, but it had no authority as the truth of Buddhism. Carus wanted to write a book that would appeal to the general reader, as Arnold's poem did, but with the academic validation that Arnold's work lacked. Hence his stress on the book's reliance on the canon, and the pseudoacademic trappings appended by the author. The biblical format precluded footnotes, but to compensate for this the author appended a "Table of Reference" in which the canonical sources for each chapter of the *Gospel* are indicated by an abbreviation. This is decoded in another table a few pages over. A casual glance reassures the reader that each chapter has a textual reference; that its truth is pinned to the Buddhist texts. But how many readers would have gone on to discover that E. A., the reference for some of the most outstanding passages, stands for "Explanatory Additions" and designates Carus's own original contributions?[4] One imaginative passage carries the reference E. H., which decoding reveals as Eitel's *Handbook of Buddhism* (1888). Few non-specialist readers would have recognized that this was actually a dictionary and that consequently this reference, an explanation of the meaning of one word, is used to validate a whole chapter as canonical. The Table of Reference not only claimed academic legitimation, it concealed the author's considerable personal contribution. The Glossary performs a similar function and it is here, along with the definitions of Buddhist names and terms, complete with diacritical marks, that we find the entry "Mahāse'tu, the great bridge. A name invented by the author of the present book to designate the importance of Christianity compared to the Hīnayāna and Mahāyāna of Buddhism" (Carus 1898, 279).

Carus's control of his text is exemplified by the chapter entitled "Maitreya," which is based on the dialogue between the Buddha Śākyamuni and his disciple Ānanda on the eve of the Parinirvāna (ch. 96). The references for the chapter are "MPNv, 1–14, concerning Maitreya see E. H. s.v. Rh. DB. pp. 180, 200; Old; G.p 153 etc." This decodes to 14 verses from T. W. Rhys Davids's *Buddhist Sutras*, another definition from Eitel's dictionary, two pages of T. W. Rhys Davids's *Buddhism*, and one page of Hermann Oldenberg's *Budda, sein Leben, seine Lehre, seine Gemeinde*. The "etc." is presumably intended to suggest that such ideas may be widely found. The chapter supports Carus's conviction that Christ is the Buddha. It opens following the *Mahāparinibbāna Suttanta* closely. Verses 1–3 of the *Gospel* correspond to vv. 3–6. Verses 7–14, that is, the rest of the verses referred to, concern gods and spirits, and have been trimmed as "apocryphal adornments." Carus has used three verses to establish the scene and characters of his own chapter. The content of the chapter thereafter diverges completely except for the repetition of Ānanda's question "Who shall teach us when thou art gone?" (96:12), which Carus uses to allow the Blessed One of his *Gospel* to predict the coming of the Buddhist Christ.

There was, however, a direct connection between the writing of this book and Japanese Buddhism. Carus had been deeply impressed by the Japanese delegates to the World's Parliament of Religions and their presentation of Eastern Buddhism.[5] The delegates, four Buddhist priests and two laymen, were representatives of the Meiji Buddhist revival movement.[6] The Buddhism they presented was a product of this movement, shaped by the imperatives of the institutional, social, and political crises of the early Meiji period, and the need to produce an interpretation of Buddhism appropriate for the new society. By the early 1890s, this Buddhism (*shin bukkyō*) was further determined by the links between Buddhist revival and emerging nationalism. The representation of Buddhism at Chicago, as the delegates planned it, was a strategic statement in the discourse of Buddhist nationalism and was given shape by the tactics and strategies implicit in this project. The Buddhism they presented, Eastern Buddhism as they called it to distance it from the existing Western constructs of Northern and Southern Buddhism, was a rationalized, secular, transsectarian, lay-oriented Buddhism consciously packaged to emphasize its compatibility with science and philosophy—especially philosophic idealism—and to emphasize the life-affirming and humanitarian aspects of Buddhism. It is no surprise, given Carus's own position, that he was particularly impressed by Shaku Sōen's paper. Its title, "The Law of Cause and Effect As Taught by the Buddha," signaled the reconciliation of religion and science; its content, an introduction to the concept of *inga rihō* (Skt. *pratītyasamutpāda*), deliberately challenged orthodox Christian arguments for the necessity of a Creator God (Shaku Sōen 1893).[7] It argued that human morality did not depend on the external authority of "divine wrath" but on self-discipline. This overlap of interests was the basis of the relationship between Carus and Shaku Sōen that led to D. T. Suzuki's presence in the United States working as Carus's assistant. Their friendship alone does not explain, however, why Shaku Sōen, chief abbot of an important Rinzai Zen temple complex and Buddhist scholar of some considerable standing,[8] should apparently endorse Carus's interpretation of Buddhism.

Budda no fukuin: The Japanese Publication

Budda no fukuin was published as a conscientiously literal translation of the original, with a Preface added by Shaku Sōen, a biography of Carus by D. T. Suzuki, and a bibliography of works on Buddhism in Western languages derived from Carus's Table of Reference. In his Preface, Shaku Sōen lists three reasons for the publication:

> Firstly, to make our readers know how much our Buddhism is understood by Western scholars; secondly, to point out a short road for studying Buddhism for the younger generation; thirdly, through the life of Śākyamuni, to sow widely the seeds of the great teaching of Buddhism. (Shaku Sōen 1895a, 280)[9]

The first of these reasons is the most compelling: it is a statement uncommitted to the quality of the work, suggesting "Let the book speak for itself," and carrying the dual implication that this is evidence of the strength of Western interest in our religion, and of the limit of Western understanding on the subject. The second and third reasons indicate that the audience targeted by the publication was the young Western-educated elite who were seeking a religion compatible with modern science and modern Western thought. In other words the book was intended precisely for those who had been interested in Christianity in the earlier decades of the Meiji era, but who were now looking for an indigenous answer to their spiritual needs. These were Japanese in search of the national spirit, who saw the future of Japan in terms of increasing nationalism. Japan was to be recognized as equal to the West in scientific, technological, and intellectual development, but as distinctly non-Western. The Western authorship of the *Gospel* was essential to the force of its communication, and testimony to the truth of Shaku Sōen's claims that "there are signs that the West might welcome Buddhism," even if "there is doubt attached" to whether or not Western scholars have fully understood the "essential principles of Buddhism" (Shaku Sōen 1895a, 280).

The importance of Western interest in Buddhism in the Meiji context of rivalry between Japanese Christians and Buddhists is shown in the address made to the Young Men's Buddhist Association (YMBA) of Yokohama by Shaku Sōen and other delegates to the World's Parliament of Religions shortly after their return from Chicago:

> The Parliament was called because the Western nations have come to realise the weakness and folly of Christianity, and they really wished to hear from us of our religions and to learn what the best religion is. The meeting showed the great superiority of Buddhism over Christianity, and the mere fact of calling the meetings showed that the Americans and other Western peoples had lost their faith in Christianity and were ready to accept the teachings of our superior religion. (Shaku Sōen 1897, 47, quoting a newspaper report from *New York Independent* 1895)[10]

The existence of the *Gospel of Buddha* was further evidence of these claims, which were repeated, though rather more subtly, in Shaku Sōen's Preface. There he connected the achievements of modern science, which had "made the truth more and more clear," with the fact that "there are many signs in the Western civilization that it will welcome Buddhism." Scientific developments were preparing Western minds to receive the truth of Buddhism. Shaku Sōen mentioned the current interest in oriental literature, history, and fine art, and the "new and powerful interest in comparative religion" as indications that "the time is at hand in which Western scholars begin to see how brilliantly our Buddhism shines in all its glory." He further writes that "the World's Parliament of Religions held in America the previous year was a great achievement that was proof of the westward advance of Buddhism" (Suzuki 1895).[11]

It is apparent from the address to the YMBA that Western interest in Buddhism was not only claimed as proof of the value of Buddhism, but was also construed by these Buddhists to imply the failure of Christianity to meet the needs of the modern world. Suzuki's biography of Carus presented him as a specific example of this, relating how Carus, the son of a prominent Christian clergyman, rejected Christianity in favor of Buddhism. The very existence of the *Gospel* was proof of the claim. Moreover, Suzuki's identification of Carus as a German philosopher and man of science challenged the position of those Japanese converts who had turned to Christianity as the natural concomitant of modernization and Westernization.[12]

Carus's book, concerned as it was with the "religion of science," was particularly valuable in Meiji religious debate because it presented Buddhism as the religion of the modern world, a claim that was the foundation of the Buddhist revival movement.[13] The *Gospel* served the Buddhist reform project in several ways. Carus had declared that the aim of the *Gospel* was not "to present Buddhism in its cradle" but to present "Buddhism up to date" in its "nobler possibilities." "It has been written to set the reader a-thinking on the religious problems of today"; it was intended "to become a factor in the formation of the future." This was precisely the aim of reform Buddhists, to establish a place for Buddhism in the modern Japanese state. The *Gospel* supported this project because it presented Buddhism as a religion suited to the modern scientific world view represented by the West, and most importantly, its Western authorship verified the claims that had been made by Japanese scholars such as Inoue Enryō for some years.[14]

Moreover, Carus had made these comments in defense of his use of Mahāyāna sources. The book therefore had added value for Japan in that it accepted the Mahāyāna sūtras as part of the Buddha's "gospel." Shaku Sōen remarked on this as a particular feature of the work (Shaku Sōen 1895a, 280). Western interest in Buddhism, upon which the benefit to the nation in taking Buddhism to the West depended, was at this stage exclusively focused on the construct of Western Pāli scholarship (Snodgrass 1996). Inoue had argued that this was because Westerners so far knew nothing of Japanese Mahāyāna, and that they could not fail to be impressed with its superior truth if it were presented to them. For their part, the delegation to Chicago had presented Japanese Buddhism as Eastern Buddhism, a new category that distanced it from the charges of nihilism leveled at Southern Buddhism by its critics, as well as from the much maligned Northern Buddhism of China and Tibet. To validate their claims that Eastern Buddhism was taught by Śākyamuni during his lifetime—the definition of what could be accepted as Buddhism under the prevailing laws of Western scholarship—they followed Inoue in referring to the Tendai teaching of the *goji* (the Five Periods of the Buddha's teachings), which established that not only were Mahāyāna sūtras indisputably the Buddha's teachings, directly transmitted to the world by Śākyamuni, but that they were his first teaching, his last teaching, and the only complete teaching of his Truth. Pāli Buddhism in this scheme is not only secondary, it is also preliminary and associated with less intellectually developed societies, people of less ability to comprehend the higher truths (Inoue 1887).[15] The question of the relationship of Mahāyāna Buddhism to the historical existence of the Buddha was contentious, and the charge that Japanese Buddhism was not really Buddhism was used by Christians, both foreign and Japanese, to discredit Buddhism (Ketelaar 1990, 3–42).[16] In his summary of the achievements of the delegation, Shaku Sōen mentioned his sense of satisfaction that "the mistaken idea that Mahāyāna Buddhism was not actually the Buddha's teaching had been put to rest" (Shaku Sōen 1895b, 6). Nevertheless, Western denigration of Mahāyāna Buddhism was a problem, and Carus's support most welcome.

The quality of Carus's representation of Buddhism was of secondary relevance in establishing the issue of Western interest in Buddhism. The points of doctrine presented in the *Gospel* that were important, however, were Carus's defense of Buddhism against the common charges of nihilism, skepticism, and atheism. The content of the *Gospel* also validated Shaku Sōen's specific claim that the delegation had shown "that Buddhism closely corresponds to modern science and philosophy" (Shaku Sōen 1895a, 5). In general it strengthened the Buddhist position against Christian criticism and provided evidence of an improved Western sympathy for Buddhism, but the value of this went just so far. In his introduction to the second edition of *Fukuin* Suzuki expressed misgivings about the quality of the work: "The book, which was not intended for Japanese hands, was unsatisfactory." One problem was its simplicity. It had been written in uncomplicated language that made it accessible to "anyone with a junior high school education," but as a consequence there were "many immature words" that, Suzuki was concerned, might hinder understanding. This was not his only complaint:

> In the translator's view, there are not a few passages where there are omissions or where there are revisions. This is the work of a Westerner, and from my personal view, it has the odour of a Westerner about it. (Suzuki 1970, 281)

Shaku Sōen, referring to the works of major Orientalists, explained how each produced an incomplete and idiosyncratic interpretation: "Swedenborg came to Buddhism through his interest in mysticism; [Edwin] Arnold through his elegant poetic vision; Olcott through his interest in superior intellect; Max Müller through his interest in the refined Sanskrit language" (Shaku Sōen 1895a, 279). Although each of them is excellent in his own field, he concluded, "as for attaining the essential meaning of the noble truths of Buddhism, there is reason to doubt whether these scholars had penetrated the secret" (Shaku Sōen 1895a, 279). If these great leaders of Western scholarship had failed in the task, what was Shaku Sōen suggesting his readers should expect of Carus?

In spite of whatever shortcomings he may have seen in the work, Shaku Sōen compared the arrival of Carus's book to "the rainbow and clouds after a serious drought." This was because "an eager demand for a concisely compiled work on Buddhism has arisen throughout the country, which it is our duty to satisfy" (Shaku Sōen 1895a, 279). As though foreseeing the assumptions of Carus's Western biographers, Shaku Sōen was explicit that it was neither absence of information on Buddhism nor a falling off in Buddhist scholarship that led to the publication of the book. As his Preface explained, "here [in Japan] the tradition is not disappearing; the writings are accumulating at a vast rate, and there is an exceedingly great superabundance of books"; "the Buddhist tradition that had existed in Japan for more than a thousand years was not disappearing; we have the complete Tripiṭaka, specialist teachers of the Sūtras, and the Commentaries." The problems were rather that the literature, already so vast, continued to accumulate, and that canonical texts required a profound skill to master. "The characters are difficult and the sentences scholarly and intricate" (Shaku Sōen 1895a, 279). Hence the scholars of today "are at a loss how to begin the study of the Tripiṭaka, the 'perfection of the ancients.'" These "scholars of today," the "up-and-coming young Buddhists" to whom *Fukuin* was directed, were the growing class of Western-educated young moderns who did not have the classical training needed to cope with the special difficulties of Buddhist texts that are not only written in Chinese, but are also further removed from even the educated general reader by specialist technical terms. For the benefit of this audience Suzuki translated the *Gospel* into "a very easy style."

Buddhist reformers recognized that there was a need for a Buddhist equivalent to the translations in Japanese of works on Christian thought and Western philosophy through which an educated reader might gain access to knowledge of Buddhism without the mediation of religious specialists. There were already some introductory books in modern language available in Japan. One of the earliest was Inoue Enryō's *Bukkyō katsuron joron* written specifically to meet the needs of this audience (1887). In 1891 Shaku Sōen, together with fellow Parliamentary delegates Toki Hōryū and Ashizu Jitsuzen, had worked with Shimaji Mokurai to compile an outline of Buddhist doctrine, a five-volume work intended to promote Buddhist unity (Shaku Sōen et al. 1896). Though this work was probably not suitable for the general distribution that Shaku Sōen envisaged for *Fukuin*, it does contradict the assumption that Japanese Buddhists went to Carus for knowledge of their religion. There were also at least three short introductions to Buddhism that had been written in Japanese before being translated into English for distribution at the Chicago World's Fair. These works were included in Carus's bibliography.[17] There had also been books on the life of Śākyamuni.[18] The fact that Shaku Sōen also saw a use for *Fukuin* as a primer of Buddhism does not detract from its primary function as a sign of Western recognition of the superiority of Buddhism as a religion for the future.[19]

One advantage of Carus's *Gospel* was that a book on Buddhism by a Western scholar could be expected to reach a wider audience than these previous works. The Buddhist content of Carus's *Gospel* was not new to Japan. The audience for a book by a Western author, however, would presumably consist of the already pro-Buddhist audience of Inoue et al., pro-Western Japanese, and also those who were curious to find out what outsiders had to say about them. Just as Carus had used the book to extend his message to the general public, beyond the restricted and intellectual readership of his journals, so Shaku Sōen's Preface to *Fukuin* could popularize and extend the audience for Buddhist reform arguments. Shaku Sōen has been described by Furuta Shokin as the founder of lay Zen in Japan, but his work was only part of the more general movement of *koji* (lay) Buddhism, bringing Buddhism out of the institutions and into the lives of the lay community. Carus's book, which was intended to introduce Buddhism/monism to the general public in America, was put to a similar task in Japan.

Validating the Chicago Mission

The Gospel of Buddha was also a sign of the success of the Japanese delegation to Chicago, a reply to conservative critics who had withheld official endorsement.[20] It was spelled out in both the Preface and the biography of Carus, which Suzuki appended to *Fukuin*, that the book had been the consequence of the meeting between the Japanese Buddhist delegation and the author. The existence of the *Gospel*—especially the fact that exposure to Eastern Buddhism had inspired Carus to write it—justified the initiative taken by the delegation, since it was proof that they had advanced Buddhist understanding by their attendance in Chicago.

In Shaku Sōen's *Bankoku shūkyō taikai ichiran* ("Outline of the World's Parliament of Religions"), where he listed the achievements of the delegation, he concluded modestly that "we have simply fulfilled our mission in spreading the wisdom of the Buddha and we will not make an announcement of this to the public" (Shaku Sōen 1895b, 6). This "private memento" was nevertheless published repeatedly in a number of editions. These, as well as addresses such as that to the YMBA, the Buddhist journals, and local newspapers, made much of the success and achievements of the delegation. The delegates became the champions of Buddhism[21] and *Fukuin* became evidence for the Japanese public of the success of the delegation, proof of the argument in the *Manifesto* that

> Quite simply, now is not the time to be conservative. It is a time to take positive action. In other words, we should not try passive resistance to the invasion of the foreign religion, but actively plan for the future of

> Buddhism. If we continue the conservative trend of the present over the next ten years, we must view the future of Buddhism pessimistically. The Parliament offers Buddhism the opportunity of external expansion and provides the means to achieve it. Why shouldn't we make a great effort and attempt the surprising strategy of expansion? (Concerned Buddhists 1893, 295)

The delegation to Chicago had been a strategy in the defense of Buddhism against Western encroachment in Japan, and it had achieved its initial, modest purpose: "It is beyond our expectations to achieve an immediate positive result from sending one or two delegates to the Conference . . . what is important is simply to make a step in the grand design for future progress." Though Christian investment in Japan was inefficient in that their immense effort had not been compensated, the *Manifesto* argued, it was nevertheless undeniable that "Christianity had built up a great latent force in our society," through this activity. Thus, the argument ran, Buddhists should also be willing to take action. Reviewing the achievements of the delegation, dealing less with transmission of doctrine than with the conversion of a New York businessman, and the cooperation of an expatriate Japanese businessman in funding extra lectures at the Exposition, Shaku Sōen mused on the possibilities for Buddhism if the wider Buddhist community could be moved to such action: "It would be a marvelous event that would change the face of the country" (Shaku Sōen 1895b, 5). The *Gospel* was an indication of the possibilities.

Creating Space for Discussion

Shaku Sōen's endorsement of the book lent it authority among Buddhist readers, but his disclaimer on the accuracy of Western understanding of Buddhism suggests that the book could have created a space for the discussion of the place of Buddhism in the modern world. Since it was written by a non-Japanese, a Buddhist sympathizer but not an educated Buddhist priest, the ideas it presented were open to freer discussion in Japan than if it had been written by Shaku Sōen himself, for example, with the responsibility his position called for within the Buddhist establishment.

The careers of the two extremely influential Meiji Buddhist scholars, Inoue Enryō and Murakami Senshō, show some of the difficulties. Inoue, though a graduate of the Buddhist Ōtani University, resigned from the Honganji institution to remain in the intellectually less restricted climate of the academic world. Murakami Senshō, whose writings also contributed to a deeper understanding among non-Buddhists, particularly intellectuals and statesmen, remained a priest but controversy caused by his scholarship forced him to resign from the Ōtani sect in 1901 (Kishimoto 1956, 150, 164). Although he always maintained his belief in the doctrinal superiority of Mahāyāna, Murakami's study of Buddhism using Western academic methods led him to question whether Japanese Buddhism had actually been taught by the historical Buddha, Śākyamuni. Some issues of importance if Buddhism was to conform to Western criteria for acceptance as truth were simply not open for discussion by institutional clergy.

In Japan Carus was respected as an authority on the West and on Western philosophy. The title page identified him as *Doitsu tetsugaku hakushi*—not just a German PhD but one whose doctorate was in the discipline of philosophy—claiming for him a share in the high esteem in which German philosophy was held among Japanese intellectuals. Shaku Sōen could enthusiastically endorse him for his goodwill in wishing to promote Buddhism, and for his achievement in avoiding some of the errors of other Western scholars, but his opinions on Japan and Buddhism could be questioned without upsetting orthodoxy. They could be easily dismissed as yet another example of the inadequacy of foreign understanding. The foreign origin of the book was signaled by the title, *Budda no fukuin*, where *fukuin* was the word coined by Christian missionaries in Japan to designate the Christian Gospels. The Japanese rendering of the characters is "glad tidings" corresponding to the etymology of the English "gospel," and current Japanese–English dictionaries indicate its close association with Christian evangelism.[22]

Shaku Sōen apparently did not choose to transmit Carus's emphasis on the similarities between Christianity and Buddhism, as *Fukuin* does not include the Table of Reference that showed these parallels. The List of Abbreviations that accompanied this was transformed into a bibliography, effectively a statement of the extent of Western scholarship on Buddhism, again an endorsement of the claims of the reformers. The bibliography was presented in both English and in Japanese, showing the extent and nature of Western scholarship in Japanese, and providing a source of reference for the Western-educated.

Budda no fukuin in Buddhist Nationalism

Paul Carus's *The Gospel of Buddha* was deployed in Japan as a sign of increasing Western approval of Buddhism as the most appropriate religion for the modern, scientific world. This idea was fundamental to Meiji Buddhist reform, but by no means the total issue. It is no surprise that Shaku Sōen's Preface also spoke on other issues in the discourse: the reinstatement of Buddhism as a state religion, and the benefits Buddhist teaching bestows upon the nation.

The Preface opened with a message of hope for Buddhism in overcoming its present problems, which included Buddhism's strength in adversity and its adaptability. "The strength of Buddhism is like fire . . . the more you beat it, the more it burns . . . if attacked it becomes more and more aroused" (Shaku Sōen 1895a, 277). Arguing from history, it described how in ancient India Buddhism survived the dissension of ninety-six heretical sects; in China, it survived the opposition it faced from the two competing religions and oppressive rulers; over the hundreds, thousands of years of its eastward advance, Buddhism had survived crushing attacks and calumny, but its real character had not been diminished in the least. The Preface suggested that the state of Buddhism in Meiji Japan, which was stripped of its power and under attack by Christians, was nothing new. Buddhism had survived greater adversity and not only had survived, but had emerged stronger for the purification. "Now, once again, although we met the crushing attack of *hai ki*[23] Buddhism's real character had not been decreased in the least."

The Preface then retold the story of an interview between an ancient Chinese emperor and a Buddhist sage who argued the virtues of Buddhism, its benefits for beings of all rank, and its benefits to the state. The emperor, convinced by the sage of Buddhism's superiority, converted to Buddhism and established it within his kingdom. The lesson of this sermon-like section of the Preface was that "the Buddha is truly the Sage of complete wisdom and virtue, and the Dharma that he preached is the true principle of *all ages and all countries, East and West*" (emphasis added). The unspoken conclusion is clearly that the Buddha Dharma, the future universal religion, must also be the true principle to guide Meiji Japan. In short, the Preface argued that Buddhism was the solution to the questions of Meiji religion, the search for an ideological base for modern Japan, a religion to assure the welfare of the nation. It also continued the campaign to reestablish the relationship between Buddhism and the state.

The Two Prefaces: The Extension of the Parliament Project

This paper so far has discussed the deployment of *The Gospel of Buddha* in the discourse of Meiji religion in Japan. But Shaku Sōen's Preface to *Budda no fukuin* was published in two versions. The second, which purported to be the English translation of the original, was reproduced in Carus's journal, *The Open Court* (Carus 1895b). This "translation" shared a few paragraphs with the original but was essentially rewritten for the American journal, suggesting that Shaku Sōen also realized the opportunity offered by the publication of *Budda no fukuin* to intervene in the Western discourse on Buddhism. In effect it was an extension of the project of the Japanese Buddhist delegates at the World's Parliament of Religions; an attempt to gain Western respect and appreciation for Buddhism, to satisfy a Buddhist missionary ideal, but more importantly, as the *Manifesto* indicated, to strengthen the position of Buddhism in Japan.

Shaku Sōen's statement of the achievements of the delegation began with the statement that "we drew the attention of both foreigners and Japanese to the following points at least . . . ," indicating his awareness that by speaking in Chicago he was also addressing a certain local audience. The Japanese and American discourses intersected for a Western-educated Japanese elite, a number of whom contributed to *The Monist* and *The Open Court* and to liberal magazines such as *Arena* and *Forum*.[24] Even non-English-speaking Japanese were brought into contact with articles of particular interest in English journals, which were translated and republished in Japan. In *The Open Court* 9, 1895, for example, a letter from Mr K. Ohara of Japan reported that he had published a translation of the "Triangular Debate on Christian Missions," an article from *The Monist*, in his journal the *Shi-Do-Kwai-Ko-Koku*. The article in *Arena* by Chicago delegate Hirai Kinzō was also translated and republished in Japan (Hirai 1893).[25] After Carus's contact with the Japanese delegation, *The Monist* regularly noted the contents of the Japanese journals it received. It was not unreasonable to assume that an article on Japanese Buddhism in *The Open Court* or *The Monist* would reach members of this particular elite, either directly or by report. Indeed, certain parts of the Preface seem directed more particularly to these readers than to a Western audience. The "translation" of the Preface to *Fukuin*, therefore, like the delegation to Chicago before it, was a strategic intervention in both discourses. Shaku Sōen not only appropriated Carus's text for deployment in the contest over the religious future of Meiji Japan, he also took the opportunity of the Japanese publication of his Preface to continue his participation in the formation of Western knowledge of Buddhism.

The Preface in *Open Court*: A Message to the West

The version of Shaku Sōen's Preface to *Budda no fukuin* reproduced in *Open Court* differed from the original in both omissions and additions. The initial historical paragraph illustrating the resilience and adaptability of Buddhism in the face of adversity, and the discussion between the emperor and the sage, was omitted, possibly as a result of Carus's editing. The sections dealing with the westward advance of Buddhism, Orientalist scholarship, and the reasons for the Japanese publication were reproduced more or less completely. There were, however, significant additions that had no parallel in the original, and these we must attribute to Japanese authorship.

The opening paragraph stressed the Buddhist belief that the Dharma predates the historical Śākyamuni, challenging the Western assumption that Buddhism was originally a secular philosophy, the creation of a historical person, an assumption that underlies Carus's vision of the Buddha as the first humanist, first positivist, etc. The Preface stated emphatically that "Śākyamuni was born in India about three thousand years ago, but Buddhism existed long before his birth . . . Buddhism is not an invention of Śākyamuni, but the Truth of the world" (Carus 1895b, 4404). Though Shaku Sōen's equation of Buddhism with the Truth of the world has a superficial coincidence with Carus's representation of Buddhism as the "religion of truth" presented in the *Gospel*, there is a fundamental difference. In Carus's vision, Buddhism and Christianity shared equally in the Truth, the results of parallel evolution, issuing in the same truth adapted to two different cultural and historical environments. For Shaku Sōen, Buddhism, the Truth of the world, was the fulfillment of all world religions. Using a fashionably scientific metaphor, he described Buddhism as the center of the solar system of religion and relegated Christianity to a position among all other religions, one of "the larger or smaller planets revolving around this brilliant sun of the Truth" (Carus 1895b, 4405).

The difference here is profound. The friendship between Carus and Shaku Sōen was apparently based on their shared commitment to the principles of the Parliament: universal religious tolerance and dedication to the search for truth. Carus wrote to Shaku Sōen that "all religions contain more or less truth, and all Bibles and sacred books more or less error. What we want is the best of them, the truth without the error, the good without the evil" (Dornish 1969, 23). This statement seems in remarkable accord with Shaku Sōen's lecture to a meeting of Japanese religious leaders, Christian and Buddhist: "In both Buddhism and in Christianity, truth and untruth are, without doubt, mingled . . . We are a people with a strong belief in truth, therefore we must search for whatever glimmer of truth there is, even amongst the rubbish, even amongst the excrement, we are willing to bow before it and rejoice" (Shaku Sōen 1896, 175).

However, the coincidence of aim between Carus and Shaku Sōen was not as close as it first appeared. Shaku Sōen advocated religious tolerance and coexistence, but he had no doubts about the relative status of the ultimate rewards of Buddhism and Christianity. In the religious crisis of Meiji Japan, he called upon both the Christian and Buddhist communities to drop their rivalry and prejudice in order to cooperate for the good of the nation. "The doctrinal arguments of philosophers cannot be reconciled . . . but men of religion should disregard this and adopt the basic position of nondiscriminating, impartial benevolence . . . Christians and Buddhists both together must meet the urgent task of today through carrying out philanthropic work" (Shaku Sōen 1896, 175).

There were for him, however, undeniable differences in belief. Both believed in the imperative of the search for truth, and both believed it was present in all religions. For Shaku Sōen, however, the unity of Buddhism and Christianity was not to be found at the level of the highest truth, which Buddhism alone possessed, but in the common belief in charity, benevolence, and compassion. "Those who have the aptitude to believe in Christianity can follow Christianity and obtain consolation. Those who are born to follow Buddhism can accept Buddhism and attain liberation" (Shaku Sōen 1896, 176).

To return to the Preface of *Fukuin*: Shaku Sōen described there his vision of their interrelationship on the basis of this firm conviction of the superiority of Buddhism in the hierarchy of world religions. Confucius is, he wrote, "a Bodhisattva that appeared in China; and Jesus and Mohammed are Arhats in the West." Here again Shaku Sōen differed from Carus. He granted Jesus a high spiritual status, but not that of a buddha. Shaku Sōen further argued that the function of each of these great teachers was to prepare their followers to receive Buddhism, and although "some religious doctrines are inferior to and less deep than others . . . as far as they are consistent with the Truth, they may freely find their place within our Buddhist doctrines" (Carus 1895b, 4405).

This is more than a restatement of the encompassing tolerance of Buddhism. In this scheme the preexistence of an established religion is a necessary condition for the entry of Buddhism into a nation: "If Brahmanism had not arisen in India, Buddhism would never have come into existence." Similarly, the existence of Confucianism in China and Shinto in Japan made it possible for Buddhism to be introduced into those countries. Without the Arhats of the West, Jesus and Mohammed, there would be no Buddhism in the countries where those religious teachers are worshiped. "For all these religions, I make bold to say, are nothing but so many conductors through which the 'White Light' of Buddha is passing into the whole universe."

Kitagawa sees the use of this typically Christian formula of fulfillment by Asian religious reformers as a legacy of the Parliament, a lesson learned from Christians (Kitagawa 1984, 187). Though this may be the case for the Indian delegates he quotes, the idea has a much earlier origin in Japan. Edward J. Reed recorded an interview with Akamatsu Renjō, a Honganji priest who had accompanied Shimaji Mokurai to England for two and a half years from 1873. Akamatsu believed, said Reed, that his sect of Buddhism contained all that was good and true in the Christian religion, and that the people of England were ripe for the reception of Buddhism (Reed 1880, 214–15). Akamatsu's statement predates the Parliament by two decades.

How did Shaku Sōen expect a Western audience to respond to this Buddhist appropriation of Carus's concept of the "religion of truth" and its claim of Asian priority? I don't believe that his argument was intended to attract converts to Buddhism. On the one hand the Preface attempted to dispute Carus's representation of Buddhism. It also challenged the Christian and Western assumption of natural superiority. On the other hand it assured Japan's pro-Western generation that Buddhism already has all that the modern West was striving for. The publication of this statement in *The Open Court* was a form of Western endorsement.

Shaku Sōen's Preface, recomposed for American publication, was a minor strategy in Western discourse, but Carus and his American readers gave no sign of noticing Shaku Sōen's vision of Buddhism as the fulfillment of Christianity and his opposition to Carus's position on Truth and the relationship of Buddhism and Christianity, or of noticing his doubts on the success of Orientalists in understanding Buddhism. What was communicated to the Western reader and entered Western discourse was that Shaku Sōen, a high-ranking Buddhist, propagated Carus's work in Japan. As Carus himself put it, "Whether or not it faithfully represents the Buddhist doctrine, it is for Buddhists to say" (Carus 1895b, 4733). As recently as 1973 the work was republished with the reassurance that, "The best evidence that this book characterizes the spirit of Buddhism correctly can be found in the welcome it has received throughout the entire Buddhist world" (Carus [1917] 1973, vi).[26]

As we have seen, however, *Gospel* was welcomed in Japan, in spite of the fact that Shaku Sōen and D. T. Suzuki both expressed doubts about the author's understanding of Buddhism. The Japanese translation was only the first of more than 13 different editions that appeared in the author's lifetime (Fader 1982, 141). Japanese reform Buddhists anticipating missions into the Chinese mainland started on a Chinese translation in 1895, and reportedly tested it out on prisoners of the Sino-Japanese war. An edition was published by nationalists in Ceylon to replace the Bible used in government schools to teach English language, the key to obtaining positions within the colonial bureaucracy. It continued to be used for this purpose until the middle of the present [twentieth] century (Peiris 1973, 327). In Ceylon, as in Japan, the *Gospel* owed its publication to reasons beyond its reliability as a source of knowledge concerning Buddhism.

Fukuin was of considerable strategic value in the campaign for a Buddhist revival. The fact that such a book had been written was itself worth bringing to public attention: it demonstrated the existence of interest in Buddhism among Western intellectuals and thus gave weight to claims that Japanese Buddhism was the religion of modernity. It also provided a vehicle to carry Shaku Sōen's plea for the reestablishment of Buddhism in the modern state beyond an existing pro-Buddhist readership. As Carus's *Gospel* was a direct consequence of the delegation to Chicago, it endorsed this initiative and encouraged support for further assertive action. The content of the book was also not without value, since it confirmed claims of the compatibility of Buddhism with science and modern philosophy, and since it promoted Buddhism as the religion of the future. It also defended Buddhism against charges of nihilism, and recognized the authenticity of Mahāyāna teachings. In its Japanese translation *Budda no fukuin* met the need for a short introductory text on Buddhism for the general reader, a need that appears to have become even more urgent by the turn of the century. For example, in Suzuki's introduction to the second edition in 1901 he apologized for the shortcomings of the work and begged his readers to understand that it was merely a first step, just one ten-thousandth part of the way towards carrying out his "earnest desire" to produce a "readable compendium of universal Buddhism," a book containing "the essence plucked from the Chinese, Indian, Tibetan, and other Buddhist texts that have been bequeathed to us." It seems that in another discursive twist across time and cultures, Carus's eclectic mixing of Buddhist texts that was a point of vulnerability in the West, now proved a point in *Fukuin*'s favor, supporting the idea that Eastern Buddhism encompassed all other teachings and that Japan was the storehouse of the Buddhist knowledge of the world. *Budda no fukuin*, as it was deployed in Japan, owed its publication and proliferation to its strategic value in the discourse of Meiji religion.

Glossary

Ashizu Jitsuzen	蘆津実全
Hirai Kinzō	平井金三
Noguchi Zenshirō	野口善四郎
Shaku Sōen	釋宗演
Toki Hōryū	土宜法龍
Yatsubuchi Bunryū	八淵蟠龍

Notes

1. *Budda no fukuin* was first published in January 1895, though it was apparently ready as early as November 1894 when Shaku Sōen sent a copy to Carus. The second edition, November 1901, is reprinted in D. T. Suzuki 1970, 271-590, henceforth referred to as *Fukuin*.
2. For a biography of Carus see Jackson 1968 and Meyer 1962.
3. *The Light of Asia* by Sir Edwin Arnold was first published in London in 1889.
4. Cf. references to M.V., which indicates *Mahāvagga*; and D.P., *Dhammapada*.
5. The World's Parliament of Religions, Chicago 1893, was one of the Auxiliary Congresses held in conjunction with the Columbian Exposition. The representation of Japan and of Japanese Buddhism at this event is the subject of my doctoral thesis (University of Sydney, History Department, 1995). There is now considerable literature available on this subject but the two most outstanding works are Seager (1995) for the significance of the event in the United States, and Ketelaar (1991), on the Japanese delegation.
6. The Buddhist priests were Shaku Sōen (Rinzai), Toki Hōryū (Shingon), Ashizu Jitsuzen (Tendai), Yatsubuchi Bunryū (Jōdo Shinshū). The two lay speakers were the *koji* (lay) Buddhists Hirai Kinzō and Noguchi Zenshirō. All of these delegates had been actively involved in the Buddhist revival and Buddhist nationalist movements of the previous

years. The delegation was deliberately transsectarian and was supported by Buddhist reform leaders. The most prominent among them are listed as Concerned Buddhists in an open letter calling for official recognition and support for the delegation, henceforth referred to as *Manifesto* (Concerned Buddhists 1893).

7. For a slightly different version see Shaku Sōen 1894. Carus had himself presented a paper called "Science as a Religious Revelation" (Carus 1893).
8. Shaku Sōen, like many of the priests prominent in Meiji reform, was a Buddhist scholar. Furuta (1967) details his extensive Buddhist studies, which led to him being one of the four editors of *The Essentials of Buddhist Teachings* (1890), a five-volume work intended to promote Buddhist unity. He also studied Western philosophy at Keio University. Fukuzawa Yukichi is listed as among the subscribers supporting his trip to Ceylon to study Pāli Buddhism (Shaku Sōen 1941).
9. Substantial passages from Shaku Sōen's "Preface" from *Budda no fukuin* were translated by D. T. Suzuki and published in *The Open Court* 9/391: 4404-4405. References to *Fukuin* are my own translations. Suzuki's translation is referenced as Suzuki 1895.
10. The YMBA (*Dainihon bukkyō seinenkai*), a network of youth organizations, was formalized in 1894. See Tamamuro 1967, 352.
11. This is modified in the English version of *The Open Court*, which reads, "This was partly shown . . ."
12. See Scheiner (1970) on the Confucian bases of Christian conversion in early Meiji, in particular the adoption of Christianity as the spiritual, ethical root of Western civilization; see Schwantes (1953) on the importance of science—the paradigm of modernity—in religious debates of mid-Meiji.
13. This is not the place to repeat the history of the early Meiji persecutions of *haibutsu kishaku* that so devastated Buddhist institutions that there were real fears for their survival in the early 1870s, nor to recount the details of the reform initiatives over the following three decades that defined Buddhism in distinction from other aspects of Japanese religiosity and recreated its function in society. For a well-researched and insightful treatment of the reconstitution of Buddhism in the second half of the nineteenth century see Ketelaar 1990.
14. On Inoue Enryō's part in Buddhist revival see Staggs 1983; Snodgrass 1997. In his influential work *Bukkyō katsuron joron*, Inoue linked the developments of the Buddhist revival taking place within specialist circles to the rapidly growing nationalist sentiments of the early Meiji 20s (Inoue 1887). Inoue, aware of the interest in Buddhism among Western thinkers seeking an alternative ethical system to orthodox Christianity—a system compatible with a scientific world view and contemporary philosophy—called upon patriots to revive Buddhism as Japan's gift to the world. It was presented as the one thing that Japan could export that could win international prestige.
15. Also see translation in Staggs 1979, 399. Based on the Lotus Sūtra, the doctrine of the Five Periods as Inoue explained it records that right after achieving *bodhi* the Buddha first preached the *Avataṃsaka sūtra* (*Kegongyō*), which revealed the truth of the Mahāyāna, but realized that the truth of this revelation was beyond the comprehension of his audience. Therefore he explained the superficial doctrines of the Hīnayāna (*agonji*). This accomplished, he was then able to teach the third stage in the gradual revelation of the truth, which is explained in the *vaipulya* sūtras (*hōdōji*); and as the understanding of his audience increased he was able to progress towards the Mahāyāna sūtras of the final two periods, the *hannyaji* and the *hokke-nehanji*. At Chicago, Ashizu, Toki, and Yatsubuchi addressed this doctrine; it is mentioned by all the delegates and by each of them more than once (Barrows 1893; Houghton 1894).

16. This charge, originally used by the *Kokugakusha* in the Tokugawa period to discredit Buddhism in favor of Shinto, had been appropriated by the Christians in the Meiji period. Christians, such as the Kumamoto band from Dōshisha who formed the Japanese Christian contingent to the Parliament, knew very little about Buddhism, since they had been brought up and educated in a strongly Confucian, anti-Buddhist tradition.
17. Carus's bibliography lists Kuroda (1893), the title page of which carries the assurance that the book had been "carefully examined by the scholars of Tendai, Shingon, Rinzai, Sōtō, and Shin sects ... for circulation among the members of the Parliament of Religions to be held in Chicago in connection with the World's Fair." He also lists Akamatsu 1893. Lay delegate Noguchi Zenshirō, under the name of Tokunaga, translated and distributed a work based on the lectures of Kiyozawa Manshi (Kiyozawa [1892] 1955). The original Japanese version of Kiyozawa ([1892] 1955) was published in 1892 and a year later the first English version was published.
18. According to Kishimoto (1956, 159), Inoue Tetsujirō wrote the first historical analysis of the life of the Buddha in 1889. Inoue (1897) was published by Inoue Enryō's Tetsugaku Shoin. This work was reprinted in Meiji bunka kenkyūkai 1954, 377-416.
19. See Ketelaar's discussion (1990, 207-212) of the importance of "Buddhist Bibles" in giving form to the ideal of doctrinal unity within the Buddhist revival. The first was Nanjō Bun'yū's *Bukkyō sei-ten*, which appeared in 1905, four years after the second edition of *Fukuin*.
20. The delegation had been unsuccessful in attempting to gain the endorsement of the All Sects Council (*Kakushū kyokai*), supposedly because of fears among conservatives that the Parliament was "a Christian conspiracy" organized to discredit the claims of other religions.
21. Ketelaar (1991) argues that the main function of the trip to Chicago was to provide the opportunity for this interpretation. While I most certainly concur with the importance Ketelaar gives the delegation to Chicago as a platform for the battle over the future religion in Meiji Japan, my principal concern is with the interaction of this delegation with Western knowledge of Buddhism at this time.
22. Sōgo (1985, 498) confirms its evangelical Christian origins.
23. *Haibutsu kishaku*, or calumny?
24. For example, Kishimoto Nobuta, Christian delegate to the Parliament, contributed articles on Japanese religion in general in *The Open Court* 8:33 (16 August 1894): "Buddhism in Japan," "Northern and Southern Buddhism," "Sacred Literature," "Present Condition," "The Zen and the Shin Sects," and "The Influence of Buddhism on the People." The scope of these articles prefigured his future work on comparative religion with Anezaki Masaharu. See Suzuki Norihisa 1970.
25. Hirai Kinzō and Noguchi Zenshirō accompanied the delegation as translators and *koji* representatives of the Meiji Buddhist reform movement. Hirai, who apparently spoke English well, delivered this highly emotional speech on the inequities of Japan's treaties under the title of "Christianity in Japan." *The Japan Weekly Mail*, 5 August 1893, noted a paper on Japanese Buddhism by Hirai had been translated and published in *Bukkyō*. *The Mail* described Hirai's paper, originally written in English and published in *Arena* as "Religious Thought in Japan," as "the best thing yet written on Japanese Buddhism." *The Mail* refers to the author as "Kinza Hirai of Los Angeles, California." The translator was Noguchi Zenshirō. The association of these two men with Buddhist reform activities goes back at least to the organization of Henry Steel Olcott's first tour of Japan. Hirai initiated the correspondence for this trip, and Noguchi was sent to accompany Olcott from India.
26. The sentiment remains in a memorial edition of *Gospel of Buddha* published by Open Court, 2004. The preface by Donald Lopez and introductory essay by Martin Verhoeven confirm the book's importance in the lineage of American Buddhism.

7

Re-membering the Dismembered Body of Tibet: Contemporary Tibetan Visionary Movements in the People's Republic of China*

David Germano

Bodies, Burial, and Renewal

We now know that religious Tibet experienced devastating material losses during the period of Chinese control from 1959 onward, a process that gradually intensified until the culminating orgy of violence that constituted the Cultural Revolution (1966–76). In addition to the many bodies of Tibetans sacrificed to the revolution's chaotic agenda, the body of Tibet herself was stripped of its web of *stūpas*, temples, and other architectural markers, and even the memories of her sacred caves, groves, and mountains were at times eradicated through the human loss.[1] Wooden and metallic bodies of buddhas, bodhisattvas, and lamas situated within these residences were destroyed or shipped off in amazing quantities to the illicit markets of Hong Kong and elsewhere, often to reappear in museum and private collections in Europe and America in a deanimated form as art dealers emptied their interiors of the sacred contents that give them life. Finally, the immense corpus of religious texts constituting the teaching bodies not only of the Buddha[2] but also of the myriad Indian and Tibetan masters who followed in his footsteps was devas-

* With permission of the author, the following elements of the original article have been omitted: all photographs, a ten-page section (Germano 1998, 58-68) with the corresponding endnotes, and discursive portions of endnotes 11, 64, 71, 78, 82, 94, 106, and 108 (as numbered in the original publication).

tated. Thus the bodies of religious Tibet were sacrificed and resacrificed on multiple fronts for a three-decade period which resulted in the literal deconstruction of an entire civilization. The sacrifice was not total, however, for not only were the essential elements of Tibetan religiosity preserved in memories and emotions buried within the individual bodies of Tibetans—and even partially in hidden valleys where Tibetans continued to practice Buddhism throughout the period—but Tibetans also concealed in the earth of Tibet an unknown quantity of buddha bodies in statuary and painting, associated ritual items, and, most important, the literary corpus of Buddhism. With the end of the Cultural Revolution in 1976 and the gradual easing of restrictions on religious expression, these buried realities of Tibetan culture have slowly been re-excavated and brought into the light of day. These excavations have played an important role in the explosion of temple building and scripture printing that has ensued in Tibet since the end of the Cultural Revolution, as well as in the equally explosive growth in the often-illicit international art trafficking that has thrived there.[3] It is this phenomenon that I would like to examine, particularly in light of how Tibetans and Tibet have been slowly trying to heal their multiple damaged bodies and reconstitute some semblance of health, despite continuing oppressive realities.

There is in fact an ancient Tibetan precedent for burying religious artifacts in the earth in the face of persecution and later re-excavating these concealed items amid a landscape of ruined temples and resurgent hope. The great Tibetan Empire (seventh to ninth century), which created Buddhism as a national religion, began to disintegrate in the mid-ninth century when the Emperor Langdarma (817–42) instituted a persecution of institutional Buddhism, traditionally said to culminate in his assassination by a Buddhist monk. During the ensuing dark period of institutional and material decay, it appears that religious artifacts such as texts and artwork were purposely concealed to ensure survival through the chaos; others were presumably lost or forgotten in caches scattered among the neglected network of temples. The following economic and cultural renaissance (beginning in the late tenth century) produced a widespread interest in re-excavating these items from the imperial past out of the Tibetan earth, particularly among the traditionalists who preferred to continue dynastic period traditions rather than adopt newly imported Indic lineages.[4] Among these groups, the excavations included a distinctive continuation of Buddhist revelatory practices that produced a wide variety of scriptures said to have been concealed by famous dynastic period saints in the consciousness of their reincarnating disciples through paranormal means. Thus these myriad new scriptures known as Ter, or treasures, were understood to have been concealed, physically *and* mystically, during the imperial period in Tibetans' bodies and the body of Tibet herself for the sake of future generations.[5] Within the Nyingma tradition, the key figure in the Ter cult came to be an eighth-century Indian master named Padmasambhava who played an important role in bringing Buddhism to the Tibetan Empire. As a distinctive mythos began to crystallize around him, from at least the twelfth century onward Padmasambhava was understood to be the main concealer of Ter in Tibet and, as such, the central devotional figure in the Nyingma Ter cult.[6] The treasure finders themselves, or Terton, were generally understood to be mystically appointed reincarnations of his main dynastic period disciples. While initially primarily a Central Tibetan phenomenon, after the sixteenth century its force largely shifted to eastern Tibet (Kham) where it became the heart of the ecumenical movement (*ris-med*) of the nineteenth century.[7]

This dyadic structure of a period of persecution-impelled decay of Buddhism followed by its renaissance obviously parallels events in Tibet over the past four decades; I will argue that these parallels have resulted in intersections of memories among Tibetans.[8] In fact, one of the most interesting phenomena in the post-1978 religious renaissance in Tibet has been that in addition to the widespread excavation of vast amounts of artwork and texts secretly buried just a few decades ago in response to Chinese-initiated repression of Buddhism, in eastern Tibet the treasure movement revealing sacred scriptures and material items from the seemingly distant imperial past has been dramatically revitalized.[9] I discuss this contemporary treasure movement in eastern Tibet by means of the story of its most prominent proponent, Khenpo Jikphun, who represents one of the most amazing stories of Tibetan endurance and survival through the Cultural Revolution, and compare its contemporary manifestations with the treasure tradition's initial parameters in eleventh- to thirteenth-century Tibet. In doing so, I highlight ways in which contemporary Tibetans *have* been able to manipulate their Buddhist past in its conflict with modernity so as to be capable of generating innovation and renewal.

The Centripetal Nature of Religious Identity in Golok

After 1978 government prohibitions against practicing religion were relaxed in the People's Republic of China, resulting in the gradual renewal of Buddhism in the areas of cultural Tibet fragmented between the contemporary provinces of the Tibetan Autonomous Region, Sichuan, and Qinghai, among others. Despite the renewal of Tibetan culture and Buddhism in particular, there remains a deep, abiding cultural depression among Tibetans, from the educated youth and religious elite to nomads and villagers. In particular, one constantly encounters feelings of alienation and inadequacy among religious practitioners and communities. There is a pervasive feeling articulated by young people with serious religious or intellectual interests, such as lay scholars educated at the Dawu Nationalities Institute in Kham, that their religious and intellectual as well as political situation is hopeless, given the continuing Chinese cultural and political onslaught. This depression often results in self-imposed exile in India; in one famous case, a prominent young scholar committed suicide, leaving behind a note that is rumored to have explicitly linked his death to the besieging of Tibetan culture by Han Chinese.[10] Among the monks, this expresses itself in the feeling that it is impossible to gain a decent religious education in Tibet today. Reasons for this situation are fairly obvious: the loss of several generations of scholars (from those who would now be in their forties to those who would be in their seventies) to death, exile, or the absence of opportunity; the consequent absence of decent study programs, even where bodies and buildings are available; the escape into exile of many of the most prominent religious figures in all traditions; the material devastation of the vast network of temples, monasteries, *stūpas*, and other sites that constituted the infrastructure of Tibet's extended religious body, often including even the culturally transmitted memory of the location of key sites; inferiority complexes created by the racism and material superiority of recent Chinese immigrants, and a host of other associated realities of modern Tibetan life. Tibet's inherent centrifugal tendencies, caused by a small population inhabiting a vast landscape with immense geographic barriers, were thus reinforced to the point of disintegration by the Cultural Revolution. This decentering of religious identity often results, at present, in emotional energy being diverted outwardly in two directions in particular, if not surrendered altogether to Chinese-approved outlets: the nostalgically remembered past or the escapist dream of refugee communities in South Asia.

Against this backdrop, before proceeding deeper into the phenomenon of Ter, we will begin by looking briefly at a particular case of religious revival of Nyingma traditions in contemporary Tibet. My comments are based on observations during extended stays in 1990–92 in Kham and Central Tibet, now politically classified as Sichuan and the Tibetan Autonomous Region respectively, as well as on contemporary hagiographies. For most of this time I was researching textual and contemplative traditions of the Great Perfection (*rdzogs-chen*) in a variety of religious communities belonging to the Nyingma sect of Tibetan Buddhism. My own experience suggests that Tibetan religious communities in Sichuan are somewhat less coercively controlled by Chinese political authorities than are their counterparts in the Tibetan Autonomous Region, particularly the monasteries and nunneries within five to six hours by road from the main urban centers of Lhasa and Shigatse. In fact, the Nyingma tradition in particular has undergone a major institutional revival in a very short time to produce an extensive network of large and small monastic communities throughout eastern Tibet. In part fueled by the general linkage of nationalistic sentiment and religious institutions along with the economic surplus recently generated in some areas, the Nyingmas' growth seems to lie in their traditional focus on nationalistic literature such as the Gesar of Ling epic and dynastic period mythology and the relative prevalence of charismatic teachers whose appeal exceeds their monastic boundaries.

The most interesting of these new communities are a religious institute and a nunnery in Golok Serta headed by Khenpo Jikphun, who is at the heart of the resurgent Nyingma tradition in eastern Tibet. I first heard of Khenpo Jikphun in the summer of 1989 when I was staying in South India at the monastery of Penor Rinpoche, the current titular head of the Nyingma sect. Khenpo Namdrol, now president of its academic college (*bshad grwa*), was Khenpo Jikphun's student, having recently traveled to Kham to study with him. Two things immediately stood out from Khenpo Namdrol's description of his teacher: he was unusually learned in the Great Perfection tradition of tantric Buddhism and he was a prolific Terton. The latter assertion particularly struck me, since the Ter movement had not for the most part been successfully transplanted in refugee Tibet, not surprising given the vast changes in the cultural and geographic landscape on which Ter was so dependent. In addition, Ter was widely rumored among refugee communities to be drastically limited in scope within Tibet itself in comparison to its exalted pre-1950 status as a visionary process of renewal that revealed massive collections of new texts interwoven with a bizarre collection of material items and esoteric *tendrel*, or interdependent supports of talismanic value.

The following year I briefly met Khenpo Jikphun for the first time in Lhasa, where he was resting with Khenpo Namdrol on his way to India for his first trip outside of the People's Republic of China. Subsequently during that year, I heard a number of vague accounts of Khenpo Jikphun while staying in Kham which generally reflected a mix of respect, awe, and jealousy. However, it was not until the following year in Dartsedo (Kangding) that I was able to talk with Khenpo and his students at greater length during a week-long series of teachings he gave there. Khenpo Namdrol's initial descriptions of him were borne out in observations of his charisma among Chinese and Tibetans as well as the miraculous nature of many of the stories told about him, which even by Tibetan standards seemed to stretch one's imagination. In particular, they centered around his status as a Terton, a revealer of treasures or new scriptures from Tibet's ancient past. It also became clear that Khenpo's community was extraordinary in terms of the propagation of Great Perfection tantric traditions, which ultimately brought me there in connection with my own research. I thus arranged for a two-month stay that summer (1990) in Golok Serta at Khenpo's institute.

What I found there proved to be in many ways startlingly different from what I had encountered in other parts of Tibet. Here the sacred landscape of Tibet was being revived in the radical way that only Ter can, and religious energy thus appeared centripetal in marked contrast to the alienated state in which institutionalized Buddhism finds itself in many parts of Tibet. Khenpo Jikphun has created a significant countermovement re-establishing the center of gravity within Tibet herself, thereby stemming the flow of authority and value toward Chinese modernity, on the one hand, and refugee Tibetan communities, on the other. Not only has he created an academic environment that in some ways surpasses what is available in refugee monasteries, but he has also managed to project an intellectual, mythic, and charismatic presence capable of competing with any of the great Nyingma lamas now living or recently deceased in exile.[11] He has constellated Tibet's fragmented cultural energy around him, reinvested it in the Tibetan physical and imaginal landscape, directly relinked the contemporary situation with Tibet's past, and thus in a major way reconstituted Tibetan identity within the realities of life in the contemporary People's Republic of China, thus reinvigorating Tibetan pride, self-confidence, and sense of purpose. He has done so in a uniquely Tibetan, and in particular Nyingma, fashion. The strategies he has employed have revolved around the identification of present figures with strings of reincarnations stretching back to the eighth-century Tibetan Empire; the reconfiguration and reanimation of the body of Tibetan sacred geography through rituals, dreams, miraculous events, and actual physical discoveries linked to that web of reincarnations; rebuilding the intellectual and material substructure of Tibetan intellectual culture within that landscape by founding temples, *stūpas*, monasteries, and retreat centers; and, above all else, his assumption of the mantle of Terton, the treasure finder who is able to establish a visceral link to Tibet's glorious past and to bring discrete products of that link into the present. In these ways, Khenpo has helped to reverse the centrifugal flow of Tibetan identity into contemporary Chinese urban culture, refugee centers in South Asia, depression, nostalgia, or even the far-off alien dream of the West, and instead revitalize a profoundly Tibetan sense of identity within a uniquely Tibetan landscape.

Beyond the Cultural Revolution[12]

Monastic Visions

The creation of a large monastic center is part of the lifelong trajectory of Khenpo's career. He himself took novice vows at the age of 14 and became a fully ordained monk at the age of 22. His life has been characterized throughout by a constant emphasis on strict monastic discipline (including celibacy), especially manifest in his advocacy of monastic renewal and strict ethical standards as the key to revitalizing Buddhism in Tibet following the Chinese destruction of existing institutions after the mid-1950s. Given his credentials as a visionary Terton, this makes him an unusual figure in the Nyingma tradition. A large number of major lamas thought to integrate both scholarship and yogic realization in the current Nyingma tradition are married or have been, especially those who are also Terton, and Khenpo Jikphun is in this way one of the few exceptions who has remained devoted to the monastic tradition. His strict monastic lifestyle is thus in stark contrast to most other treasure revealers, who generally take consorts prior to their main revelations in order to practice sexual yoga, often with reports of stormy relationships ensuing.[13]

The critical juncture in Khenpo's monastic orientation occurred in his twenties, when he encountered a young woman whom he recognized as his karmically destined consort yet declined to unite with her in favor of a lifelong commitment to monasticism. On this occasion, when he first met her, she said to him, "Since we two are intimately connected by Padmasambhava's blessing-prayers and I am thus karmically destined to be your consort, I have come here." In Tibetan tantric Buddhist lineages, women are often said to be of crucial importance as consorts for male visionaries, since it is believed that it is possible to traverse the transcendent path swiftly in reliance on the tantric techniques of sexual yoga; in addition, it is believed that sexual yoga contributes in some essential way to a Terton's ability to reveal treasures.[14] Though Khenpo Jikphun accordingly felt that the signs, circumstances, and karmic connections all indicated that the time had come to engage in sexual yoga to enhance his realization, he chose not to act on them.[15] Echoing earlier figures such as the founder of the Geluk tradition, Tsongkhapa (1357–1419), Khenpo later explained his feeling that most contemporary "yogis" were not superior to ordinary individuals and used the claim of a "tantric lifestyle" to legitimize doing as they pleased under the spell of sexual desire. He thus felt it important to set an example to preserve the teachings' integrity and refused to accept his consort despite their karmic connections, as well as the positive advantages he would have derived from their practice of sexual yoga. Shortly afterward, he related these events to a well-known master named Lodrö, who became upset and exclaimed,

> "Nowadays Tibetans have such slight virtuous merit! What can be done?! Because this has transpired, from now on you must perform the recitation and evocation rites for the Sky Dancers (*mkha'-'gro, ḍākiṇī*) and praise the merits of sexual yoga amidst large gatherings. Since later in your life your gathering of disciples will greatly increase, at that time you must propagate the sūtra and tantra teachings with an emphasis above all on the eloquent writings of Longchenpa and Mipham.[16] In this way vast benefit will accrue impartially to the teachings and to living beings."

Thus, despite being destined to take up a consort as a necessary support for his discovery of Ter, Khenpo felt forced to decline the opportunity because he perceived the need for strict ethical examples during a time of moral decay (expressed by Lodrö in the traditional terminology of Tibetans' "merits," or overall accumulation of virtuous acts and positive karmic energy).

It is not surprising, then, that a key element of Khenpo's public mission following the end of the Cultural Revolution has been to express the need for a thorough purification and ethical reform of Buddhism in Tibet as a corrective to the many corruptions he felt had developed during the preceding three decades. Monastic discipline—that is, celibacy—and serious study of classic Buddhist texts figure prominently in Khenpo's vision of Tibet's Buddhist path and future, in addition to such traditional Tibetan religious values as loyalty to one's guru. While "corruptions" in the sense of noncelibate monks, illiterate monks, disrespect to gurus, and so on, clearly predate recent Chinese influence, it seems reasonable to conclude that the close of the Cultural Revolution found the traditional ideals of Tibetan religious culture in a far worse condition than in the preceding centuries. Khenpo put forward explicit standards as to which tendencies and conduct should be encouraged and which should be rejected. Above all, in line with a resolute belief in ethical discipline as the foundation of all positive qualities, he emphasized the need for dedicated practitioners to become monks and nuns, with the exception of those special few who had already mastered tantric contemplation and were thus beyond any need for conventional morality and discipline. He also disseminated a widely read circular advising that Tibetan monks and nuns in particular needed to act in strict accordance with the Buddha's ethical teachings on monastic discipline and the tantric corpus. For those practitioners who broke their monastic and tantric vows during the Cultural Revolution (such as vows of celibacy, respect for religious structures, and reverence for one's teachers), if the corruption was not so severe as to be beyond restoration, he instructed the performance of appropriate rituals for renewing vows; for others whose actions had severely damaged their vows beyond any possibility of ritual renewal, he insisted on expulsion from monastic assemblies. He also exhorted serious religious practitioners in general—whether ordained as monks and nuns or lay tantric practitioners—to exert themselves in techniques for purifying their negative acts and transgressions and to forsake other secular activities such as agriculture which they were forced to engage in during the Cultural Revolution. He felt that people who had broken their commitments (*dam tshig, samaya*) by such acts as beating lamas should now be permitted to visit the monasteries but not to take part in empowerments, rituals, and so on, even if formerly they were high reincarnate lamas. Though he was only able to insist on adherence to the circular's prescriptions within his own centers, he actively encouraged other monasteries in eastern Tibet to commit themselves publicly to supporting his agenda. This forceful assertion of the primacy of strict monastic values and traditional standards in the post-Cultural Revolution environment has led to consistent tension with those who engaged in anti-Buddhist activities during the Cultural Revolution, since Khenpo Jikphun has advocated a hard line against such individuals. This has been the source of considerable tension with local political leaders, who argued that the Cultural Revolution constituted a special situation and thus did not involve a breach of monastic or tantric vows. However, the Panchen Lama also advocated withholding tantric teachings from those with broken commitments, suggesting that instead they be given exoteric sūtra teachings.

In this way Khenpo felt that monastic communities could purify themselves and again become worthy fields of merit for lay people to honor, offer alms, and go to for refuge. It cannot be overemphasized how central this ethical issue is in terms of the relationships between lay individuals and monks, since ethical purity (especially celibacy) is what qualifies the monks as recipients of offerings from the lay community. Even if this "purity" is always of a relative sort, when infractions are very public and extensive it can lead to lay people questioning the entire institution, at least in its local manifestation. It also guarantees in turn that such offerings constitute "religious merit making," with merit understood as positive karma that will lead to mundane benefits, better rebirths, and eventually spiritual growth. As Ronald D. Schwartz has shown, this relationship between benefactors (*sbyin bdag*) and monks as a key element of Tibetan society has been repeatedly attacked by Chinese religious policies for its political implications (see Schwartz 1994a, esp. 730-34). While Khenpo has conjoined his strong educational and ethical standards with a strict emphasis on monasticism and insistence on exposing Tibetan religious hypocrisy, even while avoiding direct complicity with Chinese rule, he has distanced his movement from any involvement with overt political protests. This contrasts sharply with Schwartz's portrayal of the conjoining of ethical aspects of Buddhism with political protest that has dominated the ongoing demonstrations in Lhasa (Schwartz 1994b, 22, 226; also Schwartz 1994a). Khenpo's brand of nationalism has not involved confrontational resistance to governmental authorities, whether in his stress on systematic education in traditional Tibetan learning as an antidote to colonialist-intensified embarrassment over Tibet's seemingly backward past or in his revival of the traditional merit-making institution of interaction between monastic and lay communities. However, Khenpo Jikphun's ethical agenda, as well as his unusually open teaching of the esoteric tantric teachings (particularly the Great Perfection), has been the source of a considerable degree of controversy among *Tibetans*, though not with Chinese authorities. At one point, Khenpo Jikphun explained his motivations to a huge monastic assembly:

> Before I began this purification and reform of the teachings, there was not even one person displeased with me among all the monks, nuns and lay people. However by force of my undertaking this purification, many people high and low have begun to consider me as almost an enemy. Even so my own motivation in doing so has been devoid of even the slightest self-interest, other than the hope that in these extreme times when the Buddhist teachings have become a setting sun by virtue of the five corruptions' pervasive spread,[17] there might emerge the means for the pure teachings to remain, even if just for a day. With the three jewels as my witness,[18] I can sincerely say that I don't feel the slightest shame for my actions, and thus even if I had to sacrifice my own life for the sake of these teachings, it is certain that I would joyfully do so without the slightest regret. My feeling is identical to that expressed by the great Bodhisattva Śāntideva in the following verse:[19]
>
> Although many beings may kick and stamp upon my head,
> Even at the risk of dying may I delight the Protectors of the World [by not retaliating].

Another outcome has been conflict with some lay tantric practitioners (*sngags-pa*) over Khenpo's criticism of their conduct, which has been linked to his advocation of strict monastic standards and conventional ethical norms as the best path to revitalization of Buddhist culture. This has been compounded by his own unusual status as a monastic hierarch deeply involved with the visionary Ter movement and the unusually tantric cast of the monastic teaching curriculum.[20] Ngakpa are often-hereditary lay practitioners of Buddhist tantra found throughout Tibetan cultural areas who have historically had a particularly close relationship to the Nyingma tradition; they at times possess considerable religious stature on the basis of the mystique of their spiritually potent family "lineage" (*brgyud-pa*) and personal achievements or charisma.[21] Although the extent of this tension is not clear to me, since a number of such figures are Khenpo's personal disciples, it appears that it derives from Khenpo's consistent criticism of supposed ethical lapses disguised in a tantric rhetoric of antinomianism and transcendence among many in their rank and file. Ngakpa have families and reside within ordinary lay communities, and I have found that it is not uncommon that entirely mundane concerns for power, sex, and money are at times masked by such figures with references to the classic tantric paradigms of the spiritual transformation of negative emotions and the violent subjugation of demonic forces. Khenpo's criticism has been particularly aggravating to some because it has been conjoined with a strong privileging of celibate clergy as the paramount ideal to which all Buddhists should aspire, with the clear implication that material and social resources should be channeled to the support of celibate monastic institutions. This criticism goes hand in hand with his criticism of married "monks," a phenomenon that apparently has traditional and recent roots.[22] This tension was reflected, for instance, in 1993 when the lay Nyingma lama Kusum Lingpa visited the United States from Golok and reportedly criticized Khenpo on several occasions, asserting that only his own "treasures" were valid.

Resuscitating the Tibetan Body

Khenpo's revival of the devastated Tibetan Buddhist systems of educational training (the Tibetan mind) has been nothing short of remarkable, and his ecumenical emphasis on monastic-centered ethics separated from political activism has offered a powerful Tibetan religious paradigm for survival in the People's Republic of China that contrasts sharply with the political activism of monks and nuns in Central Tibet. Khenpo Jikphun's most striking activity, however, has been his resuscitation of sacred pilgrimage networks in conjunction with a series of revelations of physical and literary items considered as Ter, or treasure. This contrasts, again, with the politicized brand of Buddhism Schwartz finds in Lhasa, which emphasizes "the ethical aspects of Buddhism as a religion—rather than its magical elements."[23] This treasure-driven resuscitation has been intertwined with dreams and visions of his own past lives that have governed his actions following his return to mainstream life after the Cultural Revolution. It has involved the revelation of historically important but currently forgotten or neglected geographic sites such as sacred caves, describing the forgotten significance of rooms within temples, leaving footprints and handprints in rock to create new sacred sites, and extracting treasures from the earth, all linked to his own memories of Tibetan history in the immediate fashion of recollection of previous lives. Often just his *visits* to crucial sacred spots are vital events in re-establishing this lost body of Tibetan religion for local residents, and are always marked by careful attention to the appropriate offering and ablution rituals directed to the sacred mountains considered to be the residences of Buddhist deities. Activities by lamas such as Khenpo Jikphun are thus literally reconstituting and reconnecting the extended cultural body of Tibet in its geographic landscape. The sheer density of memories evoked and personal identification with them envelop the present within a healing terrain of sacred sanctuaries, tantric deities, saints of the past, and potent buddhas adequate even to the contemporary and seemingly implacable version of the host of demons that have afflicted Tibetan lives from time immemorial.

To adequately understand these contemporary manifestations of Ter, we need first to look back into the historical context of its origins. Buddhism was first imported into Tibet on a massive, government-sponsored scale during the period of the Tibetan Empire, a time when Tibet controlled much of the Asian continent with successful military incursions even into the heart of China. This state-sanctioned importation focused on the development of monastic institutions and scholastic literature yet was intertwined with an unsanctioned diffusion of less orthodox tantric forms of Buddhist lifestyles, rhetoric, and practices. Following the gradual collapse of political centralization after the assassination of the Emperor Langdarma in 842, Tibet underwent a dark period (mid-ninth to late tenth century) during which state-sponsored Buddhism largely collapsed while lay tantric movements continued to flourish. When economic revival began to generate surplus wealth such that political centralization and concomitant large-scale cultural projects re-emerged in Tibet (late tenth century onward),[24] the glorious imperial past and its Buddhist associations became a key site of rhetorical contestation among the various groups attempting to take control of the future of Tibet. In brief, a dominant strategy for groups linked to the new centers of wealth and political power was to import current Indic traditions of Buddhism and deploy them in the Tibetan cultural field with a supporting rhetoric of purity and modernity, in the face of the supposed corruption and antiquity of previous Tibetan lineages. Thus the age of the "great translators" was born in the eleventh century under the aegis of "modernism" (*gsar-ma*, literally "new-ist") with Tibetans and Indians who traversed the Himalayas in search of teachings, fame, money, and enlightenment. This movement gradually began to dominate the Tibetan cultural arena with its powerful rhetoric and mythos centered on the grand project of the translation of Indian Buddhist scriptures into Tibetan, as well as its astute links to political and economic centers in conjunction with a monastic reinstitutionalization. This was successfully linked in reality, and in imagination, to the contemporaneous reawakening of Tibetan economic and political vitality, such that the "renaissance" of Tibetan civilization came to be linked to the modernists' "reform" of Tibetan religion. Both employed a rhetoric of the taming or control of a barbaric indigenous reality with structured language, community, practices, and belief systems derived from a more civilized India (see Samuel 1993, 217-22, 454, 571-72).

Modernist Tibetan rhetoric tended polemically to paint Buddhist groups that resisted their agenda—who came to be known as the "ancients" (Nyingma)—as passive traditionalists continuing an antinomian form of mysticism stemming from the dark period, thereby attempting socially, religiously, and intellectually to disenfranchise those groups maintaining the "old" Buddhist traditions without becoming actively engaged in the reform movement. In fact, those groups loosely organized under the rubric of the "ancients" embarked on an equally complex religious and intellectual renaissance during the same period (late tenth to fourteenth century) which continued pre-eleventh-century Tibetan traditions while revitalizing them via creative appropriation of the wealth of material flowing into Tibet through the modernist translation project. One of their most successful rhetorical weapons was the innovative adaptation of Indian Buddhist models for scriptural authentication that became known as the treasure (Ter) movement.[25] The Tibetan Ter movement thus began in earnest in the eleventh and twelfth centuries with the cultural revival that followed the dark period. As the new Buddhist groups importing teachings and authority from India put older Tibetan Buddhist lineages on the defensive, the latter, the Nyingma, developed the Ter movement as a response. Ter involved the visionary notion that during the dynastic period the literary jewels of Indian Buddhism had been embedded in the subtle bodies of Tibetans as well as the geographic body of Tibet herself,[26] so that after the dark period their only location (the fragile esoteric traditions having since disappeared in India) was this latent enfolding within the Tibetan body. In other words, many teachings hitherto unknown were said to have been brought to Tibet in the eighth century by Padmasambhava and Vimalamitra but concealed for the sake of future generations instead of being publicly disseminated at that time. These teachings were now being gradually recovered by reincarnations, particularly of Padmasambhava's and Vimalamitra's eighth-century Tibetan disciples who had been appointed as the predestined revealers of the treasures, the Terton. Thus once the darkness lifted, these treasures were said to be gradually revealed or excavated by reincarnations of these key dynastic period players. From an external perspective, it appears that the treasure cult involved innovations and adaptations of doctrinal as well as contemplative systems that creatively synthesized indigenous lineages with the new modernist material. Its historical mythos provided a legitimizing force that combated the modernist manipulation of contemporary Indic authority and lineal purity.[27]

While complex classificatory schemes developed concerning the nature and content of such rediscoveries, it is sufficient to consider two dichotomies: (1) texts versus nontexts (statues, ritual implements, etc.) and (2) texts revealed in visions without material support versus texts uncovered from the earth as physical manuscripts, though often in special encoded form known as Ḍākiṇī script. The latter distinction can be summarized in terms of earth treasures (*sa gter*) and treasures of "intention" or "wisdom" (*dgongs gter*),[28] one physically buried in the body of Tibet and the other mystically concealed in the transmigrating, embodied psyches of Tibetans. While we may readily understand the latter in terms of spontaneous composition, which by first-hand reports is accompanied by iconic flashes of past-life memories as well as intense and unusual bodily sensations, the earth treasures involve complicated searches based on visions and prophecies, discoveries of strange material items, and an often fragile process of decoding that can fail if any of the tendrel, or supporting circumstances, are disrupted. In either case, whether the texts were buried within the depths of the Tibetan earth or the depths of a Tibetan body,[29] the agent of concealment is most often Padmasambhava or Vimalamitra, while the agent of discovery is the reincarnation of one of their principal Tibetan disciples.

The functions of the early Ter movement during cultural turmoil were thus threefold:[30] (1) in the face of modernist attacks, to authorize and authenticate the Nyingmas' religious traditions by invoking a competing power structure located in culturally powerful memories of the dynastic period, headed by a reinvented Padmasambhava; (2) to appropriate and transform for a self-consciously autochthonous tradition the new intellectual and religious materials stemming from India without acknowledging them as such; and (3) to develop uniquely Tibetan theories, practices, and systems in an environment often dominated by a sense of cultural inferiority. In terms of the third point, the Ter ideology gave these traditions an Indic guise for legitimation while also creating a space in which they could transform Indic influences in Tibetan terms without simply reproducing them. Thus Ter had an important buffer function that prevented indigenous Tibetan concerns, practices, and beliefs from being overwhelmed by the immense power and authority that imported classical Indian Buddhist systems assumed in the eleventh and twelfth centuries. It was intimately concerned with formulating and sustaining Tibetan self-identity in the face of an influx of foreign culture, and thus with the value of Tibetan autonomy. Even in its invoking of Indic authority with Padmasambhava and Vimalamitra, it was precisely their presence and actions *in Tibet* that was of crucial significance, and thus this invocation simultaneously functioned to reiterate the significance of Tibetan culture in and of itself.

Finally, I would like to emphasize the role of the Great Perfection in the treasure cult: not only was it one of the most important bodies of early Ter as well as arguably the key doctrinal system in the nineteenth-century ecumenical movement that Khenpo Jikphun is heir to, but it also has been the most important Buddhist tradition in Khenpo's corpus, oral teachings, and community. The Great Perfection was central to the Ter movement as it underwent momentous transformations that clearly reflected the appropriation of the modernist importations into a characteristically Nyingma space, while its rhetorical directions offered the most sustained and clearly articulated inversions of the dominant modernist rhetorical strategies: naturalness is emphasized instead of regulated refinement, indigenous resources instead of imported civilization, advocacy of inaction instead of massive projects, spontaneous patterning instead of contrived intentional ordering, lay life instead of monasticism. What made the Great Perfection so uniquely suited to the task of interpretive assimilation was precisely its strong rhetoric of denial, which was infamous in Tibet for its apparent negation of key Buddhist beliefs and values. As I have argued elsewhere,[31] one of the key functions of this deconstructive language was to destructure the imposing intellectual coherence and authority of a given Indic system of thought and practice, thereby enabling its elements to be reconfigured within a distinctively Tibetan vision. The end result was a genuinely Tibetan transformation of Buddhist tantra that innovatively appropriated and thoroughly revised it in the cauldron of Tibetan ideologies, culture, and language. The Great Perfection's rhetorical negation thus functioned to create and sustain a bounded *Tibetan* discourse that resisted the pressure of domination from the new Indic materials flowing into Tibet and yet performed the alchemy of cultural assimilation. This process was hampered in modernist circles by the immense drains of faithfully translating primary materials from an alien culture and language (i.e., Indian Buddhist scriptures), the need to appear faithful to the transplanted paradigms, and their general rejection of the production of new canonical literature and paradigms through Tibetan authors speaking in the anonymously creative voice of a buddha (as was frequent in Ter). Ter, the Great Perfection, and the modernists' own diligent Indology were thus the three main factors that enabled the Nyingmas to create literary and intellectual works of enduring value that were as rooted in Indic forms as they were in the Tibetan soil.

Revealing Treasure in the Twentieth Century

We return now to Khenpo Jikphun's redeployment of this ancient Ter strategy of legitimation and innovation against the backdrop of the transformed landscape of the twentieth century. Some of the more remarkable accounts of these later post-Cultural Revolution events of revelation are as follows. In 1990 he identified a site in northeastern Tibet as being the location of the palace of the legendary King Gesar and directed an archaeological dig that turned up ancient building stones as well as several treasure chests (*sgrom bu*).[32] This was linked to his recall of a previous incarnation as Yuö Bumme (literally, "intense turquoise light"), the aforementioned son of Danma, one of King Gesar's ministers. Since Yuö Bumme is said to be an emanation of Mañjuśrī and Gesar an emanation of Avalokiteśvara, this reinscribes his own close relationship to the contemporary Dalai Lama, as will be seen below. During a visit to the Potala Palace on his first trip to Lhasa, he identified several historically important rooms of which even the curators were unaware. His visions while visiting Samye Monastery during the same trip are related below.

A typical discovery of an unknown sacred site happened during his visit to a place known as Sacred Site Interior Monastery, which is said to be associated with the Buddha's Enlightened Speech.[33] Here he discovered and opened up a meditation cave of Vimalamitra and a secret Ḍākiṇī cave. At dawn on the seventeenth of the first lunar month in 1987, he sat for a while in silent meditation and then suddenly said, "Bring me some ink and paper!" He then related the following manifest concerning previously unrevealed sacred sites and had it transcribed (the first and fifth lines are written in esoteric Ḍākiṇī languages):

Pu-ta-ka-ru-hu-ma-li,
To the left direction of *Me lha skya ring,*
One-third the way up a red heart,
In the middle of a bright mirror-disc and amidst trees,
Ratna pustu mudri shre dpe,
A tiger-girl with white silk and intoxicated,
Prize this time without letting it slip away.

In accordance with the mention of tiger-girls, Khenpo called together ten young girls (many of whom were born in a tiger year, according to the Tibetan calendar) and ten young boys and gave them the following instructions: "On this place's southern border, there is a cave about one-third the way up a heart-shaped rocky mountain. In front of it is a disc-shaped field, while trees surround the cave near its entrance. See if you can find it!" After sending the children to search for this meditation cave, Khenpo and his entourage went to a nearby guru meditation cave that was a sacred site of Avalokiteśvara. There Khenpo performed a ritual ablution, incense offering, and consecration of the site. He also took a chest from treasure concealment in the cave's depths, and at that time ambrosia spontaneously flowed from within the cave and the people outside clearly perceived melodious music and fragrant scents pervading the area. When the children who had been searching for the cave's location returned, he performed a ritual feast offering dedicated to Mañjuśrī.

The children related how they had found what they suspected to be the cave, and Khenpo sent several disciples to look for the sacred site's entrance with detailed instructions concerning the shapes of the mountain, cave, and surrounding field as drawn from the prophetic manifest. He predicted an additional cave would be found, a secret cave of the Ḍākiṇīs with imprints of their fingers, the syllables *Bam-ha-ri-ni-sa*, and their hand implements with offering-substances naturally engraved on its rock walls. Everything was clearly there just as Khenpo had described it. These discoveries were immediately inscribed within the web of prophecies that permeate the world of Tibetan Buddhism. The former cave was identified as a sacred site where Vimalamitra's emanation achieved contemplative realization; the latter was identified as the site where Vimalamitra taught spiritual doctrines and "turned the wheel" of feast offerings to a trillion Ḍākiṇīs such as Glorious Wisdom (Dpal-gyi blo-gros). It is said that some great figures had previously tried to find the former cave but were unable to do so. Khenpo located prophetic references to these two sites in a treasure prophecy:

> There is a meditation cave of Vimalamitra with his foot prints in stone . . .
> Esoterically it is the Glorious Copper Mountain in the Ngayab continent,[34]
> And in that glorious mountain there is an Assembly Hall of Ḍākiṇīs.

In addition, a Terton named Matiratna once revealed a treasure entitled *Prophecies Illuminating the Future, a Dialogue with the Ḍākiṇī Fierce Subduer of Demons*, which has a prophetic passage Khenpo interpreted as referring to his opening of these sacred caves to the outside world:[35]

> A power spot on the Tidro rock will be opened up, and by my, Urgyen Rinpoche's, magic powers, the door to a secret cave [an isolated sacred site of the Ḍākiṇīs] will be opened by an emanation of a small boy in eastern Tibet. Its internal door won't be opened except in the future, and the signs indicating that time are that border [i.e., foreign] troops will arrive in the hidden gorge and conquer, while religious activity will be no more present than a daytime star.

Khenpo thus identified this site as a previously unknown sister site to the famous cavern in Central Tibet within the Drigung district known as the Great Assembly of the Ḍākiṇīs Kere Yangdzong, a huge cave said to have been frequented during the dynastic period by the famous consort of Padmasambhava, Yeshe Tsogyel: both involve caverns functioning as "assembly centers for Ḍākiṇīs" and associated with the name Tidro.[36] Finally, Khenpo told his disciples how the caves' potent field of blessings meant that contemplation performed within them would be remarkably enhanced and result in direct visceral encounters with Vimalamitra and the Ḍākiṇīs respectively.

It is interesting to think of Khenpo's unusual commitment to celibacy in terms of Charlene E. Makley's argument for the importance of gendered practices in the reconstruction of Tibetan identity in contemporary China through the medium of sacred geography.[37] She argues that Tibetan women's adherence to traditional Tibetan gender distinctions with regard to the sacred space of Buddhist monasteries has played an important role in the subversive reconstruction of nationalistic models of Buddhist-derived authority that resists the "state-constructed map" of authority and identity. This is against the backdrop of emphasizing that for Tibetans "self" and "other" are played out to an unusual extent in terms of the opposition between sacred and profane, although my experience indicates that some type of distinction between domestic and public plays an equally important role, even if not as immediately visible. Clearly male-dominated institutional Buddhism is a key repository of Tibetan cultural identity (see Makley 1994, 79), in part because temple building is one of the few permissible public ways to express nationalistic pride and commitment with excess financial resources or donated labor. The complex cultural practices that then sustain these temples also play critical roles in shaping a distinctively Tibetan identity in resistance to the government's attempts to construct a suitably cleansed ethnic identity at home in the People's Republic of China. However, institutional Buddhism should not be overemphasized, given the importance of domestic residences, the fact that lay religious practices are often only peripherally connected to such institutions, including pilgrimages where such institutions are often limited to mere markers,[38] the informal nonmonastic communities that inhabit Tibet's sacred geography, the evolving strata of nonmonastic Tibetan intellectuals, and in general the pervasiveness of lay religious contemplative rituals. My analysis suggests that while Khenpo's commitment to monasticism derives in large part from the key role of such institutions in the reconstruction of Tibetan identity and community, it is his blending of the role of monastic hierarch overseeing a huge community with that of a charismatic (and generally lay) leader in the "field" that has situated him at the center of these pervasive articulations of Tibetan resistance through the medium of the Tibetan landscape itself.

The most important aspect of these activities, however, relates to the Ter phenomenon, since no contemporary Terton is more renowned than Khenpo Jikphun. The reasons are clear: his treasures include a large corpus of philosophical treatises, poetry, contemplative manuals, and ritual cycles of undeniable eloquence, precision, and power; and his discoveries have been extensive, miraculous, and public events.[39] The background to his Terton status is his frequently reiterated claim to be the reincarnation of Nanam Dorje Dudjom, one of the 25 principal Tibetan disciples of Padmasambhava in the eighth century. Thus his Ter are supposed to be actual teachings that he received in this former life but only now is able to recall and retrieve. In fact, most of his corpus has been produced by spontaneous composition, whether understood as his personal work or a transmission from figures of the past—these days disciples use a handy recorder to tape such compositions as they emerge and later transcribe them. Along with these wisdom treasures, his Ter also include material earth treasures such as yellow scrolls concealed in odd-shaped rocks and various statues or ritual implements recovered from within rocks. To give a sense of the nature of these discoveries, I will briefly describe four such events (all of which transpired in the post-Cultural Revolution period), the final two also providing some sense of his ability to galvanize Chinese and refugee Tibetan interest as well.

Ter as a source of miracles and sacred power. A famous example of public treasure occurred when Khenpo Jikphun was giving a Mañjuśrī empowerment on the tenth day of the first lunar month in 1981. In the morning while performing the preliminary recitations Khenpo kept looking up at the sky like a crazy yogi and, quite unlike his ordinary, ritually efficient conduct, he was not performing the ritual or the hand gestures properly, at times chanting the recitation very rapidly and at times very slowly. In the afternoon as the ritual feast offering was being performed, Khenpo Chöpe was acting as the attendant who handed Khenpo Jikphun the ritual items as required. Then as he presented the sacrificial cones (*gtor ma*) to Khenpo, Khenpo stood up instead of taking them and held a white offering scarf in his outstretched hands. A "chest" resembling a dark green bird egg then fell from the sky in front of his arms and landed on his desk. A number of people (several of whom I interviewed in 1991) witnessed it falling, and Lama Gakdor in particular mentioned first seeing it in the space in front of Khenpo's hands as it fell down. Khenpo then picked it up from the desk and allowed the 30 or so people there to pass it around, who found it a bit hot to the touch. This event details only one of his many reported miracles, ranging from receiving material treasures out of thin air to impressing his footprints in solid rock, and demonstrates the intense aura of power and sacrality with which his revelatory activities have imbued him. This conviction that his actions can step beyond the boundaries of corporeality and ordinary material limitations suggests to his followers that he may also be capable of a modern version of another impossible feat, namely leading them beyond the equally tangible confines of Chinese occupation, a presence now deeply rooted within the Tibetan soil and psyche.

Reawakening the geographic and mythic landscape of ancient Tibet. While on a pilgrimage to the recently restored Samye Monastery in Central Tibet,[40] Khenpo went to the Blazing Turquoise Tiled Porch on the central temple's second floor, where he suddenly experienced a past-life memory of Padmasambhava expounding the Seminal Heart Great Perfection (*snying thig rdzogs chen*) teachings to a retinue of King Tri Songdetsen and his select subjects. Saying, "Though previously Padmasambhava taught the profound teachings in this very site, now in its present form I can't even recognize it!" Khenpo wept profusely and sang a song of lament. When I asked him about it in 1991, he told me that the reconstructed Samye Monastery is unlike his past-life memories in many ways, particularly with regard to this porch. The porch is located on the second floor in the front part of the main temple as a wide balcony overhung by the roof above but without any external walls. Previously the roof below it had blue tiles, such that sunrays would reflect off its blue surface and suffuse the porch above with bluish light; at present that surface is instead covered with gold paint. His biography says that on seeing Samye in this condition, Khenpo suddenly recalled a wisdom treasure deriving from Padmasambhava's teachings to him in that very room, which his disciples immediately transcribed.

Then Khenpo went to the famous Chimphu retreat center located in the highlands near Samye Monastery. Along the way he had an intense contemplative experience of all ordinary impure appearances dissolving, followed by a vision of Padmasambhava emerging with countless Ḍākiṇīs from his pure land, the Glorious Copper Colored Mountain. Immediately after his vision he remained in meditative silence for a short time and then spontaneously sang many tantric songs. This was followed by a sudden vision of a demoness displaying unpleasant apparitions to indicate her displeasure at Khenpo's presence, such that he took the form of the fierce deity Lotus Heruka in response. Intimidating the demoness with this wrathful visualization, he confined her beneath the ground and ordered that she remain there for nine years. Finally arriving at Chimphu, Khenpo stayed at Keutshang Red Rock and became deeply absorbed in rituals of deity evocation. In the imperial period, Khenpo later said, Padmasambhava hid a treasure text at that spot in the center of two stone "chests" shaped like conch shells with clockwise spirals, the content of which summarized the contemplative triad of deity visualization, subtle body practices, and the Great Perfection, for the sake of renewing degenerated teachings in subsequent times of strife. Padmasambhava had entrusted the stones to Yeshe Tsogyel, instructing her to hand-deliver them in the distant future to an emanation of his disciple Nanam Dorje Dudjom, who would arrive at the gathering place of Ḍākiṇīs called Tidro and Chimphu. Since he recognized that the time had come for the treasure to be extracted, Khenpo Jikphun took one part of this treasure out from concealment during his stay at Red Rock. As for the other stone chest, subsequently Khenpo went to the upper part of the foot of the Drigung Tidro mountain north of Lhasa and then sent Khenpo Chöpe farther on with a white offering scarf, instructing him thus not to come back until he had found a rock exactly like the one recovered at Chimphu. Khenpo Chöpe then obtained the stone from the hand of a woman staying in retreat in the Padmasambhava meditation cave at Tidro who is widely believed to be an emanation of Yeshe Tsogyel herself.[41] Though the time had not come to extract the treasure doctrines from these two stone chests, by virtue of there being an overriding necessity Khenpo revealed an empowerment ritual and evocation ritual for the goddess Kurukullā, as well as an empowerment ritual for the Fierce Guru, in the manner of a combined earth treasure/vision treasure deriving from these chests.

These incidents illustrate how Khenpo Jikphun's reanimation and extension of Tibetan mythology and its key icons is a dynamic process performed in close relationship to the Tibetan landscape, which is understood as a series of residences (*gnas*) inhabited by the Buddhist deities, ancestral spirits, local demonic entities, and the like, who have traditionally played a major role in the history of Tibetan culture.[42] Mythic history is thus retrieved through revitalization of the sacred landscape first created in ancient Tibet, a cooperative process with other Tibetans, both human and nonhuman, that involves encounters, exchanges, physical actions, and substances understood as productive of texts, or "treasures." These texts in turn give those encounters, actions, and substances significance, jointly creating a cultural density literally grounding Tibetans in Tibet once again. Thus Ter is one of the most striking crystallizations of the marked substance orientation of Tibetan pilgrimage and other practices relating to sacred geography (see Huber 1994, 36-45).

A common ground: Ter's extension of Tibetan culture into China. In 1987 Khenpo went to the Wutai (Five Peak) Mountains in China, saying that from a very young age he had an intense desire to go there in person as it was the Bodhisattva Mañjuśrī's main pure land here on Earth. Classic Tibetan histories speak of Mañjuśrī's gazing at Tibet from his home in the Wutai Mountains in the eighth century and deciding to emanate a form there as its next ruler. This was none other than the famous Emperor Tri Songdetsen, such that the mountains are an integral part of Tibet's dynastic past and mythic present.[43] Khenpo became convinced the time had come during the late spring of 1986 when he was giving an empowerment of the *Magical Net of Mañjuśrī* tantric cycle to more than one thousand disciples,[44] after a large-scale *Wheel of Time* (*Kālacakra*) tantric initiation that he transmitted to more than six thousand people. During the blessings' descent, the phase of the ritual when the deity (the "gnostic being") is invited so that its inspiration descends and dissolves into the disciple's visualization of the deity (the "commitment being"), the empowerment deity descended in an inner visionary manifestation to Khenpo and gave him a prophecy: "Since there will be a great benefit to the teachings and living beings if you go to the Five Peak Mountains, you should go there." At that time an external sign of this vision was witnessed by everyone present: Khenpo was perceived to levitate three feet above the ground and hovered there for a short time. From that time on Khenpo encouraged all monasteries to perform thousands of ritual evocations of Mañjuśrī (involving recitation of his mantra with visualization of his form), and in the beginning of 1987 he set out for the Wutai Mountains, along with thousands of other Tibetans.[45] Along the way he visited such famous Buddhist sacred sites as the Imposing Elephant Mountain (Emeishan in Sichuan) and the huge Buddha statue at Leshan in Sichuan and finally arrived at Beijing. There Khenpo Jikphun consulted the Panchen Lama about the ongoing purification and reform of Buddhism he had undertaken and was reassured that he was on the right path. Making prayers for the sake of the teachings and living beings in front of the small *stūpa* located in a pagoda on the slopes of Beijing's Western Hills (Xishan), which is believed to contain one of the four cuspids of the Buddha, Khenpo Jikphun then departed for the Wutai Mountains.

Almost ten thousand individuals from areas in Amdo, along with members of various other regional and ethnic groups (Tibetan, Chinese, Mongolian, etc.), are said to have gathered there with Khenpo. He first taught them basic doctrines such as Tsongkhapa's *Three Principal Aspects of the Path* (*Lam gtso rnam gsum*; renunciation, the altruistic enlightened mind, and the authentic view), Tsongkhapa's *Summarized Meaning of the Path* (*Lam rim bsdus don*), and the Kadampa master Gyalse Thokme Zangpo's (1295–1369) *Thirty-seven Practices of a Bodhisattva* (*Lag len so bdun*). Then, before the Stūpa with a Nucleus of the Realized One's Relics he had all the Tibetans who had traveled there together create a virtuous foundation by reciting the *Prayer of Samantabhadra's Conduct (Bzang spyod smon lam)* 30 million times in total,[46] and Khenpo himself made potent prayers for all those spiritually related to him to be reborn in the Blissful pure land (*Sukhāvatī*), for the teaching to spread far and wide, and for all sentient beings to attain bliss. To bring benefit to the teachings in general, Khenpo had exquisite statues of Padmasambhava, Atiśa, and Tsongkhapa, among others, built with the appropriate ornaments and mantras inserted in them and also provided many such sacred objects for the other monasteries in the area. One day he traveled to a monastery on the far side of one of the key mountains, and immediately on arrival seven children are said to have magically appeared and received teachings from him, after which they suddenly disappeared into thin air. In a meditation cave called the cave of Sudhana (Shancai)[47] Khenpo kept a strict retreat for three weeks. While staying there, on the morning of the twenty-ninth of the fourth lunar month, he had a pure vision of Mañjuśrī's youthful body, accompanied by intense contemplative experiences.

Then Khenpo Jikphun went to a cave on the Eastern Terrace where the ocean can be seen which is identified with a spot mentioned in the *Avataṃsaka Sūtra* as Mañjuśrī's constant residence.[48] He did a two-week retreat there and later said that he experienced uninterrupted visions of radiant light day and night as well as other powerful contemplative experiences and visions. Then on the tenth day of the sixth lunar month when Khenpo was making a feast offering dedicated to Mañjuśrī while staying at the Clear and Cool Rock Monastery, the sky became pervaded by strange patterns of rainbow light just as explained in the Clear and Cool Mountains guidebook reference to Mañjuśrī's emanations being present as multiform light rays. While Khenpo Jikphun had a vision of Mañjuśrī himself, these strange rainbow lights, including a very unusual rainbow-colored light sphere, were witnessed by everyone there. Subsequently, everyone present witnessed an extraordinary play of rainbow light from a cloud at sunset, and photographs were taken. During Khenpo's strict retreat in the Nārāyaṇa (Naloyanku) rock cave on the Eastern Terrace's slope,[49] his retreat house was encircled by a sphere of rainbow light, which again everyone witnessed. Khenpo Jikphun uncovered a miniature statue made of exquisite gold from this cave, which he later offered to the Dalai Lama, who was delighted by it. As Khenpo had on three occasions traveled to the Wutai Mountains in a dream body prior to actually going there in person, he often told his students he was able to identify all its sacred sites during this visit. One day while staying at the meditation cave of Sudhana, he said, "That area around the central mountain over there resembles a sacred site I came to in a dream.[50] If that's it, there's a damaged deity statue in that spot." He mentioned other related signs as well. Later his disciples found it was exactly as Khenpo had described. Khenpo also hid many statues and caskets as newly concealed treasures amid the Clear and Cool Mountains during his stay.

This extension of Khenpo Jikphun's Ter activity into parts of China in which Tibetan and Chinese Buddhism traditionally interacted creates a religious prospect of common ground, a shared physical and symbolic space of resistance to government ideologies and practices crossing, or at least intersecting, ethnic boundaries. In addition, his revelation and concealment of Ter at the Wutai Mountains invests the heart of the Chinese sacred landscape with a contemporary Tibetan presence, the precise inversion of the recent massive immigration of Chinese military and peasants into cultural Tibet. Unlike the Chinese caricature of Tibetans as uncouth and unkempt barbarians, it is a highly literate textualized presence that Khenpo represents, reveals, and leaves behind, a sophisticated *maṇḍala* with the capacity to organize time and space around it even within the dominating landscape of Chinese communism. In understanding the complicated Tibetan responses to "modernity," we must take into account not only the significant role of tourism in the revival of Tibetan sacred geography (see Makley 1994, 81ff.), and the role of Chinese and Western Buddhist appropriations of Tibetan culture for their own ends but also the Tibetans as dynamic agents who construct as much as they are constructed, and who are thus both changing subjects and objects in a phenomenon of interaction that goes far beyond the pale confines of what is dismissively labeled "Orientalism." The Chinese fascination with Tibetan Buddhism is particularly important, and I have personally witnessed extremes of personal devotion and financial support by Han Chinese to both monastic and lay Tibetan religious figures within the People's Republic of China, often linked to the *qi gong* craze that continues to be an important force in Chinese resistance to the "state" (see Ots 1994; Alton 1997). While I have more frequently witnessed Chinese dismissals of Tibetan culture as backward and barbaric, the pervasive importance of the *qi gong* movements in China again raises the possibility of a common ground where Chinese and Tibetan strategies of resistance, as well as oppressive otherness, and the construction (or deconstruction) of identity, encounter each other and overlap, even within an overall pattern of divergences.

Transcendent Ter in refugee Tibet. Khenpo Jikphun in his previous incarnation as Lerab Lingpa had a particularly close spiritual and personal relationship to the thirteenth Dalai Lama, such that both Khenpo and the current

Dalai Lama reportedly felt a strong desire to meet one other on the basis of this karmic connection. Khenpo expressed intense faith in the Dalai Lama. Thus he decided to travel to India to meet with the Dalai Lama and to visit the sacred Buddhist sites there. Penor Rinpoche, who in 1993 would become head of the Nyingma tradition, had invited him to come to his monastic seat in Bylakuppe, South India, on several occasions, but Khenpo postponed accepting that invitation because of pressing duties related to his activities in eastern Tibet as well as extenuating political circumstances.[51] However, toward the end of the first lunar month after the Tibetan New Year in 1990, Khenpo Jikphun finally made the trip accompanied by Khenpo Namdrol from Penor Rinpoche's monastery.[52] When visiting the famous Yangleshö Padmasambhava cave in Nepal just outside of the Kathmandu valley, he experienced past-life memories in which he recalled a teaching cycle entitled *The Single Dagger of the Tutelary Deity's Enlightened Spirit, the Dagger in a Small Neck Bag.*[53] The name is derived from a small bag that Padmasambhava wore around his neck which contained a ritual dagger embodying the essence of his tutelary deity. When Khenpo subsequently arrived in Dharamsala, he offered its empowerment to the Dalai Lama and subsequently during conversation, an auxiliary teaching of this cycle spontaneously emerged in Khenpo's mind, which the Dalai Lama wrote out on his behalf. In addition to exchanges of teachings and wide-ranging conversations on various topics, several attendants reported one encounter during which they discussed past-life memories of their previous relationship as the thirteenth Dalai Lama and Lerab Lingpa. Just prior to Khenpo's departure, the Dalai Lama finished a supplication prayer for the *Dagger* cycle that Khenpo had requested that he compose, and thus Khenpo received the verbal transmission for it from the Dalai Lama directly. Photographs of the two were subsequently widely circulated within eastern Tibet, although I did hear rumors of the local authorities' unhappiness with this.

Also during this visit Khenpo's niece Ani Muntsho was recognized by the Dalai Lama as the reincarnation of Migyur Palgyi Dronma, a Central Tibetan emanation of Yeshe Tsogyel, who was the daughter of the important Nyingma master Terdak Lingpa (1646–1714), also closely linked to the fifth Dalai Lama (Dudjom Rinpoche 1991, vol. 2, 833; Dorje and Kapstein 1991, 81). Khenpo was also invited to the Dalai Lama's Nechung College, where he gave the *Dagger* empowerment in their assembly hall. In the ritual phase at which the gnostic deity descends, the special protector of Nechung suddenly possessed the Nechung Oracle and in a highly unusual act gave prophecies and religious offerings to Khenpo; at the same time, the goddess Dorje Yudronma suddenly took possession of her human oracle and gave prophecies. Khenpo himself experienced vivid past-life memories and wept as he recalled his former relationships and intimates. This set of events points to the deployment of Ter within Tibetan refugee communities as a rare instance of a recent movement originating from within the

People's Republic of China exerting powerful and positive effects on Tibetans still living outside its confines. His dramatic actions both within a major Tibetan monastery in India and within the sacred and political heart of refugee Tibet (Dharamsala) undercut the paradoxical notion that traditional Tibetan culture only exists outside of Tibet and points to a possible forging of unity within the fractious Tibetan community through a potent brand of myth relocated within modernity, or at least some variant thereof.

Darkness and Renewal: The Value and Limits of Contemporary Ter

I would like now to reconsider the themes of modernity, alienation, and renewal in a comparative manner that traverses the historical gap between the origins of the treasure cult in the eleventh and twelfth centuries and Khenpo's contemporary revival of Ter in the late twentieth century. I believe there is a strong subcurrent in the Tibetan imagination that associates the Chinese occupation, and above all the Cultural Revolution, with the dark period of Tibetan history following the collapse of the empire. In both cases Buddhism was persecuted, the ecclesiastical and economic structures collapsed, key religious and temporal monuments went into decay, formal education slowed to a standstill, and social chaos erupted. A key difference that is immediately evident is that between the self-engendered and self-governed collapse of central authority that occurred in the ninth century as the Tibetan Empire disintegrated for internal reasons and the coerced and other-engendered devastation brought about by Chinese invasion and occupation. As Tibetans have begun to re-emerge from this new dark period in the past two decades, there are thus unavoidable associations of this renewal of Tibetan identity with the "renaissance" of Tibetan culture beginning in the late tenth century. The points of similarity are as follows: (1) conflict with coercive temporal authorities and resistance through antinomian behavior are central; (2) a massive amount of new cultural information is flowing into Tibet from outside, much of it in literature written in alien languages (mostly Chinese and to a far lesser degree English, in contrast to the earlier predominance of Sanskrit and associated languages); (3) rebuilding monasteries and re-establishing religious lineages after an extended absence are foremost among many Tibetans' concerns; (4) there is controversy over purity in terms of religious infractions or corruptions; and (5) the institution of *tulkus*, or reincarnate lamas, has assumed renewed importance (an institution that first developed during the Tibetan renaissance). In terms of authority conflicts in early Tibet, hagiographies from eleventh- to thirteenth-century Tibet are pervaded by themes of social conflict as new religious and political institutions struggled to secure and consolidate power in the region.[54] Important themes include the strident criticisms of Nyingma traditions by the rulers of eleventh-century western Tibet (Karmay 1979, 1980), suppression of populist religious movements (Martin 1996), and the hegemonic rule of the Sakya sect under the patronage of the Mongol Yuan Empire in the thirteenth century (Petech 1990; Jackson 1994). Accusations of antinomian behavior figuring centrally within many of these conflicts involved two distinct types: social transgressions cloaked in tantric rhetoric, ranging from a supposed subculture of unbridled sexuality and even ritual murder (such as reflected in the infamous "union and liberation" [*sbyor sgrol*] slogan) to powerful religious leaders' martial engagement in social conflicts,[55] and more institutional transgressions involving populist movements that seemed to dispense with clerical leadership,[56] criticism of monastic-based scholastic education, and general rhetorical opposition to ordinary institutionally defined Buddhist ethics and intellectual systems in favor of personal realization of the transcendent truth of the Buddha's teachings (see Germano 1994, 228-34). Finally, the institution of the reincarnate lama as a peculiar form of hereditary authority took shape between the eleventh and the fourteenth century as a strategy for institutionalizing spiritual legitimacy and charisma (among other things), and precisely this institution, along with its ideology of interconnected lines of reincarnations deeply intertwined with Tibetan history, has been at the forefront of religious change in eastern Tibet following the end of the Cultural Revolution.

There are of course crucial differences as well: as Chinese authorities maintain ultimate temporal control, Tibetans are in many ways not in control of their own future. Thus the new enemies—the Chinese and modernity—are common to most Tibetans and are colonial and extrinsic others, in contrast to the largely intra-Tibetan nature of conflicts during the eleventh and twelfth centuries.[57] In addition, the continuing vitality of refugee communities in South Asia results in a fissured self-identity, especially given the continued residence of key religious leaders, above all the current Dalai Lama, in these exiled and excised appendages of Tibet. The rhetoric often heard from Tibetan leaders in Dharamsala and their Western supporters echoes this state of affairs, often resulting in a strange inversion: the real Tibet is not in Tibet anymore, since the true, authentic culture of Tibetans is only maintained in uncorrupted form among refugee groups. Leaving aside the problematic nature of such rhetoric, it does capture a powerful sense of inadequacy, alienation, and abandonment that one often encounters in Tibetan areas of the People's Republic of China, particularly among the religious elite.

Thus it is essential that we ask how Tibetans have dealt with the literally dismembered body of Tibetans and Tibet, which was torn apart in a ritual sacrifice dedicated to the gods of modernism, communism, and Han imperialism. In particular, how have Tibetans turned to, and manipulated, the past in order to cope with the peculiarly dangerous manifestation of other cultures' enforced version of modernity that has so abruptly intruded into every dimension of their lives? In the present context, I have examined just one aspect of their response: the reliance on the Ter phenomenon among Nyingma traditions in a situation closely similar to that which first elicited its historical formation in the eleventh century. Prior to the opening of Tibet to the outside world in the early 1980s, the Ter movement appeared to have become quite limited in scope. In refugee communities only a few acknowledged Terton produced mainly wisdom treasures, and as far as I know, earth treasures were almost entirely absent, as one would expect, since the refugees carried with them Tibetan bodies but not the body of Tibet herself. It was unknown to what extent the Ter tradition was active in Tibet, if at all. However, my own experience in Tibet has revealed the existence of a vibrant, multi-pronged Ter movement that has emerged as one of the most powerful and vital strategies for the renewal of traditional Tibetan culture among Nyingma traditions in Tibet. Earth treasures—physical manuscripts in Ḍākiṇī language, special containers, statues, and ritual implements—are discovered in large quantities. I was told by one prominent lama, for example, that Tsopodorlo, a well-known Nyingma lama, had shown him a large chest full of such rediscoveries belonging to his recently deceased Bonpo spouse, Khandro Khachi Wangmo.[58] The phenomenon covers the full spectrum from the sublime to the absurd: at one point while I was living in Sichuan, a well-known Nyingma lama, of whom I had heard a number of incensed complaints from young women concerning his actions toward them, revealed to me several statues that he claimed to have revealed as "Ter" while in prison. An arguably more respectable Terton is the middle-aged, female Terton Tare Lhamo from Golok, who reportedly is illiterate but has revealed a number of beautiful poetic Ter.

The contemporary Ter movement is thus similar in many respects to the initial development of Ter in the eleventh to the thirteenth century, right down to the material items taken out of the earth and the odd yellow manuscripts; both visionary retrievals also take place against the backdrop of more mundane recoveries of ancient manuscripts hidden or neglected during violent times. In addition, the movement seems to be functioning on the ground in similar ways in terms of establishing authentication and legitimacy in the face of oppressive temporal authorities.[59] The role of treasure revelations in revivifying the sacred landscape and pilgrimage sites is fundamental to the reformation of Tibetan identity—not only is the uniquely Tibetan past again yielding its gifts, but the land itself is yielding concrete fruits intertwined with that past. The religious character of many of the shared "memories" that have historically played a key role in articulating collective identity for Tibetans entails that these actions perform a central role in the reconstruction and re-membering of this identity in a time of extreme pressures following a long period of violent darkness (see Dreyfus 1994). In many ways the rebuilding of sacred sites, along with the other ramifications of Ter, is a direct response to the loss of dimensionality in Tibet: during the Cultural Revolution, or more accurately the cultural devastation, everything in Tibet was flattened out culturally, just as physically the thousands of *stūpas* and monasteries were reduced to rubble littering the landscape. The Ter movement extends the roots of the present not only in the contemporary geographic landscape but also in the landscape of Tibet's remembered past. In this way, it is of unique value in imbuing the present with greater value and resonance for a very unsettled generation of Tibetans.

The potency of Ter as a Tibetan response to modernity is particularly clear in relation to Khenpo Jikphun's impact on some Chinese.[60] Not only are there Chinese monks and nuns resident in his Golok center and Chinese lay Buddhists periodically making the long pilgrimage there, I have heard reports of Khenpo literally being mobbed by Chinese Buddhists or simply the curious seeking his blessings or teachings during visits to Chengdu. I myself witnessed "transference of consciousness" (*'pho ba*) teachings he gave in Dartsedo which were attended by many Chinese. In Golok, I became friends with one Chinese monk from Beijing who had rejected his father, a famous *qi gong* master, to study with Khenpo Jikphun. Thus here finally is a Tibetan phenomenon that reverses the standard Han dismissal of "dirty, barbaric Tibetans" and raises the possibility of an acknowledged cultural superiority, at least in some respects. Khenpo's trip in the late 1980s to the Wutai Mountains was a major spectacle involving Tibetans and Chinese, numerous publicly reported miracles, revelation of Ter, and even the hiding of future Ter on Chinese territory. This same shifting of gravity by the Ter phenomenon has occurred with regard to perceptions of refugee Tibetan religious communities. Ter is much stronger in Tibet proper than in refugee Tibet, thus reversing the general feelings of inferiority aroused in Tibet with regard to the funding, autonomy, and scholastics of refugee centers. Thus Khenpo Jikphun's 1990 trip to India and Nepal stirred considerable interest among Tibetans parallel to the type of fanfare that has marked the return of prominent exiled lamas to Tibet since the early 1980s.

There is another aspect of Khenpo's biography that is standard for a Terton: controversy. The long-standing Tibetan concern for lineal purity, a matter that Ter addresses, has been a central issue in the post-Cultural Revolution era. Against the background of a larger cultural focus on continuity and lineage in Tibet (Samuel 1993, 149-54), Tibetan Buddhism has an exceedingly strong focus on religious lineage through an unbroken continuum of masters as the means of valid transmission of an intact tradition. In the eleventh and twelfth centuries, Nyingma groups were frequently attacked as being involved in corrupt lineages that may have possessed authentic texts but whose spiritual authority to use and understand those texts had corroded during the chaos of the dark period. The treasure mythos was the Nyingmas' most potent response to such criticism, as its "direct" transmission from Padmasambhava and other dynastic period saints not only provided an authentic lineage but also could even claim to be purer than ordinary lineages whose freshness and purity were inevitably eroded by the ravages of temporality and human nature.[61] The rupture of religious lineages of all types in modern Tibet—institutional, doctrinal, yogic—caused by the recent material devastation, massive deaths, and deep social ruptures has aggravated the traditional Tibetan concern with the fragility of continuity, especially in light of continued lack of control over their own sociopolitical future. This is also reflected in the frequent claims heard from refugee Tibetans that Buddhism in Tibet has become disrupted, such that pure religious traditions at populist and elite levels have only been maintained in refugee Tibet.

While Khenpo's revival of Ter has offered a potentially potent response to such concerns, controversy inevitably stems simply from the nature of a Terton: to hold that one is the reincarnation of a famous eighth-century figure with special direct access to new sources of scripture requires real self-assertion, as well as the ability to promote oneself so as to overcome resistance to such claims (the accreditation of Ter in many ways boils down to one's contacts).[62] Thus Khenpo Jikphun's Terton status has caused a considerable subcurrent of jealousy, particularly since it is linked to his leadership of movements to purify Buddhist lineages in eastern Tibet of breaches of *samaya* (tantric vows) that arose during the Cultural Revolution by his consistent opposition to the participation of violators in major tantric empowerments or high religious positions. This has also led to at least one minor Terton skirmish (see above); and it is connected to the tensions between lay tantric practitioners and monks (*dge slong*) that have resurfaced in the resurgence of Tibetan Buddhism. However, unlike earlier Ter movements, which were the frequent locus of attacks by reformists on ethical grounds given that its proponents tended to be nonmonastic, noncelibate, and often given to seemingly antinomian behavior,[63] and earlier Great Perfection movements, which were attacked on intellectual grounds given their antischolastic rhetoric and focus on contemplative experience, Khenpo has linked Ter and the Great Perfection to ethical reform, systematic study, and monastic institutions. This linkage to institutional and ethical conservatism has meant that the Ter cult, at least in his hands, finds itself in an unaccustomed position of supporting the criticism of ethical transgressions and corrupted lineages. However, I would argue that this renovated Ter includes a strong nationalist subcurrent in its romantic-historical focus on the Camelot of Tibet's Once and Future King,[64] its reanimating of uniquely Tibetan pure lands even as Chinese technology and colonization attempt to reshape that same geography, and the millenarian overtones of its miraculous revelations indicating the re-emergence of the Buddha's potent authority and involvement with Tibet in the face of the onslaught of modernity. This unusual integration of personal charisma and authority, Buddhist rationalism and ethics, and a distinctively Tibetan cult of magic, miracles, and spontaneous manifestations of deities constitutes a revitalization movement that has managed to walk the thin line between morality and magic, charisma and institution, and, most important, Chinese authority and Tibetan tradition. The success of this integration can be seen, for example, when viewed in contrast to recent, overtly millenarian, populist movements in Tibet involving spirit possession, such as the Heroes of Ling,[65] that were quickly suppressed by alarmed Chinese authorities.[66]

A critical point of difference between ancient and contemporary Ter is the quite alien nature of the authoritarian other that current Ter combats and potentially assimilates. In the post-1978 era Tibetan horizons are dominated by a hegemonic foreign presence with a profoundly different ideological force, in contrast to the familiar, if at times antagonistic, otherness of imported Indian Buddhism and its Tibetan proponents from the eleventh century onward.[67] There is a new divide between secular scholarship and composition associated with Chinese literacy and translation activity conducted in the various Tibetan-oriented academic bureaus scattered across the landscape in modern Chinese cement-block architecture, on the one hand, and religious scholarship and praxis with its Tibetocentric concerns and agenda of institutional renewal and intellectual preservation, on the other (see Stoddard 1994; Ström 1994, 846-47). This is altogether different from the situation of the early Tibetan renaissance, when the secular/religious divide was largely absent, translation was at the heart of the religious renewal, and Ter unabashedly and successfully raided the massive materials flowing into Tibet through the modernist translation projects. Unlike this earlier period, contemporary Ter takes place within a broader movement of institutional renewal and doctrinal preservation, not the dissemination or transformation of new religious teachings from abroad; in addition, with its power hierarchy stemming from Padmasambhava and his disciples, Ter continues ideologically to look back to the dynastic period with its ensuing darkness, but these periods are no longer its own immediate historical context. Finally, the antinomian behavior of Tibetans working the twilight zone between tantric rhetoric and social reality has receded in the face of preoccupation with both colonially induced transgression of traditional Buddhist norms during the Cultural Revolution and colonially defined transgressions of Tibetan Buddhist nationalists engaged in active protest against a totalitarian state's rule.[68]

This is probably one of the primary reasons that current Ter, despite being essentially the renewal of old stories and despite its positive value in re-membering the violently dismembered body of Tibet and Tibetans, does not yet seem to involve the digestion of new materials, or the performance of the alchemy of cultural transformation. On this point it does not appear to correspond in function to earlier Ter, which served to assimilate new Indic materials available in "modern" translation, in respect to its own modern others, namely Chinese or Western traditions. The abyss between a coercive modernity and Tibet's own Buddhist past has been so sudden and abrupt that it appears we may be nearing the outer perimeter of Padmasambhava's capacity to project forward from eighth-century Tibet, such that Tibet is entering an uncharted realm where the past is no longer an authoritative guide. Despite Khenpo Jikphun's tremendous openness and efforts to weave modern America into Ter's weblike reality during his as yet sole trip to the United States in 1993—thus proving Ter can span countries as well as centuries—one will look to no avail for any trace of Chinese, Western, or even Tibetan modernity within the traditional loose-leaf rectangular confines of the several volumes of his collected Great Perfection-based revelations. In the last analysis, the modern other may simply be too foreign for the traditional Terton to digest in a Buddhist format, and at least for the moment, it appears to exceed even the capacity of the Great Perfection to create an alchemical buffer zone of rhetorical negation; only the future will tell if younger Terton may prove to be more adventurous in retrieving the enticing yet elusive intersection of Buddhism and modernity on their own terms. And then, at this imagined future moment, the long-suffering body of religious Tibet may complete its rise from the dead once again as a reconfigured gestalt with the capacity, will, and power to speak with its own distinctive yet transfigured voice in the modern arena.

Notes

I would like to express my deep gratitude to the Committee on Scholarly Communication with China for their funding and support of my research in eastern Tibet from 1990 to 1992, without which much of my present research would have been either impossible or considerably impoverished. I would also like to thank my two host institutions in the PRC—the Sichuan Research Institute of Nationalities and the Tibetan Academy of Social Sciences—as well as all the individuals who aided me so generously during my stay. Finally, I am indebted to Melvyn Goldstein and Matthew Kapstein, for their extensive and insightful comments on various drafts of this paper.

1. A very prominent Tibetan mythic history of the dynastic period presents the Tibetan landscape as a vast supine demoness, who is pinned down and controlled through a network of Buddhist temples. See Gyatso 1987.
2. The historical founder of Buddhism, Śākyamuni, was from an early period in India discussed in terms of two Bodies: his physical presence, or form bodies (*gzugs sku,*

rūpakāya), and the corpus of his teachings, or teaching bodies (*chos sku, dharmakāya*). In this paper, I play off this ancient Buddhist emphasis on the Buddha's many bodies.

3. Although there was systematic government looting of Tibetan art earlier, these days it is often Tibetans themselves who are involved.
4. The movements involved in such excavations all maintained deeply Buddhist traditions but were divided among those who maintained standard Buddhist historical discourses (known as the Nyingma [*rnying ma*]) and those who maintained idiosyncratically Tibeto-centric traditions (known as the Bonpo) that subsumed orthodox Buddhist history into a quite different account of origins and lineages.
5. See Thondup 1986 for an excellent survey of the treasure tradition in Tibet; Gyatso 1996 provides a succinct overview of the textual side of these treasures. In the standard presentation discussed by Thondup, the dynastic period concealment of these treasures was understood to have taken place via placing these texts within the Tibetan earth as well as within the transmigrating subtle bodies of Tibetans of the time. By "subtle bodies" I refer to the widespread late Indian Buddhist tantric notion that there is a more fundamental subtle body of energy currents within the ordinary physical body. By "physically" I refer to concealment that seems to have been a straightforward burial of items; "mystically" refers to the paranormal concealment of texts within solid rock, consciousness, and so on.
6. See Kunsang 1993 for a translation of an important early biography of Padmasambhava.
7. The ecumenical, or "non-partisan," movement originated in eastern Tibet in part as a reaction to the dominance of the Geluk (*dge lugs*) regime nominally headed by the Dalai Lama line of incarnations in Central Tibet. Intellectual and social in nature, it involved all the major traditions of Tibetan religion with the significant general exception of the Geluk. Particularly interesting for the present context is the fact that the Great Perfection (*rdzogs-chen*) tantric tradition in many ways formed the religious heart of the movement. The Great Perfection tradition is renowned for its strong deconstructive rhetoric undercutting analytical thought and its equally consistent positive celebration of the primordial enlightened nature of all life. It presents itself rhetorically as the "peak" of all Buddhist teachings which embraces all of them as partial truths. See Samuel 1993, 533-43, for a brief overview of the ecumenical movement and the Great Perfection's role.
8. At least one contemporary Bon scholar has explicitly identified the twentieth-century concealment of texts as a major "Treasure concealment" (Gyatso 1996, 152). Also, in an interview with the Dalai Lama printed in the 6 March 1996 edition of the *New York Times* international edition, he refers to the past 40 years as "our own dark period."
9. See Hanna 1994 for an interesting eyewitness report of a contemporary revelation in Tibet by a famous female Bonpo Terton whom I refer to below.
10. The individual in question is Dondrub Gyel (*Don grub rgyal*), whose story was repeated to me on more than one occasion by lay Tibetan scholars in Sichuan. All made a point of directly linking his death to the current domination of Tibetan cultural areas by Han Chinese (particularly the population transfer and dominance of Chinese language in education), which they claimed was made explicit in the suicide note. I have no access to the note and thus cannot verify its contents, although the rumors attest to their own social reality. See Stoddard 1994 for an interesting account of his life and death. She mentions (826) the famous note or "testament" (*bka' chems*) but appears also to have not had direct access to its contents; she adds an unhappy love life and criticism of Tibetan traditional attitudes (827) to his list of woes (in the more generalized rumors I heard, there was an exclusive focus on political problems stemming from Chinese control). See Don grub rgyal 1994 for a collection of his writings, including a biographical essay by Padma 'bum.

11. I have in mind here such eminent figures as Dudjom Rinpoche, Dingo Khyentse Rinpoche, Urgyen Tulku, and Penor Rinpoche.
12. In the original publication of this article, a detailed biography of Khenpo Jikphun was included here. The interested reader is referred to that publication (Germano 1998). *Eds.*
13. Of course the realities of such relationships are difficult to judge, but certainly in the gossip circuits there is an intense interest in the supposed quarrels and sexual infidelities that seem to be linked to so many Tertons' relationships to their sexual partners.
14. See Thondup 1986, 82-84, for a discussion of the importance of consorts in the recovery of Ter.
15. While it is said Khenpo had revealed Ter from childhood, the karmic momentum fueling these revelations was disrupted when he refused to take the aforementioned woman as his destined consort. Thus he was subsequently unable to reveal "earth treasures" until much later during a trip to the Lhangdrak power-mountain in Nyarong. Most of his treasures are understood to have been concealed by Guru Padmasambhava some twelve hundred years ago in dynastic Tibet, who transmitted his wisdom to certain advanced disciples in latent forms designed to become manifest in their future rebirths when most needed. Having arranged that wisdom in the symbolic form of written texts, he concealed them in special "adamantine" rocks, sacred lakes, inviolable containers, and so forth, sealing them with special prayers. The destined revealer was endowed with a special karmic momentum enabling him or her to reveal those texts and objects at the appropriate time when their contents could function to renew and revitalize the teachings. In general it is said that without the visionary relying on actual sexual yoga with his destined consort to intensify and enhance his energy, it is difficult to extract these treasures, which accounts for Khenpo's prolonged dry spell after refusing his destined consort. When he subsequently began to uncover treasures once again, his lack of a consort resulted in his excavated statues of Padmasambhava lacking their traditional hand-held tridents, which are symbolically understood as signifying the consort.
16. Longchenpa (1308–63) and Mipham (1846–1912) are arguably the two most prominent postdynastic figures in contemporary Nyingma circles.
17. The five corruptions relate to life span, emotional distortions, sentient beings, time, and outlook.
18. The three jewels are the traditional objects of refuge for Buddhists: the teacher (Buddha), the teachings (Dharma), and the community (Sangha).
19. This is verse 125 of the sixth chapter of Śāntideva's famous *A Guide of the Bodhisattva's Way of Life*. I have used Batchelor's 1979 translation.
20. Although, as discussed above, Khenpo Jikphun has decided against casting his community as a formal monastery, in terms of behavioral guidelines, curriculum, and residents it is for all intents and purposes a deeply monastic institution.
21. The character of Ngakpa lineages in eastern Tibet and their relationships to celibate religious institutions have been barely researched. For interesting comments on the subject in western Tibet, see Aziz 1978, 51-56.
22. Married "monks" (*grwa-pa*) have been discussed at length by Aziz (1978, 76-94), in western Tibet under the rubric *Ser khyim*, but the extent and nature of such a phenomenon in eastern Tibet is not clear to me. Certainly I have met such individuals who informed me that their clerical dress and married status was a custom in their locale, but I have also heard criticisms of such behavior which attributes it to more recent origins, such as the disruptions of the Cultural Revolution conjoined with attempts by unemployed youths to eke out a living based on performing rituals and/or begging under a clerical guise. The extent of traditional versus recent origins is thus at present unclear.

23. Schwartz 1994a, 730; Schwartz 1994b, 22. Also it should be noted that others (Samuel 1993 in particular) have argued that there is a much more ancient pattern of relative "rationalization" and "clericalization" of religion operative in Central Tibet that involved a greater stress on hierarchically governed ethical systems; Samuel argues this was in large part due to the centralization of the Lhasa-based polity with its religious stress on large monastic institutions. Based on my own experience in various parts of contemporary Central Tibet, it is clear that this highlighting of ethical and political dimensions only extends so far and in no way has elided the so-called magical element, or the individual and collective importance of tantric practices among lay and monastic populations.
24. Davidson 1994 made an excellent analysis of the initial emergence of this renaissance.
25. See Davidson 1990 for a discussion of Indian Buddhist models and Gyatso 1993 for a discussion of the use of Ter in Tibet for legitimation.
26. This notion of dual concealment within individuals' bodies and within the actual earth, rocks, and water of Tibet itself is discussed below.
27. I argue this at length in Germano 1994 and forthcoming; also see Kapstein 1992; Gyatso 1993; Davidson 1994 for related comments. Kapstein 1989 directly addresses the various Tibetan reactions to Ter, including polemical literature.
28. As noted in Gyatso 1996, 152, there was a historical transition from simple digging up of concealed objects to a complex "dependent upon visionary inspirations, the memory of past lives, and especially the compulsion exerted by the prophecy." However, it should be stressed that there continued to be a distinction made between physical recoveries and simple psychic recollections, though both were equally bound up in this complex of reincarnation and vision.
29. Gyatso 1996, 154, stresses the "Tibetan ground or Tibetan mind," but Gyatso 1986, 16 says the treasure site can be called "the adamantine body," a term for the subtle body. Given the importance tantric Buddhism places on the body, its paradigm of the body being the locus of buddha-nature and gnosis, the visceral nature of Tertons' discoveries, and my own use of the trope of the body here, I have used "body" instead of mind in this context.
30. Davidson 1994 and Gyatso 1993 both have excellent discussions of the functions of Ter, to which I am indebted.
31. See Germano 1994 for a more detailed presentation of this argument.
32. This is a technical term in the treasure cult that most commonly refers to smoothly polished medium-sized stones from which the treasure is then extracted. See Thondup 1986, 84, for a brief overview of their significance.
33. *Gnas nang*; also referred to as *Bsam gtan chos 'khor gling*. The former name derives from the monastery's foundation on a site said to be a special locus sacred to all three of the main bodhisattvas: Mañjuśrī, Avalokiteśvara, and Vajrapāṇi.
34. This is a reference to the pure land of Padmasambhava himself.
35. Matiratna is given as a sixteenth-century Terton in Thondup 1986, 194.
36. See Kapstein 1998 for an extended treatment of the more famous Tidro, which reveals interesting interpenetrations between our two accounts. The particulars of Khenpo's prophetic exegesis are that "the emanation of a small boy" referred to himself while "the hidden gorge" indicated the site was surrounded with forest.
37. See Makley 1994. Though the relevance of gendered practices here requires further thought that lies outside the parameters of my present inquiry, I would emphasize Khenpo's key role in the revival of Buddhist nunneries in eastern Tibet in addition to his role with male celibate institutions.

38. See Huber 1994 for an excellent analysis of how a Buddhist-centric analysis of Tibetan pilgrimage practices can distort our understanding of their lived reality on the ground.
39. His renown also derives from factors discussed previously: his personal charisma has been reinforced by intellectual brilliance and ecumenical learning; his religious center is one of the largest in Tibet, despite its not being founded on a preexisting institution; he has emphasized strict monastic discipline despite the traditional association of the Terton with noncelibate lifestyles; and he has created rigorous academic programs that rival those in the major refugee monasteries.
40. Samye Monastery is one of the most famous religious sites in Tibet, since it was the first Buddhist monastery constructed in Tibet at the height of the Tibetan Empire. It holds particularly important associations for the Nyingma tradition, since it is said Padmasambhava played a key role in taming the demonic forces that initially prevented the monastery's construction.
41. This woman is none other than the Tendzin Chödrön discussed in Kapstein 1998 as a pivotal figure in the revival of the community of nuns at Drigung.
42. See Huber 1994 for a discussion of the significance of sacred places in Tibet being termed "residences" (*gnas*).
43. One of the earliest examples is found in a twelfth-century history, Nyang Nyi-ma-'od-zer 1988, 272.
44. *'Jam dpal sgyu 'phrul drwa ba*. This is another title for the famous *Mañjuśrīnāmasaṃgīti*. See Davidson 1981 for a translation.
45. The number "thousands" here and the number "ten thousands" given below are difficult to evaluate. While I was assured they were accurate, traditional Tibetan hagiographies tend to use stylized enumeration and Raoul Birnbaum has informed me that it would be difficult to conceive of ten thousand individuals receiving teachings at the site in question (see below). At the same time, ten thousand was also a number given to me as attending significant empowerments at Khenpo's residence in Golok, and photographs of the event seemed to indicate at least several thousand monks in attendance. Thus I have chosen to use the numbers provided, with the above caveats.
46. The Stūpa with a Nucleus of the Realized One's Relics is a large and famous structure located in a monastery named Yuantongsi. It was built in the Ming period and is believed to contain the genuine relics of Śākyamuni Buddha, which have a complicated history of burial, reappearance, and reburial. Aside from the obvious connections to the Ter cult, the *stūpa*'s importance for Khenpo also appears to relate to its functioning as an important site for Chinese monastic ordinations.
47. Sudhana is the hero of the *Gaṇḍavyūhasūtra*, the culminating episode of the *Avataṃsaka Sūtra*. See Cleary 1993, 1135–1518, for a translation. There is an upper Shancai cave controlled by Tibetans and a lower Shancai cave controlled by Chinese; presumably Khenpo stayed at the former.
48. The Eastern Terrace is one of the five directional peaks, all of which are supposed to be sites where it is particularly easy to make contact with Mañjuśrī. The reference to the "ocean," which is far beyond visual range from Wutaishan, refers euphemistically to the "sea" of clouds visible from the peak.
49. This name occurs in the *Avataṃsaka Sūtra*'s account of dwelling places of bodhisattvas (according to a conversation with Raoul Birnbaum). It is said that long ago the Nārāyaṇa Buddha practiced here before proceeding westward. In line with the general Chinese notion of caves as sacred places linking to hidden places, there is a well-known story of a monk disappearing in this cave, indicating it to be a link to hidden worlds. Thus again we see a natural connection to the Ter activity that Khenpo performs at the site.

50. From this site the Central Terrace can be seen directly.
51. The political circumstances apparently related to the difficulty of securing government permission to travel abroad as well as the need for his personal attention during key stages in his academy's development.
52. Khenpo's original home monastery (*Gnub zur*) was actually a branch of Nyingma Palyul (*dPal yul*) lineage, currently headed by Penor Rinpoche who also is the current overall head of the Nyingma sect (base monastery in Bylakuppe, Karnataka State, India). Penor Rinpoche had met him on an earlier trip to Tibet, and Khenpo Namdrol had developed a close relationship to Khenpo Jikphun.
53. *Phur pa mgul khug ma'i thugs dam thugs kyi phur gcig.*
54. See Dudjom Rinpoche 1991 and Roerich 1976 for a wide selection of hagiographies from this period.
55. See Karmay 1979, 1980; Ruegg 1984. It is not clear how much social reality the at times lurid polemic attacks reflect, at least in terms of the nature of the actions imputed to the "transgressors."
56. See Martin 1996 for a very valuable analysis of the limited written traces of such movements.
57. I am sensitive to the problem of the essentialist reification of both the "Chinese" and the "state" in polarized opposition to "Tibetans," and would agree that the actual situation is "complicated patterns of convergences and divergences of interests and projects among the different groups encountering each other" (Makley 1994, 73). My point in the current context is that these "others" are shot through with a far stronger sense of alienness and difference than was ever the case during the Tibetan renaissance period.
58. See Hanna 1994 for a firsthand encounter with one of her revelations.
59. The religious norm in the eleventh to fourteenth century, which tended to be supported by political authorities, was to deemphasize ongoing revelation in Tibet in preference for considering a valid Indian manuscript and lineage as the necessary criteria of validity, and to embrace the scholastic norms and conventional Buddhist values of monastic institutions as primary. Thus the open canon of the treasure cult, its preference for continuing old dynastic period translations, and its predilection for the deconstructive rhetoric of the Great Perfection's emphasis on "sudden" experiences of indwelling enlightenment all rendered it the object of polemical attacks.

    While the constraints of my contemporary focus prevent a full elaboration, I would like briefly to note an important historical issue. As Dreyfus 1994 has outlined, an important element of twelfth- to fourteenth-century rhetoric is the articulation of a shared community and identity among inhabitants of Tibetan cultural zones, particularly as found within the "treasure" traditions. While these traditions themselves stemmed from groups outside of the sociopolitical mainstream, their mythic paradigms were in many cases appropriated by political powers (most famously in the ideology of the Dalai Lama as Avalokiteśvara ruling over a unified Tibet). Thus the creation of cultural identity as well as solutions to political disunity were essentially tantric in nature, involving the rhetorical manipulation of an ideology of an overarching transcendent *maṇḍala* embracing many smaller localized *maṇḍalas*. See, for example, Samuel's (1993, 61-63) discussion of the "galactic polity" (of course, this model derives from nontantric Buddhist societies, and I am only arguing that its specific form in Tibet was irreducibly tantric in flavor). These interlocked *maṇḍalas* were embodied in the web of sacred sites within which Tibetans of all types engaged in common actions (circumambulation, pilgrimage, making offerings, etc.) while an important yet often neglected subculture of monastic and lay practitioners thrived as semipermanent residents of isolated elements of this network (caves, headlands of valleys, etc.). This appropriation of the treasure cult's mythic rhetoric in relation to its current prominent role in again articulating Tibetan cultural identity in the face of oppressive authorities bears further thought.

60. I find the opposition between Tibetan "traditional" culture and an extrinsic "modernity" deeply problematic, unless this "modernity" is understood as highly rhetorical and embodying a very biased agenda, whether Chinese communist or Euro-American. This is not to deny that some version of this dialectic was present in pre-1950 Tibet, indeed even in the eleventh century, but rather to resist the tendency to lump all of Tibetan culture under the homogeneous rubric of our concept of "traditional." Dialectics between movements presenting themselves as "modern" and other cultural strata as "traditional" have been present in Tibet from at least the eleventh century onward (see Mumford 1989). I have tried to stress this at different points in my text but at times have found myself forced into language that suggests my acceptance of such a split. This note serves as a caveat.
61. See Gyatso 1996, 150. Also see Gyatso 1986 for an interesting study of lineage and interpretation in the treasure tradition.
62. In other words, simply announcing oneself to be a Terton and producing the supposed Ter is a relatively simple matter; getting others to accept the claim is more complex. A dominant factor in the process of "accreditation" is the acceptance of the individual's claim by high-ranking Nyingma lamas, who make their opinions on the relative validity of the "revelations" known in ways formal and informal; of course, the support of those who are already recognized Terton in their own right is particularly important. This support is far more than simply rhetorical, since these teachers may also begin to utilize the rediscovered rituals, contemplative handbooks, and so forth, in teaching their own students, thereby helping to create an institutionalized set of lineages that will perpetuate these traditions in future generations. See Gyatso 1996, 151 and Thondup 1986, 157-60 for remarks on the accreditation of a Terton. Aris 1988 has a fascinating study of the biography of Pemalingpa (*Pad ma gling pa*; 1450–1521), one of the most famous Terton, which focuses on his own struggle for legitimacy and acceptance. However, Aris's assumption of self-conscious deception on the part of the Terton reduces a multifaceted phenomena to a single simplistic model and largely ignores the equally interesting issues of hermeneutics, visionary experiences, and canonicity that are pertinent.
63. E.g., Thondup 1986, 157: "One cannot judge Tertons as inauthentic because of their imperfect and mercurial character, even to the slightest extent ... [A]mong the authentic Tertons there are many who are loose in speech and behavior and who, without the least hesitation, get involved in many activities that people will condemn."
64. As Schwartz 1994a, 737, notes, "The Chinese have come to realize that virtually every expression of religion [in Tibet] carries a message of political protest. Indeed, one of the salient aspects of current protest has been the ability of Tibetans to engage the secular Chinese state in a political confrontation on Tibetan terms, where religion is pitted against anti-religion. Tibetans have found that even the most innocent display of religiosity can be used to convey a powerful message of opposition to the regime. The Chinese state has been forced to contradict its own expressed policy of toleration, and Tibetans have been quick to seize on this as evidence that there is in fact no religious freedom in Tibet. Tibetans have thus been able to overcome their objective powerlessness by drawing the Chinese into a symbolic competition on terms where Tibetans control the meaning of the symbol." At a mundane level, individuals in eastern Tibet with sufficient financial resources have found making major contributions to the rebuilding of temples and monasteries to be one of the few permissible and highly visible ways to express nationalistic sentiment. This understanding of the action has been made

explicit in numerous discussions both with donors and with others. The reanimating of Tibetan mythohistorical beliefs and practices after its long suppression during the Cultural Revolution has been closely linked to this reviving landscape of *stūpas*, temples, and monasteries, such that Khenpo's actions in this light have clearly understood political implications. By "Tibetan Camelot," I refer to the close association of Ter with the mythoromantic elaboration of the activities of the dynasty's two principal kings, Songtsen Gampo (seventh century) and Tri Songdetsen (ninth century). In important Ter cycles, the first of these kings was claimed as an incarnation of the Bodhisattva Avalokiteśvara, the same patron saint who later took birth in Tibet as the Dalai Lama, the "future" king of Tibet, while the second was identified with Mañjuśrī. As mentioned above, see Kapstein 1992, 86, 88, for his suggestion that Arthurian legends are an apt analogue for understanding these elaborate mythic romances.

65. The text of this sentence has been slightly altered in light of the passages omitted in this abridgement. For an explanation of Khenpo's connection to the "heroes of Ling," see Germano 1998, 58-61. *Eds.*
66. See Schwartz 1994b, 226-31 for an interesting overview of the potential for Tibetan resistance to Chinese rule within popular religion. Also note the 1992 arrest of a woman in Lhasa simply claiming to be possessed by an important goddess (Dreyfus 1994, 218; Schwartz 1994b, 227).
67. See Schwartz 1994a, 735 for a similar analysis pointing out a crucial difference between the nature of political activity of monasteries in Central Tibet in pre-1959 and under Chinese rule. The earlier "others" were simultaneously fellow Tibetans in positions of political authority, Tibetans participating in the "modernist" (*gsar ma*) instead of "ancient" lineages of Buddhism, and the new Indic models of Buddhism they were assimilating into their own inherited traditions of Buddhism formerly drawn from Central Asia and China as well as India. The striking contrast between these familiar others and the modern variants of the "other" should be clear; the latter has a much stronger valence of being coercive, antireligious, and foreign.
68. Tantric Buddhism involves rhetorically advocating antinomian behavior, such as ritual murder, transgressing against social norms, and sexual intercourse in religious settings. The degree to which this rhetoric should be interpreted literally or symbolically was a source of tension in the Tibetan renaissance, with Nyingma groups often being attacked as adhering to literal-minded interpretations. Contemporary "transgression" is focused instead on past transgressions of Buddhist norms caused by the Chinese-forced destruction of traditional Buddhist culture in the Cultural Revolution (colonially induced) and the transgressions of Tibetan nationalists breaking Chinese laws in their defense of Tibetan autonomy and rights (colonially defined). Thus the nature of "transgression" to which current and ancient Ter is linked is quite different.

Part III

Defining Buddhist Identities

Defining Buddhist Identities: Introduction

The ways in which Buddhist persons and communities define and construct their identities through the lenses of Buddhist thought and practice are shaped by an infinite variety of factors. Just as Buddhist histories and ideologies are constructed and contested in response to complex interactions among particular historical, political, and cultural conditions, so processes of identity construction and contestation are influenced by multiple and overlapping concerns. Discourse surrounding Buddhist identities reflects the total range of human experience, from the most concrete and personal considerations to the most abstract doctrinal paradigms for understanding what it means to be a Buddhist person. But issues surrounding identity clearly do not rest solely in the realm of discourse; they have profound implications in the lives of Buddhists. As Anne Hansen's helpful notion of intersecting "landscapes of identity" in the first essay in this section suggests (231), the intricately interrelated factors contributing to the formation of identity together comprise a many-layered and always shifting map.

Contemporary theories of identity construction (as articulated in gender and postcolonial studies, for instance) recognize that the process of defining a personal or communal identity always proceeds from the identification of an "other" in contrast to which the self or community is defined. Defining identity is as much a negational process of delineating what a person or group is *not* as it is a process of claiming a particular set of qualities, values, practices, and so forth. Because identity construction involves establishing relationships of both similarity and difference with other persons or groups, it is an inherently ethical process in the sense that it entails forging commitments to support or oppose others based on shared or rejected values, traditions, practices, and so forth. Defining a Buddhist identity entails living in relation to a conception of the good life for oneself and for others, whether through modeling one's behavior on that of esteemed others or through taking an active stance against those who are perceived as a threat to personal or communal well-being. The essays in Part III investigate the construction of Buddhist identities in relation to a complex set of others, from modernity, the West, or a colonial regime, to other Buddhists—monks or lay people, adherents to a different sect, or persons of different sex or gender.

We can make a productive comparison between this general orientation in identity theory with the Buddhist theory of *anātman* (no-self), one of the three marks of existence. The theory of *anātman* denies the permanent and isolated identity of any person or thing; all entities come into being only in relation to the ever-changing conditions in which they are situated. As in contemporary academic theories, identity emerges from one's relationship with a myriad of factors. From the perspective of this foundational Buddhist theory, identity is always shifting, dependent, and relational—but as Janet Gyatso points out in her article, there is often a disjuncture between theory and lived reality. Buddhist discourse about identity is as likely as any other to reify identity and to establish norms against which others are measured.

Thus, while the notion of *anātman* is heuristically useful for thinking about Buddhist identity in broad terms, and for making connections to present-day theories of identity formation, this theory is not always invoked in Buddhist discourse about identity. In the essays that follow, the construction of Buddhist identities is governed by objectives as diverse as the development of moral discernment, the restoration of an idealized state of purity, the recuperation of Buddhist origins, or the delineation of monastic communities. The historical contexts shaping these concerns reveal not only the situatedness of all discourse on identity, but also the ideological motives for and consequences of the search for Buddhist identities.

While the essays in this section investigate very different instances of identity construction, they can be fruitfully related in terms of two overarching themes. First, each essay illuminates the tension between universal and particular understandings of identity. Motivated by particular concerns emerging from immediate historical and social circumstances, Buddhists have asked what it means to be Buddhist—a question that reaches beyond a specific local context even as it is conditioned by that context. The answers that Buddhists have given to this question are multiple, of course, but many Buddhists have understood their answers to possess universal validity and value. This tension between the notion that identity is constructed in particular contexts and visions of identity that lay claim to universality is evident on several levels within both Buddhist and scholarly discourse. As we discussed in the Introduction to this volume, the universalizing and essentializing tendencies of Orientalist scholarship have been widely critiqued in recent decades—and for good reason. When scholars defined the "true" essence of Buddhism, they concomitantly denigrated and devalued the forms of Buddhism practiced by contemporary Buddhists. The ethically motivated rejection of essentialism in scholarship on Buddhism has led to the privileging of historical and cultural context, such that any given vision of Buddhist identity is represented and studied as specific to a particular time and place. Yet the attention to particular context in identity construction need not, and should not, ignore the timeless and universal visions that Buddhists in many times and places have themselves constructed; the disposition to define a singular, essential, and universal "Buddhism" and a normative Buddhist identity is found in Buddhist communities as well, even though it is motivated by concerns arising from particular contexts. Indeed, as we will see in the essays included in this section, Buddhists have frequently viewed their "particular" visions of Buddhist identities both as rooted in the eternal and unchanging Dharma, and as possessing universal applicability and normative value. Thus, while it is possible and productive to understand a given vision of what it means to be a Buddhist as emerging from the concerns of particular times and places, and while Buddhist theories themselves (like that of *anātman*) conceive of identity as contextually determined, we need also to recognize that, for Buddhists engaged in the construction of identity, some Buddhists might ascribe such visions of what it means to be a Buddhist much broader—even universal—scope and validity.

The second theme proceeds from the first. Constructing identity, whether the scope of that identity is conceived as local or as universal, is a process of establishing or rejecting relationships with other groups and individuals. Thus we may speak of the ethics of identity formation, according to which the definition of a given identity (again, whether it aims toward inclusiveness or promotes exclusivity) has moral consequences. As each of the articles in this section reveals, the "othering" of those who are explicitly excluded from a particular identity or who fail to meet the criteria of an identity claiming normative status has real-world implications for access to power, resources, and status within a society. The definitional scope of any given identity, then, can be the grounds for its moral valuation: a formulation of identity might be judged unethical because it is not sufficiently universal, or because its claims of universal applicability impose restrictions on those without power to object. Indeed, ethical considerations often constitute the basis on which a putatively normative identity is interrogated and reformulated. The ethics of identity formation thus have relevance on a personal as well as communal level; all individuals negotiate among the multiple identities to which they lay claim and that lay claim upon them. These divergent aspects of personal and communal identity can create conflict among commitments and values that may ultimately make it impossible to hold competing identities. And yet, it is not always within the power of individuals to make those choices for themselves; as Janet Gyatso's essay on sex and gender identity makes especially clear, no matter how a person might wish to define their own identity, social definitions constrain not only what is permissible, but also, at least to some extent, what is imaginable. Recognizing the inseparability of identity formation from social norms and ethical judgments challenges us to articulate the complex connections between claims about identity and the particularities of Buddhist historical contexts and ideological commitments—and to recognize that those specific connections have also enabled Buddhists to envision universal truths about what it means to live ethically in the world as a Buddhist.

Anne Hansen's essay provides an especially helpful framework for examining these issues. Hansen examines the relationship between local interpretations of Buddhist ethics and the translocal *imaginaire* in the writings of nineteenth-century Khmer intellectual Ukñā Suttantaprījā Ind. This *imaginaire*—the "mental universe" imagined in the translocal Pāli texts of Theravāda Buddhism (226, citing Collins 1998, 61 and Faure 1996, 11-12)—is subject to interpretation in light of particular local, historical circumstances and values. Yet as Hansen points out, drawing on the essay by Charles Hallisey included earlier in this volume (111-112), "[a]lthough local Buddhist values might be produced in part as articulations of identity, they are not always meant to serve only as regional or local perspectives but, rather, as Buddhist values writ large, in a human or universalistic sense" (232). The moral "landscape of identity" articulated in Ind's manual of ethical behavior, the *Gatilok*, illustrates this complex interplay between the translocal *imaginaire* and local conditions and values—values that are set forth as having universal significance.

Indeed, in addressing what it means to be an ethical Buddhist in the particular conditions of colonial Cambodia, Ind himself draws an explicit contrast between timeless and universal values and truths of Dhamma (Sanskrit Dharma) and the "worldly," conditioned aspects of identity. According to Ind, the combination of Dhamma and worldly characteristics in a person determines his or her identity. This contrasting pair delineates a moral path according to which a person should work to diminish the worldly facets of identity and to live increasingly according to Dhamma—that is, according to the universal truths conveyed through Buddhist teachings. But just what Dhamma is and how one might approach it is a matter of interpretation. The translocal texts of the Theravāda tradition set forth authoritative answers to these questions, but those answers are read differently by particular Buddhists in particular times and places. While many of the canonical Pāli sources on which Ind draws appear to emphasize the merits of renouncing society and relationship in order to cultivate Dhamma, Ind instead stresses the fundamental interconnectedness of human beings, such that a moral identity necessitates cultivating certain kinds of relationships with others. The ethical ideal on which Ind focuses in his manual on ethical behavior, the *Gatilok*, is *satisampajañña*, a form of moral discernment that enables a person to distinguish good and evil in others and to recognize what is right and true. Again, while the Pāli texts on which Ind draws represent this form of moral discernment as one of the beneficial results of renouncing the world, Ind portrays it as a crucial resource for living ethically *within* a complicated and often deceptive society where traditional markers of virtue—none more so than monastic robes—could no longer be trusted as indicators of morality. By reinterpreting the translocal Theravāda tradition in this manner, Ind is able to promote a vision of the ethical life that is endowed with normative authority while having direct relevance to the particular challenges of his time and place.

Hansen argues that the tension between the ideal of renunciation and teachings that emphasize the profound interconnectedness of beings is present in the translocal tradition itself, enabling particular communities to interpret the teachings in light of the challenges they face and the values they espouse. Thus, Ind's interpretation of translocal ethical resources and ethical identities is endowed with universal significance and validity even as it is refracted through the specific historical conditions of Buddhists confronting the challenges of the onset of modernity and imperialism in Cambodia. Ind's allegorical tale of an orphan reasserts traditional Khmer social and ethical values in the face of these challenges, while rooting this ethical vision in the broader Buddhist tradition. For Ind, to be a Buddhist means, above all else, to recognize one's own ethical responsibility to others and to distinguish morality and immorality in others. The "others" against which this Buddhist identity is asserted are not only the European colonizers, but also those members of Khmer society who act in their own self-interest, failing to recognize their relationships with others. Ind critiques in particular corrupt Buddhist monks and the notion of detachment from the world that could be used to justify their lack of ethical engagement with others. Monks, above all others, ought to exemplify Buddhist virtues, and for Ind, the responsibility to others is paramount among those virtues. This overtly normative vision of a Khmer Buddhist moral identity resists the alternative discourses of identity—discourses shaped in part by European Enlightenment values of individualism, modernization, and capitalism—asserting instead a Buddhist way of being Khmer and a Khmer way of being Buddhist in a precarious time.

Like Ind, the Japanese monk-travelers that Richard Jaffe studies seek to establish a Buddhist identity that embodies universal, normative values. Whereas Ind does so by reinterpreting the familiar translocal tradition to which he belongs, however, the Japanese monks locate such an identity not in their own local Mahāyāna traditions, but in the relatively unfamiliar Theravāda tradition. This choice was influenced by Western scholarship of the time, much of which asserted that the Pāli canon and Theravādin monastic traditions most fully preserved Buddhism in its "true" form. These Japanese monks sought to recuperate in these regions such a "pure" and universally valid Buddhism focused on the figure of Śākyamuni and his "original" teachings by immersing themselves (to varying degrees) in the (local) Buddhist cultures of South and Southeast Asia in the late nineteenth century. Although the contours of such a Buddhism were greatly shaped by the emphases and assumptions of Western scholars, many Asian Buddhists, inspired by the apparent transregional unity of the Theravāda traditions, perceived in this "original" Buddhism an opportunity to resist Western imperialism by creating a unified, pan-Buddhist identity. For the Japanese monks, this translocal tradition practiced by their contemporaries in foreign places and cultures became the locus of their own lost Buddhist heritage; a pristine past was thought to be preserved in a (present) unfamiliar tradition.

At the same time, Jaffe notes that the writings of these Japanese travelers articulate conflicting frames of reference that reflect both Japanese anxieties and Japanese ambitions. Although the Japanese monks became students of the Theravāda tradition and worked to establish a "pure" and universal Buddhist identity, they often did so while maintaining a notion of Japanese superiority. While Japanese of the Meiji period were greatly concerned about the threat of colonialism, they responded to this threat in part through developing their own imperialistic ambitions. Thus, while the Japanese traveler-monks identified with South and Southeast Asian Buddhists as Buddhists, they also at times differentiated themselves from the colonized and downtrodden Buddhists they encountered. European imperialism constituted the other against which these Buddhists attempted to construct a unified and universal Buddhist identity that could include all Buddhists, but Japanese imperialism increasingly defined Japanese identity in opposition to other Asians; the construction of a Japanese identity constituted a frame of reference that conflicted with aspirations toward a pan-Buddhist identity. Jaffe suggests that this ambivalence grew along with Japanese power and ambition, and became increasingly apparent in the paternalistic role that Japanese Buddhists attempted to occupy in the construction of a pan-Buddhist community. Indeed, as Judith Snodgrass's study of subsequent developments makes clear, the fascination with the Theravāda was very short-lived in Japan. The shift toward a more nationalistic orientation in the efforts to reconstruct Buddhist ideologies and identities occurred within the lifetime of Shaku Sōen, who figures prominently in both these essays. Shaku Sōen and others soon sought instead to assert the superiority of Japanese Buddhism in particular as the pre-eminent modern religion. Read in light of Snodgrass's work, Jaffe's study of this earlier stage in the process of defining Japanese Buddhism illuminates how multiple and conflicting concerns and conversations shape the development of both ideologies and identities.

Sexual identity, rooted as it is (or claims to be) in concrete physical characteristics, might appear to be among the most universal and unchanging aspects of identity, even as it is perhaps the most personal and embodied aspect, one that profoundly shapes both our experience of ourselves and our engagement with the world around us. Janet Gyatso's study illuminates the complex ways in which pervasive conceptions of sex and gender intersect with the particular identities of persons, and are inflected by (or even subverted within) specific cultural, historical, and religious contexts.

The essay begins with the question of how the category of the female is conceived, especially in early Indic Buddhist monastic codes of conduct (Vinaya). In the discourse surrounding sex and gender in these texts (where "sex" refers to the differentiation of bodies in putatively natural, physical terms, while "gender" indicates the social and behavioral traits ascribed to a given sex), the female is constructed as the other against which the male claims normative status and power. Thus, monastic texts naturalize the dichotomy of male and female—a dichotomy that is always also a hierarchy in which the male is superior to and exercises control over the female. The physical differentiation of male and female provides the basis for differentiating the two in ethical terms, as well, such that male bodies become indicators of moral superiority in relation to the female other. Gyatso demonstrates, however, that the normalization of this sexual and ethical dichotomy rests on the explicit exclusion from the monastic community of a third category of sex/gender. Into this third category, the *paṇḍaka*, fall those whose sexuality is deemed deficient, unstable, or otherwise deviant from the norms of male and female—neuters, hermaphrodites, and those whose sex changes regularly, for instance. The *paṇḍaka*, then, serves as the "other other," as Gyatso aptly puts it, in contrast to which the female is defined and normalized as the admissible other within monastic institutions.

In monastic communities, whose members are defined to no small degree by the renunciation of the (specified) sexual other, the clear delineation of sexual identity is figured as critical to maintaining a religious identity. In the contexts of Mahāyāna Buddhist philosophy and Tibetan tantric practice, however, dualistic thinking is the subject of severe critique, such that the ambiguous third term that is so rigorously excluded from the monastic community becomes a central ideal toward which Buddhists strive (hence "the law of the non-excluded middle"). Similarly, in the context of Tibetan medical practice, the gendered qualities of the *paṇḍaka* (Tibetan: *ma ning*)—become unlinked from the notion of an actual ambiguously sexed body, and take on a positive connotation: ambiguity becomes equanimity, instability becomes flexibility, and the *paṇḍaka* comes to symbolize the healthy qualities of balance and suppleness that any sex might possess. Thus the ambiguities and instabilities of sex and gender that render the *paṇḍaka* inadmissible in the monastic context are precisely those that offer potential for its positive reappropriation (at least as a rich source for metaphor) in other contexts.

These instances, Gyatso suggests, offer the possibility of undermining the dichotomy, and thus perhaps the hierarchy, within the monastic context, as well—a possibility of great potential value to contemporary Buddhists who struggle with sex and gender discrimination within the tradition.

Gyatso frames her study of premodern textual sources within current discussions of gender politics in contemporary Buddhist societies, emphasizing the ongoing need to re-evaluate the normative definition of monastic identity as male and the correspondingly subordinate and devalued position of women in Buddhist communities. Her work provides a compelling demonstration of the relevance of premodern conceptions of identity to current debates; the very terms in which contemporary issues are formulated must be understood in light of trajectories from the past. Moreover, and perhaps more significantly, identity discourse from premodern sources provides valuable resources for reformulating traditional practices and institutions in the present day. Gyatso provides a compelling demonstration of the potential relevance of premodern discourse about identity to issues of contemporary concern.

Each of these essays explores circumstances in which Buddhists have called into question "given" aspects of Buddhist identity, aspects that have been taken to be natural or inherent to Buddhists. In the process, each study challenges scholars to reflect on those aspects of Buddhism that they take for granted as inherent. By illuminating moments at which Buddhists have interrogated their own assumptions, the essays help us to recognize how given aspects of identity (such as gender norms, or moral discernment) are constructed, naturalized, denaturalized, and reconstructed in accordance with the conditions and problems in different, and often conflicting, contexts. Together, these studies suggest that interrogations and reformulations of identity involve negotiating personhood within such complicated and inconsistent contexts, communities, and agendas. When people navigate such messy terrain, theoretically differentiable "landscapes of identity" overlap and sometimes override one another in exceedingly complex ways. Perhaps the only stable part of identity formation is that it always establishes difference—situating the person against that which she is decidedly not. Such attempts to reformulate identity, whether normative or subversive in intent, thereby can function to liberate some and to oppress others. These studies also suggest that identity discourse typically negotiates between the immediate needs of the local context and the translocal, transhistorical *imaginaire*. As Buddhists navigate between the intersecting terrains of the local and the translocal, they often reinterpret "tradition," transforming normative models of identity so as to address the crises of their own time. The translocal tradition enables Buddhists both to impose and to resist normative visions in particular times and places. Finally, these essays reveal that even the very notion of the translocal tradition is not immune to questioning and reformulation. Buddhists have entertained the possibility that there are other ways, or more universally valid ways, of being Buddhist, and have attempted to redefine the contours of their perceived communities by constructing new relations of similarity and difference with Buddhists and others. Creating a shared translocal identity can create solidarity, but it can also function to subjugate those who find themselves included within a normative vision to which they do not ascribe.

The insights gained through these studies of Buddhist processes of defining identity might provoke some readers to consider the constructed nature of the categories of identity they take as givens in their own times and places. If we situate particular responses to the question of what it means to be Buddhist within the broader human struggle to invest oneself and one's world with meaning and value, we open up the possibility of learning from the Buddhists we study.

8

The Image of an Orphan: Cambodian Narrative Sites for Buddhist Ethical Reflection

Anne Hansen

Much of the work in the relatively new field of Theravāda Buddhist ethics has been directed toward critiquing the Weberian characterization of Buddhism as primarily "mystical" and oriented away from social, political, and domestic attention toward the world. Ancient Buddhism, Max Weber wrote, "is a specifically unpolitical and anti-political-status religion, more precisely, a religious 'technology' of wandering and of intellectually-schooled mendicant monks" ([1958] 1996, 206). It is a tradition lacking "a concept of neighborly love," a sense of social responsibility or "any bridge to any actively conceptualized 'social' conduct," and "almost all beginnings of a methodical lay morality" (208, 213, 218). Even though Buddhism developed some formulations of a lay-oriented social ethics in order to accommodate the sponsorship of rulers beginning with Aśoka, Weber argued, it remained in its various forms throughout Asia a fundamentally mystical and magical (or nonrational) religious tradition, exhibiting a "devaluation of the world" characteristic of mysticism (330-43).

The dominance of Weber's categorization of Buddhism as a religious tradition oriented toward the achievement of an other-worldly (and thus world-devaluing) gnosis has given rise to numerous critiques that point to both texts and practices that articulate social ethical concerns (Swearer 1989; Sizemore and Swearer 1990; Darlington 1990; Queen and King 1996). Recent evidence makes clear that there *is* a tradition of social ethical thought in the Theravāda. Scholarly efforts within Buddhist studies to repudiate Weber's Eurocentric critiques and identify the social ethics of Theravāda Buddhism have not raised the question of whether or not Buddhists themselves have articulated their own versions of Weber's critique.[1] I would argue that, although the totalizing tendencies of the Weberian typology are too extreme, his characterization is not wholly without merit. There are clearly textual representations and social manifestations of world renunciation that produce a Buddhist discourse in which detachment and the individuality of enlightenment are normative concepts—which are countered with other more socially oriented values. Perhaps just as contemporary scholars of the Theravāda have chosen to emphasize the social engagement in various sources of Buddhist thought instead of Weber's readings of renunciation and detachment from the world, Buddhists in different historical contexts have also wrestled with this same tension.

Furthermore, while a number of important scholarly studies on Theravādin ethics have demonstrated the extent to which Buddhist rituals and practices contradict widely accepted doctrinal formulations of important normative ideas such as the law of *kamma* (the concept that all actions produce results) and *anattā* (the Buddhist idea of nonself) (Keyes 1983; Tannenbaum 1995), little attention has been paid to the actual production of Buddhist values in particular historical moments: *How* exactly are Buddhist values defined and generated in these moments? What are the local sites of interpretation for the *cosmopolitan* discourse of Theravāda Buddhism, by which I mean the changing body of texts and images that have moved through Buddhist cultures of Asia? How does the *imaginaire* (to invoke both Bernard Faure's work on Zen and Steven Collins's work on the Theravāda)[2] of the Pāli literary tradition intersect with local literary images, genres, and preoccupations (Faure 1996, 10-13; Collins 1998, 40-41)? How are tensions and contradictions expressed in local-historical practices and interpretations of Buddhism? How and why are certain values and virtues broadly defined as "Buddhist values"—and not others—considered important in particular contexts?

In this article, I examine how one particular late vernacular text from colonial Cambodia, which grows out of the tradition of Buddhist literature concerned with the ethics of social relationships, addresses the different normative values in the Theravāda tradition about detachment and renunciation, individuality and alterity. This article responds to recent discussions in Theravādin studies reassessing the scholarly construction and understanding of "canon" (Keyes 1983; Collins 1990; Blackburn 1999a) and to further assertions by Buddhist scholars of the central place of narrative Buddhist literature as a source of ethical reflection in the Theravāda (G. Obeyesekere 1991, 231; R. Obeyesekere 1991, x; 2001, 3; Strong 1992, xi; Hallisey and Hansen 1996; Collins 1998, 121-23, 283-85). I draw as well on the theoretical framework of Martha C. Nussbaum's claims about the inseparability of literary form and ethical context, and the appropriateness of narrative as a literary form for ethical reflection on the "world's surprising variety, its complexity and mysteriousness, its flawed and imperfect beauty . . ." (1990, 3). My examination of vernacular and local texts in Buddhist studies also flows out of a larger recent scholarly interrogation of the notion of regionalism, which highlights the dynamic relationship between core and periphery. This discussion provides a conceptual geography for viewing the interactions of canonical and local vernacular texts as textual cores and peripheries, while contributing the dimension of religious knowledge and expression to considerations of regionalism and subaltern constructions of modernity.

The text at the center of my discussion, the *Gatilok* ("Ways of the World"),[3] was written during a period in which long-standing social, religious, and political conceptions of order and value in Cambodia were under scrutiny through a newly emerging perspective of modernity. Siamese and French influences in colonial Cambodia gave rise to a new self-consciousness about ethnicity, culture, and religious orthodoxy as aspects of Khmer identity. In this historical situation, Khmer colonial interpretation of the literary images and tropes of Pāli texts reveals tensions and disagreement with the parts of the cosmopolitan ethical discourse that privilege the ideals of monastic detachment and world renunciation as normative values. In particular, Ukñā Suttantaprījā Ind's use of the morally problematic image of an orphan metaphorically expresses Khmer ambivalence regarding these themes. In a compilation meant to represent the values necessary for Buddhists to live in the modern world, the moral person, like the orphan in the text, must learn to recognize that the inextricable interconnections between self and others are what shape the world. The proper ethical orientation toward the world is, thus, recognition of the true nature and connectedness of self and others. As a result, the text puts forward the necessity of relatedness—not detachment—as a fundamental condition for the development of mature moral agency. Khmer attention to the important consideration of identity, on these multiple levels, places an ethical imperative on the cultivation of a type of moral discernment termed *satisampajañña* (mindfulness and discrimination) as a primary moral virtue for establishing one's identity as a good, moral person and a good and true Buddhist.

I conclude by suggesting that this local vernacular reinvention of the Theravāda not only articulates Buddhist ethical values that deepen our knowledge and discussions of Buddhist ethics, but it also contributes to the larger scholarly project of what Dipesh Chakrabarty calls "provincializing" our conceptions of ways of being in response to modernity (2000, 3-23).

Local Texts and the Cosmopolitan Imaginaire

Within the last decade or two of work on Buddhist cultures and texts, scholars have become increasingly sensitive to the contested meaning of the term "canon." The Christian connotations of a "canon" as a closed set of texts does not sit easily in Buddhist contexts. As Steven Collins has persuasively argued, the equation made by earlier scholars between the notion of a pre-existent Pāli canon and "original" or early Buddhism can hardly be historically supported. Rather, present-day versions of *the* Pāli canon, he suggests, are the product of the Sinhalese Mahāvihārin sect's efforts at self-preservation and legitimation during periodic downturns of royal patronage for the sect in Sri Lanka. These efforts resulted in the introduction of the concept of the Tipiṭaka as a closed and authoritative body of Theravādin scriptures (Collins 1990, 95-102). Sinhalese forms of Buddhism imported into Southeast Asia maintained the idea of the Tipiṭaka as a canon in an abstract sense only, without necessarily conflating the concepts of scriptural authority and a closed canon (102-104). Collins comments that further ethnographic and historical work is needed to understand fully the actual texts that have commanded scriptural authority in particular Theravādin contexts:

> If we wish to delineate the actual "canon" or "canons" of scripture ... in use at different times and places of the Theravāda world, we need empirical research into each individual case . . . on the actual possession and use of texts, in monastery libraries and elsewhere, and on the content of sermons and festival presentations to laity, to establish more clearly than we currently can just what role has been played by the works included in the canonical list. (104)

Collins concludes by suggesting that the importance of the Pāli canon be understood as an authoritative notion rather than as a closed body of texts.

Building on Collins's argument, Anne Blackburn's analysis of texts on monastic discipline in medieval and eighteenth-century Sri Lanka includes a carefully articulated distinction between formal and practical canons in the Theravāda. Blackburn designates Collins's notion of canon as an authoritative concept as formal canon, while referring to the texts in a given historical context that are produced, used, collected, copied, read, recited, interpreted, and understood as expressions of this larger authoritative concept as the practical canon (1999a, 283-84).

This recent shift toward examining later and vernacular texts not only frees scholars from the constraints imposed by earlier (especially colonial-era) scholarly conceptions of a dominant, frozen Pāli canon that defined the authenticity and orthodoxy of Buddhist expressions, but it also permits the tensions in Buddhist thought (such as those between individual liberation and social ethical concerns) to be explored more fully in a wider variety of Buddhist contexts and writings. The examination of particular practical canons and individual texts of later and/or vernacular composition contributes to a shifting analysis of, first, what constitutes Buddhist values and practice and, second, what forms such ethical reflection can take.

While Western ethicists and theologians have pursued for several decades the connection between ethical reflection and the narrative form, scholars of Buddhism have only recently come to this idea (Hallisey and Hansen 1996, 309-10). Within the context of Buddhist studies in the West, Buddhist narrative was long relegated to a secondary status that prevented scholars from giving it serious consideration at all beyond the evidence that it offered for the understanding of ancient Buddhist society. While T. W. Rhys Davids's first work of translation was a volume of Jātaka (birth stories), he understood its importance primarily as an unspoiled record of a primitive stage in human history.[4] Responding in 1878 to the work of evolutionists such as Herbert Spencer and E. B. Tyler, Rhys Davids suggested that, while "the accounts of modern travelers among the so-called savage tribes are often at best very secondary evidence" based on the possibly misleading cultural interpretations of native informants and passing through the "more or less able" medium of a European mind,

> in the *Jātaka* [Birth stories of the Buddha] we have a nearly complete picture, and quite uncorrupted and unadulterated by European intercourse, of the social life and customs and popular beliefs of the common people of Aryan tribes closely related to ourselves, just as they were passing through the first stages of civilization.
>
> The popularity of the *Jātaka* as amusing stories may pass away. How can it stand against the rival claims of the fairytales of science, and the entrancing, man-sided story of man's gradual rise and progress? But though these less fabulous and more attractive stories will increasingly engage the attention of ourselves and of our children, we may still turn with appreciation to the ancient *Book of the Buddhist Jātaka Tales* as a priceless record of the childhood of our race. (1925, lxxviii-lxxix)

Influenced not only by social Darwinism but also by the theoretical work of scientifically minded scholars of religion such as Friedrich Max Müller, who sought to identify the origin or essence of religion, Victorian translators of Buddhism tried to reconstruct "original Buddhism"—a Buddhism based on those texts considered to be the authentic words of the Buddha interpreted through a filter of post-Enlightenment rationalism. The translators, an amalgamation of scholars and colonial civil servants, many of whom had lived for years in Buddhist cultures, found contemporary Buddhist practice to be at odds with the canonical doctrines that they were translating and thus labeled these practices as degenerations of the original (see the essay by Charles Hallisey in this volume, 94-98). Narrative texts, even canonical versions such as the Jātaka, were qualified as "crude" and "childish," full of "inconsistencies . . . [and] many distortions in ideals . . ." (Rhys Davids [1929] 1989, xviii-xix), written for the purpose of rendering subtle philosophical writings palatable to the uneducated masses (Rice 1924, 5).

Scholars have only recently, in connection with reassessing the meaning of canon in Buddhist contexts, begun acknowledging the important role of narrative in the practical canons of Buddhist communities. In an essay on the contemporary state of Sri Lankan Buddhism, Gananath Obeyesekere commented that the "rational Buddhism" inherited from the colonial reinvention of Buddhism had robbed the tradition of what had once been its "lifeblood": the stories and rituals through which people learned what it meant to be a Buddhist. This "Buddhism as a religion of the heart," in Obeyesekere's words, needs to be recalled and re-examined not only by Buddhists but also by scholars of Buddhism (G. Obeyesekere 1991, 229-34).

This opening of the field of Buddhist studies to include greater consideration of vernacular texts (Lopez 1995a, 7), including narrative texts, is resonant with wider scholarly interests in local–global interactions and particularly in according a wider prominence to local, regional, and subaltern actors and forces (Duara 1995; Chakrabarty 2000). In the field of history this concern is evident in a recent emphasis on regionalism, a methodology that attempts to counter the rendering of the local as marginal to constructions of power and identity. An important example of the regionalist approach is found in Kären Wigen's (1995) historical study of Japanese geography. Borrowing from Richard Slotkin, Wigen characterizes regionalist analysis as the effort to examine how people articulate and represent their own local identities and ideologies, how these identities act as a social force in relation to other identity projects such as nation building or modernization, and how "the activities of symbol-making, interpretation, and imaginative projection continuously interlock with the political and material processes of social existence" (1999, 1186).

A key element of this approach is the assertion that "cultural interaction . . . [is] not a one-way process" that can be termed "Sinification" or "Indianization" (Wigen 1999, 1188). Like Chakrabarty's project of provincializing the notion of Europe as a core, Wigen wants to move away from a center–periphery perspective. In fact, she suggests, "[t]he new vision of regional dynamics is one that acknowledges more initiative and innovation in the hinterlands, that treats the core itself as a region" (1197). Thus, the central methodological approach for studies of regionalism is comparative (Rafael 1999, 1208). Since the notion of what is regional is derived from and against other loci of authority and identity that are translocal or transregional (such as the nation-state, the empire, or the global marketplace), the regional and whatever it defines itself against must be understood in relation to one another.

Although the field of Buddhist ethics may seem distinct from this project, the regional methodologies used by historians for analyzing local and translocal interactions are especially fruitful for considerations of local Buddhisms and their literary cultures in that they provide a way of thinking about the fluid and dynamic interactions between textual cores and peripheries. While the analysis of geographical conceptions of identity by historians such as Wigen (1995) and Thongchai Winichakul (1994) has played a central role in the mapping of regionalism, there are other landscapes of identity—moral, religious, domestic, linguistic, literary, imaginative—that construct what a "region" is and means to its inhabitants and which are integrally connected to the geographical. The study of local and translocal Buddhist values and ethics in fact overlaps with and could also enrich current discussions of regionalism.

The same intellectual reappraisals that gave rise to discussions on regionalism in history have also entered into discussions of Buddhist history and literature, albeit not always in the same terms or from the same starting point. Orientalist studies of the history and development of Buddhist literary cultures, rooted in the colonial enterprise, mapped a kind of core-periphery model of Buddhist history that was both temporal and linguistic, situating the "core" in the Indian origins of the religion and the "periphery" in the vernacular interpretations and practices of later Buddhists. More recent scholarship on the processes of vernacularization and the literary regions or cultures of Buddhist history has increasingly focused on the two-way process of cosmopolitan-vernacular interactions in the production of religious imaginaries, literatures, preoccupations, values, and ideologies, as well as on the ways in which, as Wigen suggests, these processes are thoroughly politicized (Wigen 1999, 1186-87; Collins 1998, 40-89; Jory 2002, 893-909; Leve 2002, 844-52). As Sanskritist Sheldon Pollock argues, the interaction between local languages and Sanskrit ultimately resulted in the production of cosmopolitan vernaculars. The use of Sanskrit receded as vernacular writings both incorporated the Sanskrit aesthetic and turned away from it. As Pollock also points out, however, Sanskrit itself became transformed by its interactions with local vernacular languages; the process was never a simple one-way Sanskritization (1998, 7).

The spread and development of Buddhism provides another arena for regionalist analysis. The region in this context becomes the local interpretations of cosmopolitan religious ideas expressed as the "Buddhist tradition," which have been transmitted, expressed, and shaped in other local Buddhist contexts. Collins's notion of the very idea of the Pāli canon is, in Wigen's words, a perfect example of "the core itself as a region" (1999, 1197). The Pāli Tipiṭaka, functioning as a locus of authority but with a shifting meaning and content depending on the ways in which it is edited, excerpted, interpreted, and translated, serves as the vertical axis by which the local defines itself. The examination of local narrative sites reveals ways in which the Pāli *imaginaire* transmitted in Tipiṭaka texts is constantly reinterpreted and used to produce local values. To suggest that these values are local, however, should be understood from a regionalist perspective rather than an Orientalist one in which the local is construed as marginal and thus easy to ignore. Although local Buddhist values might be produced in part as articulations of identity, they are not always meant to serve only as regional or local perspectives but, rather, as Buddhist values writ large, in a human or universalistic sense (see the essay by Charles Hallisey in this volume, 111-112). The rest of this article will examine one such local narrative site for the production of local values, its engagement with ethical tensions in the Theravāda, and its rearticulation of what Buddhist values are and how a Buddhist should be in the world.

Self and *Satisampajañña* in the *Gatilok*

The *Gatilok* is a narrative ethical text composed by Ukñā Suttantaprījā Ind (b. 1859), a well-known Cambodian intellectual and poet. Ind's lifetime spanned a period of great social change in mainland Southeast Asia. He lived in Kandal and then Battambang, a Khmer province under Siamese political control from the late eighteenth century until its retrocession to French-controlled Cambodia in 1907. Like most sons of Buddhist families during this period, Ind entered the monkhood as a novice at the age of ten. Unlike many young men, however, he spent a large portion of his life in the Sangha (the Buddhist monastic order), finally disrobing to marry and start a family at the relatively advanced age of 37. He began serious Pāli studies at the age of 15, and at age 18 (in 1878), he was ordained as a monk in Phnom Penh at the leading monastery in Cambodia, Vatt Uṇṇālom, associated with the Mahānikāy sect. He moved to Battambang for one rainy season to study Pāli and then in 1881 traveled from this then remote province to Bangkok, where he spent seven years as a monk and student of Pāli. Returning to Battambang in 1888, he became known as one of the foremost Khmer intellectuals of his day. Although the entire corpus of his scholarly and literary works is not known, he was an important poet who composed such works as the *Nirās Nagar Vatt* ("Journey to Angkor Vatt"), the didactic work *Cpāp' Srī* (a code of conduct for women rendered in verse), and a well-known manual on poetic meter that influenced Khmer poets of future generations. He is reported to have translated more than 44 Pāli texts into the vernacular, which, in the Khmer literary tradition of the day, consisted of a Khmer verse translation accompanied by commentary.[5] Among these translations were a Khmer poetic version of the *Paṭhamasambodhigāthā* (a Thai biography of the Buddha composed in Pāli) and the *Lokanītipakaraṇa*, apparently based on a Burmese Pāli compilation of rules of conduct.

After disrobing in 1897, he served as a provincial official in Battambang under the Siamese governor, while continuing his scholarly work and teaching. As a result of political and military pressure from the French, the Siamese were forced to return the Khmer provinces of Battambang and Siem Reap in 1907 to French colonial control, which had been established in 1863 when Cambodia became an official protectorate of the French government. In 1914, under the Franco-Khmer government, Ind received the ministerial title of ukñā suttantaprījā and was called to Phnom Penh to serve on a commission consisting of Cambodia's most distinguished scholars and officials who were charged with the task of reforming Khmer orthography and creating the first official Cambodian-language dictionary. By virtue of his work on the commission, Ind became caught up in a politically charged agenda of religious and educational reform in Phnom Penh initiated by the French colonial government. During this period, he composed what was to become his most famous and influential work, the *Gatilok*. Ind died in 1925, and shortly thereafter the *Gatilok* was serialized in the Buddhist periodical *Kambujasuriyā* ("Kampuchean Sun"). It soon appeared as a popular ten-volume set produced by the Institut Bouddhique, which was reissued at least seven more times after the early 1930s.[6] The initial publication of Ind's work in *Kambujasuriyā* gave rise to a nationwide effort to collect and publish more Khmer folklore for the next several decades, a movement that coincided with the rise of Khmer nationalism.[7]

The *Gatilok*, explicitly composed as a *tamrā*, or "manual," on how to behave, expresses the theme of emerging identities at a number of levels, moving between the articulation of authentic and inauthentic Theravādin practices among Khmer Buddhists to notions of false and true monks, corrupt and good officials, the very historically specific issues of the fakery of particular nineteenth-century millenarian figures in Cambodia and the self-degeneration caused by opium addiction—a social problem under the colonial regime in Indochina. Although the ethics of the text responds to these particular historical issues, the *Gatilok* was also clearly intended to be a universal ethical teaching on living the moral life, and its primary focus is on the recognition of individuals who are moral or pure and those who are wicked. The recognition of identity is a tricky business, the text suggests; thus, for living in the world, mature moral agency is not fully achieved except by the person who has cultivated moral discernment or *satisampajañña* as the basis for his or her perception, actions, interactions, and relationships with other people.

The ethical reflections on moral agency in the text are laid out in narrative form, giving the audience insight into the circumstances, characters, and behaviors of the moral actors in the *Gatilok*. Living in the world, as the *Gatilok* narratives make clear, involves living with others. Actions bear fruit; their consequences are felt not just by the actor but also by many others, most notably immediate family members, neighbors, and loved ones. The "self" of the *Gatilok* is not at all autonomous, but intricately interconnected with others.

The extent to which the identity of the self is interpenetrated with the world around it is explicated in the text with this analogy: "All the different beings are different from each other because *Dhamma*[8] and *lok* (world) are put together . . . in the same way that the textures of gold alloys are different because the element copper is put together with the element gold in varying large or small amounts" (Ind [1921] 1971, 1: 7-8). The parts of a human being that arise (or are born) and die, such as the body and feelings or reactions, are of the world. These aspects of the world shape human identity just as the amount and grade of copper in a gold alloy determines its overall color and appearance. Whatever knowledge or truth possessed by the being does not die because it is "of the *jāti* [category] of Dhamma" (1: 8). Like gold in an alloy, its brilliant pure color shines forth from any being possessing it. A person's unique identity is thus determined by the combination of Dhamma and *loka* that he or she constructs through thought, speech, and actions. The world itself, *loka* in Pāli or *lok* in Khmer, is defined by Ind as everything that is not Dhamma, that is, everything that is causally conditioned. It is what "arises by the power of the rebirth of *khandha* [aggregates] . . . all beings on earth, on the surface of the sky and throughout the atmosphere . . . that normally act in the world." It is also all thoughts, words, and actions that come into being (1: 2-3).

In this causally connected world, the greatest problem for human beings is the interconnectedness between the self and others. There is no escaping relationship; in a Levinasian sense, one is born into relationship with others and those relationships continue after one dies (Bloechl 2000, 3). Thus, within the text, ethical primacy is placed on the ability to recognize the nature of one's own and others' moral identities and intentions through the cultivation of a form of moral discernment known as *satisampajañña*, which becomes a precursor to living as a fully developed moral agent.

Satisampajañña can be translated in its compounded sense in terms of *sati* (mindfulness and clarity) and *sampajañña* (discrimination or attention or awareness). Ind defines the compound by drawing on a portion of the *Sāmaññaphala-sutta* (Rhys Davids and Carpenter [1890] 1949, 1: 70-71; Walshe 1987, 100), the "Sermon on The Fruits of the Homeless Life":

> People [who possess] *satisampajañña* to analyze the circumstances and occasion . . . do not falter when they are in charge of some activity; whether they are walking, sitting, sleeping, standing, lifting their arms, lifting their feet, urinating or defecating; whether eating food that is soft or tough, when chewing and when swallowing food into the stomach. If you do not have [*satisampajañña*], if you do not think first, then in all of these actions, you will falter in various ways such as falling down or getting stuck on thorns, and so on. For instance, in

respect to eating, you might choke on a fishbone or encounter a hot pepper. Those people who are without [*satisampajañña*] the world calls careless. (Ind [1921] 1971, 3: 20-21)

The play between the narrative contexts for defining *satisampajañña* in the Pāli and Khmer texts is illustrative of their interactions in a more general sense. Both texts employ different parts of the well-known Buddhist story of King Bimbisāra and Prince Ajātasattu as a frame for defining *satisampajañña*. In the *Sāmaññaphala-sutta*, Ajātasattu visits the Buddha in an effort to find relief from the turmoil of his remorse for imprisoning and torturing to death his own father. The Buddha uses the occasion to preach a *sutta* (discourse or sermon) on the "fruits of the homeless life." In this and other Pāli suttas, *satisampajañña* is explained as one of four kinds of concentration, which is one of the benefits of the homeless life led by the world renouncer. In the vernacular *Gatilok*, Ind uses a portion of the Ajātasattu story as a means of explicating *satisampajañña*. In the terms of this text, however, *satisampajañña* becomes *not* one of numerous by-products of world renunciation, but the primary aim of the moral person. Here, as in the development of every other ethical category in the text, Ind takes philosophical concepts directed at the practices and valuing of renunciation, detachment, and individual liberation and recasts them as the necessary possessions of ordinary people living in the world.

In the *Gatilok*, *satisampajañña* is explained in a passage comparing the responses of three groups of officials who are guards belonging to the retinue of King Bimbisāra. After apprehending Ajātasattu in the act of attempting to assassinate his father, the guards meet to discuss what should be done next. Two of the groups of guards advocate executing Ajātasattu on the spot, but the captain of the third group argues that, under the circumstances, the case should be brought to the king. Upon hearing the judgment of each group of palace guards, the king punishes the former two by confiscating their wealth and positions. The third group's members, however, were to be rewarded richly with an increase in wealth and status for the judgment that they put forth because their captain "was a person possessing *satisampajañña*, knowing how to analyze correctly according to the circumstances and according to the occasion" (3: 20).

While in various Pāli suttas *satisampajañña* is explained as a moral possession that must be cultivated gradually by monks who have attained higher levels of skill in meditation, in the *Gatilok* it is a moral attribute necessary to anyone who wants to live as a good person in the world. Although some exemplary characters may be endowed with *satisampajañña* by birth, for most it is a moral virtue that must be cultivated through life experience and education:

> [T]he knowledge possessed by little children is like very shallow water. As for all newborn babies, their knowledge is shallow and *satisampajañña* has not yet arisen to any great extent, and they can be deceived, as you will see . . . Sometimes adults deceive them by saying "don't cry or the scarecrow will come and bite you" . . . or . . . "Tā Breng[9] will pour rice water on your head." . . . Babies do not possess *satisampajañña* . . . and thus are ignorant of adults, who can deceive them. There is a whole category of people who are ignorant because, like babies, they do not possess *satisampajañña*. (6: 26-28)

Because most characters in the text are in dire need of even small doses of *satisampajañña*, their interactions with others tend to result in both humorous and tragic consequences.

Although *satisampajañña* can be described in terms of a general moral discernment, in a more technical sense it also involves the development of a complex of specific virtues. These are the *sappurisa-dhammā*, the sevenfold "forms of ethical recognition" that enable their possessor to recognize things such as good and evil intentions of others, truth, results of actions, and the nature of self.[10] Thus, through the development of these related virtues, the cultivation of *satisampajañña* leads to one becoming a *sappurisa* (a good person). The larger aim of the *sappurisa* in the text is to become pure (*parisuddh*), developing the dhamma aspect of one's identity—which requires a twofold obligation toward others: the absence of spreading harm and injury to others, along with "increasing the well-being of others" (1: 20). The text asserts that, although people are born into differing circumstances, the person possessing *satisampajañña* is able to discern an appropriate response for "the occasion and the circumstances," including the ability to detect the moral nature and intentions of others, an idea developed in one of the key narratives of the text, "The Story of Bhikkhu Sukh."

"The Story of Bhikkhu Sukh"

The story begins with a brief preface that explains the circumstances and context in which the story takes place, a situation that Ind regards as highly unjust, highlighting the conditions of the *loka*, in which human beings live entangled in a web composed of the reverberating results of the actions of others. Ind tells us, by way of preface to the story, that

> the law in the highland region . . . states that if someone knows sorcery and witchcraft for invoking spirits, and if someone else goes and makes an accusation to the chieftain [against him], this chieftain must, with his

authority, seize the accused to come for a deliberation of the decision. If at the deliberation it is decided that the words of the accuser are true, then according to law, the entire family [of the accused], to seven lines (*santān*),[11] must be killed. From the smallest newborn baby at a mother's breast, they must all be killed.

Furthermore, if anyone in another family threatens either to be a traitor or obstinately refuses to go along with the judgment ordered by the ruler, according to law, that entire family must be executed and their relatives must enter into hereditary slavery as slaves for the military, cutting grass for the horses and elephants. This is sealed for all time. All the beings born into this family are known as slaves and numbered as a tribute, no matter how many there are. None of them can ever escape to become free citizens. Whomsoever is born into this family, even those who are knowledgeable in some area or who possess particular intelligence, cannot claim freedom. They are known as unfortunate beings in this world. The law that is spoken of here is a lasting weight on the part of certain *dāp* [low or inferior] people.[12] . . . This is what happened in the legend of Lok Tā Sukh the Phnong.[13] (2: 47-51)

The preface to the story not only sets up the circumstances of injustice into which the protagonist, Sukh, is born but also explains his "inferior" origins—from the perspective of lowland Khmer, the dominant ethnic group—as a member of an ethnic minority group living in the highlands:

As for this story: there was a certain Phnong man who with his family inhabited the highland region, making a living in the manner of forest dwellers. After some time had passed, a group of Phnong all began to hate this man. They came together to make accusations to the chieftain of their village, saying, "that forest dweller knows how to perform witchcraft and he has caused the deaths of many villagers." When the powerful chieftain heard them say "he knows how to practice witchcraft" and so on, he ordered them to go kill the Phnong family whom they had accused. Both the husband and wife were killed, along with seven lines (*juor*) of their family, with none left alive—except one young boy named Cau Sukh. This boy was about ten or eleven years old. He had been sent to guard the rice in the forest field when he found out that by the chieftain's order, his father and mother, brothers and sisters, aunts and uncles, and grandpa and grandma had all been killed in this way. Terribly afraid, he ran up a tree and hid himself at its top, among branches entangled with creepers, and remained still and quiet. When the chieftain's band had killed the whole family, they realized that one child still remained. They went to find the child in the rice field in order to kill off and utterly eradicate the entire family. (2: 51-52)

The story tells of the boy's efforts to keep himself hidden in the tree "tangled with creepers" and his narrow escape from the chieftain's band:

> When night arrived and everything was quiet, the young boy climbed down from the tree and ran away from the garden, cutting straight through the forest to the lower village. He entered the village and pleaded with a certain household of Phnong on the front edge of the village to hide him. The occupants of the house took pity (*āṇit*) on the boy and gave him something to eat and drink, and took him inside their house to hide him. The chieftain's band walked around looking for the boy but failed to find him. When morning came, they came down to search in the lower village for him. (2: 53-54)

Convinced that the boy was somewhere in the village, the chieftain's men searched every house, "in the beginning . . . in the middle . . . and [in] the end of the village" (2: 54). Because the house in which he was hidden was located next to the headman's house, however, they neglected to search it thoroughly. The inhabitants of the house urged the boy to escape:

> "We cannot continue to protect you because our house is right next to our chieftain's. When it gets quiet, surely he cannot fail to realize you are here. If you want to escape with your life, you have no other option but to go down to the land of the Khmer. Earlier this morning, there was a Khmer merchant's cart returning to their country. If you try to run after that Khmer cart and catch up with it, you can plead with them to take you to Sruk Kraceh." The boy heard this and believed them. He took leave of the inhabitants of the house and ran after the Khmer cart until he caught up with it in the middle of the road. Utterly exhausted from going after the cart, he could walk no longer so he reached up to grasp the wheel frame under the cart and hung on to it.
>
> The merchant boss turned around and saw the young boy hanging under the cart and got down to ask him in his language: "Who are you, little child, hanging on to our cart?" The boy then told him his story from beginning to end, and the merchant boss listened, and having learned it, there arose in him horrific grief and pity (*secktī-saṅveg-āṇit*). He said, "Ah—if it's like this, you must come and live with us. We don't have any children. We will take you as our adopted child [*kun dharm*]. When others think to oppress you, I will accept responsibility. You do not have to suffer anymore." Having spoken, he let the boy ride in the wagon and drove forward to the lowland until he reached Sruk Kraceh. The merchant boss drove the cart without stopping until he reached his own house. The boy was thus freed from suffering at the hands of his chieftain.

> The merchant boss loved Cau Sukh, maintained him as his own son, and diligently taught him how to speak Khmer. Cau Sukh was also diligent and complied with the instruction of the merchant boss. They never had a single quarrel. When some time had passed, the merchant boss sent Cau Sukh to study at the temple and learn how to read and write in Khmer. Cau Sukh studied and recited diligently until he achieved his aim. When he was 15, the merchant boss allowed him to be ordained as a novice, at which time he was called "Nen Sukh." At the age of 21, his adoptive father [*pitā dharm*] had him ordained as a bhikkhu [monk], and he was called "Lok Bhikkhu Sukh." He remained contented and happy, with the profits from offerings (*lābh sakkāra*) that arise in the *sāsana* [religion] of the Lord Buddha. (2: 55-59)

The Image of an Orphan

I think that this story may likely be a historical account of an actual monk's life.[14] More strikingly, however, it can clearly be read as an allegorical narrative of spiritual liberation. The story's spareness of description and imagery highlights the few details that are given.

The story's introduction implies that the family in question is innocent and that the law of the highland in this case is not only unjust but wrongly enacted, since the motivation for the accusation was hatred, not sorcery. The ethical context of the story and the assumptions that we can make about the moral identity of the main characters are thus parallel to the problem discussed earlier of the interplay between *loka* and dhamma in the formation of human identity. Anything arising from the world, or *loka*—such as human laws—is by nature corrupt and corrupting. Only dhammic law is pure and incorruptible. The circumstances and occasions in which human beings must act as moral beings are *always* imperfect, entangled, attached, corrupted. There is no pure moral context in which human beings can perfect themselves.

Although this context employs the *loka*/Dhamma ideas of identity developed in the *Gatilok*, much of the rest of the narrative draws heavily on recognizable metaphors of spiritual development found in a variety of Pāli sources. The image of the boy guarding the rice field evokes both the imagery of the fruition of karma and the "guarding" of the sensory perceptions, a common description applied to bhikkhus in Pāli texts such as the *Sāmaññaphala-sutta* (Rhys Davids and Carpenter [1890] 1949, 1:63, 70; Walshe 1987, 100). Cau Sukh's name itself is allegorical, referring to *sukkha*, or "happiness or peace," understood as the existential condition opposite to *dukkha*, or "suffering." The oddly phrased description of the "beginning . . . middle . . . and end" of the lower village, which the chieftain's men search, must refer to the

Dhamma, or "Teaching," which is good or lovely in its beginning, middle, and end (Rhys Davids and Carpenter [1890] 1949, 1: 62), and which gives "refuge" to the young boy Cau Sukh, just as Buddhists "take refuge" in the Buddha's Dhamma. The spiritual allegory continues with the "householders" (a Buddhistic reference for lay persons) in the village telling Cau Sukh "if you want to escape with your life, you have no other option but to go down to the land of Khmer." The Khmer word "escape" (*ruoc*) used in this passage is fraught with significant religious connotations. It appears in the phrases "to escape from *dukkha*" and "to escape from *kamm*" (*kamma*) and can also mean "released," "liberated," or "finished." The boy runs after the cart—an image often used to refer to Buddhism itself—and finds it in the "middle of the path or road," or the Middle Path, another way of referring to the Buddha's teaching. He grabs onto the wheel frame—as in the imagery of the "wheel of Dhamma," another metaphor for Buddhism. The boss of the merchants, a common incarnation of the Bodhisattva in Jātaka texts, speaks to the boy "in his [own] language," like the Buddha himself, who always knows how to speak so that others will understand. He "listens to and learns" the boy's story "from beginning to end"—evoking the image of someone listening to this and other Buddhist stories and benefiting from them. With pity, grief, and compassion for the orphan's situation (the situation of all unenlightened beings), the merchant boss then offers to release him from suffering and oppression and take him as his "dhamma child," driving the cart without stopping until he has "freed him from suffering," again an image of someone who, once on the Path—often as a result of encountering the Buddha—moves forward, bent on liberation or release from the *dukkha* of *saṃsāra* (continuation of existence through rebirth). The merchant has the boy ordained as a novice and later as a bhikkhu, ritual acts which are often undertaken in Southeast Asia to produce merit for parents and relatives. Although merit making for parents is always important, its urgency is compounded if the parents have died violently; it can be a means of mitigating the suffering for all concerned, both living and dead. Bhikkhu Sukh "remained contented and happy, with the profits from offerings which arise in the *sāsana* of the Lord Buddha," through which his family's grief could be transformed into spiritual benefit.[15]

The rich interaction in this story between central metaphors of liberation drawn from the Pāli *imaginaire* and the "local" tropes of ethnicity, language, geography, and family relationship, as well as the clearly allegorical nature of the story, makes it an explicit and useful site for undertaking a specifically historically situated Khmer reading of the Theravāda path to liberation. The vernacular reading is one that revolves around the historical concerns with identity, and although it draws on symbols and imagery that are well established in a variety of Pāli texts, it simultaneously offers its own formulation of normative Buddhist values. As a site of interaction between cosmopolitan and local vernacular expressions of Buddhism, it adds to the critique of detachment and monastic renunciation that is developed throughout the *Gatilok* as well as providing an example of the necessity of *satisampajañña* (which Bhikkhu Sukh exhibits) for moral survival and development. Finally, it demonstrates the identity of a *sappurisa*, the ultimate aim of moral development, in this case in the form of the merchant boss who adopts the boy and thereby creates well-being and benefit for himself and others. I will conclude by examining these three themes in turn.

The movement in "The Story of Bhikkhu Sukh" between the images of homelessness and householder suggests that the narrative is explicitly examining these two types of individuals. Drawing the contrast between the attachment of the householder and the detachment of the bhikkhu is a common way of exalting the merits of the homeless life in various textual sources that Ind cites in the *Gatilok*. The *Dhammapada*, for example, provides vivid images of the contrast between these two ways of living in the world:

> Just as in a heap of rubbish
> Cast away on a roadside,
> A lotus there could bloom,
> Of sweet fragrance, pleasing the mind,
> So amid the wretched, blinded ordinary folk (*puthujjane*),
> Among them who have turned to rubbish,
> The disciple of the Fully Awakened One
> Shines surpassingly with wisdom.[16] (Carter and Palihawadana 1987, 144-45)

In the *Sutta Nipāta*, another of Ind's textual sources, the bhikkhu who wants to be pure must cut himself off completely from the life of the householder. Here, the ordinary person is portrayed as one who, because of attachment to friends and family members, is mired in dissatisfaction and who, because of "sympathising with friends and companions . . . misses one's goal, being shackled in mind" (Norman 1994, 4). Most companions, the text states, are like "shining bracelets of gold" which, when "two are on one arm," can be seen "clashing against each other" (7). Only by leaving aside affection toward family members, which are "like a very wide-spreading bamboo tree entangled with others," can one hope to live a pure life:

> Leaving behind son and wife, and father and mother, and wealth and grain, and relatives, and sensual pleasures to the limit, one should wander solitary as a rhinoceros horn . . .
>
> Having discarded the marks of a householder, like a coral tree whose leaves have fallen, having gone out (from the house) wearing the saffron robe, one should wander solitary as a rhinoceros horn. (5-7)

Ind reacts explicitly against this sharp delineation between the attachments and disadvantages of the lay life and the solitary, spiritually advantageous life of the monk. Even in the story of Bhikkhu Sukh, who emerges as the only virtuous and true bhikkhu among the monastic characters in the entire *Gatilok* compilation, the symbiotic relationship between monk and lay person in the story is far more evident than the detachment. The ascetic ideal of the "rhinoceros horn" appears nearly impossible in the *Gatilok* framework, since the communal life of the monks and abbots in the text and their interactions with the world appear to be just as complex and socially attached as those of their lay counterparts. For Bhikkhu Sukh, who does achieve a level of moral purity and thrives as a bhikkhu,[17] being cut off from his family and abandoning the "world" of his own people does not make him a monk. Rather, he becomes a monk through the relationships that he cultivates with virtuous lay people, first with the "householders" who give him refuge and urge him to "escape" and second with the compassionate merchant boss, his *pitā dharm*, who raises and educates him.

The overlapping in the narrative between the image of the bhikkhu and the image of the orphan reveals the ambivalence that the text attributes to the notion of detachment from society. The detachment from family idealized in certain texts is achieved here by being an orphan, which "frees" one from the bonds of society, but in the worst way (Chandler 1984, 274). In the Khmer literary context, being an orphan is not only a bad fate, but it is also a morally precarious one.

In a variety of other Khmer texts, the orphan is represented as suspect, compromised, or even dangerous to himself or herself and others: "True solitude, is being an orphan," reads a line from *Cpāp' Trīneti*, a Khmer religious poem intended to instruct children in proper moral behavior. The image is a strongly negative one, indicative of a way of life that is unbeneficial to others, explicated with illustrations such as "possessing learning, but not teaching others" or "not having children to love you" (Chandler 1984, 274; see also Pou and Jenner 1981, 152).[18] The *cpāp'* poetry in general highlights the moral relationship between parents and children; parents serve as moral exemplars for their children to emulate and are reminded that "the fruit grows not far from the tree" (Hansen 1988, 32). For children, the strong implication of the *cpāp'* is that those who lack exposure to the moral guidance sung by parents to children through the *cpāp'* lead lives that are morally unrefined and immature. A proper parent-child relationship, then, in the view of these texts, is fundamental to mature moral agency.

In several other well-known folk stories—and these are clearly gendered images of orphans—girls are abandoned in the forest by a parent or parents and assume new morally ambivalent identities in which they are incapable of achieving full agency. Lost and alone in the forest in a defenseless state, these orphaned girls become animalistic. In one story, three young girls abandoned by their mother metamorphose into birds with a cry of "kūn lok," meaning "child of the world" (Chandler 1982, 55-57). In another well-known story, the *Rathasena-jātaka* ("Birth Story of Rathasena"), 12 young orphaned sisters (after various travails and twists of fortune at the hands of an ogress that they meet in the forest) are imprisoned in a pit in the ground where 11 of the 12 must eventually resort to eating their own infants.[19] In a somewhat different vein, *Nāṅ Maraṇamātā* ("Miss Deceased-Mother"), tells the story of a young girl whose beloved mother is murdered by her father and his minor wife.[20] The mother, in her various rebirths, takes the form of animal, plant, and spirit to try to help her daughter. Even though the daughter remains a good person who is respectful toward her cruel stepmother, her existence as a *kaṃbrā-mtāy*, or "a child deprived of his or her mother," is fraught with violence and danger. She is eventually murdered by her stepmother and reborn as a bird (Jacob 1996, 164-65).[21]

As a virtuous monk, the orphaned Bhikkhu Sukh is unique in the *Gatilok.* Every other monk in the narrative collection is mired in the ways of the world instead of reaping profits from the path of the Dhamma. Several stories feature abbots who become so obsessed with material ambitions, such as building a new *vihāra* (monastery building) or choosing a silk robe, that they fail to recognize that the supposed patrons for these projects are, in reality, conning them out of the funds diligently raised by their lay followers to support the ongoing work of their monasteries (Ind [1921] 1971, 2: 30-41). In another story, an abbot implicates himself in a vile murder when he finds a corpse propped up against a jackfruit tree in his monastery. Fearful of false accusations, he shaves off the dead man's hair and dresses him as a novice. In the morning, he tells the gathered monks and lay people that a novice "without relatives or friends" passed through the monastery during the night and died. In truth, the corpse was the lover of a woman who murdered him and then tricked her husband into believing that he had inadvertently killed an intruder. Although the abbot eventually surmises the truth about the corpse, he quickly burns it anyway in order to cover up his own wrongdoing (10: 57-73). Several other stories make reference to abbots who engage in sexual misconduct, and in one case an abbot's lover hires a gambler to murder her husband (1: 46-47; 3: 55-56).

Apart from references to the Buddha, the stories of other bhikkhu that are drawn from Pāli literary sources are also corrupt and corrupting of others. Dhaniyathera, a bhikkhu who lived at the time of the Buddha, is shown "taking what is not given"—a clear violation of the Buddhist precept concerning theft. He misrepresents an edict issued by King Bimbisāra allowing monks to collect wood in the forest in order to requisition lumber from the royal foresters for a new hut. The Buddha himself chides Dhaniya for this action (3: 21-24). Kapilabhikkhu, a monk under Kassapa Buddha, is described as "a bhikkhu who knew all 84,000 [lines] of the *Braḥ Tipiṭaka* but did not know how to behave in accordance with the Dhamma and the Vinaya [Monastic code of conduct], and . . . twisted the *Braḥ Buddhavacana* [Words of the Buddha] to mean something else" (2: 60-61). His wrongdoing and consequent punishment in the Avīci hell was later explained by Gautama Buddha to fishermen who encountered Kapilabhikkhu in a rebirth as a beautiful fish with a putrid stench emitting from his mouth (2: 61). Devadattathera (the Buddha's heretical cousin) emerges as the ultimate symbol of evil within the text, one whose sins were so great that "the entire planet has taken note of this story" (2: 62). Although Devadatta's many efforts to distort the Buddha's Dhamma and to harm the Buddha himself are not narrated in the text, they are examples of the kind of stories that need no telling for Khmer Buddhist audiences. Ind's references to figures such as Dhaniyathera, Kapilabhikkhu, and Devadatta, interwoven with the narratives of more ordinary bhikkhu drawn from vernacular literature, however, seem to suggest that even Pāli textual accounts of the Buddha's time represent monastic life as fraught with the failures of monks to live according to the Dhamma.

Ind's efforts to define the true meaning of monkhood are a reaction to what he sees as a tendency among Buddhists to understand monkhood in cultural rather than spiritual terms: "Among people who believe in and follow Buddhism, when we see a shaved head and the clothing of a monk, then we recognize that he is holy and righteous . . . and we trust and believe in him" ([1921] 1971, 1: 57). The problem with complacency toward the designation of monks, Ind explains, is that it enables wicked persons to impersonate monks, easily deceiving and cheating people who assume that they are authentic because of their way of dress. Rather, the identity of a true monk is defined in an utterly different way, as "one who strives toward virtue in respect to the four kinds of morality,"[22] who is "endowed with the virtues belonging to the recluse,"[23] and so on. Then,

> he can be called a "monk" in the sāsana of Lord Buddha. But if we take shaved heads and yellow robes as signifiers of monks, the group of *upāsak*, young and old, men and women, can have shaved heads, too, and they can wear yellow robes as well. Could not this group be called by the name of monk as well? (2: 106-7)

Although the social roles and responsibilities of monks and lay people are different—and therefore the exact behaviors, occupations, and mental attitudes that constitute virtue are different for them—monks and lay people alike derive their identities from the behavior that they exhibit. Because this is the measure of personhood that is fundamental to the definition of beings in the world, the importance of sharply delineating between the lives of monks and lay people is diminished. This is not to say that the monastic life as a whole is devalued in the *Gatilok*. For Ind, on the contrary, monasticism is tied to education, which he sees as an essential component of the moral life. Monks who are not living as true monks are as pitiable and blinded as ignorant lay people, and lay people have as much need as monks for the cultivation of the *satisampajañña* that enables them to know how to live. Because detachment from society is an impossibility, the monk, like the lay person, must draw on moral discernment in order to live virtuously in relation to others, thereby improving the purity of self and others at the same time.

The second moral value highlighted in this narrative is moral discernment, or *satisampajañña*, presented here as the resource that allows the boy Sukh to survive and prosper. First, he recognizes what has happened to his family and understands the intentions of the chieftain's gang. He has the foresight to climb and hide in the tree "tangled with creepers"—exactly the same image of an entangled bamboo that is used so derisively in the *Sutta Nipāta* to describe a life lived among others. Then, he is able to escape to the lower village and, by some combination of instinct and perception, to appeal to a compassionate family who will risk their own lives to shelter him. When they ask him to leave, he quickly understands his plight and theirs and runs away, grabbing and hanging on to the right vehicle, the cart of the merchant, who introduces him to the vehicle of Theravāda Buddhism. Like other morally good protagonists in the *Gatilok*, Sukh exhibits the kind of discernment that causes moral people, possessing *satisampajañña*, to be able to respond to situations of harm in a way that avoids injury to themselves and others. Although Bhikkhu Sukh could not avoid the massacre of his family, he did live in such a way that ended rather than perpetuated the enmity associated with their deaths. What is striking here is the way in which the narrative of an orphan born into a *jāti* with little or no knowledge of the Buddhist *sāsana* is able to transform violence, loss, and disadvantage into wisdom, well-being, and purity. This contrasts with the threads of the Ajātasattu story running through the text, in which the son of a powerful Buddhist king with every advantage manages to transform advantage and benefit into violence and impurity.

Bhikkhu Sukh's story is morally powerful not because he is the only true bhikkhu in the *Gatilok*, but because, within the world view of the text, he represents the fundamental ethical problems confronting each and every person. First, all beings born into the world must live in relationship to others. Although Cau Sukh loses his natal family, he must still learn to construct appropriate and beneficial relationships in order to survive. Second, all individuals living in the world experience *dukkha* and must respond to it as they are able, given the combination of knowledge, abilities, personality, relationships, and other factors that determine their identities as beings. Bhikkhu Sukh is presented as someone who lacks every social advantage in the world that could bring him power or benefit, but he possesses the moral resource of discernment that allows him not only to survive but also to achieve spiritual development. As Katie Canon has noted in another context, because this "least-advantaged" member of society survives and prospers, others can as well (1988, 2-5).

Bhikkhu Sukh, however, is not the primary *sappurisa* of the story. More important as a moral figure is the merchant boss who becomes his *pitā dharm*. Confronting the little boy hanging on to his oxcart, the merchant heard the child's story with *secktī-saṅveg-āṇit* (horrific grief and pity),[24] and then responded compassionately. Etymologically embedded in the Khmer description of the merchant's initial response to the boy's story as *secktī-saṅveg-āṇit* is the Pāli word *saṃvega* (anxiety). In this highly allegorical context, this emotion bears religious analysis. *Saṃvega*, in various Pāli contexts, refers to the kind of emotional anxiety that one feels as a result of the "contemplation of the miseries of this world" (Rhys Davids and Stede 1986, 658), a deep distress based on the recognition of suffering and its causes (Coomaraswamy 1977, 179). One prominent context for *saṃvega* is the contemplation—presumably by monks—of decaying corpses in cemeteries, which leads them to recognize the nature of reality in terms of *anicca* or "impermanence" (Wilson 1996, 15-17). The merchant's response to the orphan's story, then, is the kind of realization that can lead one on to the Path, signifying the merchant's morally advanced and exemplary status. *Saṃvega* seems to be leading the merchant to *mettā-karuṇā*, or "loving-kindness and compassion." In contrast to the image conjured by *saṃvega* of a monk contemplating a corpse, the merchant's realization is represented in relational terms: he takes the orphan as his own child, accepting responsibility for his welfare. This moment of emotional response by the merchant seems to highlight a tension between the values of renunciation and familial responsibility but then tips the balance toward the portrayal of a *sappurisa* figure who is socially attached.

When the passage is read not allegorically but historically, the merchant boss's compassion takes on another kind of heightened significance, since he might have either sold the orphaned boy into slavery or kept him as his servant, either of which would have been seen as acceptable and even appropriate responses. Instead, he adopted him as his own son and then, displaying further generosity, had him educated and eventually sponsored his ordination. The relationship between this adoptive father and son is exemplary of *kalyāṇa-mitt*, or "virtuous friendship."[25] This type of relationship—a major concern of the text—represents the best possible kind of attachment, as it leads one to and keeps one on the Path. Because of the deceptiveness of so many people in the world, *satisampajañña* is particularly important as the moral virtue that enables one to discern who is a *kalyāṇa-mitt* and who is not.

Just as the world is produced by networks of causation, individuals are also defined by their relationships, since there is no self independent from one's response to others. Even a hermit in the middle of the forest is defined through others by his withdrawal from them—although in the *Gatilok*, all of the hermits find that they cannot really escape the social world. The text explores a number of types of relationships that the moral person must negotiate, following the "six directions" outlined in the *Siṅgālovāda-sutta* (Rhys Davids and Carpenter [1890] 1949, 3: 180-93): relationships with parents, teachers, spouse and children, friends, servants and employees, and ascetics and Brahmins (Ind [1921] 1971, 1: 23-35).[26] This fundamental reality of human interconnectedness and interaction Ind pulls from his deep knowledge of Pāli texts—in tension with the images of detachment that he finds in them as well. The nature of self and world means that relationship—even attachment—is unavoidable; thus the ability to discern the true identities of one's self and others becomes an ethical imperative.

Conclusions

My work on these stories attempts to understand the ways in which different articulations of Theravāda Buddhism and the related ethical ideas put forward by Theravādins are produced. The interactions between a cosmopolitan body of texts and images that have moved and have been carried through Southeast Asia take on particular meanings in the expression of different local Buddhisms that have emerged in various historical contexts. Currently, we know little about which Pāli texts and images were being absorbed, learned, reinterpreted, used, and taught in nineteenth- and early-twentieth-century Cambodia prior to the rise of a new formulation of Buddhist orthodoxy under French and Siamese influence. These narratives give us an opportunity to see something of the workings of the literary culture of Theravāda Buddhism during this earlier, little-studied period. Reading vernacular texts such as the *Gatilok* as textual regions enables us to view them as sites of interaction which make clear that the Pāli tradition itself is not a reified canon, but a changing set of ideas that contains and expresses contradictory ideas and tensions, giving rise to different normative values depending on the interpretations brought forward in given historical moments.

Approaching texts as sites of vernacular-cosmopolitan interaction permits the possibility of a more nuanced reading of Buddhist ethical concerns. As a form of regional history, however, it also contributes to what Chakrabarty has referred to as the task of "breathing heterogeneity into the word 'imagination,'" a process that begins "to allow for the possibility that the field of the political is constitutively not singular" (2000, 149). Buddhist literary culture is a site of imagining and interpreting the world, and in the particular context of colonial modernity in Southeast Asia, Buddhist ethical reflection becomes a critical means of constructing and articulating the new identities emerging in this period. Just as Chakrabarty argues that, in India, "being human involves the question of being with gods and spirits" (2000, 16), being in the world in colonial Cambodia involves an ethical orientation, a decision about which roads or Paths to follow: how to define one's self as a Buddhist, a modern person, a Khmer, a colonial subject, and a moral individual living in the world. Power relationships in this context are morally charged, subject to the workings of karma. Individual identity itself is attached to the complex ways in which one can and must relate to others, reciprocal relationships that are distinct from European notions of power as connected with capital. In this sense, one could see in the image of an orphan the complex imagining of an alternative or heterogeneous way of being in the modern world. This image is one of a moral being, cognizant of his or her lack of autonomy or individualism; one who survives because of his or her ability to evaluate the moral intentions of others; one whose "primitive" nature is transformed not by the encounter with European modernity, but by clinging to the frame of the right vehicle; and one whose master can speak to him or her in his or her own language.

Notes

I am indebted to Kären Wigen for her talk, "Moving Mountains: The Creation of the Modern Japanese Alps," at the University of Wisconsin-Milwaukee, October 2001, which helped the interpretive frame of this essay take shape. I am grateful to a number of colleagues for their insightful comments on earlier drafts: Susanne Mrozick, Maria Heim, Charles Hallisey, David Chandler, Charles Keyes, Mark Bradley, Amanda Seligman, and Aims McGuinness, as well as Ann Waltner and two anonymous *Journal of Asian Studies* readers. Finally, thanks are due to audiences at Harvard University, Northwestern University, the Center for Twenty-First Century Studies at the University of Wisconsin-Milwaukee, and the University of California, Los Angeles, who responded to this essay in its various oral incarnations.

1. In his early anthropological study of Sinhalese Buddhism, Richard Gombrich ([1971] 1991, 372-82) points us directly toward this question.
2. Collins (1998, 61) points out that the word *imaginaire*, drawn from French scholarship, is not easily translated, since it does not refer to what is "imaginary" in the sense of "unreal" but, rather, "what is imagined," such as the worlds of texts, which are social facts. Collins defines the Pāli *imaginaire* as "a mental universe created by and within Pāli texts" (41). Similarly, Faure (1996, 3, 12) understands the *imaginaire* as "the way beliefs are rendered in images," which, in the case of his study on the Zen master Keizan, constituted a "constellation" of images organized "around poles like awakening,

dreams, places, gods and their icons, Chan/Zen masters and their relics"—in other words, images and ideas that constitute a mental universe or system of thought. Both Collins and Faure view the *imaginaire* as being historically situated (Faure 1996, 11-12; Collins 1998, 72-89), although, as Faure argues, the *imaginaire* may understand itself as universal and unlocalized (1996, 12).

3. I am following the Pou-Martini transliteration for Khmer (Pou 1969).
4. For a fuller discussion of Rhys Davids's attitudes toward Jātaka texts, see Jory 2002, 897-905.
5. Most of these vernacular versions have not survived, and their titles and contents are unknown (Tauch 1994, 98-99; Lī-Thām 1994, 46-47).
6. As far as I have been able to determine, after the initial versions were serialized and printed by the Institut Bouddhique, the text was reissued without variation in 1936, 1961, 1965, 1971, and in a Khao I Dang version in 1981 (printed in the Khao I Dang refugee camp in Thailand). In 1982 it was reissued by Cedoreck with a new preface written by Khing Hoc Dy. The 1965 version was reprinted by the Institut Bouddique in 1995. I am grateful to Lindsay French for giving me a copy of the Khao I Dang version and to Khing Hoc Dy for giving me a copy of his preface to the 1982 version.
7. I am grateful to Penny Edwards for pointing out the associations between the *Gatilok* and nationalism, beginning in the 1930s, and to Sophea Mouth and Sotheary Duong for helping me understand the *Gatilok*'s prominence as a literary work in postcolonial Cambodia, when it became incorporated into the national secondary curriculum. Although the text continues to be well known among the older generation of Khmer, its prominence may be waning. In a July 2000 interview at the Institut Bouddhique in Phnom Penh, a Khmer scholar and publisher suggested to me that the most recent *Gatilok* imprint had not sold as well as anticipated due to, in his words, "a severe deterioration of morality in contemporary society."
8. Dhamma bears multiple interpretations in Ind's work. It is used as "Truth," or as Collins translates this sense of the word, "what is right" (1998, 450). Ind also uses Dhamma to refer to the Buddha's teachings and the transmission of these teachings. He contrasts Dhamma with *lokiya*, what is "of the world," or "worldly." Written in lower case, as in the phrase *sappurisadhammā*, dhamma here refers to "characteristics" or "attributes" of a *sappurisa*, or a "good or moral person."
9. The name apparently refers to a local village or regional *anak tā* (spirit) (Forest 1992, 22-24; Ang 1986, 201-31; Porée-Maspero 1962, 6-12).
10. Also included among the sevenfold *sappurisa-dhammā* are appropriate ways to make a living, appropriate times or circumstances, and appropriate ceremonial behavior. By comparing Ind's interpretation of the *sappurisa-dhammā* with commentarial sources, one may see that Ind is reinterpreting the concepts for application to lay persons. Whether Ind himself reinterprets the concept or is drawing on other texts such as *samrāy* (vernacular Khmer commentarial texts) is not clear. In various Pāli commentaries, the understanding of *dhammaññu*, for instance, "one who knows the dhamma," is of a person who knows the Pāli texts and commentaries. *Atthaññu* is glossed as one who knows the meaning of that which has been spoken, with an additional note in the subcommentary that this means understanding not just the words but also the meanings of *sutta-geyya* (a reference to texts). *Attaññu* is interpreted as one who knows one's self through means of meditation. By contrast, Ind explains *dhammaññuta* as the "condition of one who recognizes causes and results, who recognizes that 'this thing is the cause [which] is the origin of this result. This result is the result which arose from this cause,' and so on" ([1921] 1971, 2: 64-66). This recognition refers to the perception of the nature of reality, not to the knowledge of texts. *Atthaññuta*, in Ind's usage, refers to the ability to

make moral evaluations of actions, and *attaññuta* refers to being able to situate one's self morally in relation to others in the social world (Buddhaghosa 1920/2463, 301; De Silva 1970, 333-34).

11. This term may be used here as a synonym for *juor*, "line," which occurs later in the narrative, referring to the "extended family" of the accused, including siblings (possibly on the paternal side only), parents, and offspring. My thanks to both Sophea Mouth and Vincent Her for help in translating these two words in this context.
12. This description must refer to the sale or trade of ethnic minority members into lowland slavery.
13. Lok Tā is a title for an older monk. Ind employs *Phnong*, the commonly used Khmer designation for "hill tribe," not the tribal name for itself. This term, still in common usage, carries a pejorative connotation.
14. Unlike most of the *Gatilok* narratives, "The Story of Bhikkhu Sukh" lacks a reference to a source in the text or an obvious parallel, as far as I have been able to determine, in another compilation.
15. My reading of the ritual themes in this narrative is indebted to Charles Keyes.
16. In these verses, the commentary emphasizes that "the disciple of the Fully Awakened One" (*sammāsambuddhasāvako*) is "the monk with influxes extinct, though born among ordinary persons . . . shines surpassing the ordinary folk who have 'become blind'" (Carter and Palihawadana 1987, 145).
17. One could conclude that Bhikkhu Sukh stayed in the monkhood for a lengthy period of time or perhaps for life, since he is referred to at one point in the commentary as "Lok Tā" Sukh, indicating advanced status and age.
18. The *cpāp'* poetry was part of Ind's own literary and religious influence, and the thematic and pedagogical interconnections between the *Gatilok* and the *Cpāp' Dūnmān Khluon*, in particular, are evident.
19. This story, which I have heard in oral forms, is also referred to as the *Buddhisaen-jātaka* or as *Nāṅ Kaṅrī* ("Miss Kaṅrī"). These variations are well documented in Jacob 1996, 123, 168-69; see also Institut Bouddhique 1969, 1-39.
20. The Khmer word *kaṃbrā*, or "orphaned," refers not only to the loss of both parents but also to the loss of either the child's mother (*kaṃbrā-mtāy*) or father (*kaṃbrā-ūbuk*).
21. The story does not end here, but the versions I have encountered in oral form vary widely. In one oral version that I heard from a Khmer woman in Boston in December 1986, Nāṅ Maraṇamātā, falsely accused of adultery, turns into gold as she is about to be put to death. Her mother (who has taken the form of a bo tree) drops down a swing to her daughter, and the two "fly to heaven . . . and get enlightenment."
22. Ind goes on to refer to the "*pātimokkha-saṃvara-sīla* and the rest" ([1921] 1971, 2: 106). Apparently he is making a reference to the *catu-pārisuddhi-sīla*, the four kinds of morality for monks: *pātimokkha-saṃvara-sīla*, morality of restraint with respect to the disciplinary code; *indriya-saṃvara-sīla*, morality of restraint with respect to the senses; *ājīva-pārisuddhi-sīla*, morality of the purification of livelihood; and *paccaya-sannissita-sīla*, morality in regard to the four requisites [of robes, food, dwelling, and medicines].
23. Ind goes on to define and gloss these as "having the virtue of very little desire, meaning having few wants, a kindly disposition, and so forth" ([1921] 1971, 2: 106). Here, Ind's translation may be a Khmer rendering of the Pāli *ariya-vaṃsa.* These are translated by Nyanatiloka as the "noble usages": contentedness with any robe, any food, any dwelling, and delight in meditation and detachment (1972, 22).
24. In Khmer, *saṅveg* connotes suddenly feeling an apprehension of evil or a realization of the suffering of others that causes emotional distress or anxiety. *Āṇit* is more easily

translated, meaning "to have pity on" or "to feel compassion toward." I translate the noun form of the compound here as "horrific grief and pity" in an effort to convey the compounded emotions and realizations conveyed by the phrase without employing a cumbersome and lengthy translation. The merchant's elevated moral status is seemingly signaled linguistically by the related but different words employed to describe reactions to the orphan's story; the merchant's *secktī-saṅveg-āṇit* or "horrific grief and pity," is contrasted with the simpler *āṇit* (to feel pity or compassion) felt by the householders in the lower village.

25. Literally, "virtuous friend," from the Pāli *kalyāṇa-mitta*.
26. Ind's younger contemporary and colleague Tath Huot (1927) translated and edited a Khmer version of the sutta in the 1920s.

9

Seeking Śākyamuni: Travel and the Reconstruction of Japanese Buddhism

Richard M. Jaffe

With the opening of Japan to increased foreign contact with Europe and the United States in the 1850s, Japanese Buddhist scholars and clerics, like other members of the Japanese elite, began to travel abroad in significant numbers for the first time since the seventeenth century. Beginning in the early 1870s, Japanese Buddhists followed the imperative of the Charter Oath by fanning out to seek knowledge throughout the world. Having mastered modern philological methods, Sanskrit, and Pāli, Japanese scholars and clerics returned home to assume influential university appointments in Buddhist and Indian studies and to serve in important administrative and educational capacities in their respective denominations.

Over the last several decades, a number of scholars have described how the responses of Japanese Buddhists to increasingly bold Christian missionary efforts in Japan, their exchanges with Western Buddhologists, as well as participation in the 1893 World Parliament of Religions helped reshape the perceptions and practice of Japanese Buddhism. Many of these studies have underscored the complex interchanges and refractions that occurred as Japanese Buddhists adapted Western scholarly ideas about Buddhism for their own apologetic purposes, in the process transforming the image and practice of Buddhism in both Japan and the West (Ketelaar 1990, 136-220; Sharf 1993; Snodgrass 2003; Thelle 1987; Vita 2002). These studies have gone a long way toward answering Aijaz Ahmad's call for analyses that show how "textualities [about the non-West] might have been received, accepted, modified, challenged, overthrown or reproduced by the intelligentsias of the colonized countries: not as an undifferentiated mass but as social agents impelled by our own conflicts, distinct political and social locations, of class, gender, region, religious affiliation, and so on" (Lopez 1995b, 12, citing Ahmad 1992, 172).

The founding of academic chairs of Buddhist studies in sectarian academies and imperial universities, the publication of the Taisho canon, with its claim of philological superiority, and the redefinition of Buddhism as the most scientific and philosophically coherent of all the world's religions are but a few of the important results of the intersection of Japanese Buddhist concerns and the forces of Euro-American evangelism, Orientalist scholarship, and colonialism. The eventual Japanese reconceptualization of Buddhism as a world religion that had originated in India and reached the height of its efflorescence in Japan thus was closely linked with the emergence of Buddhist studies in Europe, the United States, and, with surprising rapidity, in Japan itself.

Because of the importance of the Euro-American-Japanese exchange in the construction of modern Japanese Buddhism, there has been a tendency to portray the network of global contacts made by Japanese Buddhists after the Meiji Restoration as almost exclusively bipolar between the West and Japan. Although most studies acknowledge the importance of interactions with Western scholars and, to a far lesser degree, Western Buddhists, little scrutiny has been given to the frequent interchanges between Buddhists within Asia. In this essay, I show how interaction with other Asian Buddhists—in this case, specifically South and Southeast Asian ones—influenced the shifting Japanese understanding of their form of Buddhism and its relationship to the broader Asian tradition.

Exchange was particularly prominent with those East Asian regions—Korea, Taiwan, Manchuria, and parts of China—that were eventually directly colonized or imperially dominated by the Japanese. But from the start of the Meiji period, Japanese Buddhists were also deeply interested in those regions of Buddhist Asia with which they had little prior direct contact. Noted Buddhist reformers such as Dharmapala, Henry Steel Olcott, Taixu, and Han Yongun as well as many other lesser-known Asian Buddhist visitors came to Japan. They sought aid in rescuing decaying Buddhist pilgrimage sites in Asia, help in expelling foreign Christian missionaries from their own countries, new pan-Asian Buddhist ties with their compatriots, or the latest methods in Buddhist scholarship.[1] The construction of modern Buddhism in Japan and, more broadly, across Asia, thus involved a wide variety of Indians, Thai, Sri Lankans, Japanese, Koreans, Tibetans, and Chinese who listened and responded not only to what Europeans and Americans said about Buddhism, but who also talked among themselves. These conversations comprised an important part of the local conditions underlying the diverse modern constructions of Buddhism.

Consideration of these exchanges in Asia reveals the emergence of a tightly linked global Buddhist culture in the late nineteenth century and illuminates the diverse "complex global loops" through which ideas were transmitted.[2] The essentialized, text-based notions of pan-Asian Buddhism created by a host of Western Orientalist scholars and Theosophists who have been described by Donald Lopez, Philip Almond, and others were not just transmitted from Europe directly to various Buddhist countries. In many instances, these ideas circulated between Buddhist countries, rather than being derived directly from their Orientalist sources. Local Buddhist practices and responses to colonial policies and missionaries of one Asian region also affected others, and Buddhists interpreted European understandings of Buddhism in light of their own experiences of these other Buddhisms. At the same time, in a process that has been labeled "intercultural mimesis," native Japanese and other Asian constructions of modern Buddhism were often transmitted to Western Orientalist scholars, reinforcing or even giving birth to certain modern Orientalist ideas about the Buddhist tradition (see the essay by Charles Hallisey in this volume, 94).

What emerged as modern Buddhism in Japan and elsewhere in Asia was a result of this complex, tangled set of exchanges that resulted in the production of a discourse that wove together traditional Buddhist self-understandings with knowledges received in a wide variety of contact zones.[3] These encounters stimulated Japanese to place their Buddhism in the context of a pan-Asian tradition at a time when contesting notions of nation and region were plentiful. The various competing Japanese Buddhist conceptions of pan-Asianism, the eastward advance of Buddhism, and the global spread of Buddhism that emerged as a result of these contacts played a significant role in the formation of radical anticolonial solidarities between the Japanese and Asian peoples but also contributed to the emergence of Japanese imperialism.

In this essay, I focus on three Japanese Buddhist clerics who traveled from Japan to other Buddhist communities or sites in Asia during the 1880s and 1890s. In particular, I examine how the travels of these individuals—Kitabatake Dōryū (1820–1907, Jōdo Shin), Shaku Sōen (1859–1919, Rinzai), and Shaku Kōzen (1849–1924, Shingon)—to India and Sri Lanka contributed to a growing interest within Japan in Śākyamuni Buddha as both a historical figure and a focal point of world Buddhism. Reports of their travels also increased awareness of other forms of Asian Buddhism and marked the start of growing Buddhist cooperation within the region.

Contact with European scholars of Buddhism no doubt also served as a catalyst for the rekindled focus on Śākyamuni as the founder of the Buddhist tradition. In part, European interest in Śākyamuni arose because the bulk of European knowledge of Buddhism derived from contacts in colonial South and Southeast Asia, where Śākyamuni was far more central to Buddhist practice than within Japan. By the mid-eighteenth century the growing body of information concerning Buddhism throughout Asia had stimulated a shift in European portrayals of the Buddha from a mythical figure to a historical personage. Through the nineteenth century, debate over Śākyamuni's biography was one important focal point in European Buddhist scholarship. European archaeologists and explorers devoted considerable energy to locating in eastern India sites associated with Śākyamuni that were described in the growing body of translated Buddhist literature.[4] The biographical turn in European Buddhist scholarship also paralleled a similar emphasis on the biography of Jesus, a prominent feature of theological studies during the second half of the nineteenth century (Tweed 2000, 119-20; Almond 1988, 54-79).[5] European scholars of Buddhism such as Émile Senart, Hermann Oldenberg, T. W. Rhys Davids, and R. Spence Hardy all wrote at length about the life of Śākyamuni. Edwin Arnold's bestselling biography of Śākyamuni, *The Light of Asia*, published in 1879, played a significant role in shaping popular European, American, and even Asian perceptions of Buddhism. It also served as a rallying message for the global Buddhist effort to "liberate" Bodh Gayā (dubbed the "Buddhist Jerusalem" by Arnold in 1896) from the hands of its Hindu owners (Trevithick 1988, 72-73).

The growing Japanese interest in the figure of Śākyamuni also can be traced back to the Edo period, when traditional biographies of Śākyamuni such as *Shaka hassō monogatari* (1666), *Shaka goichidaiki zue* (1839), *Hasshū kigen Shaka jitsuroku* (1854), and Mantei Ōga's fictionalized biography, *Shaka hassō Yamato bunko* (1845) were published. From the 1880s on, publications concerning the life of Śākyamuni were increasingly common. A number of the earlier biographies were reissued in 1883–84. By 1888, a translation of Arnold's *Light of Asia* was underway and the Buddhist Propagation Society (Senkyōkai) began a serialized biography of Śākyamuni in its English-language publication *Bijou of Asia*.[6] Interest in the biography of Śākyamuni also was demonstrated by numerous authors attempting to compile pan-sectarian histories of Japanese Buddhist history and doctrine as part of a broader effort at unifying the Buddhist community in the wake of the Meiji suppression. Many of these pan-sectarian summaries of Buddhist doctrine began with a discussion of the dates of Śākyamuni's life and at least a brief biography of the figure to whom all denominations of Buddhism could be traced (Ketelaar 1990, 200, 272, n. 65). Over the course of the Meiji era, a number of critical biographies that incorporated the latest historical and archaeological discoveries concerning Śākyamuni appeared in Japan, including Inoue Tetsujirō's *Shaka shuzokuron* (1897) and *Shakamuni den* (1902) and Itō Shundō's *Shaka jitsu denki* (1908).

But the Śākyamuni boom in Japan was triggered by more than just the academic study of Buddhism in Europe and the United States. Travel by Japanese to India and other parts of Asia and information about those regions flowing into Japan also fueled the growing interest in Śākyamuni as a figure of veneration, a historical figure, and an object of archaeological inquiry. The journeys of Kitabatake, Sōen, and Kōzen, shaped by the growing global interest in Śākyamuni, further stimulated Japanese interest in him as a rallying figure for Buddhists throughout Asia.

Kitabatake Dōryū's Pilgrimage to India

Much in the history of the late Edo period and the early Meiji (1868–1912) years impelled Japanese Buddhists to reconsider their tradition and to travel abroad. From the 1840s until the mid-1870s, the collapse of the Tokugawa regime and the restoration of imperial rule had triggered the most violent suppression of Buddhism on the local and national levels in Japanese history. Although the Tokugawa regime had regarded the Buddhist clergy as a crucial aide in the maintenance of religious and social order, nativists, Shintōists, and many members of the new Meiji regime demonized them as un-Japanese, parasitic, and corrupt. Government leaders subjected Buddhist institutions to a series of harsh measures that led to the widespread laicization of the clergy and the closure or destruction of numerous temples. By 1872 the most violent of these attacks on Buddhism had ended, but the Buddhist clergy found themselves struggling to return to the position of power and influence they once held.

Several areas of concern impelled members of the Buddhist clergy to look to Europe, the United States, and other parts of Asia as they sought to reconstruct a Buddhism that would thrive in the emerging new order in Japan. Responding to the imperative of the Charter Oath to seek knowledge throughout the world, the Meiji regime sent official delegations like the Iwakura Mission (1871–73) overseas to survey the economic, government, military, and other institutions of the Western powers that threatened Japan's independent existence. At the same time, the leadership of various Buddhist denominations and individual clerics began to look to the Western powers as a source of information for the revitalization of Japanese Buddhism. Interest within the Japanese Buddhist community in travel to Buddhist sites in other parts of Asia also increased during the first decades of the Meiji era. As commercial shipping between the ports of European colonies in Asia and Japan increased and as colonial and naval interests in those regions grew, private travel from Japan to China, Korea, India, Sri Lanka, and other Asian countries became possible in unprecedented ways.[7] European scholarly attention to Buddhist archaeological sites in India and elsewhere in Asia also contributed to a growing interest in Buddhist travel to those regions. Finally, reports of brief stops by Japanese travelers—for example, the visit by Shimaji Mokurai to India—further piqued the interest of the Japanese Buddhist community in Buddhist pilgrimage sites and the practice of Buddhism in what, from the Japanese perspective, were heretofore unexplored parts of Asia.

The leadership of the powerful and wealthy Honganji branch of Jōdo Shin was one of the most active promoters of overseas clerical travel, sending at least three clerical missions abroad between 1870 and 1880 (Mori 1983, 39-45). The leadership of both the Ōtani and Honganji branches dispatched prominent figures such as Shimaji Mokurai, Akamatsu Renjō, Nanjō Bun'yū, and Takakusu Junjirō either to tour various Western nations or to study abroad in their efforts to create modern, sectarian institutions in Japan.[8] One of the last clerics to embark on one of these early Nishi Honganji-sponsored overseas missions was the adventurer Kitabatake Dōryū.

A rather eccentric figure, Kitabatake was the son of a Jōdo Shin cleric and had studied for a number of years at the academy at the Nishi Honganji. Kitabatake left the clergy for a time, engaging in a variety of military and educational efforts that included martial arts training, fighting on the side of shogunate forces, studying German language and military science, and opening a school in Tokyo for legal studies. After becoming a confidant of Ōtani Kōson, the head of the denomination, Kitabatake re-entered the clergy. He engaged in a failed attempt to help Kōson move the administrative office of the Nishi Honganji to Tokyo and carry out a series of reforms of the denomination. Kōson then dispatched Kitabatake on a mission abroad to study church–state relations in Europe and the United States.[9]

From 1881 to 1884, Kitabatake traveled westward through much of Europe, to the United States, and then back again to Japan via Europe and India. While in Europe and the United States, Kitabatake visited a number of scholars of Asia and Asian religions, including Hermann Oldenberg in Germany and Max Müller in London. The greatest amount of time in Europe was spent in Austria, where Kitabatake regularly met with an Austrian scholar, identified only as "Stein," to discuss Buddhism and European religious institutions and history.

At least three versions of his travel accounts were published soon after his return to Japan. The earliest, *Sekai shūyū tabi nikki: ichimei Shakamuni Butsu funbo no yurai* ("A Travel Diary of a World Tour: The History of Śākyamuni's Tomb"), was published in March 1884 only a little more than one month after Kitabatake's return to Japan at the end of January that same year (Akiyama 1884, 84). The same month, in what appears to have been an attempt to advertise his adventures widely, Kitabatake also published a one-page broadside, *Kitabatake Dōryū Shi Indo kikō* ("Master Kitabatake Dōryū's India Travels"), summarizing his pilgrimage to Śākyamuni's "tomb" (*funbo*) (Emoto 1884). In 1886, a detailed version of Kitabatake's account was published as *Tenjiku kōroji shoken* ("Things Seen En Route to India") (Nishikawa and Nagaoka 1886, 287-373). The titles of these works are misleading about the nature of Kitabatake's travels, suggesting that India was the primary destination for his travel and that he spent the bulk of his time there. Although Kitabatake traveled abroad for three years, his time in India comprised just one month at the very end of his journey. Nonetheless, the India portion of his trip became the sole focus of the first two books, which Kitabatake rushed to press soon after his return to Japan. Even the lengthy travel account, two-thirds of which details Kitabatake's travels in Europe and the United States, emphasizes the India portion of the journey in the title. At the heart of all versions of his chronicles is Kitabatake's claim to have been the first Japanese to have traveled to the important Buddhist pilgrimage site of Bodh Gayā and, most important, his claim to have visited the "tomb" of Śākyamuni Buddha, an achievement that stands as the apotheosis of the three-year journey.

Kitabatake had good reason for emphasizing the India portion of his trip and the pilgrimage to Bodh Gayā. The European and American portions of his journey had been preceded by a similar trip undertaken by his bitter opponents in Jōdo Shin reform politics, Shimaji Mokurai and Akamatsu Renjō, a decade earlier. These Jōdo Shin clerics had already surveyed the religio-political scene in the United States and Europe and had brought back a considerable amount of information from those countries for the denominational leadership to use as reference for its own modernization efforts. They had also played a crucial role in the denomination's rejection of the reform agenda advocated by Kitabatake and Ōtani. But Shimaji and Akamatsu had managed only to make brief stops in South Asia during their journeys. Unlike his predecessors, Kitabatake and his fellow traveler Kurosaki Yūji, a Japanese who met Kitabatake while studying commerce in England, made a one-month trip to the interior of India that included a pilgrimage to several important sites associated with the life of Śākyamuni Buddha. It was this aspect of his trip that he chose to emphasize.

A marked shift in the language and tone of the most complete version of his 1886 travel account (the most detailed published version) occurs when Kitabatake turns his attention from the Western powers to his excursions in India. Whereas Kitabatake seemingly looked up to the various scholars, officials, and experts he met in Europe and the United States as he investigated the history of church–state relations and the state of Buddhist studies in each country, once he arrived in India, his gaze took an imperial turn. While in Europe, Kitabatake had inquired on several occasions about the general conditions in India and the state of Buddhist sites there. In his first 1884 account of his trip to India, Kitabatake reported how, in Stein's words, India was "the most dangerous place in the world," where "not only do wild beasts and poison snakes endanger and injure people, but insane barbarian bandits threaten travelers, stealing their belongings and money" (Akiyama 1884, 10-11). Reflecting on the scene from the train he took from Bombay, Kitabatake remarked on the poverty of the homes he saw and declared that even the homes of Japan's poorest mountain hamlets were greatly superior. For the first time during the whole trip, Kitabatake wrote, he felt that Japan was superior to someplace (Mori 1983, 345).

Kitabatake vacillated between scorn for the poverty and backwardness of India and sympathy for the plight of the Indians who suffered at the hands of their British rulers. Like other Buddhist travelers in Asia during the late nineteenth century, Kitabatake viewed India's modern history as a cautionary tale for the Japanese—if they failed to compete with the West successfully, they would suffer a similar fate. At the end of his earliest account of the journey to Bodh Gayā, Kitabatake entered into a lengthy description of what he considered a brutally oppressive British colonial regime in India. Observing the regressive nature of the British salt act that levied a tax on salt for all Indians, hurting the poorest Indians the most, Kitabatake concluded that the brutal British colonial policy was hypocritical and shameful. In the final sentence of the book, Kitabatake warned that "there was nothing more extremely unfortunate for the Indians or the whole Asian region than this" (Akiyama 1884, 84).

Most important, though, Kitabatake felt that rather than simply receiving knowledge, as he had in Europe, in India he could search for that which he contended had been lost—the tomb of Śākyamuni—the significance of which only a Buddhist could fully appreciate. Kitabatake emphasized that while in Europe he had asked various scholars, including Oldenberg, Stein, and Müller, about the whereabouts of the Śākyamuni tomb (*Shakashi no funbo*), but they each had responded that they did not know its location. This seems somewhat odd given that H. H. Wilson in 1854 and Alexander Cunningham in 1861–62 had tentatively identified the site of Śākyamuni's death, Kuśīnagara, with the village of Kasia in the Gorakapur region. By 1876 Cunningham's assistant, A. C. L. Carlleyle, had unearthed a large *stūpa* and a reclining statue of Śākyamuni depicting the Great Decease at the site. Cunningham's conjectures were published as early as 1871, but detailed accounts of Carlleyle's discoveries were not published until 1883.[10] Although debate over the accuracy of Cunningham's identification continued until the early twentieth century, it seems unlikely that someone as concerned with the biography of Śākyamuni as Oldenberg would have not known of the earliest of these archaeological discoveries by the time Kitabatake came to Europe in the early 1880s. But, according to Kitabatake, out of all of his inquiries into the location of Śākyamuni's tomb, only one person, an English-speaking Indian in Benares, responded positively, saying he had seen something in a local Indian paper about the discovery of the tomb. Unfortunately for Kitabatake, however, his informant had forgotten the exact location of the site (Mori 1983, 350-51).[11]

On the return trip to Japan in the autumn of 1883, Kitabatake and Kurosaki sailed from Italy to Bombay, where they boarded a train bound for eastern

India. After disembarking in Benares, Kitabatake and Kurosaki made their way by cart and on foot toward Patna, and, eventually, Bodh Gayā. As in much imperial travel literature, the inhabitants of India are rendered almost mute and invisible in Kitabatake's descriptions. Kitabatake derisively referred to the natives as *kokudo/kuronbo* (blacks) and portrayed them as nearly naked, that is, uncivilized. Much to their dismay and surprise, the Japanese found that not only did the people they encountered not speak Japanese, but they could not even understand English, French, or Chinese (Akiyama 1884, 12).

After several difficult weeks of travel, forced to resort to hand gestures and pictures to make themselves understood, the two travelers finally arrived in Bodh Gayā. There Kitabatake and Kurosaki came upon a group of Indian workers excavating in the vicinity of the Mahābodhi temple, the site of Śākyamuni's awakening. Only after encountering the site foreman did Kitabatake discover that they had indeed made it to Bodh Gayā. In an extended conversation with three English-speaking Indians directing the dig, Kitabatake and Kurosaki learned that the disrepair of Bodh Gayā was due to the ascendance of "Brahmanism" some 1,800 years ago. The Indians, according to Kitabatake's account, also informed the Japanese of the history of the discovery of "Śākyamuni's tomb" at the site some ten years earlier and of the current efforts to fully excavate it. One of the foremen explained that the two Japanese were extremely fortunate to have come upon the site when they did. Had they arrived earlier, he explained, they would have been unable to see the then unexcavated tomb. In the first 1884 account, the foreman attributed both the preservation of the tomb and the good fortune of the clerics to the power of the Buddha, who had led Kitabatake and Kurosaki to the site. The foreman then urged the Japanese to go to the tomb and offer thanks to Śākyamuni for having ensured the preservation of the tomb and for leading the men to it just as it was uncovered (Akiyama 1884, 18). The portrayal of the preservation of the tomb and its discovery by Kitabatake and Kurosaki suggests that the Japanese were destined to arrive at the site just as the structure was being unearthed.

At this juncture in the narrative, Kitabatake underwent a transformation, shedding his explorer's clothing for his Buddhist robes. Taking a copy of the Three Pure Land Sūtras (*Sanbukyō*) that had been presented to him by the head of the Honganji when he departed Japan and grasping his prayer beads, Kitabatake was led to the excavated structure, accompanied by Kurosaki. With the Indian workmen all gathered around and paying obeisance, Kitabatake opened the tomb, revealing a standing statue of Śākyamuni. From his copy of the Three Pure Land Sūtras, he performed an abbreviated reading of the texts and prostrated himself before the tomb. His service completed, Kitabatake ascended from the site of the tomb along with Kurosaki and the Indians who had gathered around him (Akiyama 1884, 20). Kitabatake then commissioned one of the stonemasons working at the site to carve a stele (*sekihi*) to commemorate his visit. The stele (see Figure 1), which was reportedly still standing at Bodh Gayā in 1933, read, "Since the founding of Japan, I am the first to make a pilgrimage to the tomb of Śākyamuni. Dōryū, December 4, Meiji 16 [1883]" (Emoto 1884).[12]

Figure 1. Kitabatake's stele at Bodh Gayā. Akiyama 1884, 1.

Kitabatake's account of his discovery is curious. I do not have space in this article to unravel how Kitabatake and Kurosaki could have gone so far astray in their assessment of what they found at Bodh Gayā. Nonetheless, it is crucial to note that the pair had made their way not to the site of Śākyamuni's tomb, but to the place of his awakening. Strangely, at no point does Kitabatake connect Bodh Gayā with Śākyamuni's enlightenment. The closest thing to the excavation of Śākyamuni's tomb may have been the excavations that took place in the late 1870s at Kuśīnagara, the site of Śākyamuni's death, which was hundreds of miles away near Gorakhpur in the vicinity of the India–Nepal border. That Kitabatake could be so wrong about Indian geography is not hard to understand. That he seemingly was so ignorant of the details of Śākyamuni's biography indicates how little was known about such matters in Japan during the mid-Meiji period, even among high-ranking Buddhist clerics.[13]

Figure 2. Kitabatake at Śākyamuni's tomb. Akiyama 1884, 2-3.

Nonetheless, Kitabatake's pilgrimage to sites associated with the life of Śākyamuni held great significance for him and had great potency as a symbol for Japanese Buddhists. The woodblock illustration (see Figure 2) of the event that is contained in the earliest published account of Kitabatake's travels provides a glimpse of how his actions were construed by one artist who read this account and, perhaps, how it was viewed by a wider Japanese audience. The illustration conflates the standing image of Śākyamuni with common images of Amida (Amitābha) Buddha, the central object of veneration for Kitabatake's Jōdo Shin denomination. In the print, Śākyamuni, although an Indian himself, is depicted as light skinned as Kitabatake and Kurosaki. As in many traditional Japanese depictions, humans are connected to the Buddha by rays of light that stream forth from him. In this particular rendering of the events, Kitabatake is shown in full Buddhist clerical garb and stands erect, receiving Śākyamuni's light for all others present. The Japanese cleric serves as an intermediary not only for other Japanese—here depicted as the half-erect Kurosaki in Western clothing, that is, the vestments of civilization—but also for the dark-skinned, almost naked and, thus, uncivilized, kneeling Indians. Curiously, the literate, English-speaking Indians directing the excavation are absent from the picture. Kitabatake, the Japanese Buddhist cleric, in timeless robes that echo those worn by Śākyamuni himself, delivers the "Light of Asia" to the Japanese, halfway to civilization and enlightenment, and to other Asians, who lag behind on the road to modernity. The woodblock illustration thus clearly demonstrates the superiority of the Japanese both as Buddhists and successful modernizers in comparison with the Indian workers. At the same time, the portrayal does not reject out of hand solidarity with Japan's less advanced Asian compatriots, who, at the very least, share a Buddhist past with the Japanese, as evidenced by their participation in the rites for Śākyamuni officiated by Kitabatake. In this way, the illustration differs from the sorts of contemporaneous pictorial and journalistic representations of other Asian groups such as the Taiwanese aborigines, who were depicted as being clearly hostile to the Japanese civilizing influence and, therefore, justifiable targets of Japan's colonial aspirations.[14]

Shaku Kōzen and Shaku Sōen in Sri Lanka

Kitabatake was but the first among what soon became a steady stream of Japanese travelers to visit important Buddhist sites in South and Southeast Asia. Following his return from India in January 1884, Kitabatake lectured to the public about his travels in Europe, the United States, and India. In a May 1885 reader survey conducted by the *Konnichi shinbun* of the most popular leaders in ten different fields, ranging from military affairs to painting, Kitabatake was the most popular Buddhist preacher (*kyōhōka*), receiving 486 votes.[15] Although the exact extent of Kitabatake's direct influence on Kōzen and Sōen is uncertain, it is clear that both clerics had heard of Kitabatake prior to embarking on their own journeys to South Asia. For example, while a student at Fukuzawa Yukichi's Keiō Gijuku in Tokyo from 1885 to 1886, Sōen expressed admiration for Kitabatake's compelling exposition of the Buddhist teaching, particularly in the context of a growing Christian presence in the Kanto region (see Inoue 2000, 41, 47). According to Noguchi Fukudō, after resolving to travel to South Asia, Kōzen attempted to consult directly with Kitabatake (Noguchi 1920, 6).

Unlike Kitabatake, who spent little over one month in India, Sōen and Kōzen practiced for extended periods in Theravāda Buddhist monasteries in Sri Lanka, which was then a British colony.[16] These two clerics also differed from Kitabatake in that they came from two primarily monastic denominations of Buddhism—Zen and Shingon respectively, rather than the nonmonastic Jōdo Shin denomination. Like Kitabatake, their contact with Buddhism in South Asia and with ideas flowing from Europe and the United States through Sri Lanka led them to reassess the importance of Śākyamuni Buddha for Japanese Buddhism. It is thus fitting that when, in the early 1870s, the Meiji regime forced all Buddhist clerics to assume surnames, both men chose the name Shaku, the Japanese transliteration of Śākya, the clan name of Śākyamuni.

The two Shakus traveled to Sri Lanka within one year of each other, with Shaku Kōzen heading to the island first in 1886.[17] Kōzen was sent to South Asia by his teacher, Shaku Unshō, a severe master who was renowned for his strict adherence to the numerous monastic regulations described in the Vinaya, behavior that was rare in the Meiji era. In 1886, having learned of the decaying state of Buddhist sites in India from an "Indian" lecturer in Tokyo and after speaking with Akamatsu Renjō, who had made a brief stop in Sri Lanka, the 59-year-old Unshō dispatched his student Kōzen to survey the situation. Unshō also requested that Kōzen study the Buddhist precepts used in Sri Lanka and Buddhist customs of the region before returning to Japan (Tsunemitsu 1968, 1: 372-73). Kōzen remained in South Asia for seven years before returning to Japan in 1893.

Sōen, ten years Kōzen's junior, traveled to Sri Lanka in 1887 to complete his Zen training, to study Sanskrit and Pāli, and to survey the state of Buddhism in Sri Lanka. Sōen had been given an additional push to head to Sri Lanka by Fukuzawa Yukichi (1835–1901), who urged Sōen to go to the island to study the "origins of Buddhism." One of Sōen's seniors notes in a farewell letter to the cleric that Sōen "had decided to sail to India's Sri Lanka in order to experience first hand the conditions of Buddhism there and later help revive the decaying teaching of this country."[18]

Official contacts facilitated Kōzen's and Sōen's trips to Sri Lanka. Hayashi Tadasu, who had met a Sri Lankan official on his way back to Japan from London in 1871, helped provide the initial contacts necessary for Kōzen and Sōen to travel to the island. Sōen also mentions in his travel diary that he brought with him a letter of introduction from Hayashi that he presented to his lay patron in Sri Lanka, E. R. Gooneratne, upon arriving on the island (Inoue 2001, 76-81; see also Satō 1999–2002). Through Kōzen's connections, both studied under the same Theravāda master, Paññāsekhara, a close associate of the learned clerical leader, Hikkaḍuvē Sumaṇgala (1826–1911). Sumaṇgala was in many ways a cosmopolitan monk who nurtured contact not only with foreigners such as Henry Steel Olcott but also, through correspondence, with clerics in Burma, Thailand, and Japan. Interested in reviving Theravāda Buddhism throughout Asia, Sumaṇgala facilitated the sojourns of numerous Japanese clerics in Sri Lanka.[19] Although Sumaṇgala served for a number of years as the head of the Buddhist Theosophical Society's clerical division, at times he disagreed strongly with Olcott, at one point even threatening to resign his position over what he considered unorthodox interpretations of Nirvana in Olcott's *Buddhist Catechism* and for Olcott's questioning the authenticity of the Tooth Relic, which devout Sri Lankans contended was Śākyamuni's tooth (Prothero 1996, 167-68).

The two Japanese clerics had gone to Sri Lanka seeking a pure, original Buddhism that they could transmit back to Japan. What they discovered in nineteenth-century Sri Lanka was a tradition undergoing radical change. In colonial Sri Lanka, Buddhism was being transformed against a background of widespread Christian missionary activity, the solidification of the British colonial administration, and, ironically, a new emphasis among Sri Lankan Buddhists themselves in reviving a decaying Buddhist tradition by returning to the "pure" origins of the tradition.[20]

At least some of the impetus for the revival of Sri Lankan Buddhism and opposition to the Christian missionaries came from the American Theosophist, Henry Steel Olcott, and his Sri Lankan associate, Dharmapala (née Don David Hevavitharana), both of whom played major roles in the creation of an increasingly rationalist reform Buddhism in Sri Lanka. Sōen's diary makes clear that he and Kōzen were in contact with both Dharmapala and Sumaṇgala. According to the diary, Kōzen, who was based in Colombo, traveled frequently to Galle, where the two Japanese clerics together visited a variety of monasteries and lay people. Within a few months of arriving in Sri Lanka, Sōen began using an English-language copy of Olcott's *Buddhist Catechism* to practice his English, writing out verbatim the first portion of the book. This text, which mimicked the primers used by Christian missionaries, presented Buddhism as a textual, rational, scientific religion centered on the founder, Śākyamuni. Olcott's approach turned Buddhism into "one religion among many. And this reified 'ism' was immediately reduced to the beliefs of the ancient Buddha" (Prothero 1996, 102-103). It is the section on Śākyamuni that is quoted by Sōen, who wrote out passages such as "Is Buddha a god? No"; "Was he a man? In form, but internally not like other men"; and "Where was Kapilavastu? In India, 100 miles northeast of the [sic] Benares, and about 40 miles from the Himalaya mountains" (Shaku Sōen 1941, 56 recto, 57 verso, 61 verso–62 recto).[21]

The Sri Lankans seem to have celebrated the visiting Japanese clerics as comrades in the struggle against the missionaries and the British colonial order. Although we do not have any account of popular reaction to Kōzen's ordination, Sōen's diary details the festivities that accompanied his own. Just as crowds all over the island lauded Olcott, one of the first white Europeans on the island formally to receive the five lay Buddhist precepts, Sri Lankans considered Sōen's ordination as a novice monk (*sāmaṇera*) a highly auspicious event. According to Sōen's diary, his ordination on 6 May 1887 was attended by a boisterous crowd of more than a thousand people, who celebrated the event with fireworks and Western-style Buddhist hymns. The geopolitical implications of the event were clearly on the mind of at least one member of the crowd. A Sri Lankan layman in attendance told Sōen that there had not been such a grand event since the British had colonized the island. The man elaborated that this celebration expressed the islanders' gratitude to the Buddha, Japanese–Sri Lankan Buddhist solidarity, and, finally, congratulations to Sōen for receiving his monastic vows. Sōen wrote that from that day forward he wore Theravāda monk's robes while in Sri Lanka (Shaku Sōen 1941, 47 recto–49 recto).

Despite the warm welcome Sōen received in Sri Lanka and his immersion in Theravāda monastic life, Sōen found some Sri Lankan customs repugnant and he was not totally enamored with the Buddhist practice on the island. Writing early in his stay, Sōen described his difficulty pronouncing Sinhala and adapting to customs such as eating with one's fingers, walking barefoot on the hot ground, washing his behind with water after defecating, and blowing his nose with his hand (41 recto–41 verso). More significant, Sōen criticized the lack of balance in Sri Lankan Buddhist practice. Noting that Buddhist training required equal attention to each of the three learnings (*sangaku*)—morality, meditation, and wisdom—Sōen wrote that in Sri Lanka the monks had totally ignored meditative practice in favor of unreflective textual study. Paying careful attention to the monastic rules (Vinaya) while lacking meditative attainment was as pointless as "a monkey donning a cap," Sōen concluded (40 verso–41 recto).

While in Sri Lanka, Sōen wrote one of the earliest Japanese-language works on South Asian Buddhism. The book, *Seinan no Bukkyō* ("The Buddhism of the Southwest") was completed in August 1888 and was published in Japan in January 1889. In this work, Sōen's familiarity with Olcott's and Dharmapala's reform Buddhism, Western Orientalist scholarship, and Sri Lankan monastic life are clearly evident. Having directly witnessed Hong Kong and Sri Lanka under British rule and having only recently learned of Britain's expansion into Burma, Sōen graphically described the plight of Buddhism in Asia: "at the front door the wolf of Christianity opens its jaws; at the back door the tiger of Islam sharpens its claws." The situation, however, was not entirely hopeless. Sōen saw the emergence of the Theosophical Society in the West as a sign of growing interest in Buddhism. To nurture this nascent sprout of the tradition and thereby ensure the future flourishing of Buddhism, Sōen urged southern and northern Buddhist clerics to unite and actively proselytize in the West (Shaku Sōen 1889, 86-88).

In a chapter entitled "Bukkyō no taii" ("The Gist of Buddhism"), Sōen noted important differences in the practice of image veneration between the Buddhists of Northeast Asia (*Tōhoku no Bukkyōsha*) and those of Southeast Asia (literally "Southwest": *Seinan no Bukkyōsha*). Whereas, for the most part, Buddhists of Sri Lanka and other Theravāda countries venerated only Śākyamuni, Buddhists of Northeast Asia venerated a host of different deities, bodhisattvas, and buddhas. Sōen saw the great diversity in images of worship as a problem for Japanese Buddhists, particularly during the period of crisis in which they found themselves. Without a sense of unity, a moral renaissance would be impossible for Buddhism. Sōen had no illusions about the difficulty in achieving this for all Buddhists, however. For this reason he argued that Buddhists in Japan should begin by choosing one figure of veneration for their own denomination of Buddhism. Members of the Jōdo Shinshū, for example, uniformly worshiped Amida, which gave their denomination a unity that was exceptional. For his own Rinzai denomination, Sōen argued that Śākyamuni should be made the central image of veneration. Not only would this unify the Zen school, it would also provide common ground with the Buddhists of Southeast Asia and with people familiar with Buddhism in Europe and the United States.

> When we ask which Buddha is most appropriate as the main image of veneration, I believe that it is Śākyamuni Buddha. (This does not apply to denominations that, like Jōdo Shinshū, already have a designated image of veneration.) That is because Śākyamuni is our Great Master to whom we are indebted for the Teaching, that is, he is the Teacher for the current cosmic age . . . What is more, today Śākyamuni's name is not valued just in Buddhist countries, it is known in all the countries of Europe and the United States. People who do not know the names of other buddhas are numerous not only in the West, of course, but also in other Buddhist countries of Asia [*Tōyō*]. In Southeast [*Seinan*] Asia those who do not even know the names of the seven past buddhas are numerous. Śākyamuni is the image of veneration that is karmically connected with the civilized world of the twentieth century.[22]

Although both Kitabatake and Sōen were ambivalent about what they saw in South Asia, Shaku Kōzen (shown in Figure 3) embraced the Theravāda Buddhism of Sri Lanka as the purest, truest form of Buddhism, becoming, for all intents and purposes, a convert. Kōzen remained in South Asia for seven years, studying under Paññāsekhara and other teachers in Sri Lanka and visiting a variety of Buddhist sites in India. Whereas Sōen lived in Galle for most of his time in Sri Lanka, Kōzen studied at the relatively new monastic training college, Vidyōdaya Piriveṇa, in Colombo, where Sumaṇgala served as principal. Kōzen also engaged more fully in Sri Lankan monastic life, receiving the full monk's (*upasampadā*) Theravāda ordination from Sumaṇgala on June 6, 1890, in Kandy, making him, according to Noguchi, the first recorded Japanese to become a full-fledged Theravāda monk (*bhikkhu*) (Noguchi 1920, 13-14).

Figure 3. Shaku Kōzen. Courtesy of Tōkeiji. Photograph by the author. (Figures 3–6 were in an album of photographs now in the collection of Tōkeiji.)

Judging from Sōen's diary entries, Kōzen was actively involved with several of the monks who headed the opposition to the Christian missionaries in Sri Lanka. Kōzen worked closely with Olcott and Dharmapala, traveling to Madras in 1890 as a Japanese representative at the Fifteenth Annual Convention of the Theosophical Society. In 1891 Kōzen traveled to Bodh Gayā for the first time, where he cofounded the Mahābodhi Society with Dharmapala, a fact given little attention in the recent works detailing Buddhist efforts to wrest control of Bodh Gayā from the Hindus.[23] Kōzen returned to Sri Lanka briefly in 1891, where he met another disciple of Unshō, Ato Yūjō, who brought funds gathered in Japan to purchase Buddhist sites in India. The following year, Kōzen and Yūjō returned to India to visit important places associated with Buddhism, but their naive plan to acquire these sites failed miserably.[24] In 1893 Kōzen headed back to Sri Lanka for another brief stay and finally returned to Japan on 6 September.

Kōzen regarded Theravāda monastic practice as the fullest expression of the true Buddhist way of life. He hoped to reinvigorate Japanese Buddhism by establishing true Theravāda practice and ordinations. Back at his home temple, Sanneji, just outside Yokohama, Kōzen set about transforming the religious artifacts, liturgy, and calendar in accordance with his new understanding of Buddhism. Soon after his return to Japan, Kōzen established the Society for the True Lineage of Śākyamuni. In an 1893 broadside announcing the creation of the society, Kōzen wrote that the purpose of the organization was to revive the true veneration of the Three Jewels (*sanbō*)—Buddha, Dharma (Buddhist teaching), and Sangha (Buddhist monastic order)—in Japan. He spelled out very clearly that by the Buddha he was primarily referring to Śākyamuni, his relics, or things closely associated with his life, for example, the bodhi tree. He also wrote that the Jewel of the Dharma first and foremost referred to the sūtras, Vinaya, and Abhidharma that had been recorded in the language spoken by Śākyamuni, which he held was Pāli. The Jewel of the Sangha, or monastic community, indicated those who were legitimate descendants of Śākyamuni, in other words, monks who had been ordained in a proper fashion and who upheld the Vinaya regulations (Shaku Kōzen 1893, 1-2).

These points were clarified further in 1898 when Kōzen, with the approval of the Shingon denomination's Great Clerical Chancellor (Daisōjō) Mikami Kaiun published the temple regulations and educational principles for Sanneji. At the beginning of the document, Kōzen warned those in charge of the various branch temples that Sanneji adhered assiduously to the "true/authentic precepts of Śākyamuni" and that it was mandatory that those at the branch temples, particularly the leaders, do the same (Shaku Kōzen 1908, 1; see also Itō 1974, 357). In the actual temple rules, Kōzen announced that Sanneji and its branch temples were Precept-Vinaya temples based on the Tathāgata's Pure School of the Elders' (Theravāda) Transmission (*Nyorai shōfū jōza denshō no kairitsu dera*).[25] In addition, Kōzen defined the Sangha as those who received and transmitted the precept lineage of Theravāda, learned Pāli, and supported the Theravāda Sangha. He also stipulated that pure Indian-style images of Śākyamuni be enshrined and venerated at Sanneji and its branch temples (Shaku Kōzen 1908, 3-6).

Kōzen's focus on using Theravāda Buddhism as a model for the reform and unification of Buddhism in Japan was given further impetus when Kōzen received an invitation from a member of the Thai diplomatic delegation for a year of study and practice in Thailand. Departing in October 1907, Kōzen and three disciples traveled to Thailand where they met with Thai monks and participated in the rainy season retreat. Returning to Japan in December 1908, he brought with him more than 50 Śākyamuni statues and numerous Pāli canonical texts (see Figure 4). The following year, Kōzen placed these items on display and encouraged Japanese regardless of their sectarian affiliation to come and view them (Shaku Kōzen 1909, 1).

Figure 4. Postcard of Thai Śākyamuni statues at Sanneji. The postcard reads, "Śākyamuni Tathāgata images imported from 'India' (*Tenjiku*). Possessions of the Shōfū Kai at Sanneji in Toriyama." Courtesy of Sanneji. Photograph by the author.

Kōzen's increasing interest in Śākyamuni images adds credence to stories that Kōzen removed the old object of veneration, a statue of the Maitreya, the future Buddha, from the main altar at Sanneji, and replaced it with a statue of a seated Śākyamuni that he had received from the king of Thailand, Chulalongkorn. According to popular accounts, the statue of Śākyamuni was placed in the main temple hall in the altar, which was decorated with a bodhi leaf design, constructed according to Kōzen's own plans.[26] (The bodhi leaf seems to have been a popular symbol with many Meiji Buddhists, who placed it not only on altars, but also used it to ornament the covers of Buddhist books and journals, particularly those works concerned with South and Southeast Asian Buddhism.)

Figure 5. Itō Chūta's plan for Thai-style Shakuōden at Sanneji.
Courtesy of Sanneji. Photograph by the author.

Kōzen planned other changes at Sanneji to increase the focus on Śākyamuni as the center of practice and veneration. Engaging Itō Chūta (1867–1954), the architectural historian and architect, Kōzen planned to build a large hall, the Shakuōden, dedicated to Śākyamuni on a hill overlooking Sanneji (see Figure 5). Itō, who had traveled through Asia in search of the roots of Japanese architecture from 1902 to 1905, drew up plans in 1912 for two possible buildings, one Japanese-style and the other reminiscent of Thai temple architecture (Itō 1974, 191, 239, n. 241; Tsunemitsu 1968, 1: 382).[27] In addition to planning the Shakuōden, Kōzen tried to shift to Śākyamuni the focus of local pilgrimage. Placing Śākyamuni statues in 32 branch temples of Sanneji in the Yokohama area—one for each of the Buddha's major distinguishing marks—Kōzen created a pilgrimage route for his parishioners and printed for distribution a broadside detailing the route. In this manner Kōzen attempted to replace the far more common Kannon- or Kūkai-centered pilgrimage routes with one devoted to Śākyamuni Buddha. He also instituted a liturgical calendar at the temple that included the fortnightly observance of the Theravāda confession ceremony (*uposatha*) and, at least as early as 1916, the celebration of Vesak (the South and Southeast Asian Buddhist festival celebrating the birth, awakening, and death of Śākyamuni) in Hibiya Kōen.

Sanneji also became something of a salon for the study of Theravāda and Indian Buddhism. Nanjō Bun'yū (who taught Sanskrit to Kōzen before Kōzen's trip to Sri Lanka), Kawaguchi Ekai (who pioneered the study of Tibetan Buddhism in Japan), and D. T. Suzuki (a disciple of Shaku Sōen who would soon travel to the United States) all communicated or worked with Kōzen at the temple at the turn of the nineteenth-twentieth century. Along with Kōzen, a number of individuals, each of them having an association with Kōzen, produced polylingual renderings in Japanese, Sanskrit, and Sinhala of the *Shichibutsu tsūkaige* ("Verse of Admonishment of the Seven Buddhas")—an expression of pan-Asian Buddhist unity—at Sanneji and elsewhere.[28] One polylingual calligraphic scroll of the verse by Nanjō Bun'yū, who had studied with Max Müller, was printed in multiple copies, apparently for distribution at Sanneji, where a number of these prints are still extant. (See Figure 6.)

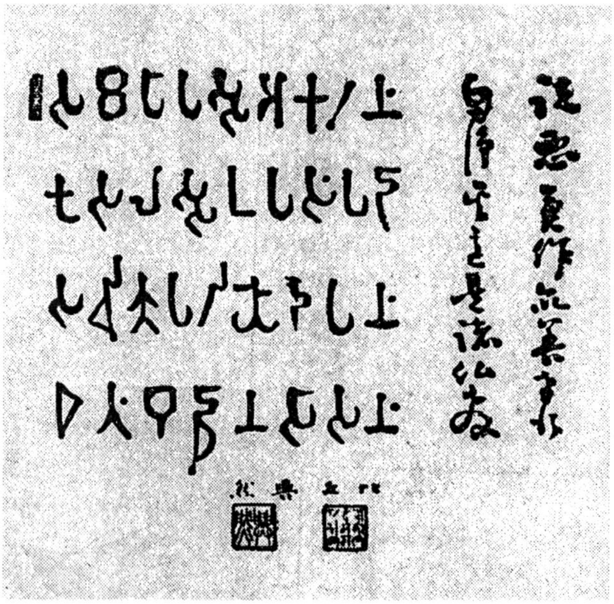

Figure 6. *Shichibutsu tsūkaige* calligraphy by Shaku Kōzen, Pāli in Aśokan Brāhmī script. From the cover of *Kaigai Bukkyō jijō* 1944, 10/6.

In a 1910 pamphlet summarizing the principles of the Shakuson Shōfū Kai and explaining the key practices of the three refuges and the five precepts, Kōzen summarized the goal of the society and, one must presume, the purpose of the various changes he had instituted at Sanneji and its branch temples.[29] Like Sōen nearly 30 years earlier, Kōzen lamented the factionalism of Buddhism in Asia, particularly in Japan. In order to create a Buddhism that could flourish in the civilized world, a Buddhism that was unified in belief, practice, and purpose was necessary. Like Sōen, Kōzen believed a return to the teachings of Śākyamuni Buddha was essential for Buddhism to recover its vitality.

> Buddhism is divided into northern and southern lineages and there are hundreds, even thousands, of denominations; however, the original founding teacher for all of them is Śākyamuni Buddha, the teacher to whom we all are greatly indebted. There is no true Buddhism that sets Śākyamuni's teachings aside. Therefore in order to make clear the true teachings of a Buddhism that is really Buddhism, one must, at all costs, return to the living Buddhism of Śākyamuni. (Shaku Kōzen 1910, 7-8)

Kōzen's experiences in Sri Lanka and India led him to question completely the legitimacy of Japanese Buddhism in its present state. His emphasis on Pāli texts as the fundamental written source for Buddhists reflects the prioritization of those materials by Sri Lankan clerics and scholars, who had turned to those materials with fervor since the eighteenth century.[30] Like such European Buddhologists as T. W. Rhys Davids, Kōzen was convinced of the primacy of Theravāda Buddhism and the teachings as they were presented in the Pāli version of the Buddhist scriptures. Unlike many European and American Orientalists, however, Kōzen did not dismiss Sri Lankan Buddhism as a decadent corruption of the pure teachings that were preserved within the Pāli canon itself. Rather, Kōzen held that the "living" Buddhist tradition in Sri Lanka transmitted the essential teachings of Śākyamuni Buddha.[31]

Believing that only the precept lineage of Theravāda Buddhism was valid, Kōzen dismissed all Japanese clerical ordinations as inefficacious and attempted to establish a Theravāda precept lineage in Japan. Maintaining a self-sustaining Theravāda order in Japan, however, necessitated having at least four other monks ordained in the same lineage in order to have the quorum necessary to conduct full monks' ordinations. To accomplish this goal, Kōzen sent five disciples to Sri Lanka for ordination. His plan never came to fruition, as only one of the disciples, Shaku Nindo, remained with Kōzen after becoming a fully ordained monk. Consequently, Kōzen was unable to conduct Theravāda ordinations in Japan. After the death of his disciple Nindo, who succeeded Kōzen as abbot of Sanneji, the Theravāda ordination begun by Kōzen in Japan consequently died out. According to the account of the current abbot of Sanneji, some time after Nindo's death the statue of Śākyamuni was removed from the main altar to a reception room for the parishioners and replaced with the former image of worship, a statue of Maitreya. The liturgical calendar reverted to the usual Shingon style and the "Theravāda" period of Kōzen's and Nindo's abbacies became little more than a historical curiosity. Today Sanneji functions as a typical Shingon temple, with regular performances of the *goma* (esoteric fire ceremony) ritual taking place in the main hall of the temple in front of several large statues of Śākyamuni brought to Sanneji from Thailand by Shaku Kōzen.

Conclusions

Today we take it for granted that Buddhism is, first and foremost, about the teachings and practices of Śākyamuni Buddha. But the extent to which Japanese Buddhists share this understanding is, in part, due to the efforts of early Japanese travelers to South and Southeast Asia such as Kitabatake, Sōen, and Kōzen. The rediscovery of Śākyamuni Buddha by late nineteenth-century Japanese Buddhists took place in the context of the Western-dominated colonial order in Asia and was indelibly shaped by the Orientalist discourse that brought an essentialized Buddhism into existence. In this sense, even when traveling to other parts of Buddhist Asia, Japanese clerics were always "traveling in the West," not only literally, but also intellectually.[32] Kitabatake like Shimaji, Nanjō, and many others, went to India *after* visiting Europe and the United States. And Kōzen and Sōen both encountered Western constructions of Buddhism in Japan. In Sri Lanka, where European and American works on Buddhism circulated, they dealt with Sri Lankan Buddhists who themselves, at least partially, saw Buddhism through the lens of Western scholarship.

But Japanese clerics and scholars approached both this Orientalist discourse and the various Buddhisms in Asia with trajectories shaped by specific historical conditions in Japan and Asia. Traditional Japanese Buddhist scholarship and the sociopolitical context for Buddhism in Japan also shaped their understanding of what they encountered in India and Sri Lanka. Their emphasis on Śākyamuni was as much a product of the need for Japanese Buddhists to find common ground with their coreligionists inside and outside Japan as it was a Japanese reaction to European and American fascination with writing a definitive historical biography of the founder and identifying those geographic sites associated with his life. Unlike Müller, Sylvain Lévi, Oldenberg, and other European scholars, Kitabatake, Kōzen and Sōen were not armchair scholars with antiquarian and philological interests. Their clerical vocation gave their search for Śākyamuni an entirely different dimension and was framed by Buddhist and Japanese idioms of pilgrimage and practice as well as by Western ideas of imperial travel. Kitabatake, for example, could do something that from his perspective was impossible for an Indian worker or British archaeologist. As a Buddhist cleric, Kitabatake was able to venerate the image of Śākyamuni, thereby serving as an intermediary for other Asians.

Similarly, Sōen and Kōzen tried to bring Śākyamuni to the center of Japanese Buddhism not just as an object of scholarly curiosity and biography, but as the foundation of Buddhist worship, practice, and continued survival.

Japanese interest in Buddhist sites in India was catalyzed by Kitabatake's journey to Bodh Gayā, and the renewed focus on Śākyamuni as the founder of the tradition and symbol of Buddhist solidarity was given further impetus by Kōzen and Sōen's reports on the condition of Buddhism in South and Southeast Asia. Kōzen and Sōen's call for a return to Śākyamuni became part of a chorus of voices in the mid-Meiji era urging the creation of a united Buddhism that transcended not only interdenominational but also international differences within the Buddhist community. In much the same manner as some Japanese Buddhists attempted to rally adherents of all denominations around the most fundamental of Buddha's injunctions, the *Shichibutsu tsūkaige*, Kōzen and Sōen sought to save Buddhism in Asia through a renewed focus on Śākyamuni and the creation of a coalition uniting all Asian Buddhists in their efforts to repel colonialism and Christianity in Asia. By the time Sōen traveled to the World Parliament of Religions in Chicago in 1893 as part of the Japanese delegation, not only was he familiar with some of the other Buddhist participants from Asia, but, as he had urged in his 1889 book, the goal of Western proselytization had become part of the group's mission (Snodgrass 2003, 173-76).

Initial contact between Japanese Buddhist clerics and other Asians, both Buddhist and non-Buddhist, reinforced the sense of peril and crisis that the Japanese, struggling to rewrite the unequal treaties, already felt. Witnessing the poverty of India, the harshness of British colonial policies, the expansion of British colonial rule into Burma, and the inroads of Christian missionaries throughout Asia, Japanese Buddhists like Kōzen, Sōen, and Kitabatake became convinced of the need to form an alliance with other Asian Buddhists. The impetus to create a united Buddhist world was fostered not only by Henry Steel Olcott, Dharmapala, and Edwin Arnold, all of whom visited Japan during the Meiji period, but also by Japanese who had themselves forged close ties with Buddhists in other parts of Asia.[33] These efforts paralleled similar attempts at modernization, cooperation, and transnational exchange occurring among Buddhists throughout South and Southeast Asia (Frost 2002, 957-63). The various inflections of Asian Buddhist modernism resulted not only from bipolar, nation-to-nation contacts between individual Buddhist countries and the Western powers. They were also conditioned by local trajectories as well as cooperation and mutual influence among Buddhists throughout the region.

These three travelers discussed in this essay were but the first among a host of Japanese Buddhist clerics, scholars, artists, and tourists to make the pilgrimage to South and Southeast Asia. Until almost the end of the Pacific War, Japanese followed in the footsteps of Kitabatake and Kōzen to Bodh Gayā and other Buddhist sites in India. Many of these pilgrims produced travel accounts of their own, creating a substantial genre of South and Southeast Asian travel literature in Japanese. Kawaguchi Ekai, Okakura Kakuzō, Ōtani Kōzui, Nanjō Bun'yū, Hioki Mokusen, Kuruma Takudō, Ōda Tokunō, and Itō Chūta are but a few of the more notable Japanese who published accounts of their travels across the region.

The relatively informal contacts between Buddhists in Japan, Sri Lanka, Thailand, and elsewhere also gave rise to more formal exchanges between Asian Buddhist countries. At the request of Inagaki Manjirō, the Japanese ambassador to Thailand, King Chulalongkorn presented the Japanese Buddhist community with relics of Śākyamuni, which were eventually enshrined in Nagoya at Nissenji (Japan-Siam Temple; today, Nittaiji, Japan-Thai Temple). Itō Chūta, who planned the never-completed Thai-style Shakuōden at Sanneji, designed the "Gandharan," Indian-style *stūpa* that housed the relics at the Nissenji. This temple became a symbol of Thai–Japanese solidarity and a required stop for Thai dignitaries who visited Japan. Itō also continued working closely with other Buddhist travelers to Asia, for example, Hioki Mokusen and Ōtani Kōzui. Through the first half of the twentieth century, he designed the Indian-influenced memorial *stūpa* housing the relics at Nissenji, the "nation protecting *stūpa*" (*gokokutō*) at the Kasuisai in Shizuoka, and the influential, architecturally eclectic Tsukiji Honganji in the 1930s, thus rendering Japan's pan-Asian Buddhist ties in stone.[34]

Contacts forged by Japanese Buddhist travelers in Asia as well as Japanese military and industrial successes drew Buddhists from other parts of Asia to Japan. Dharmapala, who had met Kōzen and Sōen in Sri Lanka, attempting to tap Japanese Buddhist sympathies as part of his anticolonial efforts in India and Sri Lanka, made several trips to Japan between 1899 and 1913. Writing to the Foreign Ministry between 1899 and 1907, Dharmapala requested that the Japanese donate money and send clerics to India to help restore Buddhist sites and counter the actions of Christian missionaries. In one letter to the foreign minister, Dharmapala wrote,

> There are nearly 200 millions of people in India sunk in ignorance and wallowing in the mire of superstition. On their behalf the Mahā Bodhi Society appeals to the Japanese Buddhists to send Japanese teachers and preachers to impart knowledge that has made Japan great. European and American missionaries, over a thousand, are all over this land imparting the doctrines of Christianity, establishing schools and making converts of the adults. The field is open to all and I earnestly appeal to all the leaders of the different Buddhist sects to organize a Society for the diffusion of Knowledge among the people of India. The Mahā Bodhi Society has done a pioneer's work and is willing to cooperate with earnest Buddhists of Japan.[35]

The relationship between Japanese Buddhists and the Buddhists in other parts of Asia remained ambiguous, however, inviting Japanese misinterpretation of entreaties such as Dharmapala's. As visible in the woodblock rendering of Kitabatake's visit to Bodh Gayā and in Sōen's dismissive comments about Sri Lankan Buddhism, triumphalism lurked beneath the surface of many versions of Japanese Buddhist pan-Asianism. Japanese collaboration with Buddhists throughout Asia continued to grow over the first four decades of the twentieth century, but Japan's imperial project gradually subsumed the fragile pan-Asian sentiments expressed by Kitabatake, Kōzen, Sōen, and other early travelers. As Japan reached parity with the Western colonial powers, Japanese Buddhist pan-Asianism turned into paternalism toward other Asian Buddhists. Just as Buddhist sites in India needed Japanese intervention to save them—Dharmapala invited the Japanese to send missionaries to India—so Asian Buddhism required Japanese assistance and evangelization, some Japanese believed. By 1940, the Vesak celebration, originally conducted by Kōzen and his disciple, Nindo, in order to spread Theravāda Buddhism in Japan, was being performed in the name of a Japanese-led order in Asia. A program for the 1945 Vesak event conducted by Nindo at Sanneji (moved from Hibiya Kōen because of Allied bombing of Tokyo) made this explicit: "creating spiritual harmony with the peoples of Southern Asia is important foundation work for us, as we are aiming to construct the Greater East Asia Co-Prosperity Sphere." Uniting Asian Buddhists in this effort, according to the program, was veneration for Śākyamuni.[36]

Notes

I am grateful to the Center for International Studies and the Asian-Pacific Studies Institute at Duke University, the North Carolina Japan Center, and the American Council of Learned Societies for grants that supported my research. I thank Andō Sonjin, Grant Goodman, Inoue Zenjō, Shaku Shinshō, Tanaka Chisei, and Tatsuguchi Myōsei for their help gathering documents for the project. An earlier version of this essay appeared as "Shakuson o sagashite: Kindai Nihon Bukkyō no tanjō to sekai ryokō" in *Shisō* 943 (2002): 64-87.

1. For a very interesting examination of many of these interchanges between Japanese and various South Asian Buddhists and the Theosophists, see Satō 1999–2002.
2. Prasenjit Duara (2001, 114) describes one later example of these intricate global loops, the transmission of an article, originally written in English by an expatriate Chinese born in Malaysia, which was translated into Japanese and then into Chinese, at which point it was published in the Chinese journal *Dongfang zazhi*. In a similar, later Buddhist case, the *Vimuttimagga* was translated into English in the mid-1930s at the suggestion of the Chinese scholar of Buddhism, Wong Mou-lam, who had spent time in Sri Lanka, by

a team of Sri Lankan Buddhists working in Kyushu with a Nichiren denomination cleric. The English text was then brought by the Sri Lankans to Burma where they used it as a meditation manual following their ordination in that country. See Upatissa [1975] 1995, ix-xxv.

3. Mary Louise Pratt (1992, 4) defines "contact zones" as "social spaces where disparate cultures meet, clash, and grapple with each other, often in highly asymmetrical relations of domination and subordination—like colonialism, slavery, or their aftermaths as they are lived out across the globe today."
4. For a description of the search for these sites and how that process influenced Western perceptions of Indian Buddhist art, see Leoshko 2003.
5. Roger Pol-Droit (2003, 37-58) asserts that the move from myth to history began with the publication of Michel-Jean-François Ozeray's *Recherches sur Buddou ou Bouddou, Instituteur religieux de l'Asie orientale* in 1817.
6. The Arnold-inspired, bimonthly, English-language journal, *The Bijou of Asia*, was first published in Japan in September 1888. Devoted to "the spread of Buddhism in other lands," the journal was published by the Buddhist Propagation Society (Senkyōkai) based in Kyoto. See the mission statement in volume 2 of the journal, published in November 1888, 3-4. That same issue announced that the translation of Arnold's *Light of Asia; or, the Great Renunciation (Mahabhinishkramana) Being the Life and Teaching of Gautama, Prince of India and Founder of Buddhism* (1879) by a Mr Nakagawa had begun. See Ishii 2002. Ishii notes that one important contributor to the journal was Sawai Jun (a.k.a. Takakusu Junjirō), the influential editor of the Taisho edition of the Chinese Buddhist canon. Takakusu studied with Max Müller in the 1890s. I am grateful to Micah Auerback for calling my attention to this journal.
7. For a description of the growth of transnational exchanges along these trade routes in South and Southeast Asia, see Frost 2002, 937-68.
8. For information concerning the Japanese Buddhist clerics and scholars studying in Europe between 1872 and 1882, see Horiguchi 1995, 121-39. A detailed study of interactions between Japanese scholars and Max Müller and Sylvain Lévi is Maejima 1985. It is significant that the first wave of Buddhist scholars and clerics to travel and study abroad all were members of either the Nishi or the Higashi sect of the Jōdo Shin denomination. As two of the largest and wealthiest denominations in the late Edo and early Meiji periods, the Nishi and Higashi Honganji establishments were probably best prepared to fund extended travel overseas. Just how the overrepresentation of Jōdo Shin clerics in early exchanges with European and American scholars of Buddhism skewed the perceptions of Buddhism of such collaborators as Müller and Lévi is an important question. The significance of this issue has been noted in Silk 1994, 194, n. 6.
9. This brief biographical sketch is based on information contained in Mori 1983, 39-42; Kashiwahara et al. 1999, 84.
10. Patil (1981, 13-14) briefly describes the British efforts to locate Kuśīnagara.
11. For a summary description of European attempts to locate sites associated with the narrative biography of Śākyamuni, see Leoshko 2003, 30-60.
12. A slightly different version of the stele, without the word *hijimete*, is found in Akiyama 1884, 1 and Mori 1983, 365. The respective drawings of the stele (*sekihi*) in the different accounts of Kitabatake's adventure vary slightly. Izumi (1933, 163) gives the same reading as in Mori, and claims that the stele still existed in 1933.
13. Izumi Hokei (1933, 163) also has noted with curiosity Kitabatake's error.
14. Robert Eskildsen has noted how in the case of the Taiwanese aborigines these portrayals "increased the perceived cultural distance that separated the Japanese from the aborigines. In the context of the 1870s, a larger cultural distance helped both to validate

Japanese claims for higher status in the Western-dominated international order and to eliminate a middle ground between civilization and savagery that might trap the Japanese in a less than salutary solidarity with other East Asian peoples." See Eskildsen 2002, 402. The relationship between Japanese Buddhist travelers in South and Southeast Asia and the natives of those regions was far more ambiguous. Nonetheless, Kitabatake and Sōen's accounts of their travels contain hints of the same sort of colonial attitudes described by Eskildsen.

15. The survey is cited in Kitabatake [1956] 1994, 79-80. I have not been able to consult the original newspaper survey to confirm the information in this source, which verges on hagiography.
16. Biographical information about Shaku Kōzen comes from Tsunemitsu 1968, 1: 371-82; Noguchi 1920; Higashimoto 1944; and the very useful Itō 1974. There is some question about the pronunciation of Shaku Kōzen's name. Shingon sources and Tsunemitsu read his name Shaku Kōnen. However, Sōen writes the name Shaku Kōzen in roman letters in the front of his diary, *Seiyu nikki* (1941), and Unshō, in an English-language letter to Sumaṇgala, also refers to Konen as Kōzen. I shall refer to him throughout this essay as Shaku Kōzen.
17. Unfortunately, a record of Kōzen's stay in Sri Lanka does not appear to be extant—the current abbot of Kōzen's temple told me there is no diary of his stay at Sanneji. However, the first two-thirds of Sōen's record of his three-year stay in Sri Lanka does exist and has recently been reissued in a modern Japanese translation. See Inoue 2001.
18. Shaku Sōen 1941, "Nantei Kūgaku Oshō o okuri kotoba." (Page numbers are not given in this portion of the original text.)
19. See, for example, the English-language letters exchanged between Sumaṇgala and Shaku Unshō, J. H. Barrows, and the Thai king, Chulalongkorn, in Prajñānanda 1947, 768-69, 774-76. I thank Anne Blackburn for providing me with copies of this correspondence.
20. The nineteenth-century Buddhist revival in Sri Lanka is examined in detail in several works, including Bond 1988; Gombrich and Obeyesekere 1988; and Malalgoda 1976. The international interests of the Sri Lankan Buddhists, especially in South and Southeast Asia, are explored by Mark Frost (2002). Although commonly referred to as "Protestant Buddhism," the usefulness of this characterization in Sri Lanka has been called into question by several authors in recent years. According to Blackburn's recent critique (2001, 200-203), portraying the shifts in Sri Lankan Buddhism as simply a response to the West denies agency to the Sri Lankan Buddhists and fails to take into account reformist trajectories well underway prior to the nineteenth century.
21. For a Japanese translation of these questions and answers, see Inoue 2001, 126, 134-35. Sōen may well have seen the Japanese translation of the *Buddhist Catechism*, *Bukkyō mondō*, which was published in April 1886. See Satō 1999–2002.
22. Shaku Sōen 1889, 46. A very similar, albeit less prescriptive, observation about the focus on Śākyamuni in Theravāda Buddhism was made in 1891 by Ōda Tokunō, a Higashi Honganji Jōdo Shin cleric who studied in Thailand from 1888 to 1891. See Ōda 1891, 46-50.
23. See Kinnard 1998; and Trevithick 1999, 635-56. Kōzen is mentioned briefly in Trevithick 1988, 87.
24. See Kusanagi (1913, 1: 126) for information concerning Unshō's efforts to oversee the purchase of Buddhist pilgrimage sites from the British.
25. *Tathāgata*, literally, "the thus come/gone one," is an honorific epithet of a Buddha.
26. According to Ishii Ryōjō, a disciple of Kōzen for many years who was interviewed by Tsunemitsu, Kōzen did not replace the statue of Miroku with one of Śākyamuni. See

Tsunemitsu 1968, 1: 379. It is unclear which version of the story is correct at this time, but given Kōzen's strong emphasis on Śākyamuni, the replacement of the Miroku statue seems likely.

27. The plans for the Thai-style building are still extant. I have not seen the plans for the Japanese-style building, however. Itō had planned the Shinshū Parishioners' Insurance Corporation building in a style reminiscent of Indian Muslim architecture. The building was completed in 1912, the same year Itō drew up the plans for the Shakuōden.
28. The verse, which is found in the *Dhammapada* v. 183, as well as numerous other sources, reads, "Refraining from all that is detrimental,/The attainment of what is wholesome,/The purification of one's mind:/This is the instruction of awakened ones" (*shoaku makusa/shuzen bugyō/jijō goi/ze shobukkyō*; in Pāli the verse reads: *sabbapāpassa akaraṇaṃ/kusalassa upasaṃpadā/sacittapariyodanaṃ/etam buddhāna sāsanaṃ*). See Carter and Palihawadana 1987, 44. According to Ketelaar (1990, 185-86), the *shichibutsu tsūkaige* was emphasized during the Meiji period by Buddhist authors hoping to bridge sectarian differences. Thanks to Anne Blackburn, Shimoda Masahiro, and Jonathan Silk for help reading several polylingual calligraphies of this verse.
29. The three refuges are taken in the Buddha, the Dharma, and the Sangha. The five precepts taken by the laity are not to take life, not to steal, not to commit adultery, not to lie, and not to use intoxicants.
30. For a detailed analysis of the textual turn in Sri Lankan Buddhism in the eighteenth century, see Blackburn 2001.
31. Rhys Davids wrote, for example, that "it is impossible rightly to understand any one phase of later Buddhism in any country, without starting from the standpoint of the earlier Buddhism of the Pāli Piṭakas. No one can write the history of later Buddhism, say in Thailand or China, without being thoroughly acquainted with the Pāli Suttas. The very interest of the later inquiries lies in the causes that have produced the manifold changes they will disclose." Cited in Welbon 1968, 225.
32. The overwhelming influence of "the West" on worldwide conceptions of travel is discussed in Clifford 1997, 4-5.
33. On Olcott's and Dharmapala's efforts to forge an alliance with Buddhists in Japan, see Prothero 1996, 116-33; Snodgrass 2003, 155-71; and Satō 1999–2002.
34. On the architecture of the Tsukiji Honganji, see Wendelken 2000.
35. Dharmapala, letter to the Buddhists of Japan, March 26, 1907. Dharmapala's last visit to Japan is discussed in Goodman 1993.
36. See Kokusai Bukkyō Kyōkai 1945. Almost identical comments by Nindo are found in Shaku Nindo 1944, 2.

10

One Plus One Makes Three: Buddhist Gender, Monasticism, and the Law of the Non-Excluded Middle

Janet Gyatso

This article addresses the need for a more specific account than we now have of how the female is conceived in Buddhism. One reason for providing such an account is so that we can better construe what has variously been perceived as the misogyny of Buddhist traditions, on the one hand, and the deification of a feminine principle in Buddhism, on the other.[1] These perceptions have important ramifications as they bear on some difficult issues that are live in Buddhist communities today. One of those would be the controversial status of women in the practice of tantric sexual yoga, and another has to do with sex and gender hierarchies in Buddhist monasticism; I will be touching on the latter, but not the former, in the present article.

But just as much as for contemporary concerns, I am interested in the matter of sex and gender for other reasons too. I find the complex—and often inextricable—relation between gender conception and sexual anatomy to be an exceptionally rich resource, not only for theory, but also for ethical reflection. Such reflection might even have salutary impact on the contemporary issues to which I just alluded. Mind you, it is only barely the case that we can say that a notion of gender as such is explicitly identified in the sources I am looking at here. With the exception of one novel usage that does indeed seem to overlap with the function of the modern sense of gender, the traditional categories I explore in what follows seem to have been understood, perhaps unreflectively, as being based specifically upon sexual characteristics. Hence I have largely used the word "sex" to refer to those categories.

Even these, however, came in many contexts to take on a metaphorical rather than strictly physicalistic denotation. Such metaphorical application already inches those categories over into the domain of what we now understand to be gender—not to mention the fact that even strict anatomical specification about sexual identity is relative and culturally constructed. Thus an occasional invocation of the idea of gender serves here to organize and highlight retrospectively the significance of a group of historical concepts and practices. To identify notions of gender in this way can provide a useful window on certain Buddhist understandings of body, personal identity, and religious meaning.

It might also be noted from the outset that this article endeavors to address a historical problem in part by a certain ahistoricism. This ahistoricism consists in taking an inchoate family of concepts from a small group of texts and, from a fairly limited period and speculating on the import of that conceptual family on the basis of how it developed later, that is, by reading back into the earlier formulation elements of how it came to be elaborated. Such a method is certainly not one that I would argue is always a good thing to do—in fact, not even one that is usually a good thing to do, especially if what one is trying to get at are the dynamics of a particular historical moment. However, in this particular case—where the early inchoate conceptual family is in fact itself about inchoateness, leading to a systematic fuzziness throughout its history; where, too, the later elaborations seem to stay close to the spirit of the earlier context and in fact salient clues from that later material draw our attention to things in the earlier material that we might not have noticed otherwise; and where, finally, we really have very little data to work with from that earlier moment in the first place—perhaps the method is felicitous.

I

The founding moment of what is at stake here would be an early pronouncement on the nature of the female that occurs in the course of a famous interchange that is ascribed to the Buddha and his disciple Ānanda.[2] It concerned the ordination of women into the monastic order. The Buddha is said to have refused at first. When pushed by Ānanda the Buddha conceded that, yes, women could indeed attain enlightenment, but their presence in the order would render Buddhism vulnerable to quicker deterioration than it would have been without women in the order. Women monastics would act like rust, or mildew, to weaken the Dharma. Hence their necessary patriarchical subordination, which came to be enshrined as the famous Eight Heavy Rules, pronounced by the Buddha as his condition for agreeing to ordain women after all. In brief, the Eight Heavies legislate that all nuns must defer to all monks and accept them as their ritual and authoritative superiors, no matter what the discrepancies in seniority or merit.[3]

This settlement has been understood by modern scholars as a nod to the demands of Indian society, and it reminds us of the central importance that the early Buddhist order gave to its public status and image in order to maintain the support of the laity. The idea is that these lay supporters would have been disturbed by the formation of a community of independent, single women and that they would be mollified—and, most crucially, would continue to respect and underwrite the order—by the reinscription of such celibate women in a submissive relationship to their male masters. Now this assessment certainly has merit, but it is by this point a truism, too easy as an explanation of all androcentrism and misogyny in Indian Buddhism. Given the stakes, the matter deserves further consideration: the Eight Heavies arguably are one of the key factors in the eventual demise of the fully ordained female order in almost every Buddhist country save China.[4] Indeed, the issue of status is especially germane today, at least for that portion of the women, both Asian and Western, who are currently attempting to revitalize the Buddhist nun's order as informed by a feminist sensibility. How are such modern female reformers going to be able to genuflect to the youngest male novice simply because he is a male—and therefore supposedly superior to them?[5] And yet if they fail to do so, how can they claim to be upholding the orthodox discipline with impunity, which is precisely what they need to do in order to regain legitimacy for the female order? Hence the possible edification in taking a closer look, not only at how exactly it was imagined that women would undermine the order in the first place, but also at what the very idea of woman represents here. Such an investigation will need to take account of both what is actually said about women, as well as the more abstract yet always revealing question of what the category of woman is defined *against*, that is, what it is defined *in contrast to*—especially in the specific context of Buddhist monasticism and the systems of ideology and practice to which it connects.

The focus of this study turns precisely on this point about definition, particularly definition *in contrast to*. It is interesting to notice that in Buddhist monasticism women were not only distinguished from men, their superiors and mentors in the order. They were also differentiated from another class of persons, persons who cannot receive ordination under any circumstances. This special class of persons who are barred from ordination includes several types of persons, but it is one such subgroup, whose description comprises the outermost bounds in sex and/or gender depiction (again, sex and gender are only partially distinguishable here), that deserves particularly close examination. This is a category of persons who are excluded from ordination on the grounds of their sex. It is my view that they can help us to appreciate the status of "normal" women in the Vinaya's rules as well. Challenging as this subgroup is to decipher, such examples at the edge take on a surplus of social meaning and provide a telling view of the terrain of sex and gender conceptions in the Vinaya overall, along with some broader insights into the implications of such conceptions.

As for the larger class of those forbidden ordination in the early Vinaya (of which the subgroup under discussion is a part), we can readily understand why the Sangha would have barred those who commit major crimes like murder, as well as those who lack permission from their parents or other masters, or who are fugitives from the law, or who are animals.[6] Another group of disqualifications is based on physical criteria: dwarfs, those missing a limb, the blind, the deaf, those with boils, or leprosy; all these may not join the order.[7] It would seem to be with these physically deficient types that the sexually marginal subgroup should be classed.[8] And yet why people whose sexuality is deficient or aberrant may not be ordained into the Buddhist order is not immediately evident. Little is said by way of explanation, but it becomes increasingly clear that more is at work here than a mere avoidance, on the part of the order, of embarrassing or unattractive abnormalities.

II

What information do we have about this subgroup of sexual excludees? Unfortunately, there is little information about actual individuals who were in this class. There are several stories and passages that suggest the defilement or dangerousness of such persons, but these say more about the conception of the group as a whole than about particular individuals; most certainly, none of these passages give a sense of actual historical people.[9] However, the fact that the Āyurvedic (and closely related Tibetan) medical tradition quite standardly speaks of three, rather than two, options for the sex of a newly born baby does tell us that an empirically observable third sex was believed to exist in the general period under discussion.[10] In fact, this medical conception of a "third sex" turns out to be closely related to the class of sexual pariahs in Buddhist monasticism.

The early monastic sources provide several subtypes within the group of people excluded from male ordination on sexual grounds. These usually include the hermaphrodite (*ubhatovyañjanaka*), a class of people called *paṇḍaka*, and sometimes a class of people called *ṣaṇḍha*. Neither of the latter terms seems ever to be precisely defined; but as the Vinaya tradition develops, *paṇḍaka* becomes the term of choice that most often stands for the excluded third sex category as a whole. The category also comes up in the exclusions for female ordination. Women with various kinds of deficiencies or irregularities in their menstrual cycle are listed here along with other types, one of which, in several versions of the list, is the "woman *paṇḍaka*." This indicates that there can be both male and female *paṇḍakas*; indeed, with the growing proliferation of subtypes within the sexually excluded class, one of the several ambiguities is whether these various terms refer to deviation from maleness, deviation from femaleness, or both.[11]

The classic Indian medical work *Carakasaṃhitā* probably represents a more mainstream Indic tendency to consider the third sex a deviation from maleness in dubbing the condition *napuṃsaka*, "not-male," but here too, Āyurveda tradition also gives indication of female varieties of this growing class of sexual aberration.[12] In general, the medical tradition attributes the third sex state to physical conditions, such as there being an equal balance of this person's mother's and father's seeds.[13] Like the monastic sources, the medical sources recognize a variety of sexual aberrations rather than portraying such a phenomenon as uniform, mentioning not only hermaphroditism but also congenital sexual dysfunctions, infertilities, and the absence of sexual organs altogether.[14] The medical tradition also describes certain congenital irregularities in sexual practice, some of which anticipate an interesting list of five kinds of *paṇḍakas* found in certain Buddhist monastic sources; but while the medical sources attribute all such anomalies to abnormal physical causes, the Buddhist sources seem less certain about the etiology of these states.[15]

A monastic list that focuses on kinds of *paṇḍakas* in particular seems to emerge in the early centuries CE in several Buddhist traditions, but its precise chronology is unclear.[16] The list singles out five main types: those who are born as either neuters or sexually indeterminate, those who have lost their sexual organ or capacities due to circumstances after birth, those whose sexuality changes every half month (in some versions from male to female and back again), those whose sexuality depends on the initiation of others (or, in another version, having oral sex), and those whose sexuality is engaged by voyeurism. Tibetan sources are familiar with this list but tend to boil down the kinds of *paṇḍaka* (generally translated as *ma ning*) into three main subtypes: the asexual neuter, the hermaphrodite, and the changing "half-monther."[17] It should be noted that neither *paṇḍaka* or *ma ning* are code words for homosexuality as such, as some have argued, and in any event same-sex sex is not singled out as distinct from other kinds of proscribed sexual activity in the Vinaya.[18] This is not to say that those who practice certain types of what is considered deviant sex are not also named by the label of *paṇḍaka*. As just seen in the list of five, they are, but there is no sign that the conception of such deviance has to do with the sexual identity of the partner. Moreover, at least as much, and perhaps more, than it is about sexual practice, *paṇḍaka*hood is also an abnormal physical condition, and indeed both lists of subtypes just mentioned betray an undecidability about what the *paṇḍaka* state most basically concerns—physical traits such as anatomy, virility, and fertility, or certain desires and practices. For all these reasons it is difficult to find one word to adequately translate the full semantic range of either *paṇḍaka* or *ma ning*. In what follows I am simply going to use the Indic or Tibetan term, as appropriate, alternating occasionally with "the third sex," a phrase also known to contemporaneous Indic sources.[19]

III

Now if the class as a whole is difficult to characterize, it is nonetheless excluded as a whole from a variety of Buddhist practices, not only from ordination. A variety of other monastic prescriptions also forbid the *paṇḍaka* and related types from acting as preceptors in ordination ceremonies, and even disqualify them from making donations to begging monks (*Mahavagga* 1.69; 38.5). There are also exclusions that go beyond monasticism altogether. Even the otherwise (and famously) inclusive *Lotus Sūtra* lists the *paṇḍaka* as someone who may not be preached to at all. Along with such other characters as heretics, hunters, magicians, dancers, and pig farmers, the *paṇḍaka* is in the unfortunate class of people whom the bodhisattva is enjoined to avoid, even when performing that most bodhisattva-like activity, teaching Buddhism (Hurvitz 1976, 209). This prohibition seems harsh and surprising indeed; even if one is convinced by yet another exclusion to which the *paṇḍaka* is subject, namely, an inability to meditate (or so claim a number of scholastic works),[20] surely such persons deserve at least to hear the Dharma! But another classic Buddhist text, *The Questions of Milinda*, specifies that *paṇḍaka*s and hermaphrodites are among those who are not able to understand the Dharma at all.[21]

The proliferation and seriousness of such exclusions, which imply that the third sex is incapable of any salvific activity whatsoever, distinguish the *paṇḍaka* from the other classes barred from ordination and signal that something special is afoot. That there is a fair amount of confusion regarding this is evident from the few terse explanations concerning the exclusions that are offered, for they are neither consistent nor satisfying. Abhidharma tradition reasons that a certain lack of restraint (*asaṃvara*) is required in order for there to be a basis for a vow of restraint. The idea seems to be that the *paṇḍaka* does not have enough sinful willfulness to have something to take a vow against.[22] Yet in the same breath the *paṇḍaka* is accused of just the opposite problem: having too much and too unstable desire.[23] And the same could be said of the monastic list of five: again, that list includes both those whose sexuality is limited physiologically and those who have perverse or extra sexuality.

If we could separate the *paṇḍaka* class into its component parts we could at least solve this last contradiction. It would be more logical if it were only the neuter *paṇḍaka* who could not take vows due to the absence of a desire to transgress (i.e., if one accepts the basic premise of this oppositional logic at all). Similarly, it should only be the *paṇḍaka* with either both or changing sets of sexual organs who is plagued by excessive or indecisive desire. But this still does not solve the most puzzling problem of all here. For it is not clear why these various *paṇḍaka* qualities are considered such a liability in the first place. Is it not a virtue in Buddhist tradition to be poor at discriminatory thought, the very attribute that so oddly disqualifies the *paṇḍaka* from meditation?[24] And would not the equanimity in the *paṇḍaka*'s lack of strong desires or intentions to transgress be a good thing, an advantage, rather than a failing, disqualifying someone from the Buddhist order?

IV

Given the seemingly universal negative gloss for the third sex category, it is surprising to discover that a positive estimation of *paṇḍaka* features did indeed come to be recognized, and in a variety of Buddhist traditions, outside monasticism. Such a recognition seems to have emerged gradually, but we can discern a developing sense that something about the *paṇḍaka* class actually mirrors virtues that Buddhism extols.[25] This development becomes notable largely in Tibetan sources, but it builds on associations and suggestions found in Indian Buddhism as well.

Most readily, there is the third sex's middleness—its equal proportion of its parents' seeds, its fetus sitting in the middle of its mother's belly, and so on (*Carakasaṃhitā Śārīrasthāna* [Agniveśa 1976] 2.18, 2.24–25)—that comes to be associated with the highly esteemed Middle Way in Buddhism. A number of early Tibetan manuals, for medical practice as well as from the yogic tradition, make just this point, extolling the middleness of the *paṇḍaka* class and using it as a marker of stability and equanimity: (here citing the Tibetan term,) *ma ning* is called the abiding breath between male exhalation and female inhalation;[26] *ma ning* is the stable psychic wind, as opposed to the shaking male wind or agitated female wind (Sa-chen Kun-dga' sNying-po 1983, 4, 266-67); *ma ning* is the balanced yogic channel, as opposed to the too tight male channel, and the too loose female one, and so on.[27]

A distinctive development in Tibetan medicine really drives home, with spectacular effect, a Buddhistically positive association with the *paṇḍaka* class. Here influenced by the Chinese diagnostics of pulse reading, Tibetan medicine introduced an innovative threefold (rather than the Chinese twofold) division of pulse types: male, female, and *ma ning*. The root Tibetan medical text sets the standard: a male pulse is thick and throbs roughly; a female pulse is fine and throbs quickly; and a *ma ning* pulse is steady, slow, and pliable (*rGyud bzhi* 1992, 560; Zur-mkhar-ba 1989, 1: 699). Given the medical tradition's high valuation of harmony and equilibrium, we are not surprised to see that this middle *ma ning* type gets such a good prognosis—a person with this pulse will live long, have few diseases, high status, and will be looked on favorably by people in power.[28] But nothing shows more how far the ostracized *paṇḍaka/ma ning* class has come than the astounding Buddhist superlative that the text goes on to provide: the *ma ning* pulse is glossed "bodhisattva pulse"—the pulse of the exalted enlightened beings who by the time of the Mahāyāna practically share the same status as a buddha.[29]

This is quite a transition from the pariah status of the *paṇḍaka* class in the Vinaya, but like much else about this elusive category, the reason for its identification with the bodhisattva is never explained. One can find a few clues, however. One is from Buddhist Abhidharma notions about the moment of a baby's conception. The classic account, famously anticipating Freud's Oedipal complex, says that the little being who gets sandwiched between the seeds of a man and woman in coitus, will, if it is to be a boy, lust for his mother-to-be and resent his future father, while the girl-to-be will do the opposite, lusting for her father and hating her mother (Kritzer 2000, 4-5). Yet when Buddhist scholastics went on to describe the moment of conception for a bodhisattva, who takes birth deliberately and out of compassion, they stipulated that this little being would realize that the mating couple is to be its parents and not the proper object of sexual desire or jealousy, and therefore would have affectionate love equally for both of them (see Kritzer 2000, 18-19, citing the *Vibhāṣā*). This distinctive specification is echoed in an early Tibetan tantric source that describes the same moment, but this source is accounting not for the bodhisattva-to-be but rather for the *ma ning*-to-be. The scene that is depicted may be indebted to the scholastic description of the bodhisattva embryo: the *ma ning* too has equal love for both parents.[30]

If the *paṇḍaka*'s association with equanimity parallels the bodhisattva's egalitarianism, the sex-changing *paṇḍaka* in particular exhibits another kind of affinity with the bodhisattva. Sex change in Buddhism is a rich issue deserving of a study on its own; the topic will come up again below. Note for now that the *Lotus Sūtra* is one of the first to associate it with the bodhisattva. The compassionate bodhisattva must be able to appear in any appropriate body so as best to teach and enlighten the full range of sentient beings; such a deliberate display often involves sex change, along with occupation, class, and even species change (Hurvitz 1976, 307-308, 314-15). Now in contrast to this exalted power, the cyclical sex changes of the *paṇḍaka* appear to be involuntary, not deliberate or compassionate. Nevertheless at least one development in Buddhism recognized the parallel. It comes up in yet another striking step in the refiguration of the sexual pariah: a rare and intriguing example of the third sex personified as a tantric Buddhist deity: mGon-po Ma-ning. Actually the texts give little indication of the grounds for construing this mysterious and probably uniquely Tibetan form of the famous Indic deity Mahākāla as in fact of the third sex. And since the deity is usually pictured fully dressed, and often standing next to a female consort, there is some reason to wonder whether it is meant to be a *ma ning* as such. But there are a few terse suggestions that do indicate its unconventional sex. One is that the special talent of this deity resides precisely in its lack of determinate sexual identity. As one visionary writes, "It is because [this deity] is not definitively either male or female that it is able to accomplish the work of all buddhas."[31] In other words, the *ma ning* deity has a sexual indeterminacy, an indeterminacy that mirrors an enlightened flexibility in its salvific power.

Connectivity, a virtue related to flexibility, also comes to be attributed to the third sex class. We can discern such an idea in the distant domain of Tibetan grammar, which nonetheless remains under the influence of Buddhist tropes. When discussing the way that consonants interact with other consonants, letters are divided into the categories of male, female, and *ma ning*, along with subtypes, which for the *ma ning* are given as "no signs" (Tib. *mtshan* and Skt. *linga* both mean either linguistic sign or genitals), "two signs," and "changing signs"; in other words, the familiar Tibetan trio for types of *paṇḍaka* persons. The point requires more discussion than space permits here. Suffice it to say for the present context that the flexibility implied by the *paṇḍaka* features of having two signs or changing signs is deployed in Tibetan grammar as a metaphor to show how sounds can join with other sounds (making for a kind of intrasyllabic *sandhi*), which makes possible phonic connection and indeed oral articulation altogether.[32] Such connectivity suggests still other enlightened virtues for the third sex category—one even counters the problematic exclusiveness of the Vinaya. This turns up again with the tantric deity mGonpo Ma-ning, whose power is said to reside in its *in*clusiveness. As one of its proponents wrote, "It is because it is complete with all three—male, female and *ma ning*—that [the mGon-po Ma-ning tantra] is held to be the tantra of the great congregation."[33]

It is not difficult to see why the middle term—which covers the gray area in between two opposite poles, and which, precisely because of its lack of strict allegiance, can assume features of either of those two poles—could come to symbolize inclusiveness. But the implications are far-reaching. They could be seen to touch on some of the most foundational ideas in Buddhism. For one exceptional example, consider the fact that a key Buddhist buzzword "nondual" is used to refer to the third sex category in both the Tibetan tantric and medical writings that valorize the category.[34] Now the locus classicus for the notion of nonduality in Buddhism is of course Buddhist philosophy, nowhere more paradigmatically worked out than in the attack on essentialism by the Buddhist philosopher Nāgārjuna. One of the principles that Nāgārjuna pretends to respect in this attack is the law of the excluded middle—the law that an entity must either be *a* or *not-a*; there is no middle ground—but actually his respect of this law is part of his reductio ad absurdum. In other words, he does mobilize the law of the excluded middle—for example, in his chapter in *Madhyamakārikā* on causation—but ends up showing that this law only pertains to positions that make dualistic, essentialist (and thereby false) assertions. If in fact one drops all such dualistic assertions, the law of the excluded middle becomes moot, or better, irrelevant.

What better instance of an actual "excluded middle" than the reviled *paṇḍaka*? Or so one might ask. Yet, inspired by the way that Nāgārjuna (and several Western philosophers too)[35] has called the law of the excluded middle into question, I submit that the third sex class can also be read as functioning to undermine its own exclusion. Such a reading would have particularly rich significance for gender theory. To recognize a middle term, with its ability to breach gaps, to connect, and to transform, is to illustrate by its very mucosity (as feminist theorist Luce Irigaray might put it) the impossibility of any definitive demarcation, least of all exclusion.[36] If indeed the two sexes are not bipolar extremes but rather are understood to be on a continuum—that is, if they do not have strict boundaries that, once crossed, become the opposite of what they started with—then they do not exclude a middle term, precisely because they are not "essential," to use the Buddhist parlance, in themselves. By the same token, just to name the third or middle term is exactly to call into question any strict separation of the other two. In this way, the same third sex that was defined as the excluded one could be turned on its head to subvert the very notion of excludability altogether.[37]

V

We have come a long way, from the social and ritual arena of Buddhist ordination to the rarified domain of theory—not to mention the fact that the points in the last paragraph were never actually made in historical Buddhist writings at all. But we still need to ask where all this would leave the hapless and excluded third sex people themselves—let alone the hapless female people, the second sex for monastic law, from whom this article took its first cue. The salvific potential of Buddhist logic notwithstanding, we cannot help but notice that the actual conditions of people, alas, do not necessarily improve in the wake of theoretical advancements. Even to argue, as some Buddhist texts actually did do, that all sexual identity is a construct and an illusion, did not historically erase all sex discrimination in Buddhism—far from it.[38]

At the very least, though, the rich theoretical potentials of the third sex category, not to mention its actual valorization in some corners of Buddhist history, makes us wonder all the more pointedly: why did the category remain a problem for monasticism? But to answer this question, the first thing we need to realize is that despite all those positive profiles of the third sex that were just marshaled—not just for philosophy but also in tantric physiology, grammar, even sacred iconography—none of these were really about actual third sex *people*: rather, in each case the third sex stands for a principle, a concept, a category—a gender. This realization will bring us to the heart of the Vinaya's litany of sexual exclusions.

Consider first, for another moment, the Tibetan medical pulse diagnostics: just where one would most expect to find actual empirical bodies. But even here, we are tipped off to the fact that it may not be sexual anatomy that is being described by the use of the term "nondual" to gloss the *ma ning* pulse—and now I will add that these same passages also connect male pulse with "skillful means" and female pulse with "gnosis" (Zur-mkhar-ba 1989, 1: 699). For these very terms—"gnosis," "skillful means," and "nonduality"—indicate that what the doctors are really looking for when they read someone's pulse is not sexual anatomy but rather the presence, somehow, in their patients of one of these three very classic tantric Buddhist virtues: gnosis, skillful means, or nonduality.[39] This is only confirmed further when the root text quite explicitly distinguishes body type from pulse type. Women can have male pulses, men can have female pulses, and both women or men can have the bodhisattva/*ma ning* pulse.

This is not to say that the pulse tradition has nothing to do with the actual sexual anatomies of bodies at all. For one thing, the pulse/sex split is not altogether neat. The medical writers still maintain that *most* males will have a male pulse, females a female pulse, and *ma ning*s a *ma ning* pulse (Zur-mkhar-ba 1989, 1: 699–700). That is because the primary issue concerns the predominance of one of these tantric patterns—that is, either skillful means, gnosis, or nonduality—in one's basic energy. Or perhaps we could call it character. This character pattern then produces certain physical manifestations, in accordance with classic tantric conceptions. So, people with dominant skillful means will tend to have male bodies, and also a male pulse. And so on. Still, most medical commentators maintained the possibility of deviance: "From one perspective," Zur-mkhar-ba Blo-gros rGyal-po (sixteenth century), one of the most influential commentators, writes, "it is uncertain" (1989, 1: 700). Here he displays the empirical bent of the medical tradition after all, for the fact of the matter is that Tibetan doctors regularly find persons whose pulse character does not match their sexual anatomy; this is already asserted by the root medical text (*rGyud bzhi* 1992, 560). But this finding proved controversial, and it prompted Zur-mkhar-ba to creatively adapt an old Buddhist scholastic term, "mind-continuum" (Tib. *sems rgyud*), for his own purposes, making it mean something like what we would call "personality," and which is something, he asserts, that can change during a person's lifetime. He distinguishes this mind-continuum from basic sex (which he labels with another scholastic category, *indriya* [Tib. *dbang po*]) and suggests that the latter cannot change.

To drive home the distinction he proclaims, "There can be a woman who possesses a man's mind-continuum, but that does not automatically mean that she has actually become a man."[40]

It is certainly striking to see a debate on the third sex category lead to the conclusion that women can have male personalities. And indeed the pulse doctrine has valorized deviation all along: men who develop a female pulse will be healthy and live long, the root Tibetan medical text proclaims; and women who have male pulses will be powerful and bear many children (*rGyud bzhi* 1992, 560). In other words, we can say that Zur-mkhar-ba in effect introduced, with his "mind-continuum" category, a working notion of gender. And this gender-like category of mind-continuum is especially germane for our purposes in this article. For in breaking the bounds of strict anatomical definition and allowing for flexibility and deviance, such an idea brings the very *in*flexibility of the Vinaya into high relief. One is tempted to propose, at the very least, that the Vinaya would have been well served by the clarity attained by the physicians: anatomical sex and personal qualities—gender, if you will—can be separated. At the very least, it seems unfortunate for the Vinaya to allow anatomy to become so determinative of spiritual value, to assume so simplistically that someone whose sexual organ was ambiguous would themselves be of ambiguous, or changing, or unreliable moral worth, incapable of taking vows or even practicing the Dharma at all.

But now this thought prompts one to go back for another look at the anatomy put forward by the Vinaya. For it is still not entirely clear why a true neuter, a person who purportedly lacks sexual organs completely, should be classed in the same category as a person who has both male and female organs, at least on biological grounds. Nor is it evident why sexual dysfunction belongs in the same class: it should not necessarily be the case that the "halfer"—the changing *paṇḍaka*—is not fully sexually active, and the same can be said of the hermaphrodite for that matter (and as already mentioned, *paṇḍaka*s are often pictured as being oversexed). And then even people whose *paṇḍaka* state is not innate but acquired, for a whole variety of nonbiological reasons, come to be included in the class. In short, this third sex *paṇḍaka* category, rather than being consistently or coherently defined, is starting to look more than anything like merely a loose catchall for an ever-expanding array of sexual aberrations on ever-shifting grounds—even psychological and social ones.

And yet this very catchall character is actually very significant, for it suggests a theoretical unity in the class after all. In other words, perhaps we can see that the Vinaya's conception of the *paṇḍaka* is, unwittingly, a gender category itself. Even though there are attempts to specify the anatomy of some of the forms of *paṇḍaka*hood, the category as a whole stands most centrally for a conceptual class, to wit, a class of people whose universal characteristic is simply to be unspecifiable and aberrational. Or to put it another way: taken as a whole, *paṇḍaka* is the category of the uncategorizable. And such a category is very relevant for Buddhist monasticism indeed.

Not only does it tell us that even for the Vinaya, the *paṇḍaka* was a conceptual category after all, rather than representing a precise or specifiable anatomical condition of particular persons. We should also note that such a gendered conceptual category has a very special meaning, one that is quite different from the tantric gender metaphors that we saw in the medical case. While for medicine and tantric yoga the third term signifies balance, flexibility, and health, I propose that for the Vinaya it is the aberrationality of the third sex that has the most salience, precisely because of its dissonance with the dominant ideology of the Vinaya. For if indeed the third sex class does stand for sexual aberration and uncategorizability, it is no wonder that it was such a pariah in the Buddhist monastic world. Why do I say that? Let us remember what the Vinaya is about.

The Vinaya represents the laws of a community of renunciates. These are people who have left home, changed their identities profoundly, and sworn off many things: taking what is not given, depriving any being of life, bragging about attainments, handling money, causing discord, and so on, all codified in a strict and extremely detailed set of rules. Arguably, the most important regulation, and the one considered the most difficult of all to maintain, is sexual abstinence—this is obvious from the premier place that sexual regulation has in the monastic lawbooks.[41] And yet it is far from fully clear what actually constitutes such a transgression. If one is raped, has one broken the vow never to have sex? If a monk has an unintentional emission during sleep, does that break the vow? What if he takes no action overtly, but passively enjoys an accidental encounter? Is it a question of intention or of what the body actually does? Are there gray areas, half-transgressions, which deserve repentance but not expulsion? Actually, such nuanced and tortured questions accompany many of the regulations in the Vinaya, not just those about sex. Read the Vinaya literature from its earliest texts onward: you cannot fail to be impressed with the utter preoccupation, nay, obsession, with trying to pin down strict dualistic distinctions. The Vinaya struggles over and over to make it clear in just what cases a transgression really *is* a transgression, exactly what kind of transgression, how it is determined that it has taken place, and precisely what or who is responsible.

And so if the *paṇḍaka* class most basically is defined as people who are not definable, who are not definitively either a male or a female[42]— and especially if, as a medical writer so pertinently put it, the *ma ning* is "the one who has no opposite" (*go ldog*)[43]—no wonder such a person in its very undefinability would have represented an abomination, as Mary Douglas surely would say. The *paṇḍaka* is an abomination, then, not to the doctors, but to the monastic legalists, because the very project of the Vinaya depends on exact definition, and decision, and vow taking, and the distinction between purity and defilement. The one whose principal defining feature is to be "whatever" in this way *had* to be excluded from the monastic order.

VI

It is far from an innovation, then, for the Tibetan pulse diagnosticians to have treated the third sex as a metaphor or idea rather than a specification about actual people; it had functioned as such all along in the chapters of Buddhism we have looked at. What *is* an advance on the medical side, however, is the recognition that characteristics associated with one sex can be exhibited by people of the opposite sex. In other words, it is the heuristic separation of sex and gender (not unlike one of the foundational moves of modern feminism) that has liberating potential both for the third—and now we can see that we could call it either sex or gender—as well as the second. But before going further, I must caution against too simplistically faulting the Vinaya out of hand for its failure to make that separation, for its conflation of body and meaning, and for placing such symbolic importance on the physical appearance of purity and disciplined order, especially given the very controversial and ground-breaking position in India that Buddhist monasticism represented. This quite understandable and in fact vital concern with public status, which as already noted, was behind the overt androcentrism of the monastic code, also explains the exclusion of sexually marginal persons.

Nor would we want, at least from a feminist perspective, to rule out generically the basic premise proposed both by Buddhist monasticism and meditative traditions that a correlation obtains between body and meaning. Such a correlation was to be explored quite precisely in both yoga and ritual as a way of bringing philosophical and ethical norms into lived bodily and social experience, and it underlies the entire tradition of personal cultivation regarding which Buddhism has made such notable contributions.

So if we must pause before insisting unilaterally that sex and gender must always be rigorously separated—a separation against which feminists themselves have cautioned, if for no other reason than to say that even sexual identity itself has no self-evident reality that is totally free of culture—what we can call for is more precision, at least to separate fact from fiction, especially concerning the material facts themselves. The current Dalai Lama has argued that Buddhism must revise its doctrine when it is contravened by modern science. I would submit that part of the problem we have been examining here is a recurring carelessness in Vinaya tradition about the facts of sex. No less influential a systematizer than Buddhaghosa can proclaim with a straight face that a woman can get pregnant by looking at a man; or by hearing, like the *balākā* bird who gets pregnant by hearing thunder; or by smell, like the cow who gets pregnant by smelling the breath of a bull (Takakusu and Nagai [1924] 1999, 1: 214). More dismaying yet, in passages that otherwise attempt to be very precise and physicalistic about sexual intercourse, there is an apparent conflation of the vagina and the urethra in some of the early Vinaya material.[44] These gaffes are surprising given what we have learned from Kenneth Zysk (1991) about the central role of the early Buddhist monastic community in developing the systems of Āyurveda, that is, the main Indian medical tradition, overall.

Still, fictions are revealing for what they betray. This is especially so for the anomalies of the third sex, which of course have long been recognized empirically, but which nonetheless have historically been subject to distortion and worse in so many societies (Herdt 1993; Fausto-Sterling 2000). And yet like other such instances, the Vinaya's images of this group—fantastical as some of its members might be—are telling for what they say about the Vinaya's larger notions of sex and gender. So in this final portion of the article I would like to pursue the meaning, and the metaphors, of the Vinaya's third sex/gender just one step further. To consider especially its more outlandish representations will also shed some light on how the Vinaya construes women.

Ponder, then, the sex-changing *paṇḍaka*, a concept in full evidence by the time of several of the Vinaya's systematizers. The image should be connected to other notions of sex change that were beginning to circulate in Buddhism, most notably the often-studied sūtra stories about women who change into men before attaining Buddhahood.[45] Less noticed in Western scholarship is another important subtype, found in Vinaya legal tracts. Salient examples can be found in the set of stories in Buddhaghosa's commentary, such as the one about a monk who wakes up one morning to find his beard and male shape gone, and female features in their place (Takakusu and Nagai [1924] 1999, 1: 273); or another, from the Mūlasarvāstivāda Vinaya tradition, about a nun who is walking alone down a path and suddenly transforms into a male.[46] The point of these passages is ostensibly to lay out the legal implications of a sex change, to reassure the aggrieved monk-turned-female that he (i.e., she) can retain status in the order (albeit now in a nunnery!), or to work out the liabilities if the person changing sex is in the middle of committing an offense that is sex-specific. For instance, the nun walking down the dangerous path is no longer in legal jeopardy when she turns into a male, because only nuns are forbidden to walk alone on deserted paths, not monks. But we might shift our focus for a moment to the underlying premise of these jurisprudential pronouncements. Since it is only at three sex changes that one must forfeit one's entitlement to monastic status altogether,[47] it appears that spontaneous sex change once or twice (and this is not about psychology or practice—it is about full anatomical transformation)[48] is something that is presumed to be a relatively innocuous event![49]

I have already noted how the sexual instability epitomized by the *paṇḍaka* marks it ineluctably as anathema and pariah for the monastic order. I would now like to add a further and I think important nuance: the same instability also renders the *paṇḍaka* a mirror of monastic fantasies about women. Most obviously, the dreaded sex change, which at least one kind of *paṇḍaka* embodies, has a lot to do with a simple male fear of becoming female; this is grossly apparent in the monastic truism, duly repeated by Buddhaghosa, that male genitals are superior to female genitals. He also expresses the view that male genitals are more stable than female ones: it takes strong negative karma for a male's organs to disappear and only a bit of weak positive karma to re-emerge as a female; conversely, even weak negative karma can cause a female to lose her female organs, and strong good karma is required for her to acquire male organs.[50] But the point can also be made on more general grounds: I am arguing that the *paṇḍaka*'s spectre of looming sex change and capricious sexuality betrays anxieties about uncontrollable sexuality period, and surely no figure is more centrally associated with sexual uncontrollability in Buddhist literature than the female. This is especially true in the Vinaya stories surrounding the celibacy rules, with their repeated cases of women raping monks, exposing themselves, running up to sit on a monk while he sleeps under a tree; even venerable female patrons try to convince monks that the gift of sex is the highest gift a lay donor can offer.[51] Nowhere is the monastic presumption of oversexed woman more overt than in the striking discrepancy in the monastic rules whereby any erotically prone physical contact with a man spells a nun's irreversible expulsion from the order, while a monk will only be expelled if he has full-fledged sexual intercourse.[52]

So sexual uncontrollability is a feature common to both *paṇḍaka* and woman. But that is not the only "female" quality that I find refracted in the *paṇḍaka*. There are even reasons to suspect that in some respects the second and third sexes/genders were virtually equated. My attention is caught by the Vinaya lists of characteristics that disqualify a woman from ordination. There are various versions of this list, but most instances provide more kinds of sexual anomaly than we find in the parallel rules on male ordination. The list amounts to a description of the class of female *paṇḍaka*s (even though at this point the term is but one member of the list); to wit: if she is without sexual organs, if she has defective sexual organs, if she is bloodless, or has stagnant blood, or is always dressed (*dhuva cola*), or is dripping, or is deformed (*sikharaṇī*), or a woman *paṇḍaka*, or a manlike woman (*vepurisika*), or one whose genitals are joined (*sambhinna*),[53] or is a hermaphrodite (*ubhatovyañjana*); in any of these cases she must be refused ordination.[54] In fact this list appears to be one of the most detailed elaborations of excluded sexual anomalies in the early strata of the Vinaya tradition altogether, apparently predating the fivefold *paṇḍaka* taxonomy. And it is suggestive indeed to realize that the most detailed early portrait of the anomalous sex that we have is of the anomalous-sex-as-female rather than as-male, especially when we remember that in virtually every other respect the Vinaya takes the male as the norm.

But there is an even more telling clue to add here: at least in its Pāli version, this very same list of female exclusions is rehearsed elsewhere in the Vinaya code as a set of abuses which men, on the whole, are prone to heap on any woman (*Suttavibhaṅga Saṃghādisesa* 3.3.1). In other words, the very same portrait of the sexually excluded class for monasticism also served as a disparaging portrait of women in general. But while in the first instance the monk preceptor is ritually entitled to interrogate a fledgling nun about her private parts and menstrual cycle in order to determine her eligibility for ordination, in the second context it is clear that the list of abuses refers rather to the kinds of afflictions and monstrosities that render a female an unacceptable—and also infertile—mate, hence men's tendency to ridicule such women.

Is the *paṇḍaka* then just a caricature of what the male finds unacceptable in the opposite sex?[55] Indeed, it is rather surprising to find concerns about procreation and female fertility reinscribed as criteria for admission to a celibate order, but perhaps it should not be too surprising, given the thoroughgoing androcentrism of the monastic code. Consider, then, one more clue that the third sex stands for the second sex in monasticism. It is in fact to be discerned in several Indic sources, but it becomes especially striking in Tibetan.[56] This is the very special ambiguity of the term *za ma*, often the Tibetan translation of the Indic *ṣaṇḍha*, one of the other words that, as already seen, names the third sex.[57] While all of those terms, including *paṇḍaka* itself, can refer to both a sexually abnormal male and a sexually abnormal female, *za ma* in Tibetan can additionally denote a normal female.[58] In this usage the term's semantic resonance implies softness, suppleness, and weakness,[59] and I take that to be very significant, for it names a key feature of what is wrong with both the female and the third sex, that is, wrong in the particular context of "rigid" monastic discipline. Both the second and third sex are in the end *napuṃsaka*, to return to the Indic medical term—that which is "not male"—but now we can see that the *paṇḍaka* is also not what the order would like the female to be either. Uncontrollability, instability, indefinability, softness, weakness: these features are common to caricatures of the second and the third sexes alike, rendering the two equally anathema to monasticism.

So why the doubling, then? Why a second second sex? Is it merely an artifact of a system of sexual discipline, a system built on the patriarchal privilege of a first sex defined against a second? Is it just such a system that calls out for a third rubric—to fill out the space in between the first two, a space that serves precisely to signal the danger of confusion and the need to patrol ever more vigilantly the borders? I am even tempted to speculate—and this is the final epiphany for now—that it was the very creation of an other to that other other that allowed the original other in through the door of ordination at all. Or in other words: I would like to suggest that the *paṇḍaka* category functioned as a scapegoat for the threat that woman was believed to pose to the monastic order. This scapegoat would have served to purify the image of woman (at least, "normal" woman) and allow her inclusion after all—even if she remained hobbled by the Eight Heavy Rules.

Now if all that is the case, we can be doubly impressed by the third sex's powers. Not only was it the proxy object of prejudice against nonconventional—that is, not fully male—sex, so that the truly discriminated sex, the second sex, could slip into an otherwise restrictive order. The foregoing theoretical speculation on a "law of the nonexcluded middle" has also revealed that this same third term ironically would work to subvert the very "order" that created it, writing slippage itself eternally into the system. And if that is true, perhaps we have really discovered some good reasons to gloss the *ma ning/paṇḍaka* as the compassionate bodhisattva, at least with regard to sex and gender ideals in Buddhist history. Perhaps the light that the curious third-term figure sheds on the nature of sex and gender discrimination will help the monastic community slowly to chip away at its roots, at the very moment that our global society finally begins to reckon with the daunting power that our conceptions about gender have. Indeed, those conceptions are proving to be almost as recalcitrant as ignorance and craving themselves, at the very heart of the Buddhist problematic.

Notes

I am grateful to Charles Hallisey and Steven Collins for help on various aspects of this article. An earlier version was first presented as a lecture at the Harvard Divinity School and then at the University of Wisconsin-Madison, both in March 2001.

1. Works critical of Buddhist misogyny and androcentrism include Paul 1979; Wilson 1996; Kabilsingh 1991; Gross 1993; and Campbell 1996. Books that take encouragement from Buddhist deifications of the feminine principle include Shaw 1994 and Simmer-Brown 2001.
2. Versions of this story and the Eight Heavy Rules appear to be present in all of our extant versions of the Vinaya. See Roth 1970, xxix-xxxi. See also Hirakawa 1982, 47-49, nn. 2 and 6. Anne Hiermann (2001, 275-304, n. 41) has pointed out that Jan Nattier (1991, 30, n. 12) was mistaken in asserting that the story postdates the Sthavira–Mahāsāṃghika split. However, Nattier maintains that the Mahāsāṃghika version of the story is garbled, suggesting it is a later interpolation (personal communication, 6 November 2002).
3. The order of the rules varies somewhat. See Roth 1970, xxxii, for the list according to the Mahāsāṃghika Vinaya. The Pāli version is in *Cullavagga* 10.1.1–6 (translated in Horner 1938–66, 5: 352).

4. See, e.g., Falk 1989. Gregory Schopen has made important contributions to our understanding of the competition between monks and nuns in the early centuries CE, as well as the active role of nuns in the image cult and patronage before their demise. See Schopen 1997, 238-57; 1996a.
5. For impressive stories of twentieth-century Thai nuns Voramai and Sara and Chongdi Bhasit, who acted on feminist sentiments, see Kabilsingh 1991. And yet many modern and international bhikṣuṇīs produce apologies for the Eight Heavy Rules. See, e.g., Wu Yin 2001, 81-89.
6. The list of what disqualifies a man from receiving ordination (Pāli, *antarāyikā dhammā*; Tib., *bar chad* [the "impediments"]) varies significantly, but it often includes some of the serious *ānantarika* crimes such as murder of parents or an arhat. Lists from Pāli Vinaya tradition may be found in *Mahavagga* 1.61; 2.22; 2.36.3; 8.30; 9.4.2 (translated in *Mahavagga* in Horner 1938–66, vol. 4). For Mūlasarvāstivāda Vinaya lists, see *Vinayavastu*, Brady 1998, text KD000111.ACT, 73; and Bapat and Gokhale 1982, sūtras 117–54. Comparative remarks on the Dharamagupta Caturvargika Vinaya are provided in Bapat and Hirakawa 1970, li. The list of impediments to ordination for women is different, but it often includes more specifications of kinds of sexual ambiguity: *Cullavagga* 10.17.1; Roth 1970, 31-33; Hirakawa 1982, 61-62. See n. 54 below.
7. Some of these are listed in *Mahavagga* 1.71, 76.
8. But in *Mahavagga* at least, being a *paṇḍaka* or hermaphrodite is listed with the first group, those who have committed crimes.
9. The *Therīgāthā* tells that one of the past lives of Isidāsī was born as neither a male nor a female (*n'eva mahiḷā na purisa*), this condition being the fruit of bad karma: Oldenberg and Pischel 1883, 166 (translated in Rhys Davids and Norman 1981, 140). *Mahavagga* 1.61 relates how a *paṇḍaka* tried to induce monks, novices, and grooms to defile him (it is not specified what that would entail), upon which he was pronounced unchaste and not to be ordained. A story in *Vinayavastu* tells of a *paṇḍaka* who wanted to take ordination so as to have opportunities for sex: Brady 1998, text KD000111.ACT, 131–32.
10. The *Śārīrasthāna* of *Carakasaṃhitā* assumes that there are three possible sexes of a child: male, female, and neuter (lit., "not male" [*napuṃsakam*]). The latter is specified by the commentary *Āyurvedadīpikā* to have a simple hole instead of a penis. See *Carakasaṃhitā Śārīrasthāna* 4.10 and 14 (Agniveśa 1976, 2: 391, 393-94). Chapter 2 of the same *Śārīrasthāna* only envisions two sexes for the newborn, male and female, but lists eight types of sexual abnormality between them: see n. 14 below. Compare the classical Tibetan medical text, probably codified in the twelfth century CE: *bDud rtsi snying po yan lag brgyad pa gsang ba man ngag gi rgyud* (hereafter *rGyud bzhi*) 1992, 17, 29. The term *napuṃsaka* is used occasionally for the third sex in Buddhist sources as well: see n. 11 below.
11. The root Pāli Vinaya texts usually mention only two main types of sexual excludees, *paṇḍakas* and hermaphrodites (*ubhatovyañjanaka*), as in *Mahavagga* 1.61, 68, 69; see also Trenckner and Jaini 1986, 310, 94-95 (translated in Horner 1963–64). The Mūlasarvāstivāda *Vinayavastu* regularly mentions the *ṣaṇḍha* (alternately, *ṣaṇḍa*) (Tib. *za ma*) along with the *paṇḍaka*. Vasubandhu lists *ṣaṇḍha*, *paṇḍaka*, and *ubhatovyañjanaka* as the three kinds of people excluded from ordination on sexual grounds: Shastri 1970, 2.1.c, 1: 137. But other than *Suttavibhanga* 1.9.1 (translated in Horner 1938–66, vols. 1–3), which specifies that there may be human, nonhuman, or animal *paṇḍakas*, I have found no definitions of the terms *paṇḍaka* or *ṣaṇḍha* as such until Yaśomitra, who distinguishes *ṣaṇḍhaka*, one who lacks either female or male genitals *by nature*, from the *paṇḍaka*, whose aberrational sex is due either to something undertaken on

purpose or to disease or injury: *Sphuṭārthā* (Law 1949), 94. The terms *ṣaṇḍa/ka, ṣaṇḍha/ka*, and *ṣāṇḍya* are also known to the classical Āyurvedic tradition, as in *Carakasaṃhitā Śārīrasthāna* (Agniveśa 1976) 2.21 and *Suśrutasaṃhitā Śārīrasthāna* (Sharma 2000) 2.41–42, 44. See also nn. 56-58 below. On the set of five kinds of *paṇḍaka*, see n. 16 below, but even there the term is not defined as such. An instance where the term *paṇḍaka* stands for the class of sexual anomalies as a whole may be found in the Mūlasarvāstivāda *Vinayavibhanga* where it repeatedly forms a trio with male and female in the specifications of kinds of proscribed sex. But the analogous Pāli text, *Suttavibhanga*, regularly lists instead four kinds of people with whom sex is forbidden: males, females, *paṇḍakas*, and hermaphrodites. *Cullavagga* 10.17 and other lists of disqualifications for female ordinands (see n. 6 above and n. 54 below) confirm that there can be a woman *paṇḍaka*. *Vinayavibhanga* also regularly distinguishes the category of male *paṇḍaka* (Tib. *ma ning pho*). *Paṇḍaka* is defined by Monier-Williams (1956) as a weakling or eunuch. "Eunuch" is a common translation for *paṇḍaka*, but this is clearly inadequate to cover its semantic range. Leonard Zwilling (1992, 204) asks if the etymology could be from *apa + aṇḍa + ka*, "with (eggs =) testicles (taken) away." But Steven Collins (personal communication, 20 February 2001) rejects this theory since there is no other example of *apa→pa* in Pāli even if *api pi* is common. Other labels for sexual anomalies that merit exclusion from ordination are also to be found in the root Vinaya texts. For example, *Vinayavastu* (Brady 1998, text KD000111.ACT, 69) characterizes the three kinds of anomaly as the state of lacking genitals (*mtshan med = animitta*), of having two genitals (*mtshan gnysis = dvinimitta?* or *ubhatovyañjanaka*), and of being a *gle 'dams*, which can refer either to a castrated man or to a woman whose vagina and anus are joined (= *saṃbhinnavyañjanā*, see also n. 53 below). Occasionally the term *napuṃsaka* is also used in Buddhist sources for sexual anomaly: Müller 1893, 260. Other terms from Mūlasarvāstivāda tradition may be culled from Sakaki (1965), including *vātāṇḍa, ekāṇḍa, anāṇḍa, puruṣānukṛtistrī, stryanukṛtipuruṣa, aṇḍalāṅgulapraticchanna, sadāprasravaṇī, alohinī*, and *naimittikī*. A widely used Indic term for the sexually anomalous person is *klība*, but it does not seem to occur in Buddhist sources: see Doniger 1991, 79-85. Compare n. 14 below.

12. *Suśrutasaṃhitā Śārīrasthāna* (Sharma 2000) 2.43 refers to the conditions for the birth of a female who acts like a man, and a comment on *Suśrutasaṃhitā Śārīrasthāna* (Sharma 2000) 2.45 asserts that there are both female (*nārī-*) and male (*nara-*) kinds of *ṣaṇḍhas*.
13. On the balance of the parents' seeds see *Carakasaṃhitā Śārīrasthāna* (Agniveśa 1976) 2.18; the same view is echoed in Tibetan medical tradition.
14. *Carakasaṃhitā Śārīrasthāna* (Agniveśa 1976) 2.17–21 indicates eight types of sexual abnormality: (1) Hermaphroditism (*dviretas*) resulting from a vitiation of the embryo's genital cells and an equal division of the parent's sperm and ovum. (2) A wind condition of the organ (*pavanendriyatva*) resulting from a wind (*vāyu*) problem in the testicles of the foetus. (3) A condition of weak sexual desire (*saṃskāravāha*) caused by a wind obstruction in the seminal passage. (4 and 5) A sexually deficient state (*klība*) in either males or females caused by weakness or insufficient seminal substances in the parents. (6) Bent shape (*vakrī*) of the male organ, caused by weakness of the father's organ and a resistance to sex on the part of the mother. (7) A condition in which pleasure derives from jealousy (in watching others have sex) (*īrṣyrati*), a proclivity produced by the parents' jealousy and reduced arousal. (8) The congenital state of being a eunuch, caused by a wind or fire condition that destroys the testicles (*vātikaṣaṇḍaka*).
15. In addition to the *īrṣyrati* mentioned in *Carakasaṃhitā* (Agniveśa 1976; see n. 14), *Suśrutasaṃhitā Śārīrasthāna* (Sharma 2000) 2.38–41 also describes other congenital aberrations in sexual practice: *āsekya*, the condition, due to weak seminal substances in the

parents, in which one gets an erection from consuming the semen of others; *saugandhika*, the condition in which one is aroused by the smell of female and male genitals, a result of being born from a putrid vagina; and *kumbhīka*, the condition in which one is aroused by receiving anal penetration. Compare the *īrṣyrati* and *āsekya paṇḍaka*s in the Buddhist monastic descriptions in n. 16 below. On the Āyurvedic attribution of all such conditions to the person's parents, see *Suśrutasaṃhitā Śārīrasthāna* (Sharma 2000) 2.47.

16. The earliest source I have found would seem to be *Vinayavastu*, from the Mūlasarvāstivāda Vinaya (Brady 1998, text KD000111.ACT, 132), although the date of this text is not known. The list is absent in the Pāli Vinaya root texts and seems first to emerge in Pāli in Buddhaghosa's Vinaya commentary, *Samantapāsādikā* (Takakusu and Nagai [1924] 1999, vol. 5, 1016). These two examples of the list diverge in their understanding of some of the types. The Mūlasarvāstivāda list is also represented in Gunaprabha's *Vinaya-Sūtra* (Bapat and Gokhale 1982), sūtras 130–33; see also sūtra 18. A later source is Yaśomitra's commentary on *Abhidharmakośa* 2.1, where he traces the list specifically to the Vinaya, but distinguishes an Abhidharma view of the *paṇḍaka*, which would focus on the (dys)function of the sexual faculty or organ (*indriya*): *Sphuṭārthā* (Law 1949), 94–95; cf. n. 40 below. The list of five is as follows: (1) The *Vinayavastu*'s *jāti*—or *jātyāpaṇḍaka* (*skyes nas ma ning*), a congenital condition in which the infant is neither male nor female, corresponds to the *Samantapāsādikā*'s *napuṃsaka*, a child born without determinate gender. Yaśomitra calls this the *prakṛtipaṇḍaka*. Compare the use of the term *jātinapuṃsaka:* Müller 1893, 271 (see n. 11 above). (2) The *Vinayavastu*'s *pakṣapaṇḍaka* (*zla ba phyed pa'i ma ning*), someone who is a female half the month and a male for the other half, corresponds to the *Samantapāsādikā*'s *pakkhapaṇḍaka*, here explained as someone who, as a result of bad karma, is a *paṇḍaka* for the dark half of the month but is relieved of their sexual cravings in the light half. On changing sex, see nn. 45-49 below. One Tibetan exegete explains this monthly cycle entirely in terms of sexual desire: this *paṇḍaka* has male sexual desire for half of the month and female sexual desire for the other: dGe-'dun 'Grub 1999, 50. (3) The *Vinayavastu*'s *āsaktaprādurbhāvi paṇḍaka* (*'khyud nas ltang ba'i ma ning*), someone who "comes out" (which could either mean becomes aroused or ejaculates) when embraced by another, has a different sense in the *Samantapāsādikā*'s "sprinkled" or *āsitta paṇḍaka*, there explained as one who performs oral sex on another and is sprinkled with impurity. Note that the Sanskrit *āsakta* would be derived from the root *ā√sañj* whereas the Pāli *āsita* would be derived from *ā√sic*. Yaśomitra aligns himself with the *ā√sic* etymology in naming this the *āsekapaṇḍaka*, but he does not discuss the term further. We should also compare here *Suśrutasaṃhita*'s sexual condition called *āsekya:* see n. 15 above. (4) The *Vinayavastu*'s *īrṣyāpaṇḍaka* (*ma ning phrag dog can*), a *paṇḍaka* with jealousy, is explained as the voyeur, someone who is aroused by watching the actions of others. This type corresponds to the *Samantapāsādikā*'s *usuyyapaṇḍaka* as well as to the condition of *īrṣyrati* listed in the Āyurvedic literature (see nn. 14 and 15 above). (5) The *Vinayavastu*'s *āpatpaṇḍaka* (*nyams pa'i ma ning*), someone who becomes a *paṇḍaka* by virtue of adventitious conditions such as illness or surgery, corresponds to the *Samantapāsādikā*'s *opakammikapaṇḍaka*. Yaśomitra calls this the *lūna* (mutilated) *paṇḍaka*. For an idiosyncratically Tibetan rendition of the list, see dBang 'dus 1983, 410. In general the list remains relatively stable across South Asian and Tibetan Buddhism, but discrepancies indicate some confusion about what the individual types refer to. Type 3 *paṇḍaka* seems more clearly conceived by *Samantapāsādikā*, while type 2 seems more clearly conceptualized in *Vinayavastu*. Yaśomitra understands types 2–4 to suffer various kinds of impairment in the functioning of their sexual faculty (*indriya*), a functioning that is signaled by the ability of the male organ to generate pleasure (in orgasm) and to produce offspring.

17. *mtshan med pa, mtshan gnyis pa,* and *'gyur ba ma ning.* The earliest occurrence of this widely used trio may be the grammatical work *rTags 'jug: Sum cu pa dang rtags kyi 'jug pa* (Yamaguchi 1973, 9). It is standard by the time of Zur-mkhar-ba 1989, vol. 1, e.g. 219, 698. As referenced above in n. 11, an almost parallel trio occurs in the Tibetan translation of *Vinayavastu: mtshan med, mtshan gnyis,* and *gle gdams pa.*
18. I study monastic prohibitions against sex in "Sex" (Gyatso 2005). It seems that people who desire conventional homosexual sex, whatever that might be, can be ordained and can stay ordained, as long as they do not actually have sex. Exactly the same would be true for people with heterosexual desires. Zwilling (1992, 205) destroys his own argument that *paṇḍakas* are homosexuals when he writes, "The *Vinaya*, in fact, goes so far as to distinguish sexual activity between normative males from sexual relations between a socially normative male and a *paṇḍaka*." Some depictions of *paṇḍakas* do show them engaging in sex with men, as in *Vinayavastu* (Brady 1998, text KD000111.ACT, 131–32), where it is also specified that a *paṇḍaka* wanted to play the role of the female. Homosexual activity is also suggested in the descriptions of the *Samantapāsādikā*'s understanding of the *āsitta paṇḍaka*; see n. 16 above.
19. *Tṛtīyaprakṛti* occurs in *Kāmasūtra* and *Nāṭyaśāstra*.
20. For example, *Visuddhimagga* 5.40–42 (translated in Buddhaghosa 1976), avers that both hermaphrodites and *paṇḍakas* are among those who cannot develop *kasina* concentration, or indeed any kind of meditation at all, due to their defilement and bad kamma. *Abhidharmakośabhāṣya* 4.43 also asserts that neither *paṇḍakas* or *ṣaṇḍhas* are subject to any of the three disciplines (from v. 13: those of monasticism, meditation, and the pure path), nor indeed the absence thereof.
21. *Milindapañha* 310 (Trenckner and Jaini 1986; and translated in Horner 1963–64). The others on this list are similar to those who cannot take ordination: see n. 6 above. But note that *Vinayavibhanga* expels from ordination monks who revile (*sun phyung ba*) *paṇḍakas*—along with, among others, *bhikṣuṇīs* (Brady 1998, text KD000311.INC, 15).
22. *Abhidharmakośabhāṣya* 4.43: *pāpe 'pyasthirāśayatvāt.* See also *Abhidharmakośabhāṣya* 4.97, where it is added that the *paṇḍaka* does not have strong enough feelings for its parents for it to be a candidate for violating the rules against the serious (*ānantarya*) crimes of patricide, etc. But cf. n. 6 above, regarding the listing of the *paṇḍaka* right next to committers of these crimes in the lists of ordination exclusions.
23. *Abhidharmakośabhāṣya* 4.43 attributes this excess to having the desires of both sexes: *ubhayāśrayakleśādhimātrata.* See also n. 9 above.
24. This connection is especially clear in Tibetan sources. For example, 'Jam-dbyangs bZhad-pa (1648–1721), *bSam gzugs kyi snyoms 'jug rnams gyi rnam par bzhag pa'i bstan bcos thub bstan mdzes rgyan lung dang rigs pa'i rgya mtsho skal bzang dga' byed* (photocopy of block print), 21-22, attributes the *paṇḍaka*'s inability to make distinctions (*so sor rtog pa mi bzod pa*) to its inability to attain meditative absorption, along with its lack of shame and circumspection (*ngo tsha* and *khrel yod pa*). The *paṇḍaka* shares these problems with the inhabitants of Uttarakuru. Thanks to Jeffrey Hopkins for this reference. Compare *Milindapañha* (Trenckner and Jaini 1986, 94-95), which maintains that *paṇḍakas* are among those who cannot keep a secret because of being fickle and indecisive. *Abhidharmakośabhāṣya* 4.80 makes similar points about the *paṇḍaka*'s inability to establish, and therefore also to destroy, virtuous roots.
25. I am preparing a separate article on the distinctive Tibetan construal of the *paṇḍaka/ma ning* class.
26. Yang-dgon-pa rGyal-mtshan dPal 1976, 2: 457. Note that this work is also published in Dor-zhi gDong-drug sNyems-blo (1991), which incorrectly identifies the author as a Sa-skya-pa.

27. Yang-dgon-pa 1976, 2: 454. Also, an early medical text, gYu-thog Yon-tan mGon-po (1976, 1: 343-50), can speak of three kinds of digestive juices—male, female, and *ma ning*—without explaining these terms; that suggests that this gendered tripartite taxonomy, in which the *ma ning* category stands for a middle point along a continuum, was already well known.
28. But apparently those below will resent them and—a curious detail—their male relatives will arise as enemies: *rGyud bzhi* 1992, 560.
29. Although the medical tradition usually uses the term *byang chub sems rtsa*, which could be rendered "*bodhicitta* pulse," the root text *rGyud bzhi* does use the longer phrase *byang chub sems dpa' ir rtsa*, "bodhisattva pulse," on 560; repeated also in Zur-mkhar-ba 1989, 1: 700. The several occurrences of the abbreviated term *byang chub sems rtsa* in the root text could be explained by metrical considerations.
30. gNubs-chen Sangs-rgyas Ye-shes 1987, 52: 131-32. I am grateful to Jake Dalton for this reference.
31. rDo-rje Gling-pa 1984, 93: *pho mo gang du'ang ma nges pas / sangs rgyas kun gyi 'phrin las bsgrubs.*
32. This argument is based on my reading of the *rTags 'jug* (see n. 17 above) and its commentaries, particularly Si-tu Paṇ-chen Chos-kyi 'Byung-gnas (b. 1699/1700, d. 1774) 1960, 74-80. It concerns the discussion of suffixes in Tibetan; in fact all letters are subject to changing degrees of strength or weakness depending on the varying phonic contexts created when they join with various suffixes, but only the terminology of the *ma ning* letters explicitly names that changeability. I am presenting this argument in detail for another publication.
33. rDo-rje Gling-pa 1984, 92: *pho mo ma ning gsum tshangs bas / 'dus pa chen po'i rgyud du bzung.*
34. For example, Zur-mkhar-ba 1989, 1: 699; cf. rTse-le sNa-tshogs Rang-grol 1978, 377-78: *pho rgyud dang mo rgyud kyi rigs dang sde tshan gang yang 'dis mi 'thul ba'i gnyen por ma gyur pa gcig kyang med cing thabs shes gnyis su med pa'i ye shes kyi sku yin pa na ma ning gi mtshan du btags pa yin pas.*
35. See, e.g., Dummett 1978; for a lucid introduction to some of the mathematical issues involved, see George and Velleman 2002, ch. 4.
36. The notion of mucosity is developed in Irigaray's essay "Sexual Difference," in Irigaray 1991, 175.
37. I would submit that the concept of a third sex accomplishes such subversion more effectively than does the often-cited goddess chapter in *Vimalakīrtinirdeśa*, which endeavors also to show the provisional nature of sexual identity, albeit merely by demonstrating it through magical fiat.
38. This point was first made in sustained form by Paul 1979.
39. Several medical writers, including Gong-sman-pa (fifteenth century) and bKra-'bum-pa (eighteenth–nineteenth century), make the point that the characterizations of a pulse as *ma ning* and so on are metaphorical (*dpe don sbyar ba*): dBang 'dus 1983, 410–11.
40. Zur-mkhar-ba 1989, 1: 699. Zur-mkhar-ba's use of these terms differs from their sense in the *Abhidharmakośa*. The Tibetan *sems rgyud* would be equivalent to the Sanskrit *cittasantati* as in *Abhidharmakośa* 3.3, but the meaning there is very general, referring to all mental activity and capacity, with no mention of gendered features. *Indriya* does serve as a label for male and female sexual identity in the Abhidharma, where it seems to be a basic force that produces, respectively, male or female genitals along with other gender-specific features: see, e.g., *Abhidharmakośabhāṣya* 2.1b. See also Zwilling 1992, 206, discussing Buddhaghosa. However, in both Sanskrit and Tibetan there is a certain

slippage whereby *indriya* or *dbang po* sometimes refers to the sexual organ, particularly the male organ, as such. An example would be Yaśomitra's definition of the castrated *lūnapaṇḍaka* as one whose *indriya* is cut (*cheda*): *Sphuṭārthā* (Law 1949) 94. The relation of *indriya* to sexual identity merits more study.

41. This point and the following are argued in Gyatso 2005.
42. This is how it is defined in the *Vinayavastu*'s description of the *jātyāpaṇḍaka* (Brady 1998, text KD000111.ACT, 132) and in Yaśomitra's gloss of the class of *paṇḍakas* and *ṣaṇḍhas* in general (*Sphuṭārthā* [Law 1949] 94); see also Zur-mkhar-ba 1989, 1: 219: *de gnyis kar ma nges pa ma ning.*
43. gYu-thog Yon-tan mGon-po (?), *rTsod bzlog gegs sel 'khor lo*, in *Gyu thog cha lag bco brgyad* 1976, 1: 327.
44. This is indicated by the repeated use of the label *passāvamagga*, "path of urine," for the vagina, e.g., *Suttavibhanga* 1.9.1. In the corresponding passage of *Vinayavibhanga*, the Tibetan translation gives *zag byed*, "defiled" for vagina, seemingly readjusting the Sanskrit semantics, and aligning itself with standard Buddhist misogynist views of female sexuality. There seems also to be some ingenious etymological acrobatics at work there: *Mahāvyutpatti* (Sakaki 1965), entry no. 9227, indicates that *zag byed* corresponds to Skt. *prasrāvaṇa[karaṇa]*, "urine maker." Normally Tib. *zag* or *zag bcas* translates Skt. *āsrava.*
45. See Paul 1979; a more recent study is Nattier 2002.
46. Mi-bskyod rDo-rje (1507–55) mentions these in passing, with reference to a larger discussion on Mūlasarvāstivāda Vinaya sources (1973, 1: 348). For the rules about what happens when a sex change takes place during an ordination session, see Guṇaprabha's *Vinaya-Sūtra* (Bapat and Gokhale 1982), sūtras 618–19. dGe-'dun Grub 1999, 381–86, provides a good example of the intricate Tibetan elaborations on the legal implications of various kinds of sex change in the Vinaya.
47. The history of this restriction deserves further study; it does not seem to be present in the early layers of the Pāli Vinaya. And it is not the same condition as the *paṇḍaka* who changes sex every month. Three-time change occurs in a list of what prevents ordination in Mūlasarvāstivāda Vinaya tradition in *Vinaya-Sūtra* (Bapat and Gokhale 1982), sūtra 617. A key early Tibetan Vinaya exegete explains that after three changes one lacks any reliable identity as either a male or a female, and so cannot take ordination in either order; it is also what renders one a *paṇḍaka:* mTsho-sna-ba Shes-rab bZang-po [1993] 1998, 214.
48. The only hint to the contrary that I have found is in dGe-'dun Grub's (1999) characterization of the half-month *paṇḍaka*: see n. 16 above.
49. It also does not render one a *paṇḍaka*: mTsho-sna-ba [1993] 1998, 214.
50. He also grants that for both sexes, the disappearance of their original genitals is a result of bad deeds and the growth of genitals of the opposite sex is a result of merit; in this he seems to be most concerned about the undesirability of having your genitals change, no matter what you are originally, and also to assume that to be left with no genitals at all (i.e., to be a *paṇḍaka*) would be a bad fate indeed. Takakusu and Nagai [1924] 1999, 1: 274.
51. A paradigmatic set of examples may be found in the first section of the *Suttavibhaṅga.*
52. A brief comparison of *bhikṣu* and *bhikṣuṇī* precepts is provided by Hirakawa 1982, 38–42; also, Kabilsingh 1984.
53. This seems to mean that her anus and vagina are joined. The term is also used for a kind of sexually inadequate male: see n. 11 above. It is also listed as an illness in *Mahāvyutpatti* (Sakaki 1965), entry no. 9514; it is the only one among the excluded sexual anomalies to be included here.

54. *Cullavagga* 10.17.1; Takakusu and Nagai [1924] 1999, 3: 548. A similar list, including the "woman *paṇḍaka*" is found in Mahāsṃghika Lokottaravāda Vinaya tradition: see Hirakawa 1982, 61, but the "quasi-Prakrit-cum-Sanskrit" (Roth 1970, lx) version in Roth (33) is quite different from the Chinese and hard to construe. A Sarvāstivāda version is found in Ridding and de La Vallée Poussin 1917–20, 131. The various lists of female sexual anomalies are interesting and deserve further study; I have not yet located one in Mūlasarvāstivāda Vinaya texts, but most of the members of the list, along with many of the other *antarāyika* states, are included in *Mahāvyutpatti* (Sakaki 1965), sec. 27.
55. Also suggesting that the *paṇḍaka* is like a potential and dangerous female sexual partner is a list of those from whom the monk may not beg for alms: prostitutes, widows, unmarried women, nuns, and *paṇḍakas*: *Mahavagga* 1.38.5. For such associations more generally in India, see Roscoe 1996.
56. An example in Indic sources suggesting that the third sex is like a female is the description of the *ṣaṇḍha* in *Suśrutasaṃhitā Śārīrasthāna* (Sharma 2000) 2.41–.42.
57. Often, like *ṣaṇḍha*, *za ma* denotes a castrated male: Zur-mkhar-ba 1989, 1: 698; dGe-'dun Grub 1999, 403. The *za ma* state is one of the sexual anomalies that prevents ordination: sometimes it is distinguished from *ma ning*, as in Mi-bskyod rDo-rje 1973, 1: 403, but it also is often used synonymously with *ma ning:* Krang-dbyi-sun et al. [1993] 1998, 2443; bTsan-lha Nga-dbang Tshul-khrims 1997, 792. See also Zur-mkhar-ba 1989, 1: 698, quoting Byang-pa bKra-shis dPal-bzang; here Zur-mkhar-ba corrects Byang-pa, arguing that to equate *ma ning* and *za ma* is a mistake and insisting that the *za ma* is someone who has been castrated whereas the *ma ning* is one of the three types: changing, hermaphrodite, or neuter. The passages of Byang-pa to which Zur-mkhar-ba refers are found in *dPal ldan phyi ma brgyud kyi 'brel pa rin po che'i bang mdzod dgos 'dod 'byung ba* (photocopied manuscript), 300-311.
58. Krang-dbyi-sun et al. [1993] 1998, 2443; *rGyud bzhi* 1992, 375; Zur-mkhar-ba 1989, 2: 309. Sometimes the term used is *za ma mo*, but I would argue that here *za ma* is in apposition to *mo* rather than modifying it. Sog-po Lung-rigs bsTan-dar (seventeenth century?) confirms the sense of *za ma* as specifically female by defining it as someone whose menstrual discharge comes out every month (1986, 296). dBang 'dus (1983, 529) interestingly explains the slippage by saying that although *za ma* in general refers to a castrated male or someone with diminished desire, the term has come to be a word for female, because (like a woman) such people's experience of sex is that their partners are consummated (*za ba*) when they experience in themselves the flavor of their desire, while they themselves are unable to arouse their own desiring organ and use it to have sex with others. In this he seems to be implying also that the *za ma* could be a male with what for dBang 'dus is a female sexual orientation.
59. Thupten Phuntsok, personal communication, March 2000, Shang-Shung Institute, Conway, MA. This resonance is reflected in the sense of the term more generally as meaning weak desire or sexual impotence.

Bibliography

Agniveśa. 1976. *Caraka Saṃhitā, Based on Cakrapāṇi Datta's Āyurveda Dīpikā*, ed. and trans. Ram Karan Sharma and Vaidya Bhagwan Dash. 7 vols. Varanasi: Chowkamba Sanskrit Series Office.

Ahmad, Aijhhaz. 1992. *In Theory: Classes, Nations, Literatures*. London: Verso.

Akamatsu Renjo. 1893. *Shisho gūeki kai: chūyō chokushi, daigakushi* (*A Brief Account of the Shin-Shiu*). Kyoto: Tanaka jihei.

Akiyama Tokusaburō. 1884. *Sekai shūyū tabi nikki: ichimei Shakamuni Butsu funbo no yurai*. Tokyo: Kyūshunsha.

Alabaster, Henry, trans. 1871. *The Wheel of the Law*. London: Trübner.

Alexander, John A. 1979. "The Archaeological Recognition of Religion: The Examples of Islam in Africa and 'Urnfelds' in Europe." In *Space, Hierarchy and Society*, ed. Barry C. Burnham and J. Kingsbury. British Archaeological Reports, no. 59, 215-28. Oxford: BAR.

Almond, Philip C. 1986. "The Buddha in the West: From Myth to History." *Religion* 16/4: 305-22.

—1988. *The British Discovery of Buddhism*. Cambridge and New York: Cambridge University Press.

Alton, John. 1997. *Living Qigong*. Boston, MA: Shambhala.

Amstutz, Galen. 1997. *Interpreting Amida: History and Orientalism in the Study of Pure Land Buddhism*. Albany, NY: State University of New York Press.

Ang Choulean. 1986. *Les êtres surnaturels dans la religion populaire khmêre* (*Supernatural Beings in Khmer Popular Religion*). Paris: Cedoreck.

Aris, Michael. 1988. *Hidden Treasures and Secret Lives*. Delhi: Motilal Banarsidass.

Arnold, Edwin. 1889. *The Light of Asia; or, the Great Renunciation (Mahabhinishkramana) Being the Life and Teaching of Gautama, Prince of India and Founder of Buddhism*. Boston, MA: Roberts Brothers.

Aziz, Barbara Nimri. 1978. *Tibetan Frontier Families: Reflections of Three Generations from D'ing-ri*. Durham, NC: Carolina Academic Press.

Badone, Ellen. 1990. Introduction to *Religious Orthodoxy and Popular Faith in European Society*, ed. E. Badone, 3-23. Princeton, NJ: Princeton University Press.

Bailey, Greg. 1991. "Problems of the Interpretation of the Data Pertaining to Religious Interaction in Ancient India: The Conversion Stories in the *Sutta Nipāta*." *Indo-British Review* 19/1: 1-20.

Bajpai, K.D. 1963. "Authority of Minting Coins in Ancient India." *Journal of the Numismatic Society of India* 25: 17-21.

Ban Gu. 1962. *Han shu*. Beijing: Zhonghua.

Bapat, P.V., and V.V. Gokhale, ed. 1982. *Vinaya-Sūtra and Auto-Commentary on the Same by Guṇaprabha. Pravrajyā-vastu*. Patna: K.P. Jayaswal Research Institute.

Bapat, P.V., with A. Hirakawa, trans. 1970. *Shan-Chien-P'i-P'o-Sha, a Chinese Version by Saṅghabhadra of Samantapāsādikā*. Poona: Bhandarkar Oriental Research Institute.

Bareau, André. 1963. *Recherches sur la biographie du Bouddha dans les Sutrapitaka et les Vinayapitaka anciens.* Paris: École française d'extrême-Orient.
Baroni, Victor. 1943. *La contre-réforme devant la Bible: La question biblique.* Lausanne: Éditions la Concorde.
Barrows, John Henry. 1893. *The World's Parliament of Religions.* 2 vols. Chicago: Parliament.
Batchelor, Stephen, trans. 1979. *A Guide to the Bodhisattva's Way of Life by Shantideva.* Dharamsala: Library of Tibetan Works and Archives.
Beal, Samuel, trans. [1884] 1981. *Si Yu Ki: Buddhist Records of the Western World.* Delhi: Motilal Banarsidass.
—[1875] 1985. *The Romantic Legend of Śākya Buddha: A Translation of the Chinese Version of the Abhiniskramanasūtra.* Delhi: Motilal Banarsidass.
Bechert, Heinz, ed. 1991–97. *The Dating of the Historical Buddha/Die Datierung des Historischen Buddha.* 3 vols. Göttingen: Vandenhoeck & Ruprecht.
Bénisti, M. 1986. "Observations concernant le stūpa no. 2 de Sāñcī." *Bulletin d'études indiennes* 4: 165-70.
Bennett, Chester, trans. 1853. "Life of Gaudama: A Translation from the Burmese Book Entitled *Ma-la-len-ga-ra-wottoo.*" *Journal of the American Oriental Society* 3: 1-164.
Bennett, Tony. 1989. "Texts in History: The Determinations of Readings and Their Texts." In *Post-Structuralism and the Question of History*, ed. Derek Attridge, Geoff Bennington, and Robert Young, 63-81. Cambridge: Cambridge University Press.
Benton, John F. 1970. *Self and Society in Medieval France: The Memoirs of Abbot Guibert of Nogent.* New York: Harper & Row.
Bigandet, Paul. 1843. "Principaux points du système bouddhiste." *Annales de philosophie chrétienne* 27. 85-94.
—1866. *The Life or Legend of Gaudama The Budha of the Burmese.* Rangoon: American Mission Press.
—1911. *The Life or Legend of Gaudama The Buddha of the Burmese.* 4th ed. 2 vols. London: Kegan Paul, Trench, Trübner & Co.
Bizot, François. 1988. *Les traditions de la* pabbajja *en Asie de Sud-Est.* Göttingen: Vandenhoeck & Ruprecht.
Blackburn, Anne M. 1996. *The Play of the Teaching in the Life of the Sāsana.* Chicago: University of Chicago Press.
—1997. "Sūtra Sannayas and Saranamkara." *Sri Lanka Journal of the Humanities* 23/1-2: 76-99.
—1999a. "Looking for the *Vinaya*: Monastic Discipline in the Practical Canons of the Theravāda." *Journal of the International Association of Buddhist Studies* 22/2: 281-309.
—1999b. "Magic in the Monastery: Textual Practice and Monastic Identity in Sri Lanka." *History of Religions* 38: 354-72.
—2001. *Buddhist Learning and Textual Practice in Eighteenth-Century Monastic Culture.* Princeton, NJ: Princeton University Press.
Blenkinsopp, J. 1989. "The Literary Evidence." In V. Tzaferis, *Excavations at Capernaum*, vol. 1, *1978–1982*, 201-11. Winona Lake, IN: Eisenbrauns in association with Pepperdine University.
Bloechl, Jeffrey. 2000. *Liturgy of the Neighbor: Emmanuel Levinas and the Religion of Responsibility.* Pittsburgh, PA: Duquesne University Press.
Bond, George Doherty. 1988. *The Buddhist Revival in Sri Lanka: Religious Tradition, Reinterpretation, and Response.* Columbia, SC: University of South Carolina Press.
Brady, John. 1998. *Asian Classics Input Project.* www.asianclassics.org. Release 4. New York.
Braun, Heinz. 1991. "The Buddhist Era in the Malālaṅkāravatthu." In *The Dating of the Historical Buddha*, vol. 1, ed. Heinz Bechert, 46-48. Göttingen: Vandenhoeck & Ruprecht.

bTsan-lha Nga-dbang Tshulkhrims, ed. 1997. *brDa dkrol gser gyi me long*. Beijing: Mi-rigs dPe-skrun-khang.
Buddhaghosa. 1920. *Sumangalavilāsinī*. Bangkok: Mahāmakutarājavidyalayena Press.
—1976. *The Path of Purification*, trans. Bhikkhu Ñyā namoli. 2 vols. Berkeley, CA: Shambhala.
Bühler, G. 1894. "Votive Inscriptions from the Sānchi Stūpas." *Epigraphia Indica* 2: 87-116.
Bukkyō Kakushū Kyōkai, ed. 1896. *Bukkyō kakushū kōyō*. 5 vols. Kyoto: Kaiba Shoin.
Burgess, James. 1883. *Report on the Buddhist Cave Temples and Their Inscriptions*. Archaeological Survey of Western India, vol. 4. London: Trübner & Co.
Burghart, Richard. 1990. "Ethnographers and Their Local Counterparts in India." In *Localizing Strategies: Regional Traditions of Ethnographic Writing*, ed. Richard Fardon, 260-74. Washington, DC: Smithsonian Institution Press.
Buswell, Robert, ed. 1990. *Chinese Buddhist Apocrypha*. Honolulu: University of Hawai'i Press.
Calvin, John. 1843. *Institutes of the Christian Religion by John Calvin*, ed. J. Allen, vol. 2. 4th ed. Philadelphia: Presbyterian Board of Publication.
—1844. "An Admonition, Showing the Advantages which Christendom might Derive from an Inventory of Relics." In *Tracts Relating to the Reformation by John Calvin*, trans. H. Beveridge, 289-341. Edinburgh: T. & T. Clark.
—1954. *Calvin: Theological Treatises*, ed. J. K. S. Reid, Library of Christian Classics, vol. 22. Philadelphia: Westminster Press.
Campbell, June. 1996. *Traveller in Space: In Search of Female Identity in Tibetan Buddhism*. London: Athlone.
Canon, Katie G. 1988. *Black Womanist Ethics*. Atlanta, GA: Scholars Press.
Carrithers, Michael. 1983. *The Buddha*. New York: Oxford University Press.
Carter, John Ross, and Mahina Palihawadana, trans. 1987. *The Dhammapada: A New English Translation with the Pāli Text, and the First English Translation of the Commentary's Explanation of the Verses with Notes*. New York: Oxford University Press.
Carus, Paul. 1890. *The Soul of Man*. Chicago: Open Court.
—1893. "Science as a Religious Revelation." In Barrows 1893, 978-81.
—1894. "Karma and Nirvāna: Are the Buddhist Doctrines Nihilistic?" *The Monist* 4: 417-39.
—1895a. "Buddhism and Christianity." *The Monist* 5: 65-103.
—1895b. "A Japanese Translation of the 'Gospel of Buddha.'" *Open Court* 9: 4404-4405.
—1897. *Buddhism and Its Christian Critics*. Chicago: Open Court.
—1898. *The Gospel of Buddha*. Chicago: Open Court.
—[1917] 1973. *The Gospel of Buddha*. LaSalle: Open Court.
Chakrabarti, Dilip K. 1988. *A History of Indian Archeology: From the Beginning to 1947*. New Delhi: Munshiram Manoharlal Publishers.
Chakrabarty, Dipesh. 2000. *Provincializing Europe: Postcolonial Thought and Historical Difference*. Princeton, NJ: Princeton University Press.
Chandler, David. 1982. "Songs at the Edge of the Forest: Perceptions of Order in Three Cambodian Texts." In *Moral Order and the Question of Change: Essays on Southeast Asian Thought*, ed. D. K. Wyatt and A. Woodside. Southeast Asian Studies Monograph Series, no. 24, 53-77. New Haven: Yale University Press.
—1984. "Normative Poems (*Chbap*) and Pre-Colonial Cambodian Society." *Journal of Southeast Asian Studies* 15/2: 271-79.
Chang Chung-yuan. 1971. *Original Teachings of Chan Buddhism: Selected from the Transmission of the Lamp*. New York: Random House.
Chappell, David. 1980. "Early Forebodings of the Death of Buddhism." *Numen* 27/1: 122-54.
Ch'en, Kenneth. 1964. *Buddhism in China: A Historical Survey*. Princeton, NJ: Princeton University Press.

—1973. *The Chinese Transformation of Buddhism.* Princeton, NJ: Princeton University Press.
Chen Yinke. 1971. *Chen Yinke xiansheng lunji.* Taibei: Zhongyang Yanjiuyuan Lishi Yuyan Yanjiusuo.
Cleary, Thomas, trans. 1993. *The Flower Ornament Scripture.* Boston, MA: Shambhala.
Clifford, James. 1980. Review of *Orientalism*, by Edward Said. *History and Theory* 19: 204-223.
—1997. *Routes: Travel and Translation in the Late Twentieth Century.* Cambridge, MA: Harvard University Press.
Coedès, George. 1968. *Mélanges d'Indianisme a la mémoire de Louis Renou.* Paris: Institut de Civilisation indienne.
Collins, Steve. 1990. "On the Very Idea of the Pāli Canon." *Journal of the Pali Text Society* 15: 86-126.
—1993. "The Discourse on What Is Primary (*Aggañña Sutta*)." *Journal of Indian Philosophy* 21/4: 301-393.
—1998. *Nirvana and Other Buddhist Felicities.* Cambridge: Cambridge University Press.
Concerned Buddhists. 1893. "Bankoku shūkyō taikai ni tsuite Bukkyō yūshika no kokuhaku." *Shūkyō* 5 April: 294-99.
Conze, Edward. 1967. "Recent Progress in Buddhist Studies." In Conze, *Thirty Years of Buddhist Studies*, 1-32. Oxford: Bruno Cassirer.
Coomaraswamy, Ananda. 1977. "Saṃvega: Aesthetic Shock." In *Coomaraswamy: Selected Papers*, ed. Roger Lipsey, 179-85. Princeton, NJ: Princeton University Press.
Cowell, E. B., ed. 1886. *The Divyāvadāna.* Cambridge: Cambridge University Press.
Cunningham, A. 1854. *The Bhilsa Topes: Or, Buddhist Monuments of Central India.* London: Smith, Elder.
Daniel, Glyn. 1981. *A Short History of Archaeology.* London: Thames & Hudson.
Darlington, Susan M. 1990. "Buddhism, Morality, and Change: The Local Response to Development in Northern Thailand." PhD dissertation, University of Michigan.
Davidson, Ronald M. 1981. "The Litany of Names of Mañjuśrī." *Mélanges Chinois et Bouddhiques* 20: 1-69.
—1990. "An Introduction to the Standards of Scriptural Authenticity in Indian Buddhism." In Buswell 1990, 291-325.
—1994. "The Eleventh-Century Renaissance in Central Tibet." Paper presented at the University of Virginia, 15-16 April 1994, at the Symposium on Esoteric Buddhism in Tibet (Center for South Asian Studies, University of Virginia).
dBang 'dus. 1983. *Bod gangs can pa'i gso ba rig pa'i dpal ldan rgyud bzhi sogs kyi brda dang dka' gnad 'ga' zhig bkrol ba sngon byon mkhas pa'i gsung rgyun gyu thog dgongs rgyan.* Beijing: Mi-rigs dPe-skrun-khang.
de Jong, J.W. 1975. "The Study of Buddhism: Problems and Perspectives." In *Studies in Indo-Asian Art and Culture*, ed. P. Ratnam, vol. 4, 13-26. New Delhi: International Academy of Indian Culture.
—1987. *A Brief History of Buddhist Studies in Europe and America.* 2nd rev. ed. Delhi: Sri Satguru.
de la Vallée Poussin, Louis. 1911. "Death and Disposal of the Dead (Buddhist)." *Encyclopaedia of Religion and Ethics*, ed. J. Hastings, vol. 4, 446-49. Edinburgh: T. & T. Clark.
de Lubac, Henri. 1952. *La recontre du bouddhisme et de l'occident.* Paris: Aubier.
Delumeau, Jean. 1971. *La Catholicisme entre Luther et Voltaire.* Paris: Presses universitaires de France. (ET = *Catholicism between Luther and Voltaire: A New View of the Counter-Reformation.* Philadelphia: Westminster Press, 1977.)
Deo, Shantaram B. and J. P. Joshi. 1972. *Pauni Excavation (1969-1970).* Nagpur: Nagpur University.
de Silva, K.M. 1965. *Social Policy Missionary Organizations in Ceylon, 1840-1855.* London: Royal Commonwealth Society.

De Silva, Lily. 1970. *Dīgha-Nikāyaṭṭhakathaṭīkā Līnatthavaṇṇana*, vol. 3. London: Pali Text Society.

dGe-'dun 'Grub, Dali Lama I. 1999. *Legs par gsungs pa'i dam pa'i chos 'dul ba mtha' dag gi snying po'i don legs par bshad pa rin po che'i 'phreng ba*. In *'Dul ṭīk rin chen 'phreng ba*. Beijing: Mi-rigs dPe-skrun-khang.

Dharmapala, letter to the Buddhists of Japan, March 26, 1907. "Shūkyō kankei zakken." Vol. 1. Gaikō Shiryōkan Doc., no. 3-10-1-8. Tokyō: Gaimūshō Gaikō shiryōkan.

Dharmasēna Thera. 1991. *Jewels of the Doctrine*, trans. Ranjini Obeyesekere. Albany, NY: State University of New York Press.

Diamond, Stanley. 1974. *In Search of the Primitive: A Critique of Civilization*. New Brunswick, NJ: Transaction.

Diskalkar, D.B. 1949. "Excavations at Kasrawad." *Indian Historical Quarterly* 25: 1-18.

Don grub rgyal. 1994. *Lang tsho'i rbab chu dang ljags rtsom bdams sgrigs*, ed. Padma 'Bum. Dharamsala: A myes rma chen Bod kyi rig gzhung zhib 'jug khang.

Doniger, Wendy. 1991. *Splitting the Difference: Gender and Myth in Ancient Greece and India*. Chicago: University of Chicago.

Dorje, Gyurme, and Matthew Kapstein, ed. 1991. *The Nyingma School of Tibetan Buddhism: Its Fundamentals and History*, vol. 2. Boston, MA: Wisdom Publications.

Dornish, Margaret H. 1969. "Joshu's Bridge: D. T. Suzuki's Message and Mission, 1897–1927." PhD dissertation, Claremont Graduate School.

Dor-zhi gDong-drug sNyems-blo, ed. 1991. *gSang chen thabs lam nyer mkho rnal 'byor snying nor*. Beijing: Mi-rigs dPe-skrun-khang.

Dreyfus, George. 1994. "Proto-nationalism in Tibet." In *Tibetan Studies*, ed. Per Kvaerne, vol. 1, 205-18. Oslo: Institute for Comparative Research in Human Culture.

Duara, Prasenjit. 1995. *Rescuing History from the Nation: Questioning Narratives of Modern China*. Chicago: University of Chicago Press.

—2001. "The Discourse of Civilization and Pan-Asianism." *Journal of World History* 12/1: 99-130.

Dudjom Rinpoche, Jikdrel Yeshe Dorje. 1991. *The Nyingma School of Tibetan Buddhism: Its Fundamentals and History*. 2 vols. Annotated translation by Gyurme Dorje and Matthew Kapstein. Boston, MA: Wisdom Publications.

Dummett, Michael. 1978. *Truth and Other Enigmas*. Cambridge, MA: Harvard University Press.

Dumoulin, Heinrich. 1988. *Zen Buddhism: A History*. New York: Macmillan.

Durt, H. 1985. "Étienne Lamotte, 1903–1983." *Bulletin de l'École Française d'Extrême-Orient* 74: 1-28.

Dymond, D.P. 1974. *Archaeology and History: A Plea for Reconciliation*. London: Thames & Hudson.

Ebrey, Patricia B. 1978. *The Aristocratic Families of Early Imperial China*. Cambridge: Cambridge University Press.

Eckel, M. David. 1994. *To See The Buddha: A Philosopher's Quest for the Meaning of Emptiness*. Princeton, NJ: Princeton University Press.

Edwardes, Michael. 1959. *A Life of the Buddha from a Burmese Manuscript*. London: Folio Society.

Eire, Carlos M. N. 1986. *War Against the Idols: The Reformation of Worship from Erasmus to Calvin*. Cambridge: Cambridge University Press.

Eitel, E. J. 1888. *Handbook of Chinese Buddhism*. Amsterdam: Trübner.

Eliade, Mircea. 1959. *The Sacred and the Profane: The Nature of Religion*. San Diego, CA: Harcourt Brace Jovanovich.

Emoto Ryūzō. 1884. *Kitabatake Dōryū Shi Indo kikō*. Tokyo: Emoto Ryūzō.

Erasmus, Desiderius. 1979. *Ten Colloquies*, trans. Craig R. Thompson. Indianapolis: Bobbs-Merrill.

Eskildsen, Robert. 2002. "Of Civilization and Savages: The Mimetic Imperialism of Japan's 1874 Expedition to Taiwan." *American Historical Review* 107/2: 388-418.

Fader, Larry A. 1982. "Zen in the West: Historical and Philosophical Implications of the 1893 Parliament of Religions." *Eastern Buddhist* 15: 122-45.
Falk, Nancy Auer. 1989. "The Case of the Vanishing Nun: The Fruits of Ambivalence in Ancient Indian Buddhism." In *Unspoken Worlds: Women's Religious Lives*, ed. Nancy Auer Falk and Rita M. Gross, 207-24. Belmont, CA: Wadsworth.
Faure, Bernard. 1996. *Visions of Power: Imagining Medieval Japanese Buddhism.* Princeton, NJ: Princeton University Press.
Fausbøll, V. 1875. *The Jātakas.* London: Trübner.
Fausto-Sterling, Anne. 2000. *Sexing the Body: Gender Politics and the Construction of Sexuality.* New York: Basic Books.
Feer, Léon, ed. 1884–1904. *The Saṃyuttanikāya of the Suttapiṭaka*, vol. 2. London: H. Frowde.
—1891. *Choix de lettres d'Eugène Burnouf consérves a la Bibliotheque Nationale.* Paris: H. Campion.
Fernando, P. E. E. 1985. "A Note on Three Old Sinhalese Palm-Leaf Manuscripts." *Sri Lanka Journal of the Humanities* 8: 146-57.
Filliozat, Jean. 1953. *L'Inde classique: Manuel des Études Indiennes.* 2 vols. Paris: École française d'extrême-Orient.
Forest, Alain. 1992. *Le culte des genies protecteurs au Cambodge: Analyse et traduction d'un corpus de texts sur les neak ta* (*The Cult of Protector Spirits in Cambodia: Analysis and Translation of a Group of Texts on Neak Ta*). Paris: Editions L'Harmattan.
Forte, Antonino. 1976. *Political Propaganda and Ideology in China at the End of the Seventh Century.* Naples: Instituto Universitario Orientale.
—1990. "The Relativity of the Concept of Orthodoxy in Chinese Buddhism: Chih-seng's Indictment of Shih-li and the Proscription of the *Dharma Mirror Sūtra.*" In Buswell 1990, 239-50.
Foucault, Michel. 1994. "Polemics, Politics, and Problematizations: An Interview with Michel Foucault." In *Ethics: Subjectivity and Truth*, 111-19. New York: New Press.
Foucaux, Philippe E. 1860. *Histoire du Bouddha Sakya Mouni.* Paris: Benjamin Duprat.
—1884. *Le Lalitavistara: Développement des jeux, contenant l'histoire du Bouddha Çakya-muni, depuis sa naissance jusqu'à sa predication*, vol. 1. Paris: E. Leroux.
Foucher, A. 1949. *La vie de Bouddha.* Paris: Editions Payot.
—1963. *The Life of the Buddha according to the Ancient Texts and Monuments of India*, trans. S.B. Boas. Middletown, CT: Wesleyan University Press.
Foulk, Theodore G. 1987. "The 'Ch'an School' and its Place in the Buddhist Monastic Tradition." PhD dissertation, University of Michigan.
Frankfurter, O. 1883. *Handbook of Pāli.* London and Edinburgh: Williams & Norgate.
Frauwallner, Erich. 1956. *The Earliest Vinaya and the Beginnings of Literature.* Rome: Istituto Italiano per il Medio ed Estremo Oriente.
Fremantle, W. H., trans. 1983. *The Principal Works of St. Jerome.* Select Library of Nicene and Post-Nicene Fathers of the Christian Church, Set 2, Vol. 4. Grand Rapids, MI: Eerdmans.
Frost, Mark. 2002. "'Wider Opportunities': Religious Revival, Nationalist Awakening and the Global Dimension in Colombo, 1870–1920." *Modern Asian Studies* 36/4: 937-68.
Furuta, Shokin. 1967. "Shaku Sōen: The Footsteps of a Modern Japanese Zen Master," trans. Kudo Sumiko. *Philosophical Studies of Japan* 8: 67-91.
Fussman, Gérard. 1969. "Une inscription Kharoṣṭhī à Haḍḍa." *Bulletin de l'École française d'Extrême-Orient* 56: 5-9.
—1980. Review of *Epigraphical Hybrid Sanskrit*, by Th. Damsteegt. *Journal asiatique* 268: 423-24.
—1989. "Gāndhārī écrite, gāndhārī parlée." In *Dialectes dans les littératures indo-aryennes*, ed. C. Caillat, 433-501. Paris: Collège de France.
Gadamer, Hans G. 1975. *Truth and Method.* New York: Seabury.

Geertz, Clifford. 1973. "Thick Description: Toward an Interpretive Theory of Culture." In *The Interpretation of Cultures*, 3-32. New York: Basic Books.

Geiger, Wilhelm, ed. 1908. *Mahāvaṃsa.* London: H. Frowde for the Pali Text Society.

George, Alexander, and Daniel J. Velleman. 2002. *Philosophies of Mathematics.* Oxford: Blackwell.

Germano, David. 1994. "Architecture and Absence in the Secret Tantric History of rDzogs Chen." *Journal of the International Association of Buddhist Studies* 17/2: 203-335.

—1998. "Re-membering the Dismembered Body of Tibet: Contemporary Tibetan Visionary Movements in the People's Republic of China." In Goldstein and Kapstein 1998, 53-94.

—Forthcoming. *Mysticism and Rhetoric in the Great Perfection: The Transformation of Buddhist Tantra in Ancient Tibet.* Monograph in progress.

Gernet, Jacques. 1956. *Les aspects économiques du bouddhisme dans la société chinoise du Ve aux Xe siècle.* Paris: École française de l'éxtrême orient.

Ghosh, A. 1979. "The Early Phase of the Stupa at Amaravati, Southeast India." *Ancient Ceylon* 3: 97-103.

gNubs-chen Sangs-rgyas Ye-shes. 1987. *Sangs rgyas thams cad kyi dgongs pa 'dus pa'i mdo'i dka' 'grel mun pa'i go cha lde mig gsal byed rnal 'byor nyi ma.* In *Rñiṅ ma bka' ma rgyas pa*, ed. H. H. Bdud-'joms Rin-po-che. 58 vols. Darjeeling: Dupjung Lama.

Gokhale, S. 1985. "The Memorial Stūpa Gallery at Kanheri." In *Indian Epigraphy: Its Bearing on the History of Art*, ed. F. M. Asher and G. S. Gai, 55-59. New Delhi: Oxford & IBH.

Goldstein, Melvin C., and Matthew T. Kapstein, ed. 1998. *Buddhism in Contemporary Tibet: Religion and Cultural Identity.* Berkeley, CA: University of California Press.

Gombrich, Richard F. [1971] 1991. *Buddhist Precept and Practice: Traditional Buddhism in the Rural Highlands of Ceylon.* Delhi: Motilal Banarsidass.

—1971. *Precept and Practice: Traditional Buddhism in the Rural Highlands of Ceylon.* Oxford: Clarendon.

—1986. Review of *The Genesis of an Orientalist*, by L. Ananda Wickremeratne. *The Indian Economic and Social History Review* 23: 121-22.

—1988. *Theravada Buddhism.* London: Routledge.

Gombrich, Richard F., and Gananath Obeyesekere. 1988. *Buddhism Transformed: Religious Change in Sri Lanka.* Princeton, NJ: Princeton University Press.

Gomez, L.O. 1987. "Buddhism in India." *Encyclopedia of Religion*, ed. M. Eliade, vol. 3, 351-85. New York: Macmillan.

Goodman, Grant Kohn. 1993. "Dharmapala in Japan." *Japan Forum* 5/2: 195-202.

Granoff, Phyllis, and Koichi Shinohara. 1988. *Monks and Magicians: Religious Biographies in Asia.* Oakville, ON: Mosaic.

Grenet, Frantz. 1984. *Les pratiques funéraires de l'asie centrale sédentaire de la conquête grecque à l'islamisation.* Paris: Editions de Centre national de la recherche scientifique.

Gross, Rita M. 1993. *Buddhism after Patriarchy: A Feminist History, Analysis, and Reconstruction of Buddhism.* Albany, NY: State University of New York Press.

Gunawardana, Ranavira. 1979. *Robe and Plough: Monasticism and Economic Interest in Sri Lanka.* Tucson: University of Arizona Press.

Guth, Klaus. 1970. *Guibert von Nogent und die hochmittelalterliche Kritik an der Reliquienverehrung.* Augsburg: Verlag Winfried-Werk in Kommissionverlag.

Gutmann, Joseph. 1961. "The 'Second Commandment' and the Image in Judaism." *Hebrew Union College Annual* 32: 161-74.

—1977. "Deuteronomy: Religious Reformation or Iconoclastic Revolution?" In *The Image and the Word: Confrontations in Judaism, Christianity and Islam*, ed. J. Gutmann, 5-25. Missoula, MT: Scholars Press for the American Academy of Religion.

Gyatso, Janet. 1986. "Signs, Memory and History: A Tantric Buddhist Theory of Scriptural Transmission." *Journal of the International Association of Buddhist Studies* 9/2: 7-35.

—1987. "Down with the Demoness: Reflections on the Feminine Ground in Tibet." *Tibet Journal* 12/4: 38-53.

—1993. "The Logic of Legitimation in the Tibetan Treasure Tradition." *History of Religions* 33/2: 97-134.

—1996. "Drawn from the Tibetan Literature, the *gTer Ma* Literature." In *Tibetan Literature*, ed. José Cabezón and Roger Jackson, 147-69. Ithaca, NY: Snow Lion.

—2005. "Sex." In *Critical Terms for the Study of Buddhism*, ed. Donald Lopez, 271-90. Chicago: University of Chicago Press.

gYu-thog Yon-tan mGon-po. 1976. *Gyu thog cha lag bco brgyad: A Corpus of Tibetan Medical Teachings Attributed to Gyu-thog the Physician.* 2 vols. Delhi: Topden Tshering.

Halbfass, Wilhelm. 1988. *India and Europe: An Essay in Understanding.* Albany, NY: State University of New York Press.

Hallisey, Charles. 1995. "Roads Taken and Not Taken in the Study of Theravāda Buddhism." In *Curators of the Buddha: The Study of Buddhism Under Colonialism*, ed. Donald S. Lopez Jr, 31-61. Chicago: University of Chicago Press.

—2005. "Buddhist Ethics: Trajectories." In *The Blackwell Companion to Religious Ethics*, ed. William Schweiker, 312-22. Oxford: Blackwell.

Hallisey, Charles, and Anne Hansen. 1996. "Narrative, Sub-ethics, and the Moral Life: Some Evidence from Theravāda Buddhism." *Journal of Religious Ethics* 24/2: 305-27.

Hanna, Span. 1994. "Vast as the Sky: The Terma Tradition in Modern Tibet." In *Tantra and Popular Religion in Tibet*, ed. Geoffrey Samuel, 1-13. New Delhi: International Academy of Indian Culture and Aditya Prakashan.

Hansen, Anne. 1988. "Crossing the River: Secularization of Khmer Childbirth Rituals." MDiv thesis, Harvard Divinity School.

Hardy, Friedhelm. 1983. *Viraha-Bhakti.* Delhi: Oxford University Press.

Hardy, Robert Spence. 1850. *Eastern Monachism.* London: Partridge & Oakey.

—1860. *A Manual of Modern Buddhism.* London: Williams & Norgate.

—1880. *A Manual of Buddhism in Its Modern Development.* 2nd ed. London: Williams & Norgate.

Hashizume Kanshū. 1969. "Mappō shisō ni kansuru yuin." *Indōgaku bukkyōgaku kenkyu* 17/2: 134-35.

Hatcher, Brian. 1992. "Yatna-Dharma: The Religious Worldview of Pandit Isvaracandra Vidyasagar." PhD dissertation, Harvard University.

Herdt, Gilbert, ed. 1993. *Third Sex, Third Gender: Beyond Sexual Dimorphism in Culture and History.* New York: Zone Books.

Hiermann, Anne. 2001. "Chinese Nuns and Their Ordination in the Fifth Century." *Journal of the International Association of Buddhist Studies* 24/2: 275-304.

Higashimoto Tarō. 1944. "Gunaratna Shaku Kōzen Wajō den." *Kaigai Bukkyō jijō* 10/3: 1-11.

Hinüber, Oskar von. 1977. "Zur Geschichte des Sprachnamens Pāli." In *Beiträge zur Indienforschung: Ernst Waldschmidt zum 80. Geburtstag gewidment*, 237-46. Berlin: Museums für Indische Kunst.

—1978. "On the Tradition of Pāli Texts in India, Ceylon, and Burma." In *Buddhism in Ceylon and Studies on Religious Syncretism in Buddhist Countries*, ed. H. Bechert. 48-57. Abhandlungen der Akademie der Wissenschaften in Göttingen, Phil.-Hist. Klasse. Dritte Folge. Nr. 108. Göttingen: Vandenhoeck & Ruprecht.

—1983a. "Die älteste Literatursprache des Buddhismus." *Saeculum* 34: 1-9.

—1983b. "Notes on the Pāli Tradition in Burma." *Nackrichten der Akademie der Wissenschaften in Göttingen*, I. Phil.-Hist. Klasse Jg. 3: 67-79.

—1983c. "Pali Manuscripts of Canonical Texts from North Thailand—A Preliminary Report." *Journal of the Siam Society* 71: 75-88.

—1985. "Two Jātaka Manuscripts from the National Library in Bangkok." *Journal of the Pali Text Society* 10: 1-22.
—1987a. "The Oldest Dated Manuscript of the Milindapañha." *Journal of the Pali Text Society* 11: 111-19.
—1987b. "The Pāli Manuscripts Kept at the Siam Society, Bangkok. A Short Catalogue." *Journal of the Siam Society* 75: 9-74.
Hirai, Kinzō. 1893. "Religious Thought in Japan." *Arena* 7: 257-67.
Hirakawa, Akira. 1982. *Monastic Discipline for the Buddhist Nuns: An English Translation of the Chinese Text of the Mahāsāṃghika-Bhikṣuṇī-Vinaya.* Patna: K. P. Jayaswal Research Institute.
Hiraoka Takeo. 1947. *Keisho no seiritsu.* Osaka: Zenkoku.
Holt, John. 1991. "Protestant Buddhism?" *Religious Studies Review* 17/4: 307-11.
Honda Shigeyuki. 1947. *Shina keigaku shiron.* Kyoto: Kōbundō.
Hopkins, Steven. 1994. "Vedāntadeśika: The Bell of Tirupati: Hymns of a Śrīnaisnava Philosopher and Poet." PhD dissertation, Harvard University.
Hori Kentoku. 1970. *Kaisetsu saikiki.* Tokyo: Kokusho kankōkai.
Horiguchi Ryōichi. 1995. "Léon de Rosny et les premières missions Bouddhiques Japonaises en Occident." *Cipango* 4: 121-39.
Horner, I.B. 1930. *Women under Primitive Buddhism.* London: G. Routledge & Sons.
—trans. 1938–66. *The Book of the Discipline* [*Vinaya-Piṭaka*]. 6 vols. London: Pali Text Society.
—1940. "The Pattern of the Nissaggiyas." *Indian Historical Quarterly* 16: 268-91.
—trans. 1963–64. *Milinda's Questions.* 2 vols. Oxford: Pali Text Society.
Horner, I.B., and B.C. Law, trans. 1975. *Buddhavaṃsa, Chronicle of the Buddhas and Cariyāpiṭaka, Basket of Conduct.* London: Pali Text Society.
Houghton, P.W.R., ed. 1894. *Neely's History of the Parliament of Religions and Religious Congresses at the World's Columbian Exposition.* Chicago: F. Tennyson Neely.
Houtman, Gustaaf. 1990. "Traditions of Buddhist Practice in Burma." PhD dissertation, University of London.
Hubbard, James B. 1986. "Salvation in the Final Period of the Dharma: The Inexhaustible Storehouse of the San-chieh-chiao." PhD dissertation, University of Wisconsin.
Huber, Toni. 1994. "Putting the *gnas* Back into *gnas-skor:* Rethinking Tibetan Buddhist Pilgrimage Practice." *Tibet Journal* 19/2-3: 23-60.
Hurvitz, Leon, trans. 1976. *Scripture of the Lotus Blossom of the Fine Dharma.* New York: Columbia University Press.
Hutterer, Karl L. 1992. Epilogue to *Southeast Asia Studies in the Balance: Reflections from America,* ed. Charles Hirschman, Charles F. Keyes, and Karl Hutterer, 135-44. Ann Arbor, MI: Association for Asian Studies.
Imam, A. 1966. *Sir Alexander Cunningham and the Beginnings of Indian Archaeology.* Dacca: Asiatic Society of Pakistan.
Ind, Ukñā Suttantaprījā. [1921] 1971. *Gatilok* (Ways of the world). 13th ed. Vols. 1–10. Phnom Penh: Institut Bouddhique.
Inden, Ronald. 1990. *Imagining India.* Oxford: Blackwell.
—2000. Introduction to *Querying the Medieval,* ed. Ronald Inden, Daud Ali and Jonathan S. Walters, 3-28. Oxford and New York: Oxford University Press.
Inoue Enryō. 1887. *Bukkyō katsuron joron.* Tokyo: Tetsugaku Shoin.
Inoue Tetsujirō 1897. *Shaka shuzoku ron.* Tokyo: Tetsugaku Shoin. Reprinted in Meiji bunka kenkyūkai, 1954.
Inoue Zenjō. 2000. *Shaku Sōen den.* Kyoto: Zenbunka Kenkyūsho.
—2001. *Shinyaku Shaku Sōen "Seiyū nikki."* Tokyo: Daihōrinkaku.
Institut Bouddhique. 1969. *Petits ouvrages cambodgiens (Short Khmer Literary Works).* Phnom Penh: Institut Bouddhique.

Irigaray, Luce. 1991. "Sexual Difference." In *The Irigaray Reader*, ed. Margaret Whitford, 165-77. Oxford: Blackwell.

Ishii Kōsei. 2002. "Thoughts and Genealogy of Ultranationalists Strongly Influenced by Buddhist Philosophy: With Special Reference to the Exchange of Japanese Nationalists and Ceylonese Buddhists." Paper presented at the American Academy of Religion, Toronto, 25 November.

Itō Hiromi. 1974. *Unshō/Kōzen ibokushū*. Tokyo: Bunka Shobō Hakubunsha.

Izumi Hōkei. 1933. "Meiji jidai ni okeru toin no Bukkyōto." *Gendai Bukkyō* 105: 163.

Jackson, Carl T. 1968. "The Meeting of East and West: The Case of Paul Carus." *Journal of the History of Ideas* 29: 73-92.

Jackson, David. 1994. *Enlightenment by a Single Means: Tibetan Controversies on the "Self-Sufficient White Remedy" (dkar po chig thub)*. Vienna: Der Östrerreichischen Akademie der Wissenschaften.

Jacob, Judith. 1996. *The Traditional Literature of Cambodia*. Oxford: Oxford University Press.

Jaffe, Richard M. 2002. "Shakuson o sagashite: Kindai Nihon Bukkyō no tanjō to sekai ryokō." *Shisō* 943: 64-87.

Johnston, E.H., ed. and trans. [1936] 1992. *The Buddhacarita or Acts of the Buddha*. Delhi: Motilal Banarsidass.

Jory, Patrick. 2002. "Thai and Western Buddhist Scholarship in the Age of Colonialism: King Chulalongkorn Redefines the Jatakas." *Journal of Asian Studies* 61/3: 891-918.

Kabilsingh, Chatsumarn. 1984. *A Comparative Study of Bhikkhunī Pāṭimokkha*. Varanasi: Chaukhambha Orientalia.

—1991. *Thai Women in Buddhism*. Berkeley, CA: Parallax.

Kaneko Hidetoshi. 1959. "Sangai-kyō no fuse kan." *Bukkyō shigaku* 7/4: 46-50.

Kant, L.H. 1987. "Jewish Inscriptions in Greek and Latin." In Part 2, *Principat*, vol. 20, v. 2 of *Aufstieg und Niedergang der römischen Welt: Geschichte und Kultur Roms im Spiegel der Neueren Forschung (Rise and Decline of the Roman World)*, ed. W. Haase, 671-713. Berlin: W. de Gruyter.

Kapstein, Matthew. 1989. "The Purification Gem and Its Cleansing: A Late Tibetan Polemical Discussion of Apocryphal Texts." *History of Religions* 28/3: 217-44.

—1992. "Remarks on the *Mani-bka'-'bum* and the Cult of Avalokiteśvara in Tibet." In *Tibetan Buddhism: Reason and Revelation*, ed. R. Davidson and S. Goodman, 79-93. Albany, NY: State University of New York Press.

—1998. "A Pilgrimage of Rebirth Reborn: The 1992 Celebration of the Drigung Powa Chenmo." In *Buddhism in Contemporary Tibet*, ed. Melvyn Goldstein and Matthew Kapstein, 95-119. Berkeley and Los Angeles: University of California Press.

Karmay, Samten. 1979. "The Ordinance of Lha Bla-Ma Ye-Shes-'Od." In *Tibetan Studies in Honor of Hugh Richardson*, ed. Michael Aris and Aung San Suu Kyi, 150-62. Warminster: Aris and Phillips.

—1980. "An Open Letter by Pho-Brang Zhi-Ba-'Od to the Buddhists in Tibet." *Tibet Journal* 5/3: 3-27.

Kashiwahara Yūsen et al., eds. 1999. *Shinshū jinmei jiten*. Kyoto: Hōzōkan.

Ketelaar, James Edward. 1990. *Of Heretics and Martyrs in Meiji Japan: Buddhism and Its Persecution*. Princeton, NJ: Princeton University Press.

—1991. "Strategic Occidentalism: Meiji Buddhists at the World's Parliament of Religions." *Buddhist-Christian Studies* 11: 37-56.

Keyes, Charles F. 1983. "Merit-Transference in the Kammic Theory of Popular Theravāda Buddhism." In *Karma: An Anthropological Inquiry*, ed. Charles F. Keyes and E. Valentine Daniel, 261-86. Berkeley and Los Angeles: University of California Press.

—1989. "Buddhist Politics and Their Revolutionary Origins in Thailand." *International Political Science Review* 10/2: 121-42.

Kimura Kiyotaka. 1978. "Shigon hōzō to sangai-kyō." *Indōgaku bukkyōgaku kenkyū* 27/1: 102.
Kimura Nichiki. 1963. "Daijō kyōten ni arawarete mappō shisō no nijūsō." *Indōgaku bukkyōgaku kenkyū* 11/1: 130-31.
Kinnard, Jacob. 1998. "When Is the Buddha Not the Buddha? The Hindu-Buddhist Battle over Bodh Gayā and Its Buddha Image." *Journal of the American Academy of Religion* 68/4: 817-39.
Kishimoto Hideo, ed. 1956. *Religion*, trans. John F. Howes. *Japanese Thought in the Meiji Era.* Vol. 2. Tokyo: Ōbunsha.
Kitabatake Dōryū Kenshōkai, ed. [1956] 1994. *Gōsō Kitabatake Dōryū.* Tokyo: Daikūsha.
Kitagawa, Joseph M. 1984. *The 1893 World's Parliament of Religions and its Legacy.* Chicago: University of Chicago Divinity School.
Kiyozawa Manshi. [1892] 1955. *The Skeleton of a Philosophy of Religion*, trans. Noguchi Zenshirō. In *Kiyozawa Manshi zenshū*, ed. Akegarasu Haya and Nishimura Kengyō, vol. 2, 45-100. Kyoto: Hōzōkan.
Kokusai Bukkyō Kyōkai, ed. 1945. *Daigokai Nanpō Butsuda matsuri.* Tokyo: Kokusai Bukkyō Kyōkai.
Kolte, V.B. 1969. "Brahmi Inscriptions from Pauni." *Epigraphia Indica* 38: 169-74.
Konow, Sten. 1929. *Kharoshṭhī Inscriptions with the Exception of Those of Aśoka.* Corpus Inscriptionum Indicarum. Vol. 2, Pt. 1. Calcutta: Supt. of Govt. Printing.
Kopf, David. 1992. Review of *Imagining India*, by Ronald Inden. *Journal of the American Oriental Society* 112/4: 674-77.
Kosambi, D.D. 1955. "Dhenukākaṭa." *Journal of the Asian Society of Bombay* 30/2: 50-71.
Krang-dbyi-sun et al., eds. [1993] 1998. *Bod rgya tshig mdzod chen mo.* Beijing: Mi-rigs dPe-skrun-khang.
Kritzer, Robert. 2000. "The Four Ways of Entering the Womb (*garbhāvakrānti*)." *Bukkyō bunka* (Buddhist culture) 10: 1-41.
Kumar, Brajmohan. 1987. *Archaeology of Pataliputra and Nalanda.* Delhi: Ramanand Vidya Bhawan.
Kumoi Shōzen. 1970. "Hometsu shisō no genryū." In *Hokugi bukkyō kenkyū*, ed. Ōchō Enichi, 287-300. Kyoto: Heirakuji.
Kunsang, Eric Pema, trans. 1993. *The Lotus-Born: The Life of Padmasambhava.* Boston, MA: Shambhala.
Kuper, Adam. 1988. *The Invention of Primitive Society.* London and New York: Routledge.
Kuroda Shintō. 1893. *Outlines of the Mahāyāna As Taught by Buddha.* Tokyo: Bukkyō Gakkuwai.
Kusanagi Zengi. 1913. *Shaku Unshō.* 3 vols. Tokyo: Tokukyōkai.
Kvaerne, Per, ed. 1994. *Tibetan Studies: Proceedings of the 6th Seminar of the International Association for Tibetan Studies.* Oslo: Institute for Comparative Research in Human Culture.
LaCapra, Dominick. 1983. *Rethinking Intellectual History: Texts, Contexts, Language.* Ithaca, NY: Cornell University Press.
Lamotte, Étienne. 1947. "La légende du Bouddha." *Revue de l'histoire des religions* 134: 37-71.
—1958. *Histoire du bouddhisme indien: Des origines a l'ère śaka.* Louvain: Universitaire de Louvain.
—1967. *Histoire du bouddhisme indien.* Louvain: Bibliothèque de l'Université, Institut orientaliste.
—1988. *History of Indian Buddhism: From the Origins to the Saka Era*, trans. Sara Webb-Boin. Louvain-la-Neuve: Université catholique de Louvain, Institut orientaliste.
Law, Narendra Nath. 1949. *Sphuṭārthā Abhidharmakośa-vyākhyā of Yaśomitra.* London: Luzac & Co.
Leclère, Adhémard. 1890. *Recherches sur la Législation Cambodgienne.* Paris: Challamel.
—1894. *Recherches sur le Droit Public des Cambodgiens.* Paris: Challamel.
—1895. *Cambodge: Contes et Légendes.* Paris: Librairie Emile Bouillon.

—1897. *Cambodge: Fêtes Civiles et Religieuses.* Paris: Librairie Hachette.
—1899. *Le Bouddhisme au Cambodge.* Paris: E. Leroux.
—1902. *Le Livre de Vesandar, le roi charitable.* Paris: E. Leroux.
—1906. *Livres sacrés.* Paris: E. Leroux.
—1907. *Les crémations et les rites funéraires au Cambodge.* Hanoi: F. H. Schneider.
—1911. *Buddhisme et Brahmanisme: Trois petits livres.* Paris: E. Leroux.
Leoshko, Janice. 2003. *Sacred Traces: British Explorations of Buddhism in South Asia, Histories of Vision.* Aldershot: Ashgate.
Leve, Lauren G. 2002, "Subjects, Selves, and the Politics of Personhood in Theravada Buddhism in Nepal." *Journal of Asian Studies* 61/3: 833-60.
Lī-Thām Teng. 1994. "Qnakniban Khmaer dael mān chmoḥ lpī" (Famous Khmer Writers). *Kambujasuriyā* 48/1: 42-60.
Lingat, R. 1937. "Vinaya et droit laïque: Études sur les conflits de la loi religieuse et de la loi laïque dans l'indochine hinayaniste." *Bulletin de l'École Française d'Extrême-Orient* 37: 415-77.
Longhurst, Albert H. 1938. *The Buddhist Antiquities of Nagarjunakonda, Madras Presidency.* Memoirs of the Archaeological Survey of India, no. 54. Delhi: Manager of Publications.
Lopez, Jr., Donald S. 1995a. *Buddhism in Practice.* Princeton, NJ: Princeton University Press.
—ed. 1995b. *Curators of the Buddha: The Study of Buddhism under Colonialism.* Chicago: University of Chicago Press.
—1998. *Prisoners of Shangri-la: Tibetan Buddhism and the West.* Chicago: University of Chicago Press.
Lüders, Heinrich. 1909. "The Manikiala Inscription." *Journal of the Royal Asiatic Society of Great Britain and Ireland* 20: 645-66.
—1912. *A List of Brahmi Inscriptions from the Earliest Times to about A.D. 400 with the Exception of Those of Aśoka.* Appendix to *Epigraphia Indica* 10. Delhi: Indological Book House.
—ed. 1963. *Bharhut Inscriptions,* rev. and ed. E. Waldschmidt and M. A. Mehendale. Corpus Inscriptionum Indicarum. Vol. 2, Pt. 2. Ootacamund: Government Epigraphist for India.
MacCormack, S. 1990. "Loca Sancta: The Organization of Sacred Topography in Late Antiquity." In *The Blessings of Pilgrimage*, ed. R. Ousterhout, 7-40. Urbana: University of Illinois Press.
MacIntyre, Alasdair. 1981. *After Virtue.* Notre Dame, IN: University of Notre Dame Press.
—1990. *Three Rival Versions of Moral Inquiry—Encyclopedia, Genealogy, Tradition.* Notre Dame, IN: University of Notre Dame Press.
Maejima Shinjī. 1985. *Indogaku no akebono.* Tokyo: Sekai Seiten Kankōkai.
Makita Tairyō. 1976. *Gikyō kenkyū.* Kyoto: Kyōto Daigaku Jinbun Kagaku Kenkyūsho.
Makley, Charlene E. 1994. "Gendered Practices and the Inner Sanctum: The Reconstruction of Tibetan Sacred Space in 'China's Tibet.'" *Tibet Journal* 19/2: 61-94.
Malalasekera, G. P. 1937. *Dictionary of Pāli Proper Names.* London: Pali Text Society.
Malalgoda, Kitsiri. 1976. *Buddhism in Sinhalese Society, 1750-1900: A Study of Religious Revival and Change.* Berkeley, CA: University of California Press.
Maraldo, John C. 1985. "Is There Historical Consciousness Within Ch'an?" *Japanese Journal of Religious Studies* 12: 141-72.
Marshall, Sir John H. 1951. *Taxila: An Illustrated Account of Archaeological Excavations Carried out at Taxila under the Orders of the Government of India between the Years 1913 and 1934*, vol. 1. Cambridge: Cambridge University Press.
Marshall, Sir John H., and Alfred Foucher. 1940. *The Monuments of Sāñchī,* vol. 1. London: Probsthain.
Martin, Daniel. 1996. "The 'Star King' and the Four Children of Penar: Popular Religious Movements of 11th to 12th Century Tibet." *Acta Orientalia Academiae Scientiarum Hung* 49/1-2: 171-95.

Maruyama Takeo. 1976. "Chūgoku ni okeru mappō shisō." In *Hokkekyō shinkō no sho keitai*, ed. Nomura Yōshō, 377-425. Kyoto: Heirakuji.
Matsumoto Masaaki. 1970. *Koten no keisei: Kodai*. Iwanami kōza sekai rekishi, vol. 4, 1-138. Tokyo: Iwanami.
McMullen, David. 1988. *State and Scholars in T'ang China*. Cambridge: Cambridge University Press.
McRae, John R. 1986. *The Northern School and the Formation of Early Ch'an Buddhism*. Honolulu: University of Hawai'i Press.
Meyer, Donald H. 1962. "Paul Carus and the Religion of Science." *American Quarterly* 14: 597-609.
Meyers, Eric M., and James F. Strange. 1981. *Archaeology, Rabbis and Early Christianity*. Nashville, TN: Abingdon.
Mi-bskyod rDo-rje. 1973. *'Dul ba ñi ma'i dkyil 'khor: A Detailed Commentary on the Vinayasutra and Buddhist Monastic Discipline*. 4 vols. New Delhi: Eighth Khams sprul Don-brgyud-ñi-ma.
Michihata Ryōshū. 1934. "Dōshaku zenshi to Sangai-kyō." *Ōtani gakuhō* 15/1: 24-49.
—1944. *Chūgoku bukkyō shi*. Kyoto: Hōzōkan.
Mitra, Debala. 1971. *Buddhist Monuments*. Calcutta: Sahitya Samsad.
Mitter, Partha. 1977. *Much Maligned Monsters: History of European Reactions to Indian Art*. Oxford: Clarendon.
Monier-Williams, Sir Monier. 1956. *A Sanskrit English Dictionary*. New ed. London: Oxford University Press.
Mori Ryūkichi, ed. 1983. *Shinshū kyōdan no kindaika*. Shinshū shiryō shūsei, vol. 12. Kyoto: Dōhō Sha.
Morris, Richard, ed. 1882. *The Buddhavaṃsa and the Cariyā-Piṭaka*. London: Pali Text Society.
mTsho-sna-ba Shes-rab bZang-po. [1993] 1998. *'Dul ṭik nyi ma'i 'od zer legs bshad lung gi rgya mtsho*. Beijing: Khrun-go'i Bod-kyis Shes-rig dPe-skrun-khang.
Müller, E., ed. 1893. *Paramatthadīpanī: Dhammapāla's Commentary on the Therīgāthā*. London: Pali Text Society.
Mumford, Stan. 1989. *Himalayan Dialogue*. Madison: University of Wisconsin Press.
Mus, Paul. 1935. *Barabudur: Esquisse d'une histoire du Bouddhisme fondée sur la critique archéologique des textes*. New York: Arno. (ET = *Barabudur: Sketch of a History of Buddhism Based on Archaeological Criticism of the Texts*. New Delhi: Indira Gandhi National Centre for the Arts, 1998.)
Naik, A.V. 1948. "Inscriptions of the Deccan: An Epigraphical Survey (*circa* 300 B.C.–1300 A.D.)." *Bulletin of the Deccan College Research Institute* 11/9: 1-160.
Nanjō Bun'yū and Maeda E'un. 1905. *Bukkyō seiten*. Tokyo: Sanseidō.
Nattier, Jan. 1991. *Once upon a Future Time: Studies in a Buddhist Prophecy of Decline*. Berkeley, CA: Asian Humanities Press.
—2002. "Gender and Enlightenment: Sexual Transformation in Mahāyāna Sūtras." Unpublished manuscript, University of Indiana.
Nishikawa Henshō and Nagaoka Senshin. 1886. *Tenjiku kōroji shoken*. Tokyo: Aranami Heijirō.
Noguchi Fukudō. 1920. *Shaku Kōzen to Shakuson shōfūkai*. Kanagawa: Sanneji.
Norman, K. R. 1984. "The Value of the Pali Tradition." In *Jagajjyoti Buddha Jayanti Annual*. 1-9. Calcutta : Bauddha Dharmankur Sabha.
—trans. 1994. *The Group of Discourses (Sutta-nipāta)*, with alternative translations by I. B. Horner and Walpola Rahula, vol. 1. London: Pali Text Society.
Nussbaum, Martha C. 1990. *Love's Knowledge: Essays on Philosophy and Literature*. New York: Oxford University Press.
Nyanatiloka, Bhikkhu. 1972. *Buddhist Dictionary: Manual of Buddhist Terms and Doctrines*. Colombo: Frewin.
Nyang Nyi-ma-'od-zer. 1988. *Chos 'byung me tog snying po sbrang rtsi'i bcud*. Gangs can rig mdzod 5. Lhasa: Bod ljongs bod yig dpe rnying dpe skrun khang.

Obeyesekere, Gananath. 1972. "Religious Symbolism and Political Change in Ceylon." In Smith 1972, 58-78.

—1991. "Buddhism and Conscience." *Daedalus* 120/3: 219-39.

—1997. "Taking the Myth Seriously: The Buddha and the Enlightenment." In *Studies in Honor of Heinz Bechert*, ed. P. Kieffer-Pülz and J. U. Hartmann, 473-82. Swisstal-Odendorf: Indica et Tibetica Verlag.

Obeyesekere, Ranjini. 1991. Introduction to *Jewels of the Doctrine*, trans. Ranjini Obeyesekere, ix-xxviii. Albany, NY: State University of New York Press.

—2001. *Portraits of Buddhist Women.* Albany, NY: State University of New York Press.

Ōchō Enichi. 1958. *Chūgoku bukkyō no kenkyū*, vol. 1. Kyoto: Hōzōkan.

Ōda Tokunō. 1891. *Shamu Bukkyō jijō.* Tokyo: Shinshu Hōwa Shūppan.

Oldenberg, Hermann, ed. and trans. 1879. *The Dīpavaṃsa: An Ancient Buddhist Historical Record.* London: Williams & Norgate.

—1882. *Buddha: His Life, His Doctrine, His Order*, trans. W. Hoey. London: Williams & Norgate.

Oldenberg, Hermann, and Richard Pischel, ed. 1883. *The Thera-and Therī-gāthā.* London: Pali Text Society.

Ōtani Shōshin. 1938. "Sangai bōzenshi gyōjō shimatsu ni tsuite." In *Shigaku ronsō.* Keijō Teikoku Daigaku Bungakkai Ronsan, vol. 7, 247-302. Tokyo: Iwanami.

Ots, Thomas. 1994. "The Silenced Body—the Expressive *Leib:* On the Dialectic of Mind and Life in Chinese Cathartic Healing." In *Embodiment and Experience*, ed. Thomas J. Csordas, 116-38. Cambridge: Cambridge University Press.

Ozeray, Michel-Jean-François. 1817. *Recherches sur Buddou ou Bouddou, Instituteur religieux de l'Asie orientale.* Paris: Brunot-Labbe.

Paranavitana, Senarat. 1970. *Inscriptions of Ceylon*, vol. 1, *Containing Cave Inscriptions from 3rd Century B.C. to 1st Century A.C. and Other Inscriptions in the Early Brahmi Script.* Colombo: State Dept of Archaeology.

Patil, D. R. 1981. *Kusinagara.* New Delhi: Archaeological Survey of India.

Paul, Diana. 1979. *Women in Buddhism.* Berkeley, CA: Asian Humanities Press.

Peiris, W. 1973. *The Western Contribution to Buddhism.* Delhi: Motilal Banarsidass.

Petech, Luciano. 1990. *Central Tibet and the Mongols: The Yüan-Sa skya Period of Tibetan History.* Rome: Istituto Italiano per il Medio ed Estremo Oriente.

Pi Xirui. 1958. *Jingxue lishi.* Beijing: Zhonghua.

Pol-Droit, Roger. 2003. *The Cult of Nothingness*, trans. David Streight and Pamela Vohnson. Chapel Hill, NC: University of North Carolina Press.

Pollock, Sheldon. 1992. Review of *Translating the Orient: The Reception of* Sakuntala *in Nineteenth Century Europe*, by Dorothy Figueira. *Journal of Asian Studies* 51: 419.

—1998. "The Cosmopolitan Vernacular." *Journal of Asian Studies* 57/1: 6-37.

Porée-Maspero, Eveline. 1962. *Étude sur les rites agraires des Cambodgiens* (*Study of the Agrarian Rites of Cambodians*), vol. 1. Paris: Mouton.

Pou, Saveros Lewitz. 1969. "Note sur la translittération du Cambodgien" (Note on the Transliteration of Cambodian). *Bulletin de l'École française d'Extrême-Orient* 55: 163-69.

Pou, Saveros Lewitz, and Philip Jenner. 1981. "Les *cpāp'* ou codes de conduite khmers" (The *cpāp'* or Khmer Codes of Conduct). *Bulletin de l'École française d'Extrême-Orient* 70: 135-93.

Prajñānanda, Yagirala. 1947. *Śrī Sumaṇgala Caritaya dvitīya bhāgaya.* Colombo: Lake House.

Prakash, Satya. 1986. *Coinage in Ancient India: A Numismatic, Archaeochemical and Metallurgical Study of Ancient Indian Coins*, vol. 1. Delhi: Govindram Hasanand.

Pratt, Mary Louise. 1992. *Imperial Eyes: Travel Writing and Transculturation.* New York: Routledge.

Prebish, Charles S. 1975. *Buddhist Monastic Discipline: The Sanskrit Prātimokṣa Sūtras of the Mahāsāṃghikas and Mūlasarvāstivādins.* University Park, PA: Pennsylvania State University Press.

Prothero, Stephen R. 1990. "Henry Steel Olcott (1832–1907) and the Construction of 'Protestant Buddhism.'" PhD dissertation, Harvard University.

—1996. *The White Buddhist: The Asian Odyssey of Henry Steel Olcott.* Bloomington, IN: Indiana University Press.

Pruitt, William. 1992. "The Study of Burmese by Westerners with Special Reference to Burmese *Nissayas.*" *International Journal of Lexicography* 5/4: 278-304.

Przyluski, Jean. 1923. *La légende de l'empereur Açoka.* Paris: P. Geuthner.

Pye, Michael. 1973. "Comparative Hermeneutics in Religion." In *The Cardinal Meaning: Essays in Comparative Hermeneutics, Buddhism and Christianity*, ed. Michael Pye and R. Morgan, 1-58. The Hague: Mouton.

Qi Youzhang, ed. 1974. *Jiazi xin shi jiaoshi.* Taipei: self-published.

Queen, Christopher S., and Sallie B. King. 1996. *Engaged Buddhism: Buddhist Liberation Movements in Asia.* Albany, NY: State University of New York Press.

Rafael, Vincente L. 1999. "Regionalism, Area Studies, and the Accidents of Agency." *American Historical Review* 104/4: 1208-20.

Rahula, Walpola. 1959. *What the Buddha Taught.* Bedford: Gordon Fraser.

Ray, Himanshu P. 1986. *Monastery and Guild: Commerce under the Sātavāhanas.* Delhi: Oxford University Press.

rDo-rje Gling-pa. 1984. *dPal ye shes kyi mgon po ma ning nag po'i gsang ba 'khor lo'i rgyud.* In *dPal ye śes kyi mgon po ma nin nag po'i chos skor.* Thimphu, Bhutan: Druk Sherig Press.

Reed, E. J. 1880. *Japan: Its History, Tradition, and Religions.* London: John Murray.

Reynolds, Craig. 1976. "Buddhist Cosmography in Thai History, with Special Reference to Nineteenth-Century Culture Change." *Journal of Asian Studies* 35: 203-20.

Reynolds, Frank E. 1972. "The Wheels of the Dhamma: A Study of Early Buddhism." In Smith 1972, 6-30.

—1976. "The Many Lives of Buddha: A Study of Sacred Biography and Theravāda Tradition." In *The Biographical Process: Studies in the History and Psychology of Religion*, ed. Frank Reynolds and Donald Capps, 37-66. The Hague: Mouton.

—1992. "Southeast Asian Studies in America: Reflections on the Humanities." In *Southeast Asia Studies in the Balance: Reflections from America*, ed. Charles Hirschman, Charles F. Keyes, and Karl Hutterer, 59-73. Ann Arbor, MI: Association for Asian Studies.

Reynolds, Frank E., and Mani Reynolds. 1982. *Three Worlds according to King Ruang.* Berkeley Buddhist Studies Series. Berkeley, CA: Asian Humanities Press.

(rGyud bzhi) bDud rtsi snying po yan lag brgyad pa gsang ba man ngag gi rgyud. 1992. Lhasa: Bod-ljongs Mi-dmangs dPe-skrun-khang.

Rhys Davids, C. A F., trans. 1922. *The Book of Kindred Sayings (Saṃyuttanikāya) or Grouped Suttas*, vol. 2. Assisted by F. H. Woodword. Translation series, vol. 10. London: Oxford University Press for the Pali Text Society.

—trans. [1929] 1989. *Stories of the Buddha.* New York: Dover.

—1938. "Editorial Note." In *Buddhavaṃsa, The Lineage of the Buddhas, and Cariyāpiṭaka, or The Collection of Ways of Conduct,* trans. Bimala Churn Law, v-vi. London: Humphrey Milford/ Oxford University Press.

Rhys Davids, C. A. F., and K. R. Norman, trans. 1981. *Poems of Early Buddhist Nuns [Therīgāthā].* Oxford: Pali Text Society.

Rhys Davids, T. W. 1877. *Buddhism.* London: Society for Promoting Christian Knowledge (SPCK).

—1882. *Lectures on the Origin and Growth of Religion as Illustrated by Some Points in the History of Indian Buddhism.* New York: G. P. Putnam's Sons.

—1896. *Buddhism: Its History and Literature.* New York: G. P. Putnam's Sons.

—trans. 1900. *Buddhist Suttas.* Sacred Books of the East, vol. 11. Oxford: Clarendon.

—1903. *Buddhist India.* New York: G. P. Putnam's Sons.

—1910. "Buddha." In *Encyclopaedia Britannica*, 11th ed., vol. 4, 737-42. Cambridge: Cambridge University Press.
—1910. "Buddhism." In *Encyclopaedia Britannica*, 11th ed., vol. 4, 742-49. Cambridge: Cambridge University Press.
—trans. 1925. *Buddhist Birth Stories*. Rev. ed. London: G. Routledge and Sons.
—trans. 1969. *Buddhist Suttas*. New York: Dover.
Rhys Davids, T. W., and J. Estlin Carpenter, eds. [1890] 1949. *Dīgha Nikāya*, vols. 1 and 3. London: Luzac.
Rhys Davids, T. W., and William Stede. 1986. *Pali-English Dictionary*. London: Pali Text Society.
Rice, Stanley. 1924. *Ancient Indian Fables and Stories: Being a Selection from the Panchatantra*. London: John Murray.
Richards, Glyn. 1985. *A Source-Book of Modern Hinduism*. London: Curzon.
Ricoeur, Paul. 1988. *Time and Narrative*. 3 vols. Chicago: University of Chicago Press.
Ridding C. M., and L. de la Vallée Poussin. 1917–20. "Bhikṣuṇī-karmavācanā, a Fragment of the Sanskrit Vinaya." *Bulletin of the School of Oriental and African Studies* 1: 131.
Rocher, L. 1978. "Max Müller and the Veda." *Mélanges Armand Abel*, ed. A. Destrée, vol. 3, 221-35. Leiden: Brill.
Roerich, G.N., trans. 1976. *The Blue Annals*. Delhi: Motilal Banarsidass.
Roscoe, Will. 1996. "Priests of the Goddess: Gender Transgression in Ancient Religion." *History of Religion* 35 Feb.: 195-230.
Roth, Gustav. 1970. *Bhikṣuṇī-Vinaya: Manual of Discipline for Buddhist Nuns*. Patna: K. P. Jayaswal Research Institute.
rTse-le sNa-tshogs Rang-grol. 1978. *dPal ye shes kyi mgon po ma ning nag po'i srog dbang bka' gtad zab mo'i las rim*. In *'Ja' tshon pod drug gi dban dpe*, by rTse-le sNa-tshogs Ran-grol and Nag-dban mthar-phyin. Leh: Tobdan Tsering.
Ruegg, D. Seyfort. 1984. "Problems in the Transmission of Vajrayāna Buddhism in the Western Himalaya about the Year 1000." *Acta Indologica* 6: 369-81.
Sa-chen Kun-dga' sNying-po. 1983. *Lam 'bras gzhung bshad sras don ma*. In *Lam 'bras slob bsad: The Sa-skya-pa Teachings of the Path and the Fruit, according to the Tshar-pa Transmission*. Dehra Dun: Sakya Center.
Sahas, Daniel J. 1986. *Icon and Logos: Sources in Eighth-Century Iconoclasm: An Annotated Translation of the Sixth Session of the Seventh Ecumenical Council (Nicea, 787)*. Toronto: University of Toronto Press.
Sahni, Daya Ram. 1937. *Archaeological Remains and Excavations at Bairat*. Jaipur: State Dept of Archaeology and Historical Research.
Said, Edward. 1978. *Orientalism*. London: Routledge & Kegan Paul.
—1983. "Roads Taken and Not Taken in Contemporary Criticism." In his *The World, the Text and the Critic*, 140-57. Cambridge, MA: Harvard University Press.
Sakaki Ryozaburo, ed. 1965. *Mahāvyutpatti*. 2 vols. Tokyo: Suzuki Gakujutsu Zaidan.
Sammons, Jeffrey. 1978. *Literary Sociology and Practical Criticism*. Bloomington, IN: Indiana University Press.
Samuel, Geoffrey. 1993. *Civilized Shamans: Buddhism in Tibetan Societies*. Washington, DC: Smithsonian Institution Press.
Sander, L. 1968. *Paläographisches zu den Sanskrithandschriften der Berliner Turfansammlung*. Verzeichnis der orientalischen Handschriften in Deutschland, Supplementband 8. Wiesbaden: F. Steiner.
Sanders, G. 1976. "Les chrétiens face à l'épigraphie funéraire latine." In *Assimilation et résistance à la culture gréco-romaine dans le monde ancien: Travaux du VIe Congrès international d'études classiques*, ed. D. M. Pippidi, 283-99. Paris: Les belles lettres.

Sarma, I. K. 1973. "A Coin Mould-Piece from Nagarjunakonda: New Light on the Silver Coinage of the Satavahanas." *Journal of the Economic and Social History of the Orient* 16: 89-106.
Sasaki Kyōgo. 1957. "Indo bukkyō ni okeru shō zō niji no shisō ni tsuite." *Ōtani gakuhō* 37/1: 83-84.
Satō Tetsuro. 1999–2002. "Ajia shisō katsugeki." http://homepage1.nifty.com/boddo/aija/all/index.html, accessed 28 June 2002.
Scheiner, Irwin. 1970. *Christian Converts and Social Protest in Meiji Japan*. Berkeley, CA: University of California Press.
Schober, Juliane, ed. 1997. *Sacred Biography in the Buddhist Traditions of South and Southeast Asia*. Honolulu: University of Hawai'i Press.
Schopen, Gregory. 1989. "A Verse from the Bhadracarīpraṇidhāna in a 10th Century Inscription Found at Nālandā." *Journal of the International Association of Buddhist Studies* 12/1: 149-57.
—1995. "Monastic Law Meets the Real World: A Monk's Continuing Right to Inherit Family Property in Classical India." *History of Religions* 35: 101-123.
—1996a. "The Suppression of Nuns and the Ritual Murder of Their Special Dead in Two Buddhist Monastic Texts." *Journal of Indian Philosophy* 24: 563-92.
—1996b. "What's in a Name: The Religious Function of the Early Donative Inscriptions." In *Unseen Presence: The Buddha and Sanchi*, ed. V. Dehejia, 58-73. Mumbai: Marg Publications.
—1997. *Bones, Stones and Buddhist Monks: Collected Papers on the Archaeology, Epigraphy, and Texts of Monastic Buddhism in India*. Honolulu: University of Hawai'i Press.
Schwab, R. 1984. *The Oriental Renaissance: Europe's Rediscovery of India and the East, 1680–1880*, trans. G. Patterson-Black and V. Reinking. New York: Columbia University Press.
Schwantes, Robert S. 1953. "Christianity vs. Science: A Conflict of Ideas in Modern Japan." *Far Eastern Quarterly* 12: 123-32.
Schwartz, Ronald D. 1994a. "Buddhism, Nationalist Protest, and the State in Tibet." In Kvaerne 1994, 728-38.
—1994b. *Circle of Protest: Political Ritual in the Tibetan Uprising*. New York: Columbia University Press.
Scott, David. 1994. *Formations of Ritual: Colonial and Anthropological Discourses on the Sinhala Yaktovil*. Minneapolis: University of Minnesota Press.
Seager, Richard Hughes. 1995. *The World's Parliament of Religions: The East/West Encounter, Chicago, 1893*. Bloomington, IN: Indiana University Press.
Senart, E. 1897. *Le Mahāvastu: texte Sanscrit publié pour la prèmiere fois et accompagné d'introductions et d'un commentaire*. Paris: Impr. nationale.
Senkyōkai (The Buddhist Propogation Society). 1888. "Mission Statement." *The Bijou of Asia* 2: 3-4.
Shaku Kōzen. 1893. *Shakuson Shōfū o kakuchō suru no shui*. Yokohama: Sanneji.
—1908. *Sanneji jihō narabi kyōyō ninka kisoku*. Kanagawa: Sanneji.
—1909. *Tenjiku Shakamuni Butsuzō oyobi sanzō shōgyō seirai no en'yu*. Kanagawa: Shōfūkai.
—1910. *Shakuson shōfū*. Tokyo: Shakuson Shōfūkai.
Shaku Nindo. 1944. "Kōzen Daiwajō o shinobite." *Kaigai Bukkyō jijō* 10/6.
Shaku Sōen. 1889. *Seinan no Bukkyō*. Tokyo: Hakubunkan.
—1893. "The Law of Cause and Effect as Taught by the Buddha." In Barrows 1893, vol. 2, 829-31. Chicago: Parliament.
—1894. "The Law of Cause and Effect as Taught by the Buddha." In Houghton 1894, 378-80.
—1895a. Preface to *Budda no fukuin*, trans. D.T. Suzuki. In *Suzuki Daisetsu zenshū*. 2nd ed., vol. 25, 277-82. Tokyo: Iwanami Shoten.
—1895b. *Bankoku shūkyō taikai ichiran*. Tokyo: Komeisha.
—1896. "Report on a Meeting of Religious Leaders." *Nihon shūkyō* Oct.: 173-77.

—1897. "A Controversy on Buddhism I, II, III." *The Open Court* 11/488: 43-59.
—1941. *Saiyū nikki*. Tokyo: Kamakura Matsugaoka Tōkeiji.
Shaku Sōen et al. 1896. *Bukkyō kakushū kōyō*. 5 vols. Kyoto: Kaiba Shoin.
Sharf, Robert. 1993. "The Zen of Japanese Nationalism." *History of Religions* 33/1: 1-43.
Sharma, Priya Vrat, ed. and trans. 2000. "Śārīrasthāna." In *Suśruta-saṃhitā*, vol 2. Varanasi: Chaukhambha Visvabharati.
Sharma, U. 1973. "Theodicy and the Doctrine of Karma." *Man* 8: 347-64.
Shastri, Swami Dwarikadas, ed. 1970. *Abhidharmakośam Bhāṣya Sphuṭārthā Sahitam*. 4 vols. Varanasi: Bauddha Bharati.
Shaw, Miranda. 1994. *Passionate Enlightenment: Women in Tantric Buddhism in India*. Princeton, NJ: Princeton University Press.
Shizutani Masao. 1979. *Indo bukkyō himei mokuroku (Catalog of Indian Buddhist Inscriptions)*. Kyoto: Hei'an gakuen kyōiku kenkyūkai.
Silk, Jonathan A. 1994. "The Victorian Creation of Buddhism: Review of *The British Discovery of Buddhism* by Philip C. Almond." *Journal of Indian Philosophy* 22/1: 171-96.
Sima Qian. 1959. *Shi ji*. Beijing: Zhonghua.
Simmer-Brown, Judith. 2001. *Dakini's Warm Breath: The Feminine Principle in Tibetan Buddhism*. Boston, MA: Shambhala.
Sircar, D.C. 1968. "Note on Chinchani Plate of Krishna III." *Epigraphia Indica* 37: 277-78.
Si-tu Pan-chen Chos-kyi 'Byung-gnas. 1960. *Yul gangs can pa'i brda yang dag par sbyor ba'i bstan bcos kyi bye brag sum cu pa dang rtags kyi 'jug pa'i gzhung gi rnam par bshad pa mkhas pa'i mgul rgyan mu tig phreng mdzes*. Dharamsala: n.p.
Sizemore, Russell F., and Donald K. Swearer. 1990. *Ethics, Wealth, and Salvation: A Study in Buddhist Social Ethics*. Columbia, SC: University of South Carolina Press.
Slotkin, Richard. 1992. *Gunfighter Nation: The Myth of the Frontier in Twentieth-Century America*. New York: Maxwell Macmillan International.
Smith, Bardwell, ed. 1972. *Two Wheels of Dhamma*. AAR Monograph Series, no. 3. Chambersburg, PA: American Academy of Religion.
Snodgrass, Judith. 1996. "Colonial Constructs of Theravada Buddhism." In *Traditions in Current Perspective*, ed. U Tun Aung Chain, 79-98. Yangon: Universities Historical Research Centre, Yangon University Press.
—1997. "The Deployment of Western Philosophy in Meiji Buddhist Revival." *Eastern Buddhist* 30: 173-98.
—2003. *Presenting Japanese Buddhism to the West: Orientalism, Occidentalism and the Columbian Exposition*. Chapel Hill, NC: University of North Carolina Press.
Snyder, Graydon F. 1985. *Ante Pacem: Archaeological Evidence of Church Life before Constantine*. Macon, GA: Mercer.
Sōgō Masaaki, ed. 1985. *Meiji no kotoba jiten*. Tokyo: Tōkyōdō.
Sog-po Lung-rigs bsTan-dar. 1986. *rGyud bzhi'i brda bkrol rnam rgyal a ru ra'i phreng ba'i mdzes rgyan*. Beijing: Mi-rigs dPe-skrun-khang.
Southwold, Martin. 1983. *Buddhism in Life: The Anthropological Study of Religion and the Sinhalese Practice of Buddhism*. Manchester: Manchester University Press.
Spink, W. 1972. "Ajanta: A Brief History." In *Aspects of Indian Art: Papers Presented in a Symposium at the Los Angeles County Museum of Art, October 1970*, ed. Pratapaditya Pal, 49-58. Leiden: Brill.
Spiro, Melford. 1970. *Buddhism and Society: A Great Tradition and Its Burmese Vicissitudes*. New York: Harper & Row.
Staggs, Kathleen M. 1979. "In Defense of Japanese Buddhism: Essays from the Meiji Period by Inoue Enryō and Murakami Senshō." PhD dissertation, Princeton University.
—1983. "'Defend the Nation and Love the Truth': Inoue Enryō and the Revival of Meiji Buddhism." *Monumenta Nipponica* 38: 251-81.

Stoddard, Heather. 1994. "Don grub rgyal (1953–1985): Suicide of a Modern Tibetan Writer and Scholar." In Kvaerne 1994, 825-34.
Ström, Axel Kristian. 1994. "Tibetan Refugees in India: Aspects of Socio-cultural Change." In Kvaerne 1994, 837-47.
Strong, John S. 1983. *The Legend of King Aśoka*. Princeton, NJ: Princeton University Press.
—1992. *The Legend and Cult of Upagupta: Sanskrit Buddhism in North India and Southeast Asia*. Princeton, NJ: Princeton University Press.
Suleri, Sara. 1992. *The Rhetoric of English India*. Chicago: University of Chicago Press.
Suzuki, D.T., trans. 1895. "A Japanese Translation of 'The Gospel of Buddha.'" *The Open Court* 9/391: 4404-4405.
—trans. 1970. *Budda no fukuin*. In *Suzuki Daisetsu zenshū*. 2nd ed., vol. 25, 271-591. Tokyo: Iwanami Shoten.
Suzuki Norihisa. 1970. "Nobuta Kishimoto and the Beginnings of the Scientific Study of Religion in Modern Japan." *Contemporary Religions in Japan* 11: 155-80.
Swearer, Donald K., ed. 1989. *Me and Mine: Selected Essays of Bhikkhu Buddhadāsa*. Albany, NY: State University of New York Press.
(Taishō) Taishō shinshū daizōkyō. 1924–1932. Ed. Takakusu Junjiro. Tokyo: Taishō Issaikyō Kankōkai.
Tajima Tokuon. 1940. "Reiji sakuhō to sangaikyū to no kankei." *Taishō gakuhō* 30–31: 188-99.
Takakusu Junjiro, and Nagai Makoto, ed. [1924] 1999. *Buddhaghosa's Vinaya commentary, Samantapāsādikā*. 7 vols. Oxford: Pali Text Society.
Takao Giken. 1937a. "Mappō shisō to shoka no taido." *Shina bukkyō shigaku* 1/1: 1-20.
—1937b. "Mappō shisō to shoka no taido." *Shina bukkyō shigaku* 1/3: 47-70.
Tamamuro Taijō. 1967. *Nihon Bukkyōshi*, vol. 3, *Kindaihen*. Kyoto: Hōzōkan.
Tambiah, Stanley Jeyaraja. 1970. *Buddhism and the Spirit Cults in North-East Thailand*. Cambridge: Cambridge University Press.
—1976. *World Conquerer and World Renouncer*. Cambridge: Cambridge University Press.
—1984. *The Buddhist Saints of the Forest and the Cult of Amulets*. Cambridge: Cambridge University Press.
—1992. *Buddhism Betrayed?* Chicago: University of Chicago Press.
Tamura Enchō. 1954. "Mappō shisō no keisei." *Shien* 63: 65-92.
Tang Yongtong. 1955. *Han Wei liang Jin nanbei liuchao fojiao shi*. Beijing: Zhonghua.
Tannenbaum, Nicola. 1995. *Who Can Compete Against the World? Power-Protection and Buddhism in Shan Worldview*. Ann Arbor, MI: Association for Asian Studies.
Tath Huot, Prah Grū Samgavicchā. 1927. *Siṅgālovādasutta (Advice to Siṅgāl)*. Phnom Penh: Publications of the Ecole Supérieure de Pāli, Bibliotèque Royale du Cambodge.
Tauch Chhuong. 1994. *Battambang during the Time of the Lord Governor*, trans. Hin Sithan, Carol Mortland, and Judy Ledgerwood. Phnom Penh: Cedoreck.
Thapar, Romila. 1966. *A History of India*, vol. 1. Harmondsworth: Penguin.
Thelle, Notto R. 1987. *Buddhism and Christianity in Japan: From Conflict to Dialogue, 1854–1899*. Honolulu: University of Hawai'i Press.
Thomas, Charles. 1971. *The Early Christian Archaeology of North Britain*. London: Oxford University Press.
Thomas, Edward J. 1927. *The Life of the Buddha as Legend and History*. London: Kegan, Paul, Trench & Trübner.
—[1927] 1975. *The Life of Buddha as Legend and History*. London: Routledge & Kegan Paul.
Thomas, Edward J., trans. and ed. 1935. *Early Buddhist Scriptures: A Selection*. London: K. Paul, Trench, Trübner & Co.
Thondup, Tulku Rinpoche. 1986. *Hidden Teachings of Tibet: An Explanation of the Terma Tradition of the Nyingma School of Buddhism*, ed. Harold Talbott. London: Wisdom Publications.

Thongchai Winichakul. 1994. *Siam Mapped: A History of the Geo-Body of a Nation.* Honolulu: University of Hawai'i Press.
Tokiwa Daijō. 1928. "Sangai-kyō no botai toshite no Hōzanji." *Shūkyō kenkyū* 4/1: 36-37.
Trenckner, V., ed. 1888. *The Majjhima-Nikāya.* London: Pali Text Society.
Trenckner, V., and P. S. Jaini, ed. 1986. *Milindapañha with Milinda-ṭīkā.* Oxford: Pali Text Society.
Trevithick, Alan Michael. 1988. "A Jerusalem of the Buddhists in British India: 1874–1949." PhD dissertation, Harvard University.
—1999. "British Archaeologists, Hindu Abbots, and Burmese Buddhists: The Mahabodhi Temple at Bodh Gayā, 1811–1877." *Modern Asian Studies* 33/3: 635-56.
Tsien, Tsuen-hsuin. 1985. "Paper and Printing." In *Science and Civilization in China*, vol. 5, *Chemistry and Chemical Technology*, ed. Joseph Needham. Pt. 1. Cambridge: Cambridge University Press.
Tsukamoto Zenryū. 1938. "Sekikyō unkyoji to sekikoku daizōkyō." *Tōhō gakuhō* 5 supplement: 1-245.
—1975a. *Chūgoku chūsei bukkyō shi ronkō.* Tokyo: Daitō.
—1975b. *Chūgoku Jōdokyō shi kenkyū.* Tokyo: Daitō.
—1975c. *Tō chūki no Jōdokyō.* Kyoto: Hōzōkan.
Tsunemitsu Kōnen. 1968. *Meiji no Bukkyōsha.* 2 vols. Tokyo: Shunjūsha.
Tuck, Andrew. 1990. *Comparative Philosophy and the Philosophy of Scholarship: On the Western Interpretation of Nagarjuna.* New York: Oxford University Press.
Tweed, Thomas A. 1992. *The American Encounter with Buddhism, 1844–1912.* Bloomington, IN: Indiana University Press.
—2000. *The American Encounter with Buddhism: Victorian Culture and the Limits of Dissent.* Chapel Hill, NC: University of North Carolina Press.
Upatissa. [1975] 1995. *The Path of Freedom (Vimuttimagga)*, trans. N. R. M. Ehara, Soma Thera, and Kheminda Thera. Kandy, Sri Lanka: Buddhist Publication Society.
Viswanathan, Gauri. 1989. *Masks of Conquest.* New York: Columbia University Press.
Vita, Silvio. 2002. "Printings of the Buddhist Canon in Modern Japan." Paper presented at the Association for Asian Studies, Washington, 7 April.
Vogel, J.Ph. 1929–30. "Prakrit Inscriptions from a Buddhist Site at Nagarjunikonda." *Epigraphia Indica* 20: 1-36.
Walshe, Maurice. 1987. *Thus Have I heard: The Long Discourses of the Buddha.* London: Wisdom Publications.
Walters, Jonathan S. 1992. "Rethinking Buddhist Missions." PhD dissertation, University of Chicago.
—1997a. "Mahāyāna Theravāda and the Origins of the Mahāvihāra." *Sri Lanka Journal of the Humanities* 23/1 & 2: 100-19.
—1997b. "*Stūpa*, Story, and Empire: Constructions of the Buddha Biography in Post-Aśokan India." In Schober 1997, 160-92.
—1998. *Finding Buddhists in Global History.* American Historical Association Essays on Global and Comparative History Series, ed. Michael Adas. Washington, DC: American Historical Association.
—1999. "Mahāsena at the Mahāvihāra: The Politics and Interpretation of History in Medieval Sri Lanka." In *Invoking the Past: The Uses of History in South Asia*, ed. Avril Powell and Daud Ali, 322-66. Oxford: Oxford University Press.
—2000. "Buddhist History: The Pāli Vaṃsas of Sri Lanka." In *Querying the Medieval*, ed. Ronald Inden, Daud Ali, and Jonathan S. Walters, 99-164. Oxford and New York: Oxford University Press.
Warder, A. K. 1961. "The Pali Canon and Its Commentaries as an Historical Record." In *Historians of India, Pakistan and Ceylon*, ed. C.H. Philips, 44-56. London: Oxford University Press.

Warren, Henry Clarke. [1886] 1992. *Buddhism in Translations*. Delhi: Motilal Banarsidass.
Wassilieff, M. 1896. "Le bouddhisme dans son plein développement d'après les vinayas." *Revue de l'histoire des religions* 17: 318-25.
Weber, Max. [1958] 1996. *The Religion of India: The Sociology of Hinduism and Buddhism*, ed. and trans. Hans H. Gerth and Don Martindale. New Delhi: Munshiram Manoharlal.
Weinstein, Stanley. 1973. "Imperial Patronage in the Formation of T'ang Buddhism." In *Perspectives on the T'ang*, ed. A. F. Wright and D. Twitchett, 265-306. New Haven: Yale University Press.
—1987. *Buddhism Under the T'ang*. Cambridge: Cambridge University Press.
Welbon, Guy Richard. 1968. *The Buddhist Nirvāna and its Western Interpreters*. Chicago: University of Chicago Press.
Wendelken, Cherie. 2000. "Pan-Asianism and the Pure Japanese Thing: Japanese Identity and Architecture in the Late 1930s." *Positions: East Asia Cultures Critique* 8/3: 819-28.
West, W. 1862. "Description of Some of the Kanheri Topes." *Journal of the Bombay Branch of the Royal Asiatic Society* 6: 116-20.
Wickremeratne, Ananda L. 1984. *The Genesis of an Orientalist: Thomas William Rhys Davids and Buddhism in Sri Lanka*. Delhi: Motilal Banarsidass.
Wickremesinghe, K.D.P. 1972. *The Biography of the Buddha*. Colombo: Priyanka Lakshman Wickremesinghe.
Wigen, Kären. 1995. *The Making of a Japanese Periphery, 1750-1920*. Berkeley and Los Angeles: University of California Press.
—1999. "Culture, Power, and Place: The New Landscapes of East Asian Regionalism." *American Historical Review* 104/4: 1183-1201.
Wijayaratna, Mohen. 1983. *Le moine bouddhiste selon les textes du Theravāda*. Paris: Editions du Cerf. (ET = *Buddhist Monastic Life: According to the Texts of the Theravada*. Cambridge and New York: Cambridge University Press, 1990.)
Wilson, Liz. 1996. *Charming Cadavers: Horrific Figurations of the Feminine in Indian Buddhist Hagiographic Literature*. Chicago: University of Chicago Press.
Woods, J.H. and D. Kosambi, ed. 1928. *Papañcasūdanī nāma Majjhimanikāyaṭṭhakathā of Buddhaghosācāriya*. London: Pali Text Society.
Wright, Arthur F. 1973. "T'ang T'ai-tsung and Buddhism." In *Perspectives on the T'ang*, ed. A.F. Wright and D. Twitchett, 239-63. New Haven: Yale University Press.
Wu Yin, Venerable Bhiksuni. 2001. *Choosing Simplicity: Commentary on the Bhikshuni Pratimoksha*. Ithaca, NY: Snowlion Publications.
Wyatt, David K. 1982. "The 'Subtle Revolution' of King Rama I of Siam." In *Moral Order and the Question of Change: Essays on Southeast Asian Thought*, ed. David K. Wyatt and Alexander Wordside. Yale University Southeast Asia Studies Monograph, no. 24, 9-52. New Haven: Yale University Press.
Yabuki Keiki. 1926. "Sangai-kyō." *Shisō* 60: 49-53.
—1927. *Sangai-kyō no kenkyū*. Tokyo: Iwanami.
Yagi Kōkei. 1942. "Eshin kyōgaku ni okeru Sangai-kyō no kōsatsu." *Shina bukkyō shigaku* 6/2: 38-58.
—1943. "Eshin kyōgaku ni okeru Sangai-kyō no kōsatsu." *Shina bukkyō shigaku* 6/2: 10-17.
Yamada Ryūjō. 1957. "Mappō shisō ni tsuite—Daijikkyō no seiritsu mondai." *Indōgaku bukkyōgaku kenkyu* 4/2: 54-63.
Yamaguchi Zuiho, ed. 1973. *rTags 'jug: Sum cu pa dang rtags kyi 'jug pa*. Tokyo: Toyo Bunko.
Yampolsky, Philip B. 1967. *The Platform Sutra of the Sixth Patriarch*. New York: Columbia University Press.
Yan, Zhitui. 1968. *Family Instructions for the Yen Clan: Yen-shih chia-hsün*, trans. Deng Siyun. Leiden: Brill.

Yanagida Seizan. 1967. *Shoki zenshū shisho no kenkyū*. Kyoto: Hōzōkan.

—1978. "Shinzoku toushi no keifu." *Zengaku kenkyu* 59: 1-39.

Yang-dgon-pa rGyal-mtshan dPal. 1976. *rDo rje lus kyi sbas bshad*. In vol. 2 of *The Collected Works (Gsun 'bum) of Yan-dgon-pa Rgyal-mtshan-dpal*. 3 vols. Thimphu: Kunsang Topgey.

Yuki Reimon. 1936. "Shina bukkyō ni okeru mappō shisō no kōki." *Tōhō gakuhō* 6: 205-16.

Zaehner, R.C. 1974. Foreword to *The Origin and Early Development of Buddhist Monasticism*, by P. Olivelle, vii. Colombo: M.D. Gunasena.

Zürcher, Erik. 1982a. "Perspectives in the Study of Chinese Buddhism." *Journal of the Royal Asiatic Society* 2: 161-76.

—1982b. "Prince Moonlight: Messianism and Eschatology in Early Medieval Chinese Buddhism." *T'oung Pao* 68/1-3: 1-59.

Zur-mkhar-ba Blo-gros rGyal-po. 1989. *rGyud bzhi'i 'grel pa mes po'i zhal lung*. 2 vols. Beijing: Krung-go'i Bod-kyi Shes-rig dPe-skrun-khang.

Zwilling, Leonard. 1992. "Homosexuality as Seen in Indian Buddhist Texts." In *Buddhism, Sexuality, and Gender*, ed. José Cabezón. Albany, NY: State University of New York Press.

Zwingli, Ulrich. 1981. *Commentary on True and False Religion*, ed. S.M. Jackson and C.N. Heller. Durham, NC: Labyrinth.

Zysk, Kenneth. 1991. *Asceticism and Healing in Ancient India: Medicine in the Buddhist Monastery*. New York: Oxford University Press.

Index of Names

Ahmad, Aijaz 252–53
Ajātasattu 235, 245
Akamatsu Renjō 171, 257–58, 264
Alabaster, Henry 101, 115 n. 25
Āḷāra Kālāma 47, 51–52, 55–59, 62–64, 69–70, 74, 76n. 9; 77n. 16, 17, 19, 21; 79nn. 28, 34
Almond, Philip 92–93, 98, 113n. 15, 254
Amitābha (Japanese: Amida) Buddha 132, 262, 267
Ānanda 46, 71–73, 159, 282
Ani Muntsho 199
Ārāḍa Kālāma. *See* Āḷāra Kālāma
Arnold, Edwin 158, 173n. 3, 255, 275, 278n. 6
Ashizu Jitsuzen 164, 173n. 6, 174n. 15
Aśoka 45, 55, 148, 225
Aśvaghoṣa 50, 67, 69; 76nn. 7, 8; 78n. 21
Atiśa 197
Ato Yūjō 268–69
Avalokiteśvara 190–91, 209n. 33, 211n. 59, 213n. 64

Bailey, Greg 53–54, 56–58, 74
Ban Gu 128
Bareau, André 96
Barrows, J. H. 279n. 19
Bigandet, Paul 94–96, 100–2, 104, 109–10, 114nn. 20–22, 115n. 31
Bimbisāra 52, 70, 235, 243
Blackburn, Anne 54, 64–65, 74, 228, 279
Bodhidharma 83
Bodhisattva (the) 46–52, 56–58, 63–69, 77n. 17; 79nn. 29, 34
Brahmā 55–57, 67, 72, 77n. 16
Buddha (the) (Gotama, Śākyamuni)
  bodies of 176–77, 206n. 2
  bodily characteristics of 48–49, 72, 271
  Buddhaghosa's conception of 70–75, 80n. 36
  Paul Carus's conception of 157, 159, 169–70
  in *Gatilok* 240, 243–44
  historical 2, 44–45, 48, 51, 59–60, 67–68, 73–74, 79n. 34, 96, 99
  images of 130, 135, 176–77, 196, 262, 267, 269–70, 273–74
  and Mahāyāna Buddhism 163, 167, 174n. 15
  in Meiji Japan 167, 221, 254–65, 267, 269–77; 278nn. 5, 10, 11; 279nn. 21, 22, 26
  Henry Steel Olcott's conception of 265
  as one of Three Jewels 134, 208n. 18, 269
  on ordination of women 130, 282–83
  in Orientalist scholarship 3, 16–17, 29, 229
  as preacher of sūtras (suttas) 44–47, 235
  previous lives of 66, 99, 110, 154n. 19, 229
  as rationalist 2, 105–6, 157, 169–70, 265
  as refuge 280n. 29
  relics of 196, 210n. 46, 269
  royal status of 67
  Shaku Sōen's conception of 160, 168, 171
  as source of textual authority 119, 121–22, 162–63, 167, 229
  in Three Stages sect 131–35, 140–42, 144
  See also related headings in the "Index of Subjects"
Buddhaghosa 44, 48, 50, 59–60, 70–74, 76n. 6, 79n. 29, 80n. 36, 294–96, 304n. 50
Bühler, Georg 26–28
Burnouf, Eugène 25, 104, 110, 116n. 37

Index of Subjects

Orientalist constructions of 2, 51–52, 97–98, 101–5, 157
T. W. Rhys Davids on 95–98, 105
as source for social history 44–45, 54–58, 78n. 21
sources for, vernacular versus classical 95–104, 113n. 17, 232
supplementation and 65–70, 74–75, 79n. 34
suttas as sources for 44–45, 47
Buddhacarita 50, 67, 76n. 7, 77nn. 17–19, 78n. 21, 96
Buddhadharma. *See* Dharma
Buddha-eye 47, 49, 51, 56
buddha-nature 133–35, 142, 209n. 29
buddhas
bodies of 72, 176–77
Buddhaghosa on 71–72
in Japanese Buddhism 267
previous 20, 66, 77n. 16, 82, 84, 89, 99
in Three Stages sect 132–36, 139
in Tibetan Buddhism 186, 190
Buddhavaṃsa 50, 69, 76n. 7, 77n. 16
Buddhism(s)
Buddhist definitions of 1–13, 16–19, 21–23, 103–12, 118, 121–23, 125, 155–56, 159–65, 168–73, 216–21, 223–24, 226, 247–48, 252–56, 265, 267, 269, 273–75
dialogical process of defining 1–4, 7–11, 13, 17, 19, 23
and Hinduism 54–55, 67, 106–7
local and translocal 5–6, 22, 111, 219–21, 223–24, 230–32, 247
and modernity. *See* modernity
multiplicity versus unity of 1–6, 10, 12, 22, 112, 118–19, 122, 125, 217–21, 223–24, 232
Orientalist definitions of 2–3, 5, 7–8, 10, 12, 16–17, 21–22, 93, 95, 98, 103–12, 113n. 15, 122, 155–59, 163, 169–72, 217, 220–21, 231–32, 253–55, 273–74
pan-Asian 253–54, 272, 276–77
premodern 6–7, 9–11, 60, 119–21, 223
"pure," "original," or "true" 2–3, 8, 12, 16–17, 21–22, 33, 95, 122, 220–21, 228–29, 264–65, 267, 269, 273
as rational 2, 105–9, 122, 160, 229–30, 265
as religion of the future 122, 157, 164, 168, 172
and resistance to state power 12, 119–20, 123–24, 184, 186, 192–93, 198, 200, 204–6; 211nn. 57, 59; 212n. 64; 213nn. 66–68
as scientific 2, 73, 122, 157, 160–63, 167, 170, 172, 174n. 14, 253, 265
state support of 12, 119–22, 127–29, 146–51, 162, 167–68, 172, 186–87, 201, 211n. 59, 213n. 64
and women. *See* women
as world-renouncing religion 26, 225–26. *See also* renunciation
See also Chan, Japanese Buddhism, Mahāyāna Buddhism, Sinhalese Buddhism, tantric Buddhism, Theravāda Buddhism, Three Stages sect, Tibetan Buddhism
Buddhist ethics. *See* ethics, Buddhist
Buddhist studies 1–13, 16–23, 25, 32–33, 36–38, 94–112, 113n. 8, 115n. 29, 225–27, 229–30, 253
Buddhology 8, 60, 68, 73–74
Burmese Buddhist literature 95, 97, 100–1, 103–4, 110, 114n. 23, 116n. 37

cakravartin king 148–51
Cambodia
colonial 219–20, 227, 232–33, 247
highland versus lowland 237, 250n. 13
Khmer folk stories from 242–43, 250nn. 19–21
Khmer nationalism in 233, 249n. 7
Phnong in 237–38, 250n. 13
See also Khmer Buddhist literature
canon
Anne Blackburn on 65, 228
Chinese conceptions of 126–28
as closed 227–28
Steven Collins on 45, 65, 228, 231
formal versus practical 228, 230
as historical source 17–19, 29–32, 39nn. 4–6, 40n. 7, 44–46, 75
in Japan 164
Orientalist privileging of 2–3, 17, 97, 103–4, 231–32, 273
Pāli (Tipiṭaka) 39nn. 4–5, 40n. 7, 44–46, 49, 60–61, 97, 104, 220, 226–28, 231, 247, 273

Printed in the United States
201660BV00006B/1-84/A

9 781845 530556